Microsoft® Windows® Workflow Foundation Step by Step

Kenn Scribner

PUBLISHED BY
Microsoft Press
A Division of Microsoft Corporation
One Microsoft Way
Redmond, Washington 98052-6399

Library of Congress Control Number: 2006940677

Printed and bound in the United States of America.

1 2 3 4 5 6 7 8 9 QWE 2 1 0 9 8 7

Distributed in Canada by H.B. Fenn and Company Ltd.

A CIP catalogue record for this book is available from the British Library.

Microsoft Press books are available through booksellers and distributors worldwide. For further information about international editions, contact your local Microsoft Corporation office or contact Microsoft Press International directly at fax (425) 936-7329. Visit our Web site at www.microsoft.com/mspress. Send comments to mspinput@microsoft.com.

Microsoft, Microsoft Press, Active Directory, ActiveX, BizTalk, DataTips, Developer Studio, FrontPage, IntelliSense, Internet Explorer, Jscript, MSDN, MSN, SQL Server, Visual Basic, Visual C#, Visual C++, Visual SourceSafe, Visual Studio, Visual Web Developer, Win32, Windows, Windows NT, Windows Server, Windows Vista, and WinFX are either registered trademarks or trademarks of Microsoft Corporation in the United States and/or other countries. Other product and company names mentioned herein may be the trademarks of their respective owners.

The example companies, organizations, products, domain names, e-mail addresses, logos, people, places, and events depicted herein are fictitious. No association with any real company, organization, product, domain name, e-mail address, logo, person, place, or event is intended or should be inferred.

This book expresses the author's views and opinions. The information contained in this book is provided without any express, statutory, or implied warranties. Neither the authors, Microsoft Corporation, nor its resellers, or distributors will be held liable for any damages caused or alleged to be caused either directly or indirectly by this book.

Acquisitions Editor: Ben Ryan
Project Editor: Lynn Finnel
Copy Editor: Roger LeBlanc
Technical Reviewer: Kurt Meyer
Peer Reviewer: Scott Seely
Editorial and Production Services: Waypoint Press

Body Part No. X12-64035

To my wonderful family, Judi, Aaron, and Katie,
without whose love and support life has little meaning.
Thank you all for always being there.

Table of Contents

What do you think of this book? We want to hear from you!

Microsoft is interested in hearing your feedback so we can continually improve our books and learning resources for you. To participate in a brief online survey, please visit:

www.microsoft.com/learning/booksurvey/

Part II **Working with Activities**

What do you think of this book? We want to hear from you!

Microsoft is interested in hearing your feedback so we can continually improve our books and learning resources for you. To participate in a brief online survey, please visit:

www.microsoft.com/learning/booksurvey/

Foreword

To me, workflow engines such as Microsoft BizTalk always seemed like a really expensive thing that I didn't need for many projects. I always thought, "How hard can it be to actually code the logic you draw on the screen?" As a result, I spent a lot of time not learning what a workflow engine could do for me and, instead, lived with "just code." Still, I was intrigued and would bug my friends about what they saw as the value of BizTalk. They would usually get me excited enough to try installing the product and learning how it worked. Every time I tried to make the plunge and learn how to use BizTalk, I backed away because it seemed too complex for what I perceived as a flowchart execution engine.

Sometime around 2003, while working at Microsoft on what was to become Windows Communication Foundation, I heard about a general-purpose workflow engine being built within Microsoft. Rumor had it that the workflow engine might even be integrated into the operating system! The reason: Prior to then, groups within Microsoft had created their own workflow engines for their own problem domains. Most of the engines were written in C++ and exhibited limited flexibility outside of their domain area. BizTalk, which had a general-purpose engine, was not then designed to have its engine separated from the BizTalk product. What Microsoft discovered was there was a real need for a single, general-purpose workflow engine so that internal Microsoft teams could stop reinventing workflow. This realization (which occurred prior to me hearing anything) helped create what would eventually become the Windows Workflow Foundation team.

As a part of .NET Frameworks 3.0, Windows Workflow Foundation is a freely distributable .NET component. On Windows Vista and later, it ships as a part of the operating system. What does this mean for developers? It means that they can learn how to use a workflow engine and distribute their applications while being able to rely on a workflow engine just being present on the client machine. Bigger applications will still need tools such as BizTalk Server to manage workflows. But, for smaller applications that could use some of the benefits of workflow (such as state machines and the ability to suspend and resume a workflow), Windows Workflow Foundation is a godsend.

The book you now hold shows all the little things that Windows Workflow Foundation can do. Because it is the introductory book to Windows Workflow Foundation, it takes a tour of the feature set and lets you know what is available. For me, this book has served as a great introduction to the technology. I have discovered that most projects would benefit from a healthy dose of workflow somewhere. The samples in this book proved as much to me.

Kenn, congratulations on finishing up a great book. Thank you for making me a part of the process. I believe many more .NET developers will finally understand what workflow can do for them thanks to your introduction to the topic.

Scott Seely

Acknowledgments

If you ever have the opportunity to write a book, aside from the tremendous amout of work it takes, you'll find it's a lonely business. You'll spend hour after hour after hour, typing, writing, debugging... You can easily be fooled into believing the world consists of only two entities: yourself and your computer.

But the simple truth is you're not an island, and literally dozens of people are behind you, working long hours, night and day, to help you. Some, you know. Others, you may not know, but they're helping just the same. Everyone has a single goal in mind, and that's to help you craft the best book you can possibly write. If you're one of the many people who helped me with this effort and I didn't mention you by name here, rest assured you have my undying thanks and gratitude. If you've remained nameless to me, it's only because we haven't had the good fortune to meet. Forgive me any oversights...your help and support were invaluable to me, and what's more, I have no misunderstandings regarding how hard you worked on my behalf. Thanks to all of you!

Happily, I do happen to know a few people who were instrumental in this process. First and foremost, I'd like to humbly and most appreciatively thank my wife, Judi, who encouraged me to take the plunge yet another time. She knows how much work it is to write one of these and sacrificed our time together on many evenings so that I could hurridly work to meet deadlines. I'd like to thank my children Aaron and Katie, who sacrificed many backyard baseball and football games with Dad and put up with my evil alter-ego, Mr. Stressed, for the months it took me to complete this manuscript. Their understanding and encouragement kept me going as well.

To my editor, Lynn, words can't express how thankful I am, certainly in part because of your efforts with this book, but also for our friendship. Lynn and I have worked together on many books (me being a technical editor), and they've all been a treat because of your care and guidance. Sometime dinner's on me, unless I find you atop Mt. Ranier (she's an avid climber). Then you're on your own, unless you're good with freeze dried!

Thank you Roger for taking my raw, grammatically incoherent text and turning it into something I can claim I wrote. We both know better, but let that be our secret. I can't tell a dangling participle from a misplaced modifier, but I boldy went forth and wrote them anyway. Thanks for kindly fixing things!

And thank you, Kurt, for your dogged determination to root out every bug I cleverly hid in the text and code. I know well the work you did for me. Sometimes I could almost hear you say "Technical editor turned author, correct thyself!" when you ran into the more obvious of my technical errors. I have a new appreciation for the author's side of the technical editing job, and any errors that remain are mine alone and were probably stealthily injected under the cover of darkness, hidden from your keen eye. Either that or...Roger did it. Yeah...Roger did it! That's the ticket.

I owe a special thanks to Scott Seely, who not only suffered through my misplaced protection levels and laughable coding style while reviewing this manuscript, but is also for being a tremendous friend. For once, I don't owe him a beer. Come to think of it, I think I paid up on that debt for quite some time to come. Welcome back home, Scott.

If you stop and take a look at the printed material—not what I've written, but how it's formatted and became wonderfully readable—that's due to Steve Sagman's hard work. Looking at it makes it hard for me to believe I am the one who wrote it, it looks so nice. It's hard to do, Steve, but you made me look good!

We all want to be supermen (and women), but the fact is you can't do everything in a 24 hour day. Sometimes my work with this book affected my daily job. Okay, it really affected my daily job. I'd like to thank Dave Pledger, Keith Stafford, and Steve Held at Strategic Data Systems for sticking with me through this process and helping me to explain why I missed other deadlines. I hate missing deadlines, but superman I am not, or so I am learning. Thanks guys!

Thanks to all of my friends at Wintellect, including Lewis Frazier, Paula Daniels, Jeffrey Richter, John Robbins, Todd Fine, and most especially Jeff Prosise, who keeps the same awful hours I do. He says I work longer, but I know the truth when I get e-mails back from him at 2:00 in the morning. You guys rock!

And where would this book be without the fine work of the Microsoft Windows Workflow Foundation team? Someday I hope to have the pleasure of meeting all of you. If I didn't describe some functionality you played a hand in creating quite well enough, believe me it wasn't for lack of trying. If there is a second edition, you can be sure I'll get it right the second time around! Totally clever code, dudes.

Finally, I can't forget to thank you for picking up this book off the shelf and shelling out your hard-earned money for the copy. No, I'm not thinking about the royalties—computer books are notorious for not making money. I write software for a living, just like you, and I know what it takes to meet deadlines, crush bugs, and stand and deliver. It's for you I wrote this book, and I hope you'll find it useful when learning Windows Workflow Foundation programming. It's a great technology, and one I know we'll all find incredibly diverse and eminently useful. Thank you.

Introduction

Before diving into programming with Microsoft Windows Workflow Foundation, or WF, it's important to understand what workflow is and why you'd want to invest the effort to learn how to use it. After all, learning new technology means that you have to, well, take the time to learn the new technology. The learning curve can be painful. There are new tools, new ways to think about your applications, and so forth. Given your time investment to learn WF, what sort of return on your investment can you expect? Is it worth learning, or is it just a passing fad?

Workflow, at least as I believe WF most closely defines it, is simply a term that is applied to software that executes in a more rigorous environment. What software? Essentially, the same software you have already been writing. Have you ever written code to take information from a database, process the information, and then write the processed data to another database or data sink? Or how about taking files and moving them from place to place once a person or process approved or otherwise manipulated them? Actually, the examples I could come up with are nearly infinite, limited only by my ability to invent them. *Anything* you write could be considered workflow at some level.

The environment WF provides you with is of great value, if only because it allows for easy multithreaded processing. Your services or user interfaces don't need to worry about creating worker threads and monitoring their use and ultimate demise.

But WF offers other tantalizing features, such as the ability to stop an executing workflow process and shuttle it to a database for safekeeping while a long-running approval or other external process completes. It can automatically record tracking information to a database. It facilitates the development of neatly compartmentalized and readily reusable code. It has nice transactional support. And it's already a part of Microsoft Windows Vista, so you don't have to install it on the next generation of Windows. Even if you're using Microsoft Windows XP or Microsoft Windows Server 2003, it's part of the latest version of .NET, which is something you'd probably be installing anyway at some point.

Oh, and did I mention it's free? The cost to you is the cost of the download and your time investment to learn to use it.

Speaking personally, the investment in learning and using WF is proving to be worth the effort. I write software, and I'd guess that you do as well or you wouldn't be reading this. I'm finding that customers and clients want this technology. From that standpoint, it's not a hard decision, really. I chose to take the time to learn this technology, and I'm applying it in my software solutions today.

So how best to learn WF? I like to write code and experiment. If you do also, you should find this book useful, because with it you'll be able to write code and experiment as well. This book isn't designed to go into great depth regarding any particular topic. Rather, it's designed to get you up and running with WF as quickly as possible. You'll find other books over time that provide much greater exposure to the whys. This book targets the hows. I recommend reading any workflow-related book that comes out, but for starters, this book should provide you with enough detail to get going.

Who This Book Is For

This book is best suited for software developers working with Microsoft-based technologies, especially those who are already familiar with .NET and programming for the .NET platform using Microsoft Visual Studio. While I occasionally discuss general workflow or software development topics, I'll always back those discussions with .NET code. Not Java. Not Ruby. All C#, all the time.

Finding Your Best Starting Point in This Book

This book is designed to help you build skills in a number of essential areas. It assumes that you are new to WF and takes you step by step through the fundamental concepts of WF feature by feature, activity by activity. It is recommended that you follow the chapters in sequence and perform each of the exercises, as the techniques and ideas that you see in one chapter are extended in subsequent chapters. However, if you have specific requirements or are interested only in certain aspects of WF, you can use the following table to find your best route through this book.

If you are	Follow these steps
New to workflow processing and need to gain a basic understanding of WF	1. Install the code samples as described in the "Code Samples" section of this Introduction. 2. Work through Chapters 1 through 4 sequentially, and perform the exercises. 3. Complete Chapter 7 and Chapters 9 through 14 as your level of experience and interest dictates.
Familiar with WF but want to learn more about integrating WF into your applications	1. Install the code samples as described in the "Code Samples" section of this Introduction. 2. Skim the first chapter to get an overview of WF, but perform the exercises. 3. Read Chapter 2 and perform the exercises. 4. Skim Chapters 3 and 4. 5. Read Chapters 8 and 10, and complete the exercises. 6. Skim Chapter 17, performing the exercises.
Familiar with WF but want to learn more about how it can be used declaratively (for example, by using XML-based workflow definitions)	1. Install the code samples as described in the "Code Samples" section of this Introduction. 2. Skim the first three chapters. 3. Read Chapter 16 and perform the exercises.

If you are	Follow these steps
Referencing the book after working through the exercises	1. Use the index or the Table of Contents to find information about particular subjects.
	2. Refer to the "Quick Reference" section at the end of each chapter to find a brief review of the concepts and techniques presented in the chapter.

Conventions and Features in This Book

This book presents information using conventions designed to make the information readable and easy to follow. Before you start, read the following list, which explains conventions you'll see throughout the book and points out helpful features that you might want to use.

Conventions

- Each exercise is a series of tasks. Each task is presented as a series of numbered steps (1, 2, and so on). A round bullet (●) indicates an exercise that has only one step.

- Notes labeled "tip" provide additional information or alternative methods for completing a step successfully.

- Notes labeled "important" alert you to information you need to check before continuing.

- Text that you type appears in bold.

- A plus sign (+) between two key names means that you must press those keys at the same time. For example, "Press Shift+F6" means that you hold down the Shift key while you press the F6 key.

System Requirements

You need the following hardware and software to complete the practice exercises in this book:

- Microsoft Windows XP with Service Pack 2, Microsoft Windows Server 2003 with Service Pack 1, or Microsoft Windows Vista.

- Microsoft Visual Studio 2005 Standard Edition or Microsoft Visual Studio 2005 Professional Edition, including SQL Server 2005 Express.

- 600-MHz Pentium or compatible processor (1-GHz Pentium recommended).

- 192 MB RAM (256 MB or more recommended).

- Video monitor (800 × 600 or higher resolution) with at least 256 colors (1024 × 768 High Color 16-bit recommended).

- DVD-RW (readable/writable) drive.

- Microsoft mouse or compatible pointing device.

You also need to have the following additional software installed on your computer. This software is available on the companion CD supplied with this book. Installation and configuration instructions are provided later in the Introduction—as well as in Chapter 1 along with additional information and locations from which you can download the software from the Internet. The order in which you install the supporting software matters. It should be installed in the order listed here.

1. Microsoft .NET Framework 3.0.

> **Note**   If you are using Windows Vista, the .NET Framework 3.0 is automatically installed as part of the operating system. You do not need to install it again.

2. Microsoft Windows Software Development Kit for Windows Vista and .NET Framework 3.0 Runtime Components.

3. Visual Studio 2005 Extensions for .NET Framework 3.0.

4. Visual Studio 2005 Extensions for Windows Workflow Foundation.

5. SQL Server Management Studio Express Edition.

> **Note**   If you are using the full retail version of SQL Server 2005, SQL Server Management Studio is installed for you.

You will need to create a DVD yourself to install the Microsoft Windows Software Development Kit for Windows Vista and .NET Framework 3.0 Runtime Components (step 2). As downloaded, it will come to you as a DVD image file suitable for DVD creation (note you may have to change the file extension to .iso to be compatible with some DVD creation software packages). You can download this software from the Microsoft Download Center site at *www.microsoft.com/downloads/details.aspx?FamilyId=C2B1E300-F358-4523-B479-F53D234CDCCF&displaylang=en*. If you'd rather not type in such a lengthy Internet address, I've placed the locations of the software for download in the first chapter's page in the accompanying code manual on the CD.

Code Samples

The companion CD inside this book contains the code samples that you'll use as you perform the exercises. By using the code samples, you won't waste time creating files that aren't relevant to the information being presented. The files and the step-by-step instructions in the lessons also let you learn by doing, which is an easy and effective way to acquire and remember new skills.

Installing the Code Samples

Follow these steps to install the code samples and required software on your computer so that you can use them with the exercises:

1. Remove the companion CD from the package inside this book, and insert it into your DVD-RW drive. (You may use a CD-ROM to install the book's contents, but keep in mind you'll require a DVD-RW to install the Windows SDK, which is required for creating and executing WF projects.)

> **Note**   An end-user license agreement should open automatically. If this agreement does not appear, open My Computer on the desktop or Start menu, double-click the icon for your DVD-RW drive, and then double-click StartCD.exe.

2. Review the end-user license agreement. If you accept the terms, select the accept option and then click Next.

    A menu will appear with options related to the book.

3. Click Install Code Samples.

4. Follow the instructions that appear.

    The code samples are installed to the following location on your computer if you are using Windows XP:

    My Documents\Microsoft Press\WF_SBS

    The code samples are installed to the following location on your computer if you are using Windows Vista:

    Documents\Microsoft Press\WF_SBS

Installing and Configuring the Microsoft .NET Framework 3.0 (Windows XP Only)

 Note If you are using Windows Vista, the .NET Framework 3.0 is automatically installed as part of the operating system. You do not need to install it again.

The exercises and samples in this book have been tested against the release-to-manufacturing (RTM) version of the .NET Framework 3.0. If you have previously installed an earlier version of the .NET Framework 3.0, you must uninstall it and use the software provided on the companion CD. Follow these instructions to install the Microsoft .NET Framework 3.0.

 Note These installation procedures are mentioned again in Chapter 1, along with additional information and locations from which you can download the software from the Internet.

1. Using Windows Explorer, move to the \Software folder on the companion CD.
2. Double-click the file dotnetfx3setup.exe. If the Open File – Security Warning dialog appears, click Run.
3. In the Welcome To Setup page, read the license agreement. If you agree with the license terms, click "I have read and ACCEPT the terms of the License Agreement," and then click Install.

   Installation continues in the background.
4. When the Setup Complete page appears, click Exit.

Installing the Visual Studio 2005 Extensions for .NET Framework 3.0

 Important You should download and install the Microsoft Windows SDK before installing the Visual Studio 2005 Extensions for .NET Framework 3.0. Because the SDK comes as a DVD image, it was too large to place on the book's CD. You can find the Web location for downloading the image for burning onto your own DVD in Chapter 1, or you can alternatively click the link in the first chapter's page in the code manual that is installed with the book's code.

The exercises and samples in this book have been tested against the November 2006 RTM version of the Visual Studio 2005 Extensions for .NET Framework 3.0. Follow these instructions to install this software:

1. Using Windows Explorer, move to the \Software folder on the companion CD.
2. Double-click the file vsextwfx.msi. If the Open File – Security Warning dialog appears, click Run.

3. On the Welcome To The Visual Studio 2005 Extensions For .NET Framework 3.0 (WCF WPF) November 2006 CTP Setup Wizard page, click Next.

4. On the License Agreement page, read the license agreement. If you agree with the license terms, click I Accept and then click Next.

5. On the Confirm Installation page, click Next.

6. When the Installation Complete page appears, click Close.

7. Close the Internet Explorer window displaying the release notes.

Installing the Visual Studio 2005 Extensions for Windows Workflow Foundation

The exercises and samples in this book have been tested against the November 2006 RTM version of the Visual Studio 2005 Extensions for Windows Workflow Foundation. Follow these instructions to install this software:

1. Using Windows Explorer, move to the \Software folder on the companion CD.

2. Double-click the file Visual Studio 2005 Extensions for Windows Workflow Foundation (EN).exe. If the Open File – Security Warning dialog appears, click Run.

3. On the Visual Studio 2005 Extensions For Windows Workflow Foundation screen, click Visual Studio 2005 Extensions For Windows Workflow Foundation.

4. On the License Agreement page, read the license agreement. If you agree with the license terms, click I Accept and then click Next.

5. On the Component Installation page, click Next.

6. On the Summary page, click Install.

7. When the Installation Complete page appears, click Finish.

Installing the SQL Server Management Studio Express Edition

Some of the applications in this book require the use of SQL Server or SQL Server Express. If you're using SQL Server Express, you can install the very useful SQL Server Management Studio Express Edition application to make administering your SQL Server Express databases much easier. This application will be necessary later in the book for running database creation scripts that ship with .NET 3.0 as well as with this book. Note the installation package is provided on the book's CD.

1. Using Windows Explorer, move to the \Software folder on the companion CD.

2. Double-click the file SQLServer2005_SSMSEE.msi. If the Open File – Security Warning dialog appears, click Run.

3. When the Welcome To The Install Wizard For Microsoft SQL Server Management Studio Express dialog box appears, click Next.

4. On the License Agreement page, read the license agreement. If you agree with the license terms, click I Accept and then click Next.

5. When the Registration Information page appears, verify the registration information and click Next.

6. When the Feature Selection page appears, make sure all features are marked as This Feature Will Be Installed On Local Hard Drive and click Next.

7. When the Ready To Install The Program page appears, click Install.

8. After all the files have been installed and your system has been configured, click **Finish**.

Using the Code Samples

Each chapter in this book explains when and how to use any code samples for that chapter. When it's time to use a code sample, the book will list the instructions for how to open the files. The chapters are built around scenarios that simulate real programming projects, so you can easily apply the skills you learn to your own work.

Because a book such as this involves writing a lot of code, I've included the code samples in two forms. The first form is as Visual Studio projects, both completed (fully working) and incomplete (requiring you to complete the steps in the chapter). If in the chapter you build the application entirely from scratch, the CD contains only the completed version of that application.

The other form is a bit different, and that is as a "code manual" you can load into Internet Explorer. When you open the Default.htm file located in the \Manual folder of the code samples, you'll find each chapter has an entry in a navigation bar to the left of the page, and when you select a chapter, all of the code you would normally type into Visual Studio is shown, suitable for copying to the clipboard and pasting into Visual Studio. The code is identified by chapter, section, and step number. Any Internet links mentioned in the chapter are also repeated in the code manual for your convenience as well.

 Note   Note that the files are actually based in XML, so if you're not using Internet Explorer, and therefore cannot use the Internet Explorer behavior files that render the XML as Web pages, you can still load the XML into your browser of choice (or even Visual Studio) and copy and paste the code from there. The XML tags containing the code and links are self-evident.

For those of you who like to know all the details, here's a list of the sample Visual Studio projects and solutions, grouped by the folders where you can find them.

Solution Folder	Description
Chapter1	
PCodeFlow	This solution gets you started. Creating the PCodeFlow project leads you through the process of building a simple WF application. The workflow enables you to test candidate postal codes using both U.S. and Canadian values.
Chapter2	
WorkflowHost	This solution builds a custom workflow host application rather than using the wizards built into the Visual Studio workflow extensions. The purpose is to show you what your host application is required to do to support the workflow runtime.
Chapter3	
WithoutParameters	The WithoutParameters application starts a workflow instance without initialization input parameters.
WithParameters	The WithParameters application shows you how to initiate a workflow instance using initialization input parameter values.
GetStatus	The GetStatus application, like all the applications in Chapter 3, is based on the WorkflowHost application from Chapter 2. GetStatus simply shows how to obtain workflow status information from a workflow instance.
Terminate	The Terminate application is designed to show you how to terminate an executing workflow instance.
Chapter4	
StateFlow	Chapter 4 discusses the different types of workflows you can create using WF. The previous applications were all sequential by nature. The StateFlow application builds a very rudimentary state-based workflow to show how this type of workflow is started.
Chapter5	
WorkflowTracker	WF has the ability to store tracking points in a SQL Server database. As your workflow progresses, you can have WF store information along the way in a manner similar to tracing. This application shows how this is done.
WorkflowTrackerUserEvents	WF comes prewired to store certain information for specific well-known tracking points, but it can't know beforehand about any data you might also want to record in SQL Server as your workflow executes. This application shows you how to provide your own user-defined tracking information to be recorded.
WorkflowTrackerProfile	You might not want all the possible tracking points stored in SQL Server as your workflow progresses. This application shows you how to filter the tracking information through a profile you create and store in SQL Server.

Solution Folder	Description
Chapter6	
WorkflowPersister	Although many workflows could conceivably load, execute, and finish in a relatively short period of time, other workflows might take longer to complete. In those cases, you can, if you want, shuttle your executing workflow out of memory and into a SQL Server database for safekeeping until the conditions that merit its return are met. This application demonstrates this WF capability.
WorkflowIdler	In this solution, you learn how *Delay* activities can be configured to automatically persist your workflow to a SQL Server database, allowing you to remove long-running workflows from your computer's memory while the workflow waits.
Chapter7	
Sequencer	This application demonstrates a simple sequential workflow.
ErrorThrower	What do you do when your workflow encounters a runtime condition it can't handle? Why, use the *Throw* activity, of course! In this application, you see how this is done.
ErrorHandler	This solution demonstrates how workflow-based exceptions thrown using the *Throw* activity are handled by your workflow.
ErrorSuspender	Should you need to do so, you can suspend the execution of your workflow using the *Suspend* activity. This application demonstrates the *Suspend* activity.
ErrorTerminator	As with workflow suspension, you have the capability to completely terminate your workflow. This application demonstrates this capability.
Chapter8	
MVDataChecker	Workflows ultimately work with some form of data. If your host application needs to retrieve data directly from your workflow, this application demonstrates the technique.
WorkflowInvoker	If you've ever wondered whether an executing workflow can invoke another workflow, this application shows you that indeed you can do so.
Chapter9	
IfElse Questioner	This chapter's focus is on workflow logic flow. The application for this chapter is written using three different workflows that accomplish the same task. In this case, the *IfElse* activity directs program flow.
While Questioner	This version of the application uses a *While* activity to direct program flow.
Replicator Questioner	Finally, this application uses the *Replicator* activity to direct program execution flow.

Solution Folder	Description
Chapter10	
eBroker	The application from Chapter 8 shows you how data is sent from your workflow to your host application. This application demonstrates the reverse, where your host application sends data to an already-executing workflow.
Chapter11	
ParallelHelloWorld	This application demonstrates parallel workflow branches, which is in contrast to the sequential workflows demonstrated thus far in the book.
SynchronizedHelloWorld	If you have the ability to create parallel workflow execution branches, you probably will at some point need to synchronize them. If so, this application shows you how.
TankMonitor	WF ships with a fascinating activity called the *ConditionedActivity-Group* activity, or CAG. Part parallel and part event-driven, this activity allows for the monitoring and control of many workflow branches and conditions. This application demonstrates the CAG by monitoring the level of chemical in a storage tank, alerting the user if the level falls below or rises above specified boundary levels.
Chapter12	
RuleQuestioner	This application revisits the applications demonstrated in Chapter 9 by using a rule condition to determine workflow flow rather than the code conditions used previously.
PlasticPolicy	This solution demonstrates the built-in rules processing WF is capable of performing. It builds on an example mentioned in the first chapter.
Chapter13	
FileGrabber	As good as the built-in WF activities are, they can't possibly encompass your every need. Therefore, you can create your own custom activities. This application shows how you might create an FTP-based custom activity to retrieve files from an FTP server.
Chapter14	
SodaMachine	Throughout the book, all the workflows have been sequential by nature, which is to say the workflow tasks went from beginning to end in the order they were assigned. But there is another workflow type, that being the state machine workflow, which has the ability to execute workflows based on finite-state machines. This application simulates a vending machine, a classic finite-state machine example.
Chapter15	
WorkflowATM	Although you might write a hundred workflows that don't require transactional processing, when you find a workflow that does require transactional support, this application is for you. It demonstrates both traditional and compensated transactions as it simulates an automated bank teller machine.

Solution Folder	Description
Chapter16	
DirectXmlWorkflow	This application uses a XAML-based workflow directly.
CompiledXmlWorkflow	If you've studied Windows Presentation Foundation, also a part of .NET 3.0, you might be familiar with XAML, which is the XML vocabulary used to lay out user interfaces and presentation layer logic. What you might not know is WF also accepts XAML, and this chapter shows you several techniques you can use to incorporate XAML-based workflows into your applications. This particular application uses the workflow compiler to take XAML as input and creates a .NET assembly containing your workflow definition.
PCodeXaml	With this application, you revisit the application from Chapter 1 as you re-create that workflow using XAML. What's important here is learning how XAML-based workflows are started using input parameters.
XmlnsDefFlow	This application shows you how you can create custom activities and access them from XAML-based workflows.
Chapter17	
TruckTracker	This chapter examines the concept of correlation and how applications and workflows communicate when more than one workflow is executing in concert with the host application. In this application, you'll execute multiple workflows that monitor the movement of trucks using simulated Global Positioning System tracking capabilities. Each vehicle is represented by a single workflow, and WF keeps the data for an individual vehicle straight using correlation.
Chapter18	
QuoteRetriever	In Chapter 10's application, stock values were updated using a simulation. This application uses a Web service from within the workflow to request the stock quote values.
Chapter19	
QuoteGenerator	This application builds on the previous chapter by driving a Web service to return stock quotes using workflow. WF has the ability to create Web services directly from workflow definitions, which when considering state machine workflows isn't as simple as it might at first appear.

In addition to these projects, most of the projects have completed solutions available. The completed solution for a project is included in the folder for that chapter in a subfolder labeled "{Application Name} Completed."

Uninstalling the Code Samples

Follow these steps to remove the code samples from your computer:

1. In Control Panel, open Add Or Remove Programs.

2. From the list of Currently Installed Programs, select Microsoft Windows Workflow Foundation Step By Step.

3. Click Remove.

4. Follow the instructions displayed to remove the code samples.

Online Companion Content

The online companion content page has content and links related to this book, including a link to the Microsoft Press Technology Updates Web page. The online companion content page for this book can be found at

www.microsoft.com/mspress/companion/0-7356-2335-4/

> **Note**   Code samples for this book are on the companion CD.

Support for This Book

Every effort has been made to ensure the accuracy of this book and the contents of the companion CD. As corrections or changes are collected, they will be added to a Microsoft Knowledge Base article.

Microsoft Press provides support for books and companion CDs at the following Web site:

www.microsoft.com/learning/support/books/

Questions and Comments

If you have comments, questions, or ideas regarding the book or the companion CD, or questions that are not answered by visiting the sites above, please send them to Microsoft Press via e-mail to

mspinput@microsoft.com

Or via postal mail to

Microsoft Press
Attn: Microsoft Windows Workflow Foundation *Step by Step Editor*
One Microsoft Way
Redmond, WA 98052-6399

Please note that Microsoft software product support is not offered through the above addresses.

Part I
Introducing Windows Workflow Foundation (WF)

Chapter 1
Introducing Microsoft Windows Workflow Foundation

After completing this chapter, you will be able to:

- Understand workflow concepts and principles
- Be able to compare Windows Workflow Foundation (WF) to BizTalk and Windows Communication Foundation (WCF)
- Have begun programming with WF
- Know how to use Visual Studio workflow support

Workflow. It sounds like some new technological buzzword, and in a sense, it is. But the concept of workflow stems from the need to process data quickly and accurately. If I were to conjure a definition for the term, I would define *workflow* as the basic tasks, procedures, people and organizations, system informational input and output, policies and rules, and tools needed for each step in a business process. That's a very broad definition, but it often takes all these components to make a business process work. Or not work. Our goal, of course, is to automate the interworkings of these business process elements with software to improve the odds of a given process's success.

Workflow Concepts and Principles

The origins of workflow processing come from document processing, where documents need to go from place to place for approval or review. But the notion of executing a specific set of tasks, coupled with decision making (such as approved or not approved), is something we can generalize. In fact, if you've ever written a piece of software that processed information, made decisions based on system inputs, and took into account the rules and practices of the system in which the software executed, I'd argue that you've written workflow software.

But I'd also hazard a guess that this task wasn't easy for you because for most of us it seldom is. The task involves writing a lot of the support and infrastructure ourselves. And because of this, budget and schedule concerns likely prevented us from writing the performance-minded application we wanted to write. Unfortunately, this happens more often than we'd like. This is simply how business is—time truly *is* money, and the faster we implement our application the more quickly it will be used and benefit the organization.

Enter the Operating System

In the early 1980s, personal computer operating systems did well to introduce hard drives and organize file systems. That was their primary function, in addition to maintaining the runtime environment for a single executing program. Later, innovative developers found ways to write "terminate and stay resident" programs that would pop up given a command key sequence, but still the operating systems were crude by today's standards.

Today, the operating system is expected to be a multitasking one, with virtual memory for each of many concurrently executing tasks. Printing must be seamless. Networking, over Ethernet and other networking mediums, is required. And of course we expect great graphics.

Operating systems have grown in complexity, then, to meet the demands of the consumer as well as to grow with the capabilities of the hardware platforms in which they execute. The business community, which is one of the largest consumers of software and software technology, recognizes this and places even greater demands on operating system vendors.

Microsoft has recognized the need for stronger operating system support for coordinating processes within organizations and decided to include a fantastic capability in the Microsoft Windows Vista operating system, the next release of Microsoft Windows—the *Windows Workflow Foundation*, or WF. This foundational component will ship with every copy of Windows Vista. Moreover, Microsoft has also provided the world with separate distributable copies we can use for existing versions of Windows, including Windows XP and Windows Server 2003. No longer will we have to write all the infrastructure for our business processes!

Multithreading and Workflow

WF is many things, but when you put it under a microscope and examine its most basic functionality, WF essentially provides you with a parallel execution path for your code. Without WF, either you execute your workflow tasks in the same thread that runs your user interface or main process or you write multithreaded software yourself and have the separate threads execute the process logic. But multithreaded software isn't easy to write, and in more cases than we would like to admit, we introduce latent defects (okay, *bugs!*) when we forget even the most seemingly minor detail.

WF, in it's most basic form, provides you with multithreading capability without the hassle. If you follow some basic rules for passing data into and out of WF, you can easily benefit from multithreading without the pain.

> **Note**   Passing data between multiple threads is like handing a cheeseburger to a car next to you when traveling at 70 miles per hour. You can do it, but you'd better know what you're doing, and it's not inherently safe to do. Special synchronization techniques are required, and when there are bugs, they're not often easily found.

"But wait," you ask, "what about BizTalk?" Excellent question. Let's explore that for a moment. In fact, let's also look at Windows Communication Framework (WCF) while we're at it.

Comparing WF with Microsoft BizTalk and WCF

If you've ever worked with BizTalk Server, Microsoft's business to business (B2B) connection platform, you've undoubtedly worked with *orchestration*. Orchestration is BizTalk's term for workflow. Using BizTalk Server, you can use a graphical editor to lay out business processes, and some of these processes might even include external agencies, such as a trading partner, through external communications protocols. Communication with your trading partners is easy and seamless with BizTalk.

But that's the key to the difference between WF and BizTalk Server. BizTalk Server is designed to integrate multiple businesses, or put another way, to facilitate electronic commerce. WF, on the other hand, is designed to work at the operating-system level and is therefore appropriate for integration into a single application within a single domain. That's not to say you can't communicate with external processes and servers using WF, but WF's primary focus is facilitating workflow functionality within your application. BizTalk is designed for *inter*application (multiple applications) use, while WF is focused on *intra*application (single application) functionality.

> **Note**   WF can be used in an interapplication workflow scenario, but doing so requires additional logic and structure, which BizTalk readily provides. In fact, the BizTalk team is even rewriting BizTalk to use WF "under the hood" so that there is a single workflow technology used by Microsoft products.

From a communications standpoint, WF provides you with some basic tools to use XML Web Services. Using WF, you can expose a workflow as a Web Service, and you can consume other Web Services quite easily. Isn't this the same functionality as WCF, though?

Yes, WCF provides you with the basic tools you need to implement and consume XML Web Services, but WCF is a great deal more powerful than that. While the primary goal of WCF is to unify the programming model for all electronic communications processes, certainly one could argue a secondary goal of WCF is to implement the Internet standards for Web Services and allow you to build connection-based *service-oriented architectures*, or SOAs.

With SOAs, software moves from a "call this method" mentality to a "use this service" mentality. If I change a given method's signature, whether I change the method name or the types or numbers of input parameters, I must recompile all the software that depends on (uses) that method. As you know, in large software systems, this process can be difficult and painful. Quite often the process doesn't go right and the software fails during execution, which is a nice way of saying it crashes when the users need it the most.

Service-based software, however, is integrated using contracts and policy. It's expected that services will morph and change, and the goal is to have dependent processes recognize changes and adjust accordingly. *Contracts* identify *what* services are available. *Policy* describes *how* the services are to be used. A contract might tell me there is a service available that I can use to order stock for my shelves. The policy associated with that service would tell me that I have to authenticate before I use the service and that the information flowing between the remote server and my local system must be encrypted and digitally signed. When contracts or policies change, ideally service consumers automatically adjust and change as well.

Note   Actually, when contracts or policies change, things don't magically fix themselves. In reality, service providers should communicate how many previous versions they'll support and service consumers should update their code to the most up-to-date version as soon as possible.

Communication functionality within WF isn't this grand. If you require strong SOA support, by all means use WCF! I do. But for more simplistic "get this data from that Web Service," or "expose this process as a Web Service" needs, WF is able to help, and toward the end of the book we'll look at how WF supports these needs.

Note   This book is designed to get you up and running with WF but not necessarily to explain in great detail *why* you're doing something. We'll have to save that level of detail for another book.

Beginning Programming with WF

With this brief introduction in mind, let's start working with WF. Unless you are using Windows Vista (or later), you will need to download and install the runtime environment for WF. To write software that uses WF, you'll also need to download several additional components to Microsoft Visual Studio 2005. The Introduction contains detailed installation instructions, and you'll find all of the necessary software on the book's CD with the exception of the Windows SDK. It was excluded due to size constraints. The workflow support software on the CD was current at the time this was written, but it's best to check to see if updates are available. As long links you see are easily mistyped, I included them in the section for Chapter 1 in the CD-based manual for your convenience. They were also valid at the time this was written and are also subject to change.

Downloading and installing Windows Workflow Foundation

1.   Download the following files from the links provided:

   ❑   .NET Framework 3.0 runtime components (file: dotnetfx3setup.exe):

   http://www.microsoft.com/downloads/details.aspx?familyid=10CC340B-F857-4A14-83F5-25634C3BF043&displaylang=en

> **Note**   The dotnetfx3setup.exe file is necessary only if you're using Windows XP or Windows Server 2003. If you're using Windows Vista, the .NET Framework 3.0 runtime is already installed.

❑ Windows software development kit, or SDK (file: 6.0.6000.0.0.WindowsSDK_Vista_rtm.DVD.Rel.img, which you can burn to DVD or install from the .img file directly. (To burn the DVD image, you might first have to change the file extension from "img" to "iso".) *http://www.microsoft.com/downloads/details.aspx?familyid=7614FE22-8A64-4DFB-AA0C-DB53035F40A0&displaylang=en*

❑ Visual Studio extensions for presentation and communication ("Orcas") (file: vsextwfx.msi)

This package is described as optional, but if you want to use the visual designer to create workflows (versus creating them entirely through code), you'll need to install it: *http://www.microsoft.com/downloads/details.aspx?familyid=F54F5537-CC86-4BF5-AE44-F5A1E805680D&displaylang=en*

❑ Visual Studio extensions for workflow (file: Visual Studio 2005 Extensions for Windows Workflow Foundation (EN).exe): *http://www.microsoft.com/downloads/details.aspx?familyid=5D61409E-1FA3-48CF-8023-E8F38E709BA6&displaylang=en*

2. Install the downloaded software packages in the following order:

❑ Double-click the dotnetfx3setup.exe file to begin installation of the .NET Framework, version 3.0. Follow the on-screen wizard's instructions to complete the installation. This installation application will download additional components from Microsoft at the time you install it and when complete will prompt you to download and install the latest related service packs and security updates.

❑ Place the DVD you created with the Windows SDK into your DVD-ROM player and follow the provided installation instructions.

❑ Double-click the vsextwfx.msi file to merge the installation files for the Visual Studio enhancements into Visual Studio. If you receive an error stating you don't have the prerequisite software already installed, ignore the error and continue.

❑ Execute Visual Studio 2005 Extensions for Windows Workflow Foundation (EN).exe to install the Windows Worflow Foundation components. Follow any on-screen instructions.

Once you've downloaded and installed these components, you will have installed the WF runtime on your system and loaded the development tools that both you and Visual Studio 2005 will need to create workflow-enabled software.

Visual Studio Workflow Support

We'll build a quick little workflow application in a moment, but first let's look at the workflow support Visual Studio 2005 provides.

Visual Studio 2005 support for WF falls into two main categories: visual editing and templates. The visual editor, called the workflow designer, is very much like the forms designer you're probably accustomed to using. You drag workflow-related items from the toolbox onto your workflow, change some properties, compile, and go. Visual Studio 2005 also supports visual debugging by allowing you to set breakpoints in the designer to debug and test while executing your workflow objects. You'll see the designer in action when you build your first workflow application in the next section.

As for templates, Visual Studio provides templates for adding workflow-based projects as well as inserting a great variety of workflow-related objects once you have a project open. You'll also take a look at the various templates as you build your first workflow application.

Building Your First Workflow Program

Here is a small code snippet that performs postal code validation, and it's one you've no doubt written before or probably very much like one you would write if asked to do so:

```
protected const string USCode =
    @"^(\d{5}$)|(\d{5}$\-\d{4}$)";
protected const string CanadianCode =
    @"[ABCEGHJKLMNPRSTVXY]\d[A-Z] \d[A-Z]\d";

public static bool ValidatePostalCode(string str)
{
    return (Regex.IsMatch(str, USCode) ||
            Regex.IsMatch(str, CanadianCode));
}
```

Nothing special here—"Test the input string against a properly formatted US ZIP code or Canadian postal code and return false if improperly formatted for either postal system." It's a nice chunk of procedural code, and in fact you could drop it into your ASP.NET validation logic as is if you weren't using some other validation control that already uses regular expressions. We'll now build a workflow application that performs this same validation and reports back the pass/fail status.

Create a console-based workflow project

1. In Microsoft Windows, click the Start button, move the cursor to All Programs, and then select Microsoft Visual Studio 2005 from the resulting menu.

2. Click the Microsoft Visual Studio 2005 icon to start Visual Studio 2005.

Note   If this is the first time you've run Visual Studio 2005, you might see a dialog box that asks you to select certain default development system preferences, such as Microsoft Visual C# as your preferred development language. Visual Studio tailors its user interface to match your preferences. Once configured, the Visual Studio integrated development environment (IDE) will appear.

3. On the File menu, select New and then Project. The New Project dialog box appears. This dialog box contains many project templates, including Windows Forms applications, console applications, class libraries, and so forth. It might even contain templates for different languages if you installed them.

Note   The templates installed on your system result from the combination of the version of Visual Studio you are using and any additional software you might have installed, such as for WF. You can even define your own project templates, but that is a topic for another book.

4. In the Project Types pane, click Visual C# to expand the tree node to show the project types available for the C# language.

5. Under the Visual C# node, click the Workflow node to display the workflow-based project templates.

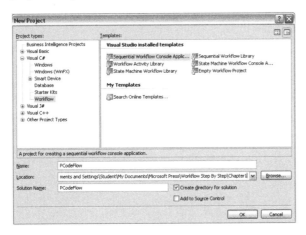

> **Note**   Because you're learning to use WF, I'll sometimes have you build a workflow-based project from scratch to demystify what's required to host WF in your applications. But in this case I'll use one of the WF-provided templates (a console application). The other templates include projects for building workflow libraries, other types of workflow projects (primarily a "state machine" project, which we'll tackle starting in Chapter 4), and one template for an empty project, which references the WF assemblies but provides no source code files. Notably absent is a graphical user interface project that includes WF support. That you'll need to build on your own (but you'd probably use a workflow library to house your workflow code anyway).

6. In the Templates pane, click Sequential Workflow Console Application.

7. In the Name field, type **PCodeFlow**.

8. In the Location field, type **C:\Documents and Settings***YourUsername***\My Documents\Microsoft Press\Workflow Step By Step\Chapter1**.

    Replace the text *YourUsername* with your Windows user name. Because this directory name is lengthy, and to save some space in the book, we will refer to the path "C:\Documents and Settings\YourUsername\My Documents\Microsoft Press \Workflow Step By Step" as your "\Workflow" directory.

> **Note**   The directory path I've provided is just a suggestion. Feel free to place the project anywhere on your local drive that you feel is appropriate if you'd rather not use the directory I've specified. If the directory does not exist, Visual Studio will create it for you. But do keep track of this directory path name, as we'll need it later to execute the application we create here.

9. If the Create Directory For Solution check box is not already selected, select it.

10. Click OK. Visual Studio 2005 will now create the basic project for you and bring up the workflow visual designer user interface.

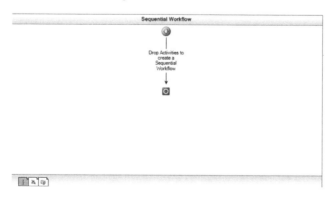

This is the basic process for creating any type of Visual Studio project, and we'll use it throughout the book. Most of the sample projects we'll create will be console applications simply because there is less automatically generated code to wade through to build our examples. But from time to time we will create other types of projects, such as for custom workflow services, activities, and even a few Windows Forms applications.

> **Note**   If you're new to Visual Studio 2005, welcome! You'll find it to be a rich development environment with a host of features and capabilities. You might find an additional resource handy, though, to guide you as you learn the system. John Sharp's excellent *Microsoft Visual C# 2005 Step by Step* (Microsoft Press, 2006) will prove invaluable as you learn Visual Studio 2005.

Before editing code or inserting workflow items, take a moment and look at two of the files the workflow project generator created for you:

Program.cs   This, in many respects, is a typical console application source file. However, the template added a great deal of code to support workflow operations. Understanding the code that is here is a major goal of this book, but we'll at least get a feel for what it's doing in this chapter.

Workflow1.cs   This is the workflow component we'll modify to validate the incoming postal code. It is the first of many you could add, but for now we'll just use this single workflow.

The other files are typical of Visual Studio 2005 console projects. Something that is atypical, however, is the references Visual Studio 2005 automatically created for you. In addition to the *System* assembly, which any common console application would have referenced, Visual Studio 2005 added references to these assemblies:

- *System.Data*
- *System.Design*
- *System.Drawing*
- *System.Drawing.Design*
- *System.Transactions*
- *System.Web*
- *System.Web.Services*
- *System.Workflow.Activities*
- *System.Workflow.ComponentModel*
- *System.Workflow.Runtime*

This is a nice feature to have when creating workflow applications using Visual Studio 2005. It's easy to forget to include an assembly when assigning references, so having the references created for you automatically helps speed your development process.

Let's now turn our attention to building our workflow using the workflow visual designer.

Building a workflow

1. With the workflow visual designer showing, move the mouse cursor to the Visual Studio Toolbox and allow it to expand. If the workflow visual designer is not showing, select Workflow1.cs in the Solution Explorer pane and click the Solution Explorer's View Designer toolbar button.

2. Drag the *IfElse* activity component onto the workflow designer's surface. *Activities* are the building blocks of workflow applications, and the Toolbox contains the activities that are currently appropriate for your workflow. As the mouse approaches the Drop Activities To Create A Sequential Workflow area, the designer view changes slightly to indicate that you can drop the *IfElse* activity icon onto the designer surface.

> **Note**   Visual Studio 2005 will place only the activities appropriate for your workflow application into the Toolbox. Other activities in fact are available, but Visual Studio won't present them in the ToolBox because they're not designed for use with the workflow type currently being edited. (We'll look at the different workflow types in Chapter 4, "Introduction to Activities and Workflow Types.")

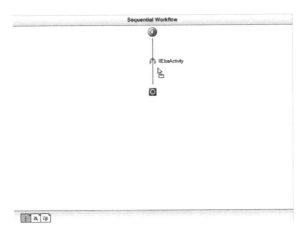

3. Release the mouse button to drop the *IfElse* activity icon into the sequential workflow.

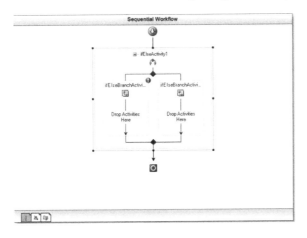

We're now going to use the *IfElse* activity component to ask the following question: "Does the string we've provided contain a valid postal code?" We'll actually ask this question in code, using the regular expression code snippet you saw previously.

Before we do, though, look closely at the workflow visual designer. The workflow designer is reminding us that we've not yet provided code to make this decision. If you look at the upper-right corner of the left branch, named *ifElseBranchActivity1*, you'll see a small circular icon with an exclamation mark inside. This is the workflow visual designer's way of telling you that the workflow is incomplete. If you attempt to compile a workflow project with these reminder icons active, you'll receive compilation errors. The workflow visual designer will tell you more about the error condition if you move the mouse over the icon and then click the down arrow that appears:

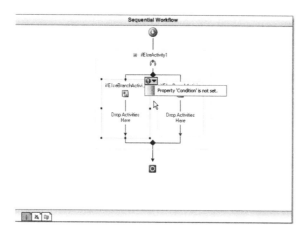

Let's correct this situation and add some code to our workflow.

Adding code to the *IfElse* activity's conditional branch

1. Move the mouse cursor over the left branch, named *ifElseBranchActivity1*, and click to activate the properties for this branch in the Properties pane. If the Properties pane isn't visible, select View and then Properties Window from the main Visual Studio menu.

> **Note** Visual Studio 2005 provides default names for objects when you insert them into your workflow. However, the names might not be adequate (they're placeholders). At any time, you can easily rename activities and activity components by changing the *Name* property, shown in the Visual Studio Properties pane, to something more appropriate. For this example, we'll go with the default names.

2. We need to add a condition, which is to say a test that forces the workflow to take the actions in the left branch (condition evaluates to *true*) or the right branch (condition evaluates to *false*). To do this, click the *Condition* property to activate the *Condition* type property drop-down list. From that list, you can select a code condition type, a rule condition type, or none. Click the Code Condition option.

3. The *Condition* type property user interface will now change to include a plus sign (+) that, when clicked, drops a child property, also named *Condition*. This child *Condition* property is where we'll begin adding code. Click the child *Condition* property to again activate the property drop-down list.

4. The *Condition* property is requesting a name for the internal event we want to add. This event will fire when the condition requires evaluation. For this example, type **EvaluatePostalCode** into the Condition property field.

Behind the scenes, Visual Studio 2005 added the event you identified in the *Condition* property to the workflow source file. Later, we'll need to actually add the regular expression code snippet that is executed in response to this event.

Before we do, though, let's continue working in the workflow visual designer, as we have more to do here. We just added a condition that will cause the workflow to choose one path or the other through our workflow, but neither path has any identifiable action. We need to add activities to the left branch, *ifElseBranchActivity1*, and the right branch, *ifElseBranchActivity2*.

Adding conditional code activities

1. Move the mouse cursor to the Toolbox, and allow it to expand. After the toolbox has been expanded, select the *Code* activity.

2. Drag the *Code* activity icon into the workflow visual designer, and drop it in the Drop Activities Here area in the left branch (*ifElseBranchActivity1*). You might need to enlarge your Visual Studio window in order to see both the ToolBox and the left branch. This creates a *Code* activity and associates it with the branch that will be taken if the condition evaluates to true.

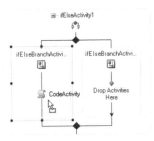

The result looks like this:

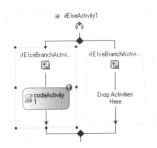

3. Just as we did when adding code to evaluate the condition, we'll add code that will execute when this branch is taken. To do that, click the *codeActivity1* icon to activate its properties in the Visual Studio Properties pane.

4. Click the *ExecuteCode* property, and activate it by clicking in the edit portion of its drop-down list as you did with the *Condition* property. The workflow runtime will execute the conditional code you specify here in response to an event, and we'll again have the opportunity to name the event. Type **PostalCodeValid** in the *ExecuteCode* property.

To review, at this point Visual Studio 2005 has inserted events that, when fired, will execute code we'll provide in a moment. The first event handler, *EvaluatePostalCode*, executes when the workflow runtime needs to evaluate the test condition. The second event handler, *PostalCodeValid*, executes when the left branch is taken (that is, the test condition evaluated to true).

We could, at this point, add code to the right-hand branch, which would be executed if the test condition evaluated to *false* (that is, the postal code was not valid). To do so, retrace the last set of steps but add the *Code* activity to the right branch and name the event **PostalCodeInvalid**. This adds a third event handler to our workflow, *PostalCodeInvalid*.

If you're familiar with how events are handled in .NET, the next set of steps should be familiar. The event handlers we added will be called by the workflow runtime at the appropriate locations in our application. We'll need to add code to the event handlers Visual Studio added for us to intercept the events and take action. Let's see how that's done.

Adding event handler code to our workflow

1. In the Visual Studio Solution Explorer pane, click Workflow1.cs to select it in the Solution Explorer tree control. Then click Solution Explorer's View Code toolbar button to open the Workflow1.cs C# file for editing.

2. With the C# source code loaded in the editor, locate the *Workflow1* constructor:

```
public Workflow1()
{
    InitializeComponent();
}
```

3. The *InitializeComponent* method is called within the constructor to assign and initialize the events we inserted using the designer. If you opened the file Workflow1.designer.cs, you would find a line of code similar to the following (you must expand the Designer Generated Code block):

```
codecondition1.Condition +=
 new System.EventHandler<System.Workflow.Activities.ConditionalEventArgs>
 (this.EvaluatePostalCode);
```

> **Tip**   The Workflow1.designer.cs file is similar to the code-behind files for Windows Forms applications. If you prefer editing this code in the editor rather than in the designer, by all means feel free to do so. If you wondered how the code in the events was managed, this is where you'll find the code to hook the events into the .NET and workflow runtime.

4. We'll next add the regular expression code snippet in slightly modified form. Locate the newly inserted *EvaluatePostalCode* method in Workflow1.cs, and insert the following code into the blank method:

```
string USCode = @"^(\d{5}$)|(\d{5}$\-\d{4}$)";
string CanadianCode = @"[ABCEGHJKLMNPRSTVXY]\d[A-Z] \d[A-Z]\d";

e.Result = (Regex.IsMatch(_code, USCode) ||
            Regex.IsMatch(_code, CanadianCode));
```

> **Tip**   For simplicity, I added the regular expressions as locally declared strings within the *EvaluatePostalCodeHandler* event handler. In reality, you'd probably declare them as constant strings in the enclosing workflow activity class. Keep in mind that the manual included on the CD has text you can copy and paste into Visual Studio if you'd rather not type it in by hand.

The variable *e* is an instance of *ConditionalEventArgs*, which is used to tell the *IfElse* activity which branch to take. Setting *e.Result* to true means the left branch will be executed. Conversely, the right branch is executed if you set *e.Result* to false.

5. *Regex* is an object exported by *System.Text.RegularExpressions*. For our program to compile, we need to add the appropriate *using* clause at the top of the Workflow1.cs source file:

```
using System.Text.RegularExpressions;
```

6. We also need to add the ability for our workflow activity to accept the incoming string for evaluation. To do this, we'll add a public string property named *PostalCode* to the class, just prior to the *EvaluatePostalCode* method:

```
private string _code = String.Empty;

public string PostalCode
{
    get { return _code; }
    set { _code = value; }
}
```

7. At this point, our workflow application would compile, but it's still incomplete. We've not added code to the handlers for the conditional branches. Locate the *PostalCodeValid* method Visual Studio inserted in Workflow1.cs, and insert the following code into the empty implementation you find there:

```
Console.WriteLine("The postal code {0} is valid.", _code);
```

8. Repeat step 7 to add a *Code* activity to the right condition (the *false* condition), but add the following code to the false condition handler, *PostalCodeInvalid*:

```
Console.WriteLine("The postal code {0} is *invalid*.", _code);
```

We're nearly there! To this point, we've created a complete workflow application, with one notable exception. Although the workflow portion is now complete, we've not added any code to properly call the workflow into execution. To do that, we'll need to add some code to the application startup method, *Main*, which is found in the Program.cs file. That's next.

Calling your workflow into execution

1. Click Program.cs in the Visual Studio Solution Explorer and then click the Solution Explorer View Code toolbar button.

2. Locate the following code in the *Main* method:

```
WorkflowInstance instance =
    workflowRuntime.CreateWorkflow(typeof(PCodeFlow.Workflow1));
```

3. Replace the code you just located with the following:

```
// Added to basic code provided by Visual Studio and .NET 3.0 ("WinFX")
Dictionary<string, object> wfArgs = new Dictionary<string, object>();
wfArgs.Add("PostalCode", args.Length > 0 ? args[0] : "");
```

```
// Modified to accept the input parameter "wfArgs"
WorkflowInstance instance =
    workflowRuntime.CreateWorkflow(typeof(PCodeFlow.Workflow1), wfArgs);
```

> **Note** The startup code Visual Studio 2005 inserted into the *Main* method would have been perfectly adequate had we not wanted to pass the postal code found on the command line to the workflow. We'll look more closely at passing startup arguments to our workflows in the next chapter.

4. Compile the application by selecting Build PCodeFlow from the Visual Studio Build menu.

That's it! The code we just added allows us to process a postal code that's provided on the command line. Let's try it.

Executing your workflow application

1. In Microsoft Windows, click the Start button, move the cursor to Run, and click to open the Run dialog box.

2. In the Run dialog box Open field, type **cmd** and click OK.

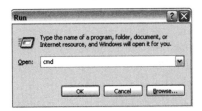

3. This opens a Windows Command Shell. At the command prompt, type **cd \Workflow\Chapter1\PCodeFlow\PCodeFlow\bin\Debug** and press the Enter key. This changes the current directory in the command window to the directory containing our workflow application. If you compiled the application using the Release mode, then be sure to change to the Release directory rather than the Debug directory.

> **Note** Don't forget our convention regarding directory names: "\Workflow" indicates the root directory you selected when you created the PCodeFlow project. You'll need to replace "\Workflow" with the full path name you chose.

4. Type the following command at the prompt, followed by the Enter key: **pcodeflow 12345**. The application should take a moment (to spin up the .NET Framework as well as the workflow runtime) and then spit out "The postal code 12345 was valid."

5. Type the following command at the prompt, followed by the Enter key: **pcodeflow 1234x**. The application should respond with "The postal code 12345 was *invalid*."

6. Type the following command at the prompt, followed by the Enter key: **pcodeflow "A1A 1A1"**. The application should tell you "The postal code A1A 1A1 was valid."

7. Type the following command at the prompt, followed by the Enter key: **pcodeflow "A1A ABC"**. The application should sadly indicate "The postal code A1A ABC was *invalid*."

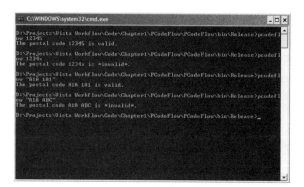

If you want to continue to the next chapter, keep Visual Studio 2005 running and turn to Chapter 2. I recommend grabbing some spicy cheese crackers and a cold Diet Mountain Dew, my caffeinated beverage of choice.

If you want to stop, exit Visual Studio 2005 now, save your spot in the book, and close it. (Personally, I'd also reward myself with a malted beverage brewed with barley and hops, but feel free to go for any chilled beverage you prefer.)

Chapter 1 Quick Reference

To	Do This
Create a new console (sequential) workflow application	From the Visual Studio menu, choose File and then New, selecting Project as the new item type. From the New Project dialog box, select Visual C# and Workflow from the Project Types pane and Sequential Workflow Console Application from the Templates pane. Select a location for the project files in the Location field. Type a name for the project in the Name field. Click OK.
View your workflow process in the workflow visual designer	Select the workflow you want to view from the Visual Studio Solution Explorer, and click the View Designer toolbar button.
Add activities to your workflow	With the workflow visual designer open in Visual Studio, drag activities from the Toolbox into your workflow.
To modify activity properties	Select the activity whose property you want to modify, and change the property in the Visual Studio Properties pane.
To edit activity code directly	Select the activity whose code you want to edit in the Visual Studio Solution Explorer pane, and click the Solution Explorer View Code toolbar button.

Chapter 2
The Workflow Runtime

After completing this chapter, you will be able to:

- Be able to host the workflow runtime in your applications
- Understand the basic capabilities of the *WorkflowRuntime* object
- Know how to start and stop the workflow runtime
- Be able to connect to the various workflow runtime events

When you execute tasks in the Workflow Foundation (WF) environment, *something* needs to oversee that execution and keep things straight. In WF, that something is an object known as *WorkflowRuntime*. *WorkflowRuntime* starts individual workflow tasks. *WorkflowRuntime* fires events for different situations that pop up while your tasks execute. And *WorkflowRuntime* keeps track of and uses pluggable services you can hook in to the execution environment. (We'll look at some of these pluggable services starting in Chapter 5, "Workflow Tracking.")

The overall WF architecture is shown in Figure 2-1.

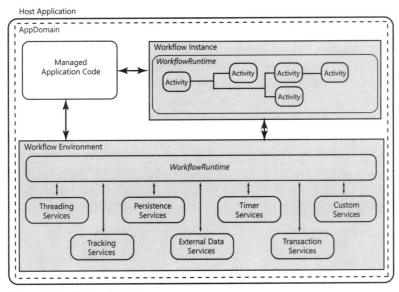

Figure 2-1 WF architecture

WF and your application execute concurrently. In fact, WF requires your application as a host. The host application might be a Windows Forms application, a console application, an ASP.NET Web application, or even a Windows service. The WF runtime and your application execute together in a .NET AppDomain, and there can be only one instance of *WorkflowRuntime* per AppDomain. Attempting to create a second instance of *WorkflowRuntime* in a single AppDomain results in an *InvalidOperationException*.

You build workflow applications—"workflows"—by creating logical groupings of *activities*. These logical groupings work to complete the workflow task you require. When you host the workflow runtime, you essentially hand the workflow your activities and tell it to execute them. This results in a workflow *instance*. The workflow instance is a currently executing workflow task, which is itself composed of logically grouped activities. And, as you recall from the first chapter, activities can execute code you provide as well as make decisions based on input data. We'll cover workflow instances in the next chapter and activities in the chapters to follow.

Hosting WF in Your Applications

In the last chapter, we used the Microsoft Visual Studio workflow project template to build a basic workflow application for us. And in practice you would likely do just that. But if you're like me, just executing wizards and such is fine *only* if you understand the code they're inserting. After all, the code is *yours* to maintain and understand once the code generator's job is complete.

So what does it take to host WF in your application? Well, aside from building the workflow tasks that WF is to run (that's your job), all you really need to do is reference the WF assemblies and provide the necessary code to bring *WorkflowRuntime* into execution, start it, and manage the operational conditions you're interested in managing. In that sense, hosting WF isn't a lot different from using other .NET assemblies. The operational condition management amounts to handling events that the runtime will fire from time to time given specific conditions, such as when the runtime goes idle or an instance sustains an unhandled exception. There is quite a list of available events you can handle, and we'll see some of those a bit later in the chapter, with still others introduced in Chapter 5, "Workflow Tracking," and Chapter 6, "Loading and Unloading Instances."

 Note   WF can be hosted in a variety of applications, including Microsoft Windows Forms and Windows Presentation Foundation applications, console applications, ASP.NET Web applications, and Windows Services. The basic process remains the same as far as WF is concerned for all of these (very different) host application types.

For now, though, let's build a basic .NET console application and host the workflow runtime ourselves. This will help make the code the Visual Studio workflow project template inserts a little less mysterious.

Creating a basic console application

1. Start Visual Studio 2005 as you did in the previous chapter.

2. From the File menu, select New and then Project.

3. When the New Project dialog box appears, expand the Visual C# tree control node and then select Windows from the Project Types pane.

4. Select Console Application from the Templates pane.

5. In the Name field, type **WorkflowHost**.

6. In the Location field, type **\Workflow\Chapter2**.

> **Note**   Remember that the path *\Workflow* represents the path you are using to store the book's sample applications.

7. Click OK to create the WorkflowHost project.

At this point, we have a basic console application, but of course it does nothing interesting. Now let's begin adding workflow components. Speaking personally, I truly love the Visual Studio IntelliSense functionality. But for that to take effect, you have to first reference the assemblies IntelliSense will interpret to help you write code. So a great place to start is to reference the workflow assemblies before adding any code. This way, when we do add code, we can take advantage of the Visual Studio code assistance capabilities.

Adding the workflow assembly references

1. In the Visual Studio Solution Explorer pane, right-click the References tree node and select Add Reference.

> **Tip**   Selecting Add Reference from the Visual Studio Project menu achieves the same result.

2. This activates the Add Reference dialog box. Using the vertical scrollbar's thumb control, scroll down until you find System.Workflow.Runtime. Select that using a single mouse click.

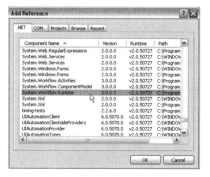

3. Click OK to add the reference.

Visual Studio has now added the workflow runtime reference you'll need to execute workflow tasks. What we've *not* done is actually bring the workflow runtime into execution. To do that, we need to add some code to our application—here's what we'll do.

Hosting the workflow runtime

1. If it's not already open, open the Program.cs file for editing as you did in the previous chapter.

2. Locate the following code (which is located at the top of the source file):

```
using System;
using System.Collections.Generic;
using System.Text;
```

3. Add the following line of code, just after the *System.Text* line:

```
using System.Workflow.Runtime;
```

4. Locate the *Main* method, and add the following line of code after the opening curly brace:

```
WorkflowRuntime workflowRuntime = new WorkflowRuntime();
```

5. For now, we'll just compile the program to make sure there are no errors. We'll use this application throughout the chapter, so keep Visual Studio running, or reload this application as necessary while progressing through the chapter. To compile, select Build WorkflowHost from the Visual Studio Build menu.

A Closer Look at the *WorkflowRuntime* Object

Now that we have an instance of *WorkflowRuntime* created in our WorkflowHost application, it's time to take a brief look at how we interact with this object. Like most useful objects, *WorkflowRuntime* exposes a set of methods and properties we use to control the workflow runtime environment. Table 2-1 lists all the *WorkflowRuntime* properties, while Table 2-2 lists the methods we typically use.

Table 2-1   *WorkflowRuntime* Properties

Property	Purpose
IsStarted	Used to determine whether the workflow runtime has been started and is ready to accept workflow instances. *IsStarted* is *false* until the host calls *StartRuntime*. It remains *true* until the host calls *StopRuntime*. Note you cannot add core services to the workflow runtime while it is running. (We'll address starting services in Chapter 5.)
Name	Gets or sets the name associated with the *WorkflowRuntime*. You cannot set *Name* while the workflow runtime is running (that is, when *IsStarted* is *true*). Any attempt to do so will result in an *InvalidOperationException*.

Table 2-2   *WorkflowRuntime* Methods

Method	Purpose
AddService	Adds the specified service to the workflow runtime. There are limitations regarding what services can be added as well as when. We'll look at services in more detail starting in Chapter 5.
CreateWorkflow	Creates a workflow instance, including any specified (but optional) parameters. If the workflow runtime has not been started, the *CreateWorkflow* method calls *StartRuntime*.
GetWorkflow	Retrieves the workflow instance that has the specified workflow instance identifier (which consists of a Guid). If the workflow instance was idled and persisted, it will be reloaded and executed.
StartRuntime	Starts the workflow runtime and the workflow runtime services and then raises the *Started* event.
StopRuntime	Stops the workflow runtime and the runtime services and then raises the *Stopped* event.

There are more methods associated with *WorkflowRuntime*, but the methods shown in Table 2-2 are the ones most commonly used and the ones we'll focus on both here and in the remainder of the book. There are also a number of events *WorkflowRuntime* will raise at various times during workflow execution, but we'll examine those a bit later in the chapter.

Basically, then, working with *WorkflowRuntime* involves calling a few simple methods and handling some events of interest. There is a significant limitation *WorkflowRuntime* imposes, however, which we'll look at next.

Building a Workflow Runtime Factory

I mentioned this previously in the chapter, but it is important enough to mention again—there can be only a single instance of *WorkflowRuntime* per AppDomain. And because the majority of .NET applications use only a single AppDomain, it necessarily follows that you can generally use only a single instance of *WorkflowRuntime* in your application.

Whenever I hear "use only a single instance," I naturally think of using a combination of the singleton and factory patterns. The *singleton pattern*, if you're unfamiliar with patterns, is simply a mechanism for assuring that no matter how many times your application requests instances of the singleton object, only one instance of the singleton is ever given out. This is typically done for objects that are considered "expensive" to create, such as objects that consume a large number of resources or take a significant amount of time to be created.

The concept of a singleton, which is to say only a single object is ever created and handed to your application, dovetails nicely with the *factory pattern*. The factory pattern involves an intermediate object that's used to create instances of other objects. Most of us, for example, don't build our own cars. Instead, we purchase them from the automobile manufacturer, at least indirectly. (Many of us, I'm sure, wish we could buy them directly!)

The combination of the singleton and factory is powerful because the factory can make sure only a single instance of the singleton object is ever created. This is perfect for our needs, because within our application it's entirely possible that different pieces of the application might try to load and start the workflow runtime (independent application modules, for instance). Let's see how we might create a *WorkflowRuntime* factory.

Creating the *WorkflowRuntime* factory object

1. We'll need to add a new class to our WorkflowHost poject. To do that, right-click on the project name (WorkflowHost) in the Visual Studio Solution Explorer and select Class from the Add menu item.

> **Tip**   Selecting Add Class from the Visual Studio Project menu achieves the same result.

2. The Add New Item dialog box should now appear, and because we requested that a new class be created, the Class item in the Templates pane should already be selected. Therefore, we'll only need to name the source file (which indirectly also names the object we're creating). Type **WorkflowFactory.cs** into the Name field and click Add.

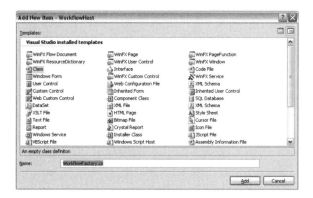

3. As we did with the main application source file, Program.cs, we'll need to add the *using* directive for the workflow assembly to the top of the *WorkflowFactory* source file. The *WorkflowFactory* source file should be open for editing because we just created it, but if not, open it for editing using the techniques we used for opening Program.cs in the previous chapter. To add the *using* directive, locate this code at the top of the WorkflowFactory.cs file:

```
using System;
using System.Collections.Generic;
using System.Text;
```

After the *using* directive for *System.Text*, add the following line:

```
using System.Workflow.Runtime;
```

4. The using directive introduces the workflow runtime assembly to our source file, but it does little more. We need to add the code to represent the singleton object to the *WorkflowFactory* class. To do that, locate the *WorkflowFactory* class definition:

```
class WorkflowFactory
{
}
```

Not much of a class yet! But we'll fix that. Just after the opening curly brace of the class definition, add these lines of code:

```
// Singleton instance of the workflow runtime.
private static WorkflowRuntime _workflowRuntime = null;|

// Lock (sync) object.
private static object _syncRoot = new object();
```

5. Notice that the field *_workflowRuntime* is initialized to *null*. Our factory will sense this and create a new instance of *WorkflowRuntime*. If *workflowRuntime* is not *null*, our factory won't create a new instance but will hand out the existing instance. To do this, we'll need to add a method designed to create and return our singleton object. Moreover, we'll make the method static so that objects requesting the workflow runtime object don't need to create instances of the factory. To do this, we'll add the following code just after the *_syncRoot* field:

```
// Factory method.
public static WorkflowRuntime GetWorkflowRuntime()
{
    // Lock execution thread in case of multi-threaded
    // (concurrent) access.
    lock (_syncRoot)
    {
        // Check for startup condition.
        if (null == _workflowRuntime)
        {

            // Not started, so create instance.
            _workflowRuntime = new WorkflowRuntime();
        } // if

        // Return singleton instance.
        return _workflowRuntime;
    } // lock
}
```

6. Almost there! When the Visual Studio class template builds a new class, it omits the *public* keyword on the class definition, making it a private class. Because we want other classes to be able to request instances of *WorkflowRuntime*, we'll need to make the factory class public. While we're at it, we'll also mark the class as *static* to prevent direct

instantiation (it's a factory class, after all). To make all this happen, we'll change the class definition from this

```
class WorkflowFactory
```

to this:

```
public static class WorkflowFactory
```

With *WorkflowFactory* in hand, any part of your application can request the workflow runtime without getting slammed with an *InvalidOperationException*. Later, starting in Chapter 5, we'll make slight revisions to this class to account for other startup services we might want to include.

Tip   I like placing all the startup and shutdown code in this factory because it puts all the runtime initialization code in one place, making future changes and maintenance easier. No matter what object requests access to the workflow runtime, we know the runtime has been initialized according to our design.

Starting the Workflow Runtime

Of course, no sooner have you created your *WorkflowFactory* object than I'll ask you to modify it. I've done this intentionally because I wanted to single out how the workflow runtime is started. Referring back to Table 2-2, we see that there is a method called *StartRuntime*, and making that method call from within our factory object makes a lot of sense. External objects requesting the workflow runtime object (presumably to create new workflow instances) do not need to deal with or worry about the initialization state of the runtime environment. We have a one-stop place to establish the environment as required by our application. The external objects requesting the workflow runtime object can simply use it without making further changes to the environment as they receive it.

Calling *StartRuntime* is not absolutely required. If we were to create a workflow instance, *StartRuntime* would be called internally for us. And if all we ever did was create an instance of *WorkflowRuntime*, I probably wouldn't worry about calling *StartRuntime* explicitly. Once we add services, however (starting in Chapter 5), I think the explicit call makes a lot of sense, if only for code-maintenance purposes and to ensure the runtime environment's state is properly established as the workflow runtime object is passed out to whoever asks for it.

So let's make the slight change to our factory object and call *StartRuntime* directly.

Starting the workflow runtime

1. With Visual Studio running and WorkflowFactory.cs open for editing, locate this line of code:

```
_workflowRuntime = new WorkflowRuntime();
```

2. Following this line of code, add this new line:

```
// Start the runtime.
_workflowRuntime.StartRuntime();
```

Stopping the Workflow Runtime

If there is a way to start the workflow runtime, it makes sense that there is a way to stop it as well. And in fact there is. Looking back at Table 2-2, we see there is a *StopRuntime* method that matches, and countermands, *StartRuntime*. Calling *StopRuntime* unloads all executing work-flows and services and shuts down the runtime environment. Of course, the appropriate place to call *StopRuntime* is just prior to or during your application shutdown logic, or as the AppDomain is being torn down.

 Tip   Just as calling *StartRuntime* is not mandatory (but not a bad idea), calling *StopRuntime* also isn't mandatory (but is similarly a good idea). As the WF runtime assembly unloads, *StopRuntime* is called automatically.

 Note   You cannot call *StopRuntime* once the *WorkflowRuntime* object is marked as disposed. Doing so results in an *ObjectDisposedException*. Depending on the timing of your application termination, this might be something to watch out for.

A great place to provide for this is in the *WorkflowFactory* object. Let's modify *WorkflowFactory* to automatically shut the workflow runtime down for us.

Stopping the workflow runtime

1. With Visual Studio running and WorkflowFactory.cs open for editing, locate this line of code:

```
_workflowRuntime = new WorkflowRuntime();
```

2. Prior to this line of code, add these lines of code:

```
// Provide for shutdown
AppDomain.CurrentDomain.ProcessExit += new
                        EventHandler(StopWorkflowRuntime);
AppDomain.CurrentDomain.DomainUnload += new
                        EventHandler(StopWorkflowRuntime);
```

3. Then add the *StopWorkflowRuntime* to the *WorkflowFactory* class:

```
// Shutdown method
static void StopWorkflowRuntime(object sender, EventArgs e)
{
    if (_workflowRuntime != null)
    {
```

```
            if (_workflowRuntime.IsStarted)
            {
                try
                {
                    // Stop the runtime
                    _workflowRuntime.StopRuntime();
                }
                catch (ObjectDisposedException)
                {
                    // Already disposed of, so ignore...
                } // catch
            } // if
        } // if
    }
```

The entire listing for the *WorkflowFactory* object is shown in Listing 2-1. We'll not make any further changes until Chapter 5.

Listing 2-1   The Complete *WorkflowFactory* Object

```csharp
using System;
using System.Collections.Generic;
using System.Text;
using System.Workflow.Runtime;

namespace WorkflowHost
{
    public static class WorkflowFactory
    {
        // Singleton instance of the workflow runtime
        private static WorkflowRuntime _workflowRuntime = null;

        // Lock (sync) object
        private static object _syncRoot = new object();

        // Factory method
        public static WorkflowRuntime GetWorkflowRuntime()
        {
            // Lock execution thread in case of multi-threaded
            // (concurrent) access.
            lock (_syncRoot)
            {
                // Check for startup condition
                if (null == _workflowRuntime)
                {
                    // Provide for shutdown
                    AppDomain.CurrentDomain.ProcessExit += new
                            EventHandler(StopWorkflowRuntime);
                    AppDomain.CurrentDomain.DomainUnload += new
                            EventHandler(StopWorkflowRuntime);

                    // Not started, so create instance
                    _workflowRuntime = new WorkflowRuntime();

                    // Start the runtime
```

```
            _workflowRuntime.StartRuntime();
        } // if

        // Return singleton instance
        return _workflowRuntime;
    } // lock
}

// Shutdown method
static void StopWorkflowRuntime(object sender, EventArgs e)
{
    if (_workflowRuntime != null)
    {
        if (_workflowRuntime.IsStarted)
        {
            try
            {
                // Stop the runtime
                _workflowRuntime.StopRuntime();
            }
            catch (ObjectDisposedException)
            {
                // Already disposed of, so ignore...
            } // catch
        } // if
    } // if
}
}
}
```

Now that we have a workflow runtime factory, let's modify our main program to use it.

Using the workflow runtime factory object

1. With Visual Studio running and Program.cs open for editing, locate this line of code:

    ```
    WorkflowRuntime workflowRuntime = new WorkflowRuntime();
    ```

2. Replace this line of code with the following:

    ```
    WorkflowRuntime workflowRuntime = WorkflowFactory.GetWorkflowRuntime();
    ```

Subscribing to Workflow Runtime Events

It might seem like there isn't a lot to *WorkflowRuntime*, at least from a methods and properties perspective. You can start it, you can stop it, and you can ask it to initiate workflow instances. That's about it.

It's a bit more interesting than that, however, and you begin to see the complexity of the runtime environment when you look at the events *WorkflowRuntime* exposes. Table 2-3 doesn't provide an exhaustive list, but it does indicate the events you'll use most often.

Table 2-3 *WorkflowRuntime* Events

Event	Purpose
Started	Raised when the workflow runtime is started.
Stopped	Raised when the workflow runtime is stopped.
WorkflowCompleted	Raised when a workflow instance has completed.
WorkflowIdled	Raised when a workflow instance enters the idle state. When workflow instances go idle, you have the opportunity to unload them from memory, store them in a database (in case they're waiting for a long-running task), and bring them back into memory at a later time. We'll tackle this in Chapter 6.
WorkflowTerminated	Raised when a workflow instance is terminated. The workflow can be terminated by the host through a call to the *Terminate* method of a workflow instance, by a *Terminate* activity, or by the workflow runtime when an unhandled exception occurs.

We'll look at additional events *WorkflowRuntime* exposes as we progress through Chapters 4 and 5 as well.

As we add handlers for these events, you begin to see the same code (or nearly the same code) that you saw when Visual Studio generated the sequential workflow console application we built in the previous chapter. For one thing, to see the effects of these events, we'll need to stop the main application thread for awhile. To do this, both we and Visual Studio use a kernel-based automatic reset event. In a moment, we'll type in some code to use a few of these events. From time to time, glance back at the first chapter's PCodeFlow's Program.cs file and compare what's there with what we'll type here. Although it's not identical, you'll find the same ingredients in both applications.

Note   For clarity, I'll avoid the use of anonymous methods as I add code to this chapter's WorkflowHost application. PCodeFlow, on the other hand, uses anonymous methods. (They were placed there by Visual Studio when PCodeFlow's Program.cs file was created.) The functionality of each, however, is the same.

Handling workflow runtime events

1. With Visual Studio running and WorkflowHost's Program.cs source file open for editing, locate the line of code we added to call our *WorkflowFactory*:

```
WorkflowRuntime workflowRuntime = WorkflowFactory.GetWorkflowRuntime();
```

2. If you've worked with .NET delegates, this code will look familiar. What we need to do is to add event handlers for the events we're interested in observing. Let's add handlers for the workflow idled and workflow completed events for now. We can add other handlers later as we need them. With that in mind, type in the following line of code after the line from step 1:

```
workflowRuntime.WorkflowIdled += new
    EventHandler<WorkflowEventArgs>(workflowIdled);
```

> **Tip** As it happens, Visual Studio can add the handler for you. Nice! Here's how it works: After you type the equal sign (=), press the tab key to let IntelliSense add the EventHandler keyword and name. It will leave the name highlighted. Without changing the highlight, type in the name you want to use (workflowIdled in the preceding example). Then just press the Tab key when Visual Studio prompts you, and Visual Studio will insert the handler with the matching name immediately below whatever procedure you are coding. Of course, you can always modify the handler method name after the handler has been inserted into your code if you need to.
>
> ```
> me.WorkflowIdled +=
> ```
> `new EventHandler<WorkflowEventArgs>(workflowRuntime_WorkflowIdled);` (Press TAB to insert)

3. Following the code you just added, type in this line of code to add the handler for workflow completion:

```
workflowRuntime.WorkflowCompleted += new
    EventHandler<WorkflowCompletedEventArgs>(workflowCompleted);
```

4. And now add the handler for the *WorkflowTerminated* event:

```
workflowRuntime.WorkflowTerminated += new
    EventHandler<WorkflowTerminatedEventArgs>(workflowTerminated);
```

5. If you compile and run WorkflowHost, the application should compile and execute. But there is no workflow executed because we didn't ask the workflow runtime to start a workflow instance. (We'll add this in the next chapter.) In preparation, though, let's add some code. First, we'll add the automatic reset event we'll need to stop the main thread long enough for the workflow events to fire (so that we can observe them). The *AutoResetEvent* class is perfect for the job. Following the two lines of code you just typed in (in steps 3 and 4), add these lines of code. (We'll define the waitHandle object in the next step.)

```
Console.WriteLine("Waiting for workflow completion.");
waitHandle.WaitOne();
Console.WriteLine("Done.");
```

6. We'll need to create the *_waitHandle* object, so add this static class member just prior to the *Main* method:

```
private static AutoResetEvent waitHandle = new AutoResetEvent(false);
```

7. *AutoResetEvent* is exported by *System.Threading*, so add the *using* directive to the list at the top of the Program.cs source file:

```
using System.Threading;
```

8. The three event handlers (created by Visual Studio 2005) both contain "not implemented yet" exceptions. We need to get rid of those and implement some code. Locate the first handler we added, *workflowIdled*, and replace the exception you find there with the following lines of code:

```
Console.WriteLine("Workflow instance idled.");
```

9. We'll perform a similar edit to the *workflowCompleted* handler. Replace the "not implemented yet" exception with this:

```
Console.WriteLine("Workflow instance completed.");
waitHandle.Set();
```

10. The *workflowTerminated* handler rounds out the set of handlers. Replace the "not implemented yet" exception with the code you see here:

```
Console.WriteLine("Workflow instance terminated, " +
                  "reason: '{0}'.",e.Exception.Message);
waitHandle.Set();
```

The completed main application is shown in Listing 2-2.

Listing 2-2   The Complete *WorkflowHost* Application

```csharp
using System;
using System.Collections.Generic;
using System.Text;
using System.Workflow.Runtime;
using System.Threading;

namespace WorkflowHost
{
    class Program
    {
        private static AutoResetEvent waitHandle =
                                    new AutoResetEvent(false);
        static void Main(string[] args)
        {
            WorkflowRuntime workflowRuntime =
                WorkflowFactory.GetWorkflowRuntime();
            workflowRuntime.WorkflowIdled +=
                new EventHandler<WorkflowEventArgs>(workflowIdled);
            workflowRuntime.WorkflowCompleted +=
                new EventHandler<WorkflowCompletedEventArgs>
                                            (workflowCompleted);
            workflowRuntime.WorkflowTerminated +=
                new EventHandler<WorkflowTerminatedEventArgs>
                                            (workflowTerminated);
            Console.WriteLine("Waiting for workflow completion.");
            waitHandle.WaitOne();
            Console.WriteLine("Done.");
        }

        static void workflowTerminated(object sender,
                                        WorkflowTerminatedEventArgs e)
        {
            Console.WriteLine("Workflow instance terminated, " +
                  "reason: '{0}'.",e.Exception.Message);
            waitHandle.Set();
        }

        static void workflowCompleted(object sender,
```

```
                                WorkflowCompletedEventArgs e)
        {
            Console.WriteLine("Workflow instance completed.");
            waitHandle.Set();
        }

        static void workflowIdled(object sender,
                                  WorkflowEventArgs e)
        {
            Console.WriteLine("Workflow instance idled.");
        }
    }
}
```

What are we missing? A workflow to execute! We'll dive into workflow instances in the next chapter. For now, though, if you execute this application, it hangs. Why? The events we tapped into never fire because we never execute a workflow instance. That means the event handlers never handle the events. And because of that, *waitHandle* is never tripped—the application hangs forever (or until you terminate it yourself). We'll revisit this application in the next chapter when we add a workflow instance and execute it.

Chapter 2 Quick Reference

To	Do This
Host the workflow runtime in your application	Add a reference to the *System.Workflow.Runtime* assembly. Create a single instance of *WorkflowRuntime* per AppDomain, and start the runtime by calling *WorkflowRuntime.StartRuntime* or by creating a workflow instance.
Stop the workflow runtime	Call *WorkflowRuntime.StopRuntime*, or simply exit the host (that is, tear down the AppDomain).
Monitor workflow health and status	Subscribe to the various workflow runtime events. Chapter 5 covers *SqlTrackingService*, which is used to gather even more workflow health and status information.
Subscribe to workflow runtime events	Workflow runtime events are no different from other .NET object events, and they are subscribed to as any event would be subscribed to.

Chapter 3
Workflow Instances

After completing this chapter, you will be able to:

- Initiate a workflow instance, both with and without startup parameters
- Determine the status of your running workflow instances
- Stop workflow instances
- Determine why your workflow instances were idled or terminated

The workflow runtime, when it comes right down to it, is really there for one purpose—supporting your workflow-based tasks. Workflow tasks, called *instances* when they are executing, are the heart of the workflow system. They're why the workflow runtime exists in the first place.

A workflow instance is composed of one or more *activities*. (We'll look at the various activities starting in Chapter 7, "Basic Activity Operations.") The primary activity, or *root activity* is referred to as the *workflow definition*. The workflow definition normally acts as a container for the other activities that will actually do the work.

> **Note** A *workflow definition* is what you ask the workflow runtime to execute, whereas an *instance* is an executing workflow definition. There is a distinct difference. One is executing and the other is not. However, I'll use the terms interchangeably throughout this chapter, and even in the rest of the book, because in the end we're interested in executing software, not just in writing it. Besides, "instance" rolls off the tongue more easily than does "workflow definition."

Where do instances come from? They come from you. You have problems to solve and software to write to solve those problems, and if workflow processing fits the needs of your application requirements, at least part of the software you'll write is the workflow task or tasks that the workflow runtime will execute for you. Microsoft provides the workflow runtime. You provide the rest. After all, it's *your* application.

Windows Workflow Foundation (WF) is there to help. Not only will WF execute the workflow instances you create, but it will also help you create them. WF has a rich graphical designer that's there to help you lay out workflow software in much the same way as you build ASP.NET Web forms, Windows Forms, or Windows Presentation Foundation software. You roll the mouse cursor over the Toolbox, select one of the many activity items you find there, drag that item over to the design surface, and drop it. If the item has configurable properties, you can tailor those to suit your purpose using the Microsoft Visual Studio Properties pane.

We used the workflow designer briefly in Chapter 1, "Introducing Microsoft Windows Workflow Foundation," and we'll use it again here. After all, working with WF is all about building workflow tasks, and the workflow visual designer is a huge part of that development process.

> **Note**   Although we won't look at rehosting the workflow visual designer in this book, you can host the workflow visual designer in your own applications, outside Visual Studio. However, we will look in some detail at creating our own custom activities and how we integrate those into the workflow visual designer's Toolbox in Chapter 13, "Custom Activities."

Workflow instances are like any other piece of software. They begin executing and run until they hit some terminal condition. Maybe all the rows of the database have been processed, or all the files the instance is supposed to crunch have been crunched. Or the documents the workflow routed to the various approval authorities were returned, approved or disapproved, and that process has been completed. There is a natural starting place and one or more natural stopping places.

Instances can sustain errors. Exceptions. And maybe you handled those exceptions and maybe you didn't (oops). In some cases, maybe you didn't want to handle exceptions because the workflow runtime reports the stoppage of an instance differently if it sustains an unhandled error and you'll deal with it then.

Sometimes, a workflow process can take a long, long time to complete. For example, maybe a process places an order for parts and then waits for the order to be received. The number and type of parts are confirmed before the workflow terminates. Depending on the type of part, it might take days, weeks, and even months to receive the order. So should a workflow instance remain active in memory for days, weeks, or months? What happens if the server crashes or the power goes out in the meantime? Do you lose your workflow instance? Your data? Your application state?

Workflow instances can also participate in transactions, and to be honest, this is a critical piece of the workflow puzzle for those of us writing business software. Imagine a workflow process that coordinates financial transactions between the accounting department and the shipping department while awaiting approval from the department heads of research and design and engineering. Any time we deal with funds, we're probably also dealing with transactions so that if anything goes wrong in the process, the money is left in a known place. Just participating in a long-running transaction is an amazing feat, but handling failure conditions is even more amazing. (We'll see how transactions are handled in Chapter 15, "Workflows and Transactions.")

So working with workflow instances and the activities that instances are composed of is an important part of workflow processing. It's no surprise, then, that WF has strong support for building workflow instances as well as executing them. We'll start by looking at the *WorkflowInstance* object.

Introducing the *WorkflowInstance* Object

WorkflowInstance is the WF object that gives your individual workflow task context. This is the object you use to find out how things are going with your process. Just as we have methods and properties to control the workflow runtime, so too do we have methods and properties we can use to interact with our workflow instances. Table 3-1 lists most of the *WorkflowInstance* properties, while Table 3-2 lays out the commonly used methods. We'll look at additional properties and methods in Chapter 5, "Workflow Tracking."

Table 3-1   *WorkflowInstance* Properties

Property	Purpose
InstanceId	Gets the unique identifier for the workflow instance (a Guid).
WorkflowRuntime	Gets the *WorkflowRuntime* for this workflow instance.

Table 3-2   *WorkflowInstance* Methods

Method	Purpose
ApplyWorkflowChanges	Applies changes to the workflow instance specified by the *WorkflowChanges* object. This allows you to modify the workflow (add, remove, or change activities) while it's executing, although the workflow instance is suspended while the dynamic changes are being made.
GetWorkflowDefinition	Retrieves the root activity for this workflow instance.
Resume	Resumes execution of a previously suspended workflow instance. If the workflow instance is not in the suspended state, nothing happens. If the workflow instance is in the suspended state, the workflow runtime raises the *WorkflowResumed* event just before the workflow instance execution is resumed.
Start	Starts the execution of the workflow instance, calling *ExecuteActivity* on the root activity of this workflow instance. (We'll start putting activities under the microscope in the next chapter.) If *Start* encounters an exception, it terminates the workflow instance by calling *Terminate* with the *Message* property of the exception passed as the reason for the termination.
Suspend	Synchronously suspends the workflow instance. If the workflow instance is already suspended, nothing happens. If the instance is running, the workflow runtime suspends the workflow instance, sets *SuspendOrTerminateInfoProperty* to the string (*reason*) passed into *Suspend*, and raises the *WorkflowSuspended* event.

Table 3-2   *WorkflowInstance* Methods

Method	Purpose
Terminate	Synchronously terminates the workflow instance. When the host requests termination of the workflow instance, the workflow runtime kills the instance and tries to persist the instance's final state. Then *WorkflowInstance* sets *SuspendOrTerminateInfoProperty* to the string (*reason*) passed into *Terminate*. Finally, it raises the *WorkflowTerminated* event and passes *reason* in the *Message* property of a *WorkflowTerminatedException* contained in the *WorkflowTerminatedEventArgs*. If another, different, exception is raised during persistence, the workflow runtime passes that exception in *WorkflowTerminatedEventArgs* instead.

There are more methods associated with *WorkflowInstance* than I've shown here. We'll look at those in more detail when we persist workflow instances to a Microsoft SQL Server database in Chapter 6, "Loading and Unloading Instances."

Let's build a workflow task and see how we kick it off.

Starting a Workflow Instance

Before we can start a workflow instance, we must have a workflow task for WF to execute. In the first chapter, we asked Visual Studio to create a workflow-based project for us that automatically included a raw workflow task we modified to validate U.S. and Canadian postal codes. We could, if we wanted, go back to that project and physically copy the workflow source code, or we could reference the resulting assembly *PCodeFlow.exe* and try to use the workflow we created directly. And, in practice, you might do that.

In this case, however, we're attempting to learn to write workflow applications. What fun is swiping existing workflow code when we can build new? Let's simulate a long-running task by using a sequential workflow that contains a delay. We'll execute some code prior to the delay to pop up a message box. After the delay, we'll again pop up a message box to indicate our work has finished. (We'll know our workflow instance finished anyway because WorkflowHost handles the *WorkflowCompleted* event, but this way we get to write a bit more workflow code.) As we progress through the book, our examples will become more detailed and richer, but for now because we're still new to it, we'll keep the examples on the "type in less code" side to concentrate more on the concept than on improving typing skills.

 Note   Remember, a *sequential workflow* is one that executes activities one after another. This process is in contrast to a *state machine workflow*, which executes activities based on state transitions. If this sounds like so much nonsense right now, don't worry. We'll get into all this in the next chapter.

Adding a sequential workflow project to the WorkflowHost solution

1. If Visual Studio isn't running, start Visual Studio 2005 as you did in the previous chapters. If the WorkflowHost project isn't loaded, select it from the Visual Studio Recent Projects menu, which you can access from the main File menu. Visual Studio will grind for a moment as it reloads WorkflowHost for editing.

2. We could, if we wanted, add a workflow-based class directly into our WorkflowHost project. This is precisely what Visual Studio did when it created the PCodeFlow application in Chapter 1. Instead of simply adding a workflow component to our existing WorkflowHost application, however, let's add an entirely new workflow project to our solution. To do that, select Add and then New Project from the Visual Studio File menu. This will activate the Add New Project dialog box.

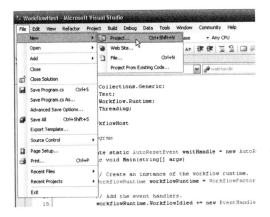

> **Note**   It's generally a better practice to build your workflow into separate assemblies. For one thing, it neatly compartmentalizes your code along assembly lines. But for another, at the time this was written there is a bug in WF that prevents you from executing secondary workflows from within a primary workflow if the two workflows in question are in the same assembly.

3. When the Add New Project dialog box appears, expand the Visual C# tree node and then select Workflow from the Project Types pane.

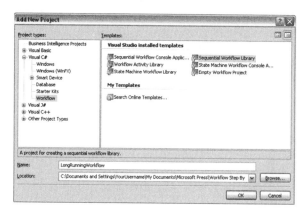

4. Select Sequential Workflow Library from the Templates pane.

5. In the Name field, type **LongRunningWorkflow**.

6. In the Location field, type **\Workflow\Chapter3**.

> **Note** Remember that the path *\Workflow* represents the file system directory path you are using to store the book's sample applications.

7. Click OK to add the LongRunningWorkflow project to your WorkflowHost solution.

Visual Studio then adds the new library assembly project to our solution and opens the workflow visual designer in preparation for creating our workflow task. Just to give you the big picture, we're going to add three activities to this new workflow task—two *Code* activities and one *Delay* activity. The *Delay* activity will be sandwiched between the *Code* activities, allowing us to pop up message boxes before and after the delay. We'll delay a fixed amount of time at first, but we'll later modify the workflow task to accept a delay value we specify when we initiate the workflow.

Building the simulated long-running sequential workflow

1. With the workflow visual designer active, move the mouse cursor to the Visual Studio Toolbox and allow it to expand. If the workflow visual designer is not showing, select Workflow1.cs from the LongRunningWorkflow project in the Solution Explorer pane and click the Solution Explorer's View Designer button.

2. Select Code from the Toolbox, and drag the *Code* activity component onto the workflow designer's surface.

As the mouse approaches the area marked "Drop Activities to Create a Sequential Workflow," the designer view changes slightly to indicate that you can drop the *Code* activity component on the designer surface.

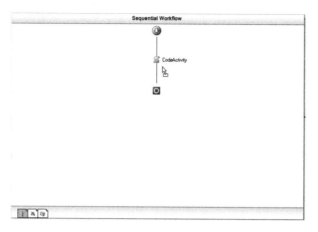

3. Release the mouse button to drop the *Code* activity component into the sequential workflow.

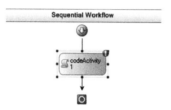

4. As we did in the first chapter, we're going to add some code to our workflow task via the *Code* activity. If the *Code* activity's properties aren't showing in the Visual Studio Properties pane, click the *Code* activity you just inserted into your workflow once to select it. This will bring this activity's properties into view.

5. Click the *ExecuteCode* property to activate the property drop-down edit box, which allows us to name the event that will fire when the code in the *Code* activity is to be executed.

6. Type **PreDelayMessage**. This adds the event to the workflow code. Later, we'll modify the code and show a message box. For now, though, we'll continue working in the workflow visual designer because we need to add two more activities.

7. Select Delay from the Toolbox, and drag the *Delay* activity component onto the workflow designer's surface. Drop it below the *Code* activity that we just placed there.

> **Note**   A sequential activity, such as the one we're working with here, executes activities in order. The order is determined by the activity's location in the workflow visual designer. The activity at the top of the designer's window is executed first, with other activities executed in order as you progress toward the bottom of the designer window. We'll revisit this process in the next chapter.

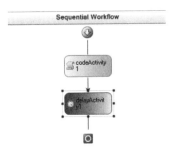

8. We'll need to establish a delay value for our *Delay* activity to use. To do that, we change the *TimeoutDuration* property in the Visual Studio Properties pane. If the *Delay* activity's properties aren't showing in the Visual Studio Properties pane, as you did with the *Code* activity, click the *Delay* activity you just inserted into your workflow once to select it. Change the last two zeros ("00") to "10", which means the *Delay* activity will wait 10 seconds before allowing workflow processing to continue.

 Note   With the *Delay* activity's properties showing, note the activity name *delayActivity1*. We could change that if we like, but for now we'll leave it. Later, when we change the delay value dynamically, we'll need to remember this name. Here, we'll just set the time-out duration and continue.

9. To briefly review, we have an initial *Code* activity that we'll use to display a message box prior to a delay. We have the *Delay* activity that will wait 10 seconds and then allow our workflow processing to move on. What we need now is the second *Code* activity to show the second message box. To add that, repeat steps 2 through 6, dropping the new *Code* activity following the *Delay* activity you placed in the preceding two steps. However, when you name the event in the *ExecuteCode* edit control (step 6), type **PostDelayMessage** as the event name. The final workflow as it exists in the workflow visual designer should appear as you see here:

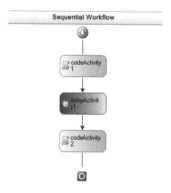

We have a couple of tasks remaining. Eventually, we'll need to introduce our workflow assembly to our main application so that we can execute it. But first, we must add the code necessary to show the two message boxes. We've created two events in our workflow code: *PreDelayMessage* and *PostDelayMessage*. We'll now add the event handler code for those, which is where we'll actually fire up the message boxes.

Adding code to our pre- and post-delay events

1. In the Visual Studio Solution Explorer pane, click the LongRunningWorkflow project's Workflow1.cs file to activate the property grid's control buttons. Click the View Code button to open the Workflow1.cs C# file for editing.

2. So that Microsoft IntelliSense works for us when we try to add the message boxes, we'll need to add a reference to *System.Windows.Forms* and add the *using* declaration using the techniques we learned in the previous chapter. Therefore, to the LongRunningWorkflow project, add a reference to *System.Windows.Forms* and add the following *using* declaration to Workflow1.cs:

    ```
    using System.Windows.Forms;
    ```

3. Now we'll add some code. First, locate the *Workflow1* constructor:

    ```
    public Workflow1()
    {
        InitializeComponent();
    }
    ```

4. Locate the newly inserted *PreDelayMessage* method, which follows the constructor, and insert the following code:

    ```
    MessageBox.Show("Pre-delay code is being executed.");
    ```

5. As you did for the previous event handler, locate the newly inserted *PostDelayMessage* method and insert the following code:

    ```
    MessageBox.Show("Post-delay code is being executed.");
    ```

If you compiled the solution, which you can do by selecting Build Solution from the Visual Studio Build menu, everything builds without error. But the WorkflowHost application still hangs as it did in the previous chapter. Why? It hangs because although we did just create a workflow assembly we can use, we didn't ask the main application to execute it. The *WorkflowCompleted* event will never fire, so the automatic reset event won't release the main application thread.

To execute our workflow task, we'll need to reference the new workflow assembly we created and add the code that the *WorkflowRuntime* object will need to kick off the workflow job. Let's work through that now.

Host a custom workflow assembly, and start a workflow instance without parameters

1. First we'll add a reference to our LongRunningWorkflow assembly that supports our simulated long-running workflow task. We'll start by adding the reference as we have in the past, but instead of selecting an assembly under the .NET tab, we'll use the Projects tab. There is no need to add a *using* directive for this assembly.

> **Tip**   If you prefer, you can add a project-level reference to the LongRunningWorkflow project using the Add Reference dialog box's Browse tab. Using the file system navigation controls, browse to \Workflow\Chapter3\LongRunningWorkflow\bin\Debug and select LongRunningWorkflow.dll. Then click OK.

2. If we were to compile the application now, WorkflowHost would fail to compile! Why? Well, when we built WorkflowHost in the previous chapter, we added only enough references to make it compile at that time. That is, we added a reference to *System.Workflow.Runtime*. However, we've now introduced a live workflow assembly to our host application, and as it happens, we'll need to add a couple more workflow-related reference assemblies to WorkflowHost. So as you have done in the past, open the Add Reference dialog box, select the .NET tab, and scroll until you find *System.Workflow.Activities*. Select this with a single mouse click. Then, while holding the Control key down, click *System.Workflow.ComponentModel* as well. This selects the two assemblies at one time. Click OK to make the reference. There is no need to add *using* directives for these assemblies, however.

> **Tip** You can combine this step with step 1. After you select the LongRunningWork-flow assembly using the Browse button, simply click the .NET button and search for the system assemblies as described here in step 2.

3. Now let's get down to coding. Click Program.cs for the WorkflowHost project in the Visual Studio Solution Explorer, and then click the Solution Explorer's View Code button.

4. When the source file is displayed for editing, locate the following code in the *Main* method:

```
Console.WriteLine("Waiting for workflow completion.");
```

5. After this line of code, add the following:

```
WorkflowInstance instance =
workflowRuntime.CreateWorkflow(typeof(LongRunningWorkflow.Workflow1));
instance.Start();
```

6. Compile and execute the WorkflowHost application.

> **Tip** If you execute the WorkflowHost application by pressing F5 in Visual Studio, the application will complete and the console window will be destroyed before you could possibly read all of the messages. Setting a breakpoint so that the application stops and breaks into the debugger (so you can access the console window while the application has stopped) or executing the compiled application from the command prompt should allow you to see the screen output.

You should find that you had to dismiss both message boxes. Meanwhile, in the console window, WorkflowHost sent various messages to the console that we can review:

```
Waiting for workflow completion.
Workflow instance idled.
Workflow instance completed.
Done.
```

The golden nugget in all this is rolled into these few lines of code:

```
WorkflowInstance instance =
    workflowRuntime.CreateWorkflow(typeof(LongRunningWorkflow.Workflow1));
instance.Start();
```

Here, we're using the *WorkflowRuntime* object to create a workflow instance by passing into the *CreateWorkflow* method the workflow definition (by its type) we want to execute. When we receive the *WorkflowInstance* object in return, we call its *Start* method to initiate workflow processing. Notice that the workflow instance required no input from us prior to executing. Wouldn't it be nice to be able to pass in a variable delay value? That's the topic of the next section.

Starting a Workflow Instance with Parameters

Workflow instances that take input parameters upon startup accept those parameters as public properties. That is, to pass in a variable delay value, we need only to create a public *Delay* property on our workflow instance and then provide the delay value when we create the instance. If you're familiar with XML Serialization and the *XmlSerializer* in .NET, the process for creating a workflow instance is similar to the process of deserializing an XML stream into a living .NET object. In fact, this is very nearly what happens.

The arguments that a workflow instance expects are passed in as values in a dictionary object that uses a string as a key and a simple *object* type as the value. Typically, code such as this is used:

```
Dictionary<string, object> parms = new Dictionary<string, object>();
```

You then use the *Add* method of the *Dictionary* object to insert the parameters. The key must be a string representation of the name of a public property the workflow root activity exhibits. Additionally, the value must be compatible with the activity's property type. For example, if we pass in an integer-based delay value and our workflow instance exposes a *Delay* property, the code to add the parameter to the dictionary would be the following:

```
parms.Add("Delay", 10); // 10 second delay.
```

Once again, time to write some code. The changes we'll make are relatively minor, but they add a lot of functionality. We could get fancy and add a custom form to our host application to request a delay value. However, to keep it simple, we'll accept an integer value on the command line. So that our application doesn't run forever, we'll limit the value to be from 0 to 120, meaning from no delay to a delay of up to 2 minutes. We'll also modify the workflow itself to add our *Delay* property, and we'll accept that as the time delay before continuing. Let's look at the modifications to our workflow component first.

Adding an input property to a workflow

1. In the Visual Studio Solution Explorer pane, click the LongRunningWorkflow project's Workflow1.cs file to activate the property grid's control buttons. Click the View Code button to open the Workflow1.cs C# file for editing.

2. After the *Workflow1* constructor, add this code:

```
private Int32 _delay = 10;

public Int32 Delay
{
    get { return _delay; }
    set
    {
        if (value < 0 || value > 120)
        {
            value = 10;
```

```
        }

        if (ExecutionStatus == ActivityExecutionStatus.Initialized)
        {
            _delay = value;
            delayActivity1.TimeoutDuration = new TimeSpan(0, 0, _delay);
        }
    }
}
```

That's it for the workflow piece. We check the incoming integer value, and if it's out of range, we assign a default value. From there, we check to see that we're about to execute (but not already executing). This prevents someone from changing the delay value once our workflow task is actually running. Then, of course, we set the *TimeoutDuration* on our *Delay* activity, *delayActivity1*.

We need to modify the *Main* method slightly to account for the input parameter as well. We use the first command-line argument as the delay value. If it's not an integer, we quit. If it is, we accept it as is. If it's out of range, the workflow activity applies its bounds (0 through 120 seconds) as necessary. With that in mind, the next procedure shows what we do to *Main*.

Starting the workflow instance with a parameter

1. In the Visual Studio Solution Explorer pane, click the WorkflowHost project's Program.cs file to activate the property grid's control buttons. Click the View Code button to open the Program.cs C# file for editing.

2. With the file open in the code editor, locate the code we added in *Main* to hook up the three event handlers (idle, completed, and terminated).

```
workflowRuntime.WorkflowIdled += new
    EventHandler<WorkflowEventArgs>(workflowIdled);
workflowRuntime.WorkflowCompleted += new
    EventHandler<WorkflowCompletedEventArgs>(workflowCompleted);
workflowRuntime.WorkflowTerminated += new
    EventHandler<WorkflowTerminatedEventArgs>(workflowTerminated);
```

3. Now we'll add some logic to test the incoming command-line argument, if there is one, and to create the *Dictionary* object we need to pass in the delay value. After the code to add the event handlers, insert this code:

```
Int32 delay = 0;
string val = args.Length > 0 ? args[0] : "10";
if (!Int32.TryParse(val, out delay))
{
    // Not an integer value.
    Console.WriteLine("You must pass in an integer value!");
    return;
}

Dictionary<string, object> parms = new Dictionary<string, object>();
parms.Add("Delay", delay);
Console.WriteLine("Waiting for workflow completion ({0} seconds...).",val);
```

4. Next, find this line of code a bit further down:

```
WorkflowInstance instance =
    workflowRuntime.CreateWorkflow(typeof(LongRunningWorkflow.Workflow1));
```

5. Change this line of code to match the following:

```
WorkflowInstance instance =
    workflowRuntime.CreateWorkflow(typeof(LongRunningWorkflow.Workflow1), parms);
```

With that last step, we're done adding code. Compile the application by selecting Build Solution from the Visual Studio Build menu, and execute it by pressing the F5 key. Did it work?

It should have, because we added code to account for the situation where no command line was provided. If you were to execute the application as we did in Chapter 1 (in the "Executing your workflow application" section), by adding different delay values on the command line you would see the delay's effects reflected in the time lag between instances of the message boxes.

Determining Workflow Instance Status

Interestingly, if you look at the methods and properties of both the workflow runtime object and the workflow instance object, you don't find a status property. How do you know if there is a workflow executing, and if there is one, where is that workflow in its process? Is it idled? Is it executing? How do we know?

I'm jumping ahead a little, but this is the most logical place to discuss workflow status determination. As it happens, the workflow definition of a given workflow instance provides you with the execution status. The base class *Activity* exposes an *ExecutionStatus* property that sports a member of the *ActivityExecutionStatus* enumeration. I've listed the *ActivityExecution-Status* values with their meaning in Table 3-3.

Table 3-3   *ActivityExecutionStatus* Values

Property	Purpose
Canceling	The *Activity* is in the process of canceling.
Closed	The *Activity* is closed.
Compensating	A transaction has failed, causing the compensation action to be initiated. (We'll learn more about this in Chapter 15.)
Executing	The *Activity* is currently running.
Faulting	The *Activity* has sustained an exception.
Initialized	The *Activity* has been initialized but is not yet running.

The enumerated values in Table 3-3 all refer to an activity object, but remember that the workflow definition *is* an activity. That means if we query the workflow definition for its status, we're effectively determining the status of the entire instance. The following process shows how we add the code we need to query the workflow definition.

Determining workflow instance execution status

1. In the Visual Studio Solution Explorer pane, open the WorkflowHost project's Program.cs file for editing.

2. With Program.cs open in the code editor, look for the code we added in *Main* to start the workflow instance:

   ```
   instance.Start();
   ```

3. So that we can see the workflow instance status, we'll print the result of the workflow definition status query directly to the console. Place the following below the code we inserted in Step 2:

   ```
   Console.WriteLine("The workflow is: {0}",
     instance.GetWorkflowDefinition().ExecutionStatus.ToString());
   ```

> **Tip**   You could do more with this status information than merely print it to the console window. If you wanted to take specific action depending on the status of the workflow instance, simply add a conditional branch (such as *if/else*) and perform whatever action your application requires.

Terminating a Workflow Instance

Should you need to do so, you can easily terminate a workflow instance by executing the *Terminate* method on the *WorkflowInstance* object. The string you pass into *Terminate* is folded into an exception. If you added the *WorkflowTerminated* handler to your application, you can pull the reason for the termination from the *Message* property of the exception. You'll find the exception wrapped in the *WorkflowTerminatedEventArgs* that are passed into your *WorkflowTerminated* event handler. This code is already in WorkflowHost, so let's give it a try. We'll need to add a single line of code to actually terminate the instance.

Terminating a workflow instance

1. If the WorkflowHost project's Program.cs file isn't still open in Visual Studio, open it again for editing.

2. Within Program.cs, look for the code we just added in *Main* to display the workflow instance execution status:

   ```
   Console.WriteLine("The workflow is: {0}",
     instance.GetWorkflowDefinition().ExecutionStatus.ToString());
   ```

3. Following this line of code, add this new line:

   ```
   instance.Terminate("User cancellation");
   ```

Now, if you compile and execute the WorkflowHost application, providing a delay of 25 seconds, you won't see any message boxes and the console window's output will appear as follows:

```
Waiting for workflow completion (25 seconds...).
The workflow is: Initialized
Workflow instance terminated, reason: 'User cancellation'.
Done.
```

Dehydration and Rehydration

Before we leave the topic of workflow instances, I want to touch on the concept of *dehydrating* and *rehydrating* an instance. If you have long-running workflow tasks or have a large number of tasks executing, you can unload tasks and store the necessary execution context information in a SQL Server database using a service that ships with WF. The goal is to unload workflow tasks and store them temporarily only to later reload them when the time is right.

We'll save a detailed discussion for Chapter 6, but I mention it here because, for one thing, this process targets the workflow instance. But for another, you might hear the terms, and I didn't want you to have to wade too far into the book without understanding their basic meaning.

When you dehydrate an instance, you're removing it from execution status and storing it away for later recall. Typically, we use the persistence service that comes with WF for this, but you can write your own service to perform the same task. Later, when your application senses the trigger for restarting the workflow instance, you rehydrate the instance and bring it back into an executing state. There are a number of reasons for doing this, all of which we'll examine briefly later in the book.

Chapter 3 Quick Reference

To	Do This
Start a workflow instance without parameters	Use the *WorkflowRuntime* object's *CreateWorkflow* method, passing in the type of the workflow definition.
Start a workflow instance with parameters	Use the *WorkflowRuntime* object's *CreateWorkflow* method, passing in the type of the workflow definition along with a generic *Dictionary* object that contains the parameters. The key for each value should be a string that matches a public property of the workflow definition. The value should simply be an object.
Determine workflow status	Request the workflow definition from the executing workflow instance, and query the activity's *ExecutionStatus* property.
Terminate an instance	Call the *Terminate* method exposed by the *WorkflowInstance* object.

Chapter 4
Introduction to Activities and Workflow Types

After completing this chapter, you will be able to:

- Explain how activities form workflows
- Describe the differences between a sequential and a state machine workflow
- Create a sequential workflow project
- Create a state machine workflow project

As I write this, I have young children who love Legos. Legos, if you've not seen them, are intricate building blocks and components from which you build larger and more complex systems. (See *www.lego.com*.) There is a rather complete line of *Star Wars* Lego sets, for example. I even have a Lego Yoda I was given to assemble while I recuperated from knee surgery—for injuries incurred the only time I ever was thrown from my horse (don't ask). Yes, you caught me. My children aren't the only Lego fans in the house.

Activities are the Lego blocks of Windows Workflow Foundation (WF) workflow processing. If you divide a business process (or workflow task) into pieces, you typically find it's composed of smaller, more granular tasks. If a high-level business process is designed to route information through some data processing system, the sublevel tasks might include such things as reading data from a database, generating a file using that data, shipping the file to a remote server using FTP or an XML Web service, marking the information as having been processed (through a write to a database and an entry into an audit trail), and so forth. These sublevel tasks are typically focused on a specific job. Read the database. FTP the file. Insert an audit trail entry. In a word, they are *activities*. Actions. Focused tasks.

When you build workflows, you gather the individual activities together and move from one activity to the next. Some activities act as containers for other activities. Some activities perform a single task, as I've described here. One container-based activity is chosen to hold all the rest, and that's the *root activity* I mentioned in the previous chapter. The root activity will either be a *sequential activity* or a *state-machine activity*, and we'll examine those types of activity in this chapter.

How the activities choose what to accomplish as the next step in the process they model is a primary focus of this chapter. Perhaps the activities are executed in an order you specified when you created the root activity. Or it's just as likely you'll need a workflow designed such that specific activities will execute only after certain events have occurred. So that we have a pretty good understanding of activities in general, let's look first at the WF *Activity* object by itself and then look at how activities are connected together.

Introducing the *Activity*, the Basic Unit of Work

Moving from conceptual notion to concrete implementation, WF provides you with the *Activity* object. By itself, *Activity* implements a simplistic-looking base class. It doesn't do much taskwise, but it does allow for workflow interaction (which is *not* simple). However, activity objects that derive from *Activity* do provide tremendous functionality, and that's just using activities that ship with WF. You are certainly free to create your own activities, a topic we'll visit in Chapter 13, "Custom Activities." In fact, the entire second part of the book is dedicated to activities. But looking for now at the base *Activity* object, Table 4-1 lists many of the *Activity* properties of general interest, and Table 4-2 lays out the methods you'll typically encounter. In Chapter 13 you'll see a couple more that are useful when creating your own activities.

Table 4-1   *Activity* Properties

Property	Purpose
Description	Gets or sets the user-defined description of the activity.
Enabled	Gets or sets a value that indicates whether this instance is enabled for execution and validation.
ExecutionResult	Gets the *ActivityExecutionResult* of the last attempt to run this instance (*Canceled, Compensated, Faulted, None,* and *Succeeded*).
ExecutionStatus	Gets the status of the workflow in the form of one of the *ActivityExecutionStatus* values (*Canceling, Closed, Compensating, Executing, Faulting,* and *Initialized*).
Name	Gets or sets the name of this activity instance.
Parent	Gets the activity that encloses this activity.
WorkflowInstanceId	Gets the workflow instance identifier associated with this activity.

Table 4-2   *Activity* Methods

Method	Purpose
Cancel	Cancels the execution of an activity.
Clone	Returns a deep copy of the activity ("deep copy" means the clone contains all of the internal data from the cloned activity).
Execute	Synchronously runs the activity.
GetActivityByName	If executed on a composite activity, this method returns the named activity if it is contained by the composite activity.
Load	Loads an instance of an activity from a stream.

Table 4-2 *Activity* Methods

Method	Purpose
RaiseEvent	Raises an event associated with the specified *DependencyProperty*.
RaiseGenericEvent<T>	Raises the event associated with the referenced *DependencyProperty*. The effect of *RaiseEvent* and *RaiseGenericEvent* is the same—fire an event. *RaiseEvent* uses the dependency property directly, while *RaiseGenericEvent* is the generic (templated) version.
Save	Saves a copy of the activity to a stream.

The activity methods are generally all both *virtual* and *protected*. The intention is for you to override them and provide implementations specific to your own activity's needs. By far the most critical method is *Execute*. This method, when called by the workflow runtime, is *the* method where your activity's magic happens.

Activities can be grouped into two primary camps: *composite* and *basic*. Composite activities contain other activities, and an excellent example of this is the sequential activity we've been using throughout the book so far. All the sample applications so far have implemented their workflow instances as sequential activities that contained other activities, such as if-else, delay, and code activities.

Basic activities, such as the delay and code activities I just mentioned, are the single-minded task-based activities I referred to earlier in the chapter. Ultimately, you'll need basic activities to actually carry out specific pieces of work. Composite activities might direct the flow of work and data, but it's the basic activity that does the number crunching.

The *ActivityExecutionContext* Object

Many of the *Activity* object's methods require an *ActivityExecutionContext* object as input. The *ActivityExecutionContext* object is created when the workflow runtime queues your workflow instance for execution. Therefore, it isn't something you create directly. The workflow runtime creates it for you.

The *ActivityExecutionContext* object's purpose is to provide the activity with methods and services tied to the workflow instance, such as for initialization, timers, and general execution flow. It's essentially a helper object. Chapter 13 discusses activity context in a bit more detail. For now, though, it's enough to think of it as a collection of runtime properties and helper methods the workflow runtime maintains so the entire workflow process stays on track.

> **Note**   If you're familiar with ASP.NET programming, this context object serves essentially the same purpose as the *System.Web.HttpContext* object. Those familiar with .NET Framework programming may find similarities between this context object and *System.Threading.Thread.CurrentContext*. The goal of all of these context objects is the same—to provide a place to store and easily recall information specific to a currently executing instance. In this case, it's an instance of an executing activity.

Dependency Properties 101

Within Table 4-2, you'll also see something known as a *DependencyProperty*. If you've looked at the code we've used so far in the preceding chapters, sprinkled into the workflow code that Visual Studio generated for you are events based on dependency properties. What is a *DependencyProperty*?

Normally, if you create a property for a class, you also create a field within the class to store the property value. This type of code is common:

```
class MyClass
{
    protected Int32 _x = 0;
    ...
    public Int32 X
    {
        get { return _x; }
        set { _x = value; }
    }
}
```

The field *_x* is more formally called a *backing store*. Your class, in this example, provides the backing store for the *X* property.

Both WF and Windows Presentation Foundation (WPF), however, quite often need access to your class's properties. WPF will need to determine the sizing and spacing of controls in a container so that things will be optimally rendered. WF needs dependency properties to facilitate *activity binding*, which is a process that allows different activities to reference (and be bound to) the same property. The WF *ActivityBind* class facilitates this for you.

To facilitate the chaining and binding of properties, the backing store for your class properties can be shifted from your class down to the .NET runtime itself. The property data is still stored—it's just that .NET stores it for you. In a sense, it's like having a room full of lockers. You didn't build the building and install the lockers, but you can use them when you need to. In this case, you register your locker request with .NET, and .NET provides you with the locker and the means to access what's inside the locker. These lockers, so to speak, are called *DependencyProperties*.

To revisit the bit of code I provided earlier, this code uses a *DependencyProperty* as the backing store for *X*:

```
class MyClass
{
    public static DependencyProperty XProperty =
        DependencyProperty.Register("X", typeof(System.Int32),
            typeof(MyClass));
    ...
    public Int32 X
    {
        get { return ((Int32)(base.GetValue(MyClass.XProperty))); }
        set { base.SetValue(MyClass.XProperty, value); }
    }
}
```

To register to use a "locker," you call the static *Register* method on the *DependencyProperty* object. To access the "locker," you use *GetValue* and *SetValue* instead of writing to the field in your class directly. These methods access the underlying backing store, giving both you and the .NET runtime (or the workflow runtime, as the case may be) access to your activity properties. Visual Studio will insert a *lot* of code like this for you as you use WF. When we create our own custom activity in Chapter 13, we'll write this sort of code ourselves as well.

Activity Validation

As you might recall from Chapter 1, activities often have validation capabilities, as shown in Figure 4-1.

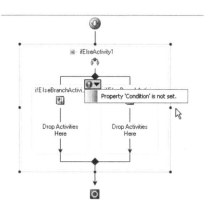

Figure 4-1   An example of the validation capabilities of activities

In this case, the *IfElse* activity is telling us that we've not specified a condition that will cause one branch or the other to be taken. Other activities implement different validation algorithms. No matter the activity, if we were to compile our code with validation errors, our compilation would fail. We must correct the deficient validation condition before we can compile and execute our workflow code.

Workflow Types

Because you've now created a small handful of workflow applications, you've undoubtedly looked at the New Project dialog box as we've created our applications. You've likely noted there are different types of workflow applications that we could create. The type of workflow application you develop depends in large part on the root activity you choose.

Even though you'll note only two types of workflow applications in the New Project dialog box, there are actually three main types. You've built sequential workflows so far in this book, so they're hopefully not too mysterious. Your activities are executed in the order you prescribe when you build the workflow.

The other type of workflow you see from the New Projects dialog box is the state-machine workflow. I'll discuss this in more detail in this chapter, but it's basically a workflow that depends on external events to move forward.

The third type of workflow is based on the sequential workflow, but it is rules-driven. Instead of merely executing tasks you specify, the rules-based workflow combines the *Policy* activity and rule conditions to execute workflow tasks based on business rules you specify. We'll learn much more about this workflow type in Chapter 12, "Policy Activities." Because this type of workflow stems from the sequential activity as the root, there is no special New Project dialog box selection for building such a workflow application. Instead, you start with the basic sequential workflow and add the rules-based activities.

Selecting a Workflow Type

So when is one type of workflow better than another? How do you know which workflow type to choose? Table 4-3 gives you a basic decision matrix. I'll address the table with some discussion to clarify things.

Table 4-3   Basic Workflow Type Decision Matrix

Workflow Type	Conditions
Sequential	Workflow tasks can execute autonomously with little outside direction. The workflow itself primarily controls the execution of the tasks. Some or no user interaction is required. The root activity is the *SequentialWorkflow* activity.
State-machine	Workflow tasks depend heavily on outside control to guide execution. Much user interaction is expected (or other outside control will dominate the task flow). For state-based workflow, the root activity is the *StateMachineWorkflow* activity.
Rules-based	Business rules exist to resolve complex decisions, and neither a sequential nor state-machine workflow directly applies. Rules-based workflow can have either a sequential or state-based root activity.

Sequential workflows are ideal for implementing business processes. If you need to read data from a source, process that data, send notifications, and write results to another data sink, the sequential workflow probably will suit your needs. This does not imply that a sequential workflow is inappropriate for processes that depend on user interaction for approval or disapproval of specific tasks. But such user interaction should not be the focal point of the workflow itself.

If you need a lot of user interaction, the state-machine workflow is likely a better alternative. When your workflow sends notifications to users or other systems (for whatever reason—to notify, to request approval, to select an option, and so on), as the users or other systems respond, their responses form *events*. These events trigger the workflow to move forward from processing state to processing state. I'll discuss this a bit more later in the chapter and again in Chapter 14, "State-Based Workflows."

The final type of workflow we'll look at (in Chapter 12) is the rules-based workflow, where the decisions whether to move forward with the workflow and in what direction are based on business rules. These workflows are usually reserved for more complex scenarios. For example, suppose that a customer orders custom-built formed plastic components, perhaps to install into new automibiles. Your job is to build a workflow task that monitors customer orders and component production.

Let's throw a little complication in, though. Plastics are long polymer chains created using a relatively complex chemical process. In this process, a plasticizing compound is used to facilitate the long polymer chains to form into even longer chains (making the plastic less brittle). The plasticizer easily evaporates, so the process is completed in a low-vapor pressure system.

The customer orders this plastic part, and your system tells you there should be enough plasticizer to complete the order. However, when you check the tank, you find more plasticizer has evaporated than you expected (perhaps because of a leak in the tank) and you cannot fill the order quite yet.

Do you ship a partial order, sending the remainder of the order later at your expense? Or do you have an agreement in place to hold orders until complete? Do you order more plasticizer at great expense (overnight shipment) to meet the customer's need, knowing that several suppliers offer quick shipments of plasticizer for increased cost? Do you offer the customer a way to participate in this process?

What the rules enforce isn't truly the point here. It's only important that there are rules and that they are applied under the given circumstances.

You might believe that all workflow could be created from a rules-driven approach, and indeed many can be. We typically don't always use this approach because other workflow styles, such as the sequential workflow and the state-machine workflow, are easier to build and test. They offer far fewer internal, automated decisions. In the end, it amounts to complexity. Rules-based workflows are often complex and are therefore more costly to create and adequately test. The other workflow types are less complex and therefore easier to build and test.

The goal is to model your system using the most appropriate workflow type. Often, you will find yourself using some combination of all three types in many real-world scenarios.

The *Sequence* Activity

So let's dig into the sequential composite activity a little more. Although we've used this activity throughout the book so far, I intentionally delayed talking much about it until this point. Now that we have an understanding as to how the workflow runtime works with workflow instances, and know that workflow instances are really running versions of our workflow activities, we can better understand what's happening.

Performing tasks sequentially means those tasks are executed in a specific order. First things first, last things last. A sequential activity is something like a to-do list. Record the first thing you need to do, then the next, and the next, until finally you record your last task. If these tasks are stored in a *Sequence* activity, WF will execute each and every task in precisely the order in which the tasks are specified.

Note   We won't be looking at dynamically adding activities in this book, but you should know this is possible. For our purposes, we'll be adding activities using Microsoft Visual Studio and executing them statically.

In the case of Visual Studio, the workflow visual designer helps you lay out your workflow. When you create a sequential workflow application and open the root activity in the designer, the tasks you place at the top of the screen are executed first. Those toward the bottom are executed later. From a visual perspective, the sequence of activities runs from top to bottom. The *Sequence* activity is, of course, a composite activity.

Note   A specialized version of the *Sequence* activity is used as the root for sequential workflows—*SequentialWorkflow* activity. The only difference between the two is that the *SequentialWorkflow* activity accepts parameters when it begins execution, allowing you to initialize your workflow with runtime initialization information.

Building a Sequential Workflow Application

Because we've created a few sequential workflow applications so far in the book, I won't belabor their creation here. I will, however, repeat the steps for completeness.

Creating a sequential workflow application

1. In Microsoft Windows, click the Start button, move the cursor to All Programs, and then select Microsoft Visual Studio 2005 from the resulting menu.

2. Click the Microsoft Visual Studio 2005 icon to start Visual Studio 2005.

3. On the File menu, select New and then Project. The New Project dialog box will appear.

4. In the Project Types pane, expand the Visual C# tree node to show the project types available for the C# language.

5. Under the Visual C# node, click the Workflow node to display the workflow-based project templates.

6. In the Templates pane, click Sequential Workflow Console Application or Sequential Workflow Library. The former creates an executable application designed to execute in the Console window, while the latter creates a dynamic-link library other applications can use.

> **Note**   Currently, you don't have the option of creating a Windows Forms application that contains workflow. If you need a graphical user interface with your workflow, either you'll need to create a sequential workflow console application and add the Windows Forms you require, or you'll need to create a typical Windows Forms application and add the workflow components as you did in the previous chapter as a library assembly. Because my personal style is to create workflows within individual assemblies, I prefer the latter approach, but either will do.

7. In the Name field, type the name of your project or application.

8. In the Location field, type the file system location where you would like your project files stored.

9. If the Create Directory For Solution check box is not already selected, select it.

10. Click OK. Visual Studio 2005 will now create the basic project for you and bring up the workflow visual designer user interface.

At this point, you have the makings of an application that will execute sequential workflow instances. Simply drag and drop the activities you need from the Toolbox, adjust their properties to your needs, and continue with your application development. If you need to add more workflow library projects, you can do that as I described in the previous chapter, or simply add new workflow classes directly to your application. We'll see a great many more examples in the pages to follow because most workflow examples I'll present will be sequential by nature.

The *State* Activity

A type of workflow we've not seen so far in this book is one based on the model of a deterministic *state machine*. Crusty old digital microelectronics engineers (and I sadly admit I am one) well understand the design and implementation of state machines. However, if you're not a crusty old digital microelectronics engineer, the concept might be new to you. Chapter 14 is entirely dedicated to working with state-based workflows, but I'll introduce the concept here. We'll build a quick little state-based workflow as well.

People have dedicated their entire lives to the study of *finite state machines*. There is a language specific to finite state machines, custom mathematical notation, and a specific way they're diagrammed. I can't possibly hope to provide you with everything you might need to build state-based workflows, but I can provide enough information so that you can make sense of them as we build one or two.

> **Tip**   There are many resources on the Internet that better and more deeply describe finite state machines. One that's worth looking into is *en.wikipedia.org/wiki/Finite_state_machine*.

Breaking the term down, we have three words: finite, state, and machine. *Finite*, in this case, means we have a limited number of states we're willing to transition to. *States* are logical conditions our application transitions to as events occur. And *machine* implies automation. Let me illustrate by using an example.

In engineering school, you might be asked to design any number of digital systems using a finite state machine. The two classic examples are the vending machine and the washing machine. Looking at the vending machine, think about the steps the machine has to take to provide you with its product (soda, candy, snacks...whatever it's designed to dispense). As you insert coins, it counts the money until you've provided at least enough to pay for your selection. As you make your selection, it checks inventory (if it didn't already indicate it was out of a specific choice). If there is inventory, it dispenses your selection. And if you provided too much money, it makes change and dispenses that as well.

We can model the vending machine using a finite state machine. To diagram a finite state machine, we use circles as states and arrows as transitions between states. The transitions are triggered by events. There is a logical starting point and one or more logical stopping points. If we stop somewhere in between, our application is said to be in an indeterminate or invalid state. Our job is to prevent invalid states. We can't give our product away for free, and we shouldn't ask for more money than the product is worth, or worse, "eat" the user's money. Users have been known to get violently angry at vending machines that take their money but don't provide the goods.

So imagine a simplified vending machine. Let's lay out our states and events that lead to transitions between those states. States, as I mentioned, are represented by circles. Events, which move your machine from state to state, are represented by arrows. Both are named so that we know which states and which transitions are related. Tying all of this back to the vending machine, we certainly have a starting state, as we can see in Figure 4-2.

Figure 4-2   The symbol for the starting state of a finite-state machine

This state represents the machine as it sits there, waiting for someone to come along and put in a coin. So let's say someone does come along and puts in a coin, but it's not enough money to purchase an item. We simulate that by creating a new state, WaitCoins, which we transition to through the CoinInserted event, as shown in Figure 4-3.

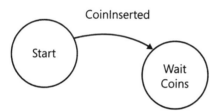

Figure 4-3   A diagram showing the transition to the WaitCoins state

The machine stays at the WaitCoins state, accepting CoinInserted events, until it has enough money to complete the purchase of the product the user chose. This triggers the Sufficient-Coins event, which transitions our machine to the WaitSelection state. Here our vending machine waits patiently for the user to make a selection. (In a real machine, the user could also ask for money back at any time, but let's keep it simple.)

When the user makes a selection, the item is dispensed and our transaction is complete. The completion state, or *terminal state*, as it's sometimes called, is indicated by a double circle. The complete, albeit simplified, vending machine state diagram would then appear as shown in Figure 4-4.

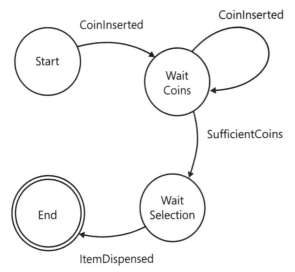

Figure 4-4   A complete machine state diagram for a vending machine

Although this might be an oversimplification of a real-world vending machine, hopefully this brief description provides you with an idea as to how state machines work. When we design state machines, we identify discrete states, or logical places to wait for events, and we then identify the events that shift the machine from state to state. Some events take the machine back to the same state it was in to begin with. Others move the machine to new states with new events to be handled. No state transitions are ever made without some event trigger, which ideally is not an unforeseen event or exception.

This model is very different from the one used for a sequential workflow. In sequential workflows, activities are executed in the order in which they are specified. Once one activity in the chain has completed its task, the next activity in the chain begins its work. There might be events involved with the workflow processing, but they're simply related to the workflow task at hand (timer events, for example).

State machines, however, spend a lot of their time waiting. They wait for events, and depending on the event, they shift from state to state. The states themselves *do not* fire events (although they might call into play external code that does). They are event handlers. So they patiently wait for the events they need to transition from state to state. It's entirely possible to shift from one state to any one of a number of different states in a nonlinear fashion, depending on the event. Our vending machine, if it's in the WaitCoins state, would do very different things if it received a CoinInserted event versus a RefundRequested event, or even an ImminentPowerdown event. I didn't show those events in my simplified model in Figure 4-4, but I'm sure you can see how different events can drive your finite state machine into different states.

In WF, the individual state in a state-based workflow is modeled by the *State* activity. The *State* activity is a composite activity, but it limits the child activities it will contain. You'll learn much more about state-based workflows in Chapter 14.

> **Note**   Just as sequential workflows used a specialized version of the *Sequence* activity to contain the entire workflow, so too do state-based workflows have a specialized root activity—the *StateMachineWorkflow* activity, which is a specialization of the *State* activity. The specialization is again necessary so that the root activity can accept initialization parameters when it is initially executed.

Building a State Machine Workflow Application

So how do we build state-based workflows? As it happens, Visual Studio is, as always, there to help. Creating a state-based workflow project is as easy as creating a sequential workflow. Let's build a basic state-based workflow project to see how it's done. We won't add any code to the project quite yet—we need to progress a bit further in the book for that. But when we need it, we'll know how state-based workflows are created.

Creating a state machine workflow application

1. Start Microsoft Visual Studio 2005 as you did for building a sequential workflow.

2. On the File menu, select New and then Project, which activates the New Project dialog box.

3. As you typically do when creating new projects, expand the Visual C# node in the Project Types pane to show the project types available for the C# language.

4. Under the Visual C# node, click the Workflow node to display the workflow-based project templates.

5. In the Templates pane, click State Machine Workflow Console Application or State Machine Workflow Library. As with sequential workflows, the first template creates a full-fledged application designed to work within the Console window. The second template creates a dynamic-link library you can use from other workflow-based applications.

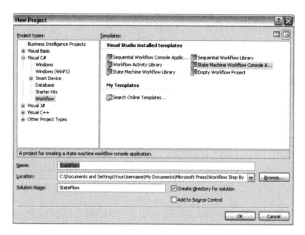

6. In the Name field, type the name of your project or application.

7. In the Location field, type the file system location where you would like your project files stored.

8. If the Create Directory For Solution check box is not already selected, select it.

9. Click OK. Visual Studio 2005 will now create the basic project for you and bring up the workflow visual designer user interface.

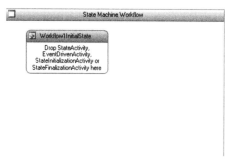

As with the sequential workflow application, Visual Studio is now ready for us to build a state-machine workflow. We're not quite ready to actually build a state-machine workflow at this point in the book. Why? Because we need to trigger the events that cause the workflow to change state. To do that, we'll need to understand how workflow instances communicate with their host applications so that our host application can perform the trigger actions. We'll begin looking at host and workflow communication in Chapter 8, "Calling External Methods," but it's in Chapter 10, "Event Activities," that we learn what we need to know to drive state-machine workflows.

Chapter 4 Quick Reference

To	Do This
Select the appropriate workflow type	Model your system, and look closely at what is controlling the process. If the workflow is controlling the process, select a sequential workflow model. If external inputs are controlling the workflow, select a state-machine workflow. If complex behavior is to be modeled, a rules-based approach might be the best. Often a combination of workflow types will be necessary.
Build a sequential workflow application	Start Visual Studio 2005, and select the New and then Project menu items from the main File menu. From the resulting New Project dialog box, select the Workflow node from the Visual C# subtree shown in the Project Types pane. From the Templates pane, select either the Sequential Workflow Console Application or the Sequential Workflow Library type.
Build a state-machine workflow application	Follow the steps for building a sequential workflow application until you choose the template. In the Templates pane, select either the State Machine Workflow Console Application or the State Machine Workflow Library type.
Build a rules-based workflow application	Create a sequential workflow application, and then skip to Chapter 12 to learn how to apply the *Policy* or rule condition.

Chapter 5
Workflow Tracking

After completing this chapter, you will be able to:

- Describe workflow-pluggable services
- Create an event tracking database and populate it with tables and scripts
- Activate the event-tracking service
- Create a custom tracking profile
- View your workflow's tracking information

So far we've seen the basic objects that workflows are built from and controlled by. We build workflow tasks from activities, which when executing are managed by a *WorkflowInstance* object. Workflow instances are queued and controlled by the *WorkflowRuntime*. But Windows Workflow Foundation (WF) doesn't just provide us with objects—it also provides us with services that work alongside our objects.

Pluggable Services

Workflow services are additional software functions that your workflows can, and will, use to complete their tasks. Some of the services are optional, like the tracking service we'll work with in this chapter. Other services are required for your workflow to execute at all.

Workflow services are *pluggable*. A pluggable service is a service that can be selected a la carte to perform specific tasks. For example, there are services that manage threading, tracking, transactions, and so forth. You select the service that's right for your workflow. You can even create your own.

So what do these services look like? What do they do for us? Table 5-1 lays out the available base services and gives you a better idea which services are available and what they do.

Most of these services we don't use directly. We'll typically use services derived from these base services.

Table 5-1   Base Workflow Services

Service	Purpose
WorkflowPersistenceService	The abstract base class from which all persistence services are derived.
WorkflowQueuingService	The base class that provides methods you can use to manage the workflow queues associated with a workflow instance.
WorkflowRuntimeService	The abstract base class from which the workflow runtime core services are derived.
WorkflowSchedulerService	The base class for all classes that create threads that run workflow instances on the workflow runtime host.
WorkflowSubscriptionService	The base class for classes that manage subscriptions for a workflow runtime.
WorkflowTransactionService	The base class for all transaction services.
TrackingService	The abstract base class that provides the basic interface between a tracking service and the runtime tracking infrastructure.

Remember that these are *base* classes. The services we actually use are derived from these. For instance, when we run a workflow instance, something needs to create a thread for that instance to use. *DefaultWorkflowSchedulerService* does just that, using *WorkflowSchedulerService* as its base. But if you want to provide the thread yourself, you can use *ManualWorkflowSchedulerService* instead. In this chapter, we'll look at the tracking service provided by *SqlTrackingService*, which has *TrackingService* for a base class.

The "pluggable" part comes in when you consider that at any given time you might need to use a scheduler service (one that prepares threads for your workflow instance to use), the runtime service, and queueing and subscriptions (timers). But you can add persistence (saving in-progress workflow instances) and tracking, as well as external data communication services. They all just plug in and work together.

Workflow Tracking

In this chapter, we'll concentrate on the tracking service. Other chapters will look at other available services. Regarding tracking, WF ships with one primary tracking service—*SqlTrackingService*. However, should you need them, there are two additional services available as samples. These services, *ConsoleTrackingService* and *SimpleFileTrackingService*, allow you to write tracking information to the console window or to files instead of to a Microsoft SQL Server database. We won't use those services here, but they are available if you need to use them.

> **Note**   The samples are installed with the Windows SDK—see Chapter 1, "Introducing Microsoft Windows Workflow Foundation" for installation instructions. See also the section in this chapter entitled "Viewing Tracking Information with WorkflowMonitor" for accessing the samples. The tracking services to which I refer, "Console" and "File," are located in the Technologies directory under "Tracking."

Workflow Event Tracking Using *SqlTrackingService*

You track your workflow processes by adding a tracking service to the workflow runtime—typically, *SqlTrackingService*. As your workflow instance progresses, it fires events, as do individual activities within your workflow. If you have specific tracking needs, you can create your own user-defined tracking events. If the events that are captured provide you with more tracking data than you require, you can filter the tracked data using a tracking profile you establish.

As tracked events fire, WF creates and manages *tracking records*. Although you're not required to do so, you can easily access the tracking records directly from WF. Note that the information is recorded in the database as well, so retrieving the information directly from the database is also a possibility. Queries for tracking information are normally made at a later date using an external tracking monitor tool, such as *WorkflowMonitor* (a tracking tool that comes with WF as a sample, with source code) or a tool of your own design.

Table 5-2 lists the objects you'll typically use when working with WF event tracking, and we'll use some of these as we progress through the chapter. If all you ever do is use WF's out-of-the-box event tracking capabilities, you won't directly use many of the objects shown in Table 5-2, but they will be used by WF on your behalf. However, if you need to customize your workflow's event tracking capabilities, it's nice to know WF provides a strong library of tracking-related objects for you to use.

Table 5-2   Event Tracking Objects

Object	Purpose
ActivityDataTrackingExtract	Specifies a property or a field to be extracted from an activity and sent to the tracking service together with an associated collection of annotations when a track point is matched.
ActivityTrackingCondition	Represents a condition resulting from comparing the value of an activity property with a known value by using a specified comparison operator.
ActivityTrackingLocation	Defines an activity-qualified location that corresponds to an activity status event in the executing root workflow instance.
ActivityTrackingRecord	Contains the data sent to a tracking service by the runtime tracking infrastructure when an *ActivityTrackPoint* is matched.
ActivityTrackPoint	Defines a point of interest that is associated with an activity execution status change to be tracked.

Table 5-2 Event Tracking Objects

Object	Purpose
SqlTrackingQuery	Provides methods and properties that you can use to access certain kinds of tracking data stored in a SQL database by the *SqlTrackingService*.
SqlTrackingQueryOptions	Contains properties that are used to constrain the set of *SqlTrackingWorkflowInstance* objects returned by the *SqlTrackingQuery.GetWorkflows* method.
SqlTrackingWorkflowInstance	Returned by a call to either *SqlTrackingQuery.TryGetWorkflow* or *SqlTrackingQuery.GetWorkflows* to provide access to the tracking data collected by the *SqlTrackingService* in a SQL database for a specific workflow instance.
TrackingProfile	Filters tracking events, and returns tracking records based on this filtering to a tracking service. There are three kinds of tracking events that can be filtered: activity status events, workflow status events, and user events.
UserTrackingLocation	Specifies a user-defined location that corresponds to a user event in the executing root workflow instance.
UserTrackingRecord	Contains the data sent to a tracking service by the runtime tracking infrastructure when a *UserTrackPoint* is matched.
UserTrackPoint	Defines a point of interest that is associated with a user event.
WorkflowDataTrackingExtract	Specifies a property or a field to be extracted from a workflow and sent to the tracking service together with an associated collection of annotations when a track point is matched.
WorkflowTrackingLocation	Defines a workflow-qualified location that corresponds to a workflow event in the executing root workflow instance.
WorkflowTrackingRecord	Contains the data sent to a tracking service by the runtime tracking infrastructure when a *WorkflowTrackPoint* is matched.
WorkflowTrackPoint	Defines a point of interest that is associated with a workflow event.

These objects can be thought of as belonging to two main categories: tracking data retrieval and tracking specification. Tracking retrieval objects, such as *SqlTrackingQuery*, help you gather tracking data once it is stored in the database. Tracking specification objects, such as the track points and locations, allow you to dictate what is tracked from your workflow code.

The tracking specification objects, such as the point and location obects, are organized into three main groups: activity events, workflow events, and user events. The activity-related tracking objects, such as *ActivityTrackingPoint* or *ActivityTrackingLocation*, are designed to record activity-related event information to the tracking database. These events include such things as activity cancellation, unhandled exceptions, and execution events. Workflow event-tracking objects work in a similar manner but for workflow-related events, such as the workflow starting and stopping; instances being created, idling, and finishing; and other similar things. And finally, user event tracking, which is where you customize the tracking needs of your particular workflow, is specific to your workflow and depends entirely on how you want your workflow tracked. You can allow as many or as few tracked user events in your workflow as you require. We'll see a couple of these when we look at tracking profiles later in the chapter.

The tracking records are decorated with *annotations*. Annotations are just strings that are kept with the tracking record and recorded into the tracking database. The activity-related and workflow-related tracking records have an established collection of annotations, but you might want to provide additional annotations for user-related event tracking records.

Tracking in WF terms isn't that dissimilar to the notion of *tracing*. Tracing, as you might know, is a useful debugging tool, and ASP.NET and .NET client technologies—such as Windows Presentation Foundation (WPF) and Windows Forms—all support tracing capabilities. Tracing embodies the concept of trace levels, where you specify what is traced for varying degrees of severity, such as tracing on an error, tracing to record a warning, and writing trace entries for informational purposes. This allows people reviewing the trace records to filter the trace information according to their desires. They can see only exception trace information, or they can see the entire trace stack.

WF tracking is based on a similar concept, at least as far as the filtering is concerned. As you might imagine, both activity-related and workflow-related events will generate all manner of tracking records, some of which you might find interesting (such as records for unhandled exceptions or idle status). You might decide other events are not as necessary for tracking purposes.

To filter the tracked events you don't want, you create a *tracking profile*. Ultimately, a tracking profile is an XML document that identifies what is to be tracked and what is to be excluded. Unlike tracing, the tracking profile dictates what is written to the tracking database, not what is later to be viewed. If you exclude events, nothing regarding the excluded events is written to the database. Also unlike tracing, the tracking profile XML document is recorded in the tracking database and recalled when the workflow is executed. Tracing, on the other hand, records everything designated to be traced but categorizes the trace information for later filtered viewing.

Setting Up SQL Server for Tracking

Although you could build custom tracking services that record tracking data to various repositories (such as a message queue or data file), in this chapter we'll concentrate on WF's ability to record event data in a SQL Server 2005 database. WF comes with built-in support for using SQL Server 2005.

Note   Because SQL Server 2005 and SQL Server Express both use SQL Server Management Studio, the steps will be identical for either database service, at least as far as establishing the event tracking database itself is concerned. SQL Server Express doesn't ship with SQL Server Management Studio, but you can download the Express version from this site: *www.microsoft.com/downloads/details.aspx?displaylang=en&FamilyID=C243A5AE-4BD1-4E3D-94B8-5A0F62BF7796*

We'll begin by creating a new database in SQL Server Management Studio (or the Express version). We'll then need to run some SQL scripts that ship with the WinFX components (or that come prepackaged with Windows Vista). These scripts will create the database roles, the tables and views, and the stored procedures necessary to interact with your workflow. Let's start by creating a new database and running some preliminary scripts; then we'll record tracking data to that database using the WF tracking service.

Note   I'll refer to SQL Server Express in the steps that follow, but for those of you using the full version of SQL Server, the steps remain the same. When you read "SQL Server Express," think to yourself "SQL Server."

Create a SQL Server 2005 tracking database

1. In Microsoft Windows, click the Start button, move the cursor to All Programs, and then select Microsoft SQL Server 2005 from the programs menu.

2. Click the SQL Server Management Studio Express icon to start the SQL Server management application (or if you have SQL Server installed, click the SQL Server Management Studio icon).

3. We'll need to connect to the database server we want to use, using the SQL Server Connect To Server dialog box:

(If SQL Server Management Studio Express is already running, click the Connect button and then choose Database Engine in the Object Explorer pane.) The Server Type drop-down list should indicate Database Engine (the default value). The Server Name drop-down list should display the server's name and the instance of SQL Server 2005 you want to use on that server. My server is named "Redbarron," and the SQL Server instance I want to use is "SQL2005." If you want to use the default instance, simply provide only the server's name. As for authentication, you should use the authentication methodology you selected when you installed SQL Server (or see your database administrator for any assistance you might require). Click Connect to connect to your database server.

4. SQL Server Management Studio Express's user interface typically consists of two panes. The left pane mimics Windows Explorer and shows the databases and services associated with your database server. The right pane is the work pane, where you'll type in scripts, set up table columns, and so forth. The left pane is known as the Object Explorer, and if it is not visible, you can activate it by selecting Object Explorer from the View menu.

5. Right-click on the Databases node to activate the context menu, and select New Database.

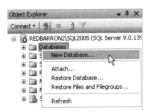

6. The New Database dialog box appears. Type **WorkflowTracking** in the Database Name field, and click OK.

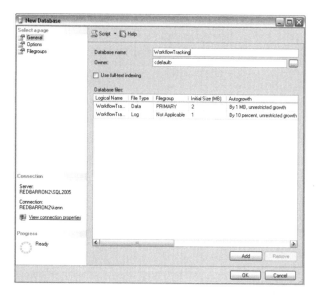

If you expand the Databases node in the Object Explorer, you will find that the new WorkflowTracking database has been added.

7. Next we'll need to execute the scripts Windows Workflow Foundation provides for setting up tracking, starting with the schema script. (This builds the tables and views, as well as creating workflow tracking roles.) The scripts are located in <%WINDIR%>\ Microsoft.NET\Framework\v3.0\Windows Workflow Foundation\SQL\EN, where <%WINDIR%> is your Windows directory (typically, C:\Windows). From SQL Server Management Studio Express's File menu, select Open and then File, which brings up the common Open File dialog box. Using the controls in the Open File dialog box, locate the schema script, Tracking_Schema.sql. Select that from the available scripts, and click the Open button. Note you'll need to connect to your database server once again.

8. SQL Server Management Studio Express should have loaded the script into a new window, but before we actually run the script, we need to specify which database we want the script to run against. Naturally, we want to use the WorkflowTracking database we just created. So locate the WorkflowTracking database in the drop-down list of databases, and select it as the target, as shown below.

Note   Don't forget this step! If you forget to specify the database, the tables, views, and roles will be created on whichever database is active in the drop-down list at the time. You will need to delete the inserted elements by hand. Don't ask how I know…

9. With the script loaded and ready to execute, and with the WorkflowTracking database designated as the target of the script, execute the script by clicking the Execute button on the toolbar.

Tip   You can alternatively execute the script using the Execute menu option, found under the Query main menu item, or just press the F5 key.

10. Repeat steps 7 through 9 to execute the Tracking_Logic.sql script. This loads the necessary stored procedures into the database.

We now have a database in which we'll record tracking information, but how does the information get recorded? What component is responsible for that? Let's find out!

Using the *SqlTrackingService* Service

With the workflow tracking database in place, it's time to actually use it. Let's create a new workflow and see how we track events. We'll start by creating a slightly more complex workflow so that we have a few events to play with. After we have the basic workflow built, we'll add the necessary tracking code.

Create a new workflow for tracking

1. To make it easier, I've created two versions of this sample application. (In fact, I'll try to do that for the remainder of the book.) The WorkflowTracker application has two different versions: one incomplete and one complete. The complete version is entirely finished and ready to run, and you will find it in the \Workflow\Chapter5\ WorkflowTracker Completed\ directory. The incomplete version is yours to modify when completing the steps I've outlined here, and you'll find it in the \Workflow\Chapter5\Workflow Tracker\ directory. Feel free to use either one. Whichever version you choose, you can open it for editing by dragging its .sln file onto an executing copy of Visual Studio.

2. After Visual Studio opens the WorkflowTracker solution for editing, create a separate sequential workflow library project as you did in Chapter 3 to house our new workflow. (See the section in Chapter 3 entitled "Adding a sequential workflow project to the WorkflowHost solution".) Name this workflow library **TrackedWorkflow** and save it in the \Workflow\Chapter5\WorkflowTracker directory.

> **Note** This will turn out to be a common theme—creating a workflow to go with a basic application. The good news is you'll become quite adept at creating workflow host applications, which isn't a bad thing, I think. If you prefer, you can create a workflow-based console application directly within Visual Studio, but you should still create a separate workflow library. This arrangement will make it easier to monitor your workflow when we use WorkflowMonitor later in the chapter.

3. After you have completed the steps to add the workflow library project, Visual Studio opens the visual workflow designer for editing. If it doesn't, locate the Workflow1.cs file in Visual Studio's Solution Explorer and click the View Designer toolbar button to activate the designer.

4. For this workflow, let's combine some aspects of previous workflows we've built. This should give us a slightly more complex workflow without pushing us too far away from what we've seen. Let's begin by dragging an *IfElse* activity from the Toolbox onto the designer's surface.

> **Tip** Building this part of the workflow will be a lot like building the workflow from Chapter 1.

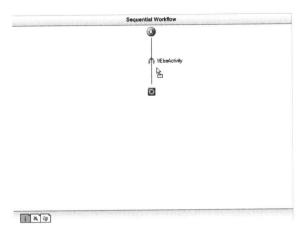

5. Click once on the left branch, *ifElseBranchActivity1*, to activate its properties in the Visual Studio Properties window.

6. Look for *ifElseBranchActivity1*'s *Condition* property. Open the drop-down list by clicking the down arrow, and select Code Condition.

7. The *Condition* property should now display a plus sign (+) to its left. Click the plus sign to expand the property grid and expose the *Condition* property's *Condition* name field. (It may seem confusing to have a property of a property use a name that is identical to its parent, but that's how the WF team chose to name things.) In the edit control, type **QueryDelay**. We'll use this method to decide which path we'll take through the *IfElse* activity.

8. Next we'll add some activities to the left branch (which is the branch that is executed when the condition evaluates to *true*). First, drag a *Code* activity from the Toolbox and drop it onto the left *IfElse* branch, *ifElseBranchActivity1*.

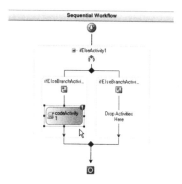

9. The exclamation mark (!) you see in the preceding figure means we have work to do. In this case, it indicates we need to to add a method to be called when the code activity we just placed into our workflow is executed. In the Visual Studio Properties pane, locate the *ExecuteCode* property and type **PreDelayMessage** into its edit control.

10. You probably see what I'm doing... I'm essentially adding the delay workflow we created in Chapter 3 to this workflow. And as we did in Chapter 3, drop a *Delay* activity and

another *Code* activity into *ifElseBranchActivity1* and set their properties. The *Delay* activity should delay 10 seconds (00:00:10), as in Chapter 3, and the second *Code* activity should execute a method called **PostDelayMessage**. When completed, the designer should look like the following:

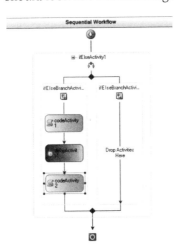

11. With our designer work complete, let's add some code. Click the View Code toolbar button in the Visual Studio Solution Explorer toolbar to bring up the C# code for Workflow1.cs. Begin by adding a reference to *System.Windows.Forms* as well as the corresponding *using* statement at the top of the Workflow1.cs file.

```
using System.Windows.Forms;
```

12. As you scan through the file, you should see the three event handlers Visual Studio added for you as activity properties: *PreDelayMessage*, *PostDelayMessage*, and *QueryDelay*. As you did in Chapter 3, add message boxes to the *Code* activity methods so that the application notifies you when the workflow is executing. To *PreDelayMessage*, add this code:

```
MessageBox.Show("Pre-delay code is being executed.");
To PostDelayMessage, add this code:
MessageBox.Show("Post-delay code is being executed.");
```

13. The slightly more interesting case is the code we'll add to *QueryDelay*:

```
e.Result = false; // assume we'll not delay...
if (MessageBox.Show("Okay to execute delay in workflow processing?",
    "Query Delay",
    MessageBoxButtons.YesNo,
    MessageBoxIcon.Question) == DialogResult.Yes)
{
    // Allow progression
    e.Result = true;

    // Show message
```

```
        Console.WriteLine("Delay path taken...");
    } // if
    else
    {
        // Show message
        Console.WriteLine("Delay path NOT taken...");
    } // else
```

14. With the workflow complete, we'll need to add a reference from our main application, WorkflowTracker, to the workflow, TrackedWorkflow. A project-level reference is easiest, and to add the reference right-click the References folder in the WorkflowTracker project in Visual Studio's Solution Explorer and select Add Reference. When the Add Reference dialog box appears, select the Project tab and then click the TrackedWorkflow project from the list. Click OK.

15. Open Program.cs in the WorkflowTracker project for editing and then look for this line of code:

```
Console.WriteLine("Waiting for workflow completion.");
```

16. To create a workflow instance, add this code following the line of code you just located:

```
// Create the workflow instance.
WorkflowInstance instance =
    workflowRuntime.CreateWorkflow(typeof(TrackedWorkflow.Workflow1));

// Start the workflow instance.
instance.Start();
```

17. Compile the solution by pressing F6. Correct any compilation errors.

18. To execute the application, press F5 (or Ctrl+F5) and respond "Yes" to the delay query. You should see this console output:

We now have a basic workflow we can use to experiment with WF's tracking capabilities. Let's turn now to adding the code we'll need to actually perform the tracking.

Add *SqlTrackingService* to your workflow

1. WF ships with activity and workflow event tracking capability, so we won't need to do much to track those events. Nonetheless, we will still need to add some logic to the main program application file. Start by adding a reference to *System.Configuration* to the WorkflowTracker application. We'll need this to access the database connection string we'll store in the application configuration file. Do this by clicking Add Reference for the WorkflowTracker project. When the Add Reference dialog box comes up, select the .NET tab and then *System.Configuration* from the list of available .NET assemblies. Click OK.

2. Next, add an application configuration file to the WorkflowTracker application. To do this, right-click the WorkflowTracker tree control node in Visual Studio's Solution Explorer and select Add and then New Item. When the Add New Item dialog box appears, select Application Configuration File from the list and click OK. This adds a new app.config file to your application.

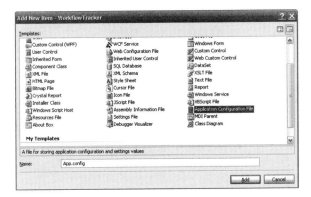

3. Visual Studio will create the new app.config file and open it for editing. Insert this XML between the *configuration* opening and closing tags. Note that printing limitations prevent the *connectionString* attribute from being shown as a single line, but the line you insert should be a single line with no line breaks:

```
<connectionStrings>
<add name="TrackingDatabase"
    connectionString="Data Source=(local)\SQLEXPRESS;
        Initial Catalog=WorkflowTracking;Integrated Security=True;"/>
</connectionStrings>
```

> **Note** The connection string I've shown might or might not work for you. If you're using a different server or a named instance, you'll need to adjust the Data Source value accordingly. Or, if you're using SQL Server authentication, you'll want to replace the Integrated Security value with the UID and PWD (user ID and password, respectively) values that correspond to the SQL login you want to use.

4. Click WorkflowFactory.cs for the WorkflowTracker project in the Visual Studio Solution Explorer, and then click the Solution Explorer's View Code button.

5. So that we can use the Visual Studio IntelliSense capability, add the following lines of code to the top of the file, following the last *using* directive you find there:

```
using System.Workflow.Runtime.Tracking;
using System.Configuration;
```

6. While in the WorkflowFactory.cs file, scan down and find the line where we create the *WorkflowRuntime* instance. We'll need to introduce *SqlTrackingService* to the workflow runtime at this point. Add this line of code following the line of code calling *GetWorkflowRuntime*:

```
String conn = ConfigurationManager.
                ConnectionStrings["TrackingDatabase"].
                ConnectionString;
_workflowRuntime.AddService(new SqlTrackingService(conn));
```

With that last step, we're done adding code that we'll need to actually perform the tracking. (In a moment, we'll add more code to display the tracking results.) Compile the application by selecting Build Solution from the Build menu, and execute it by pressing the F5 or Ctrl+F5 keys.

Note   If the program crashed with an *ArgumentException* telling you that the runtime can't access the given database, you probably need to add the login account you're using as a valid database user (as specified in the connection string we added to the workflow code a moment ago) or otherwise adjust the connection string. If you're unsure how to do this, the online reference material can help (*http://msdn2.microsoft.com/en-us/library/ ms254947(VS.80).aspx*), or see your local database administrator for assistance.

Assuming the workflow runs as expected, you should find entries in the WorkflowTracking database's *ActivityInstance* table, as shown in Figure 5-1.

Note   To see the table, open SQL Server Management Studio Express (if not already open) and expand the Databases tree control node. Locate the WorkflowTracking database and expand its tree node. Expand the Tables node and right-click the ActivityInstance tree node. From the resulting context menu, select Open Table.

| Table - dbo.ActivityInstance | Summary | | | ▾ × |
WorkflowInsta...	ActivityInstanc...	QualifiedName	ContextGuid	ParentContext...
1	1	Workflow1	4d943215-18d0-...	4d943215-18d0-...
1	2	ifElseActivity1	4d943215-18d0-...	4d943215-18d0-...
1	3	ifElseBranchActi...	4d943215-18d0-...	4d943215-18d0-...
1	4	codeActivity1	4d943215-18d0-...	4d943215-18d0-...
1	5	delayActivity1	4d943215-18d0-...	4d943215-18d0-...
1	6	codeActivity2	4d943215-18d0-...	4d943215-18d0-...
*	NULL	NULL	NULL	NULL

Figure 5-1   ActivityInstance table

If all you ever want to do is record tracking data in the tracking database, the steps we've completed so far are enough to accomplish this. But let's take a minute and use a couple of the objects listed in Table 5-2 to draw tracking data from the database from within our application.

Retrieve tracking records from your workflow

1. To begin, with the application we just created open and ready for editing in Visual Studio, open the WorkflowTracker project's Program.cs file for editing.

2. Add the *using* statements for configuration and workflow tracking to the top of the file:

```
using System.Configuration;
using System.Workflow.Runtime.Tracking;
```

3. In the *Main* method, locate this line of code:

```
waitHandle.WaitOne();
```

4. Add these lines of code following the line of code you found in step 3:

```
ShowWorkflowTrackingEvents(instance.InstanceId);
ShowActivityTrackingEvents(instance.InstanceId);
```

5. Because we've called a couple of methods that don't yet exist, we need to implement those methods. Add these methods to the *Program* class:

```
static void ShowActivityTrackingEvents(Guid instanceId)
{
    SqlTrackingQuery sqlTrackingQuery =
            new SqlTrackingQuery(ConfigurationManager.
                    ConnectionStrings["TrackingDatabase"].
                    ConnectionString);

    SqlTrackingWorkflowInstance sqlTrackingWorkflowInstance = null;
    sqlTrackingQuery.TryGetWorkflow(instanceId,
                            out sqlTrackingWorkflowInstance);
    if (sqlTrackingWorkflowInstance != null)
    {
        Console.WriteLine("\nActivity Tracking Events:\n");
        Console.WriteLine("  Status :: Date/Time :: Qualified ID");

        foreach (ActivityTrackingRecord atr in
                        sqlTrackingWorkflowInstance.ActivityEvents)
        {
            Console.WriteLine("  {0} :: {1} :: {2}", atr.ExecutionStatus,
                            atr.EventDateTime, atr.QualifiedName);
        } // foreach
    } // if
}

static void ShowWorkflowTrackingEvents(Guid instanceId)
{
    SqlTrackingQuery sqlTrackingQuery =
            new SqlTrackingQuery(ConfigurationManager.
                    ConnectionStrings["TrackingDatabase"].
                    ConnectionString);
```

```
    SqlTrackingWorkflowInstance sqlTrackingWorkflowInstance = null;
    sqlTrackingQuery.TryGetWorkflow(instanceId,
                                out sqlTrackingWorkflowInstance);
    if (sqlTrackingWorkflowInstance != null)
    {
        Console.WriteLine("\nWorkflow Instance Events:\n");
        Console.WriteLine(" Description :: Date/Time");

        foreach (WorkflowTrackingRecord wtr in
                        sqlTrackingWorkflowInstance.WorkflowEvents)
        {
            Console.WriteLine(" {0} :: {1}", wtr.TrackingWorkflowEvent,
                                        wtr.EventDateTime);
        } // foreach
    }
}
```

We blew out a lot of code in that last step, but in reality what we're doing isn't terribly complex. We first create an instance of *SqlTrackingQuery*, providing it the same connection string we provided to *SqlTrackingService*. Then we effectively query the database for tracking information for our current workflow instance, identified by the instance's ID (a *Guid*). The query is performed by *SqlTrackingService.TryGetWorkflow*. If tracking information for our workflow instance is located in the database, we loop through the tracking records (returned to us as a collection of *WorkflowTrackingRecord* objects) and extract the information of interest. If no records are found, no tracking information is written to the console window. The screen output should look something like the screen you see in Figure 5-2 (you might need to set a breakpoint and run the code in debug mode to see the output).

Figure 5-2 WorkflowTracker application screen output

Tracking User Events

SqlTrackingService, because it is a part of WF, is capable of tracking events that are inherently a part of WF. That is, it can track standard events fired from activities and workflow instances. But what about events your workflow generates? How do we track those?

As it happens, the *Activity* activity supports a method named *TrackData*. *TrackData* has two overloaded versions: one that takes an object to be stored in the tracking database and one that accepts a string as a key as well as the object to be stored.

If you execute *TrackData* and pass in data for tracking purposes, usually a string, the information will be stored in the tracking database as user-event data. Try the procedure below with the WorkflowTracker project we created earlier in the chapter.

Retrieve tracking records from your workflow

1. With the WorkflowTracker project open in Visual Studio for editing, open the Workflow1.cs C# file for editing.
2. Scroll down until you find the *PreDelayMessage* and *PostDelayMessage* methods we added when we created the workflow.
3. After the code to display the message box in *PreDelayMessage*, add this code:

```
this.TrackData("Delay commencing");
```

4. Similarly, add this code following the message box code in *PostDelayMessage*:

```
this.TrackData("Delay completed");
```

5. Compile and execute the program using F5 or Ctrl+F5.

Now open the *UserEvent* table in the WorkflowTracking database, following the procedure outlined for the *ActivityInstance* table (Figure 5-1). There should be two rows, one for each time we called *TrackData* in our workflow, as shown in Figure 5-3.

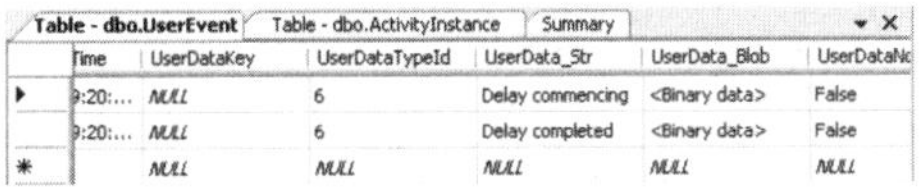

	Time	UserDataKey	UserDataTypeId	UserData_Str	UserData_Blob	UserDataNc
▶	9:20:...	NULL	6	Delay commencing	<Binary data>	False
	9:20:...	NULL	6	Delay completed	<Binary data>	False
*		NULL	NULL	NULL	NULL	NULL

Figure 5-3 UserEvent table showing results of calling TrackData

Building Custom Tracking Profiles

I've mentioned tracking profiles a few times already in this chapter, but I intentionally didn't get into the details. I left those for this section.

As you might recall, a tracking profile is a mechanism for limiting the amount of information the WF tracking architecture will store in the tracking database. Ultimately, a tracking profile is no more than an XML document that stipulates what is to be included or excluded from a given workflow's tracking perspective. But to make things easier in code, there is a *Tracking-Profile* object as well as the rest of the objects you saw in Table 5-2. You can use these objects to create this XML document.

Because there is a tracking profile object, you might naturally assume that there is also an XML serializer available to convert the *TrackingProfile* object into the XML document you'll need to store in the database. And in fact, there is—*TrackingProfileSerializer*. There is no inherent WF support for writing the XML information to the database once it's serialized, but that's easily accomplished using typical ADO.NET techniques and a stored procedure you'll find in the tracking database.

If you glance back at Table 5-2, you'll find objects named using words such as "location" and "point"—one each for activity, workflow, and user events. What do we mean when we talk about locations and points?

Well, locations refer to specific places in your workflow where events occur, whether activity-related, workflow-related, or user-related (with "user-related" referring to events you coded into your workflow, not end users of your workflow-based application). Locations describe the events to be tracked. Using a location object, you can specify more precisely which events you want included and at what location in your workflow you want those events included in the tracking database, as well as which events you want excluded from tracking consideration.

Track points collect locations, and as such they can trigger tracking information in one or many places within your workflow. You can think of a track point as a point of interest that can span different places in your workflow code. Given the conditions and locations you assign to the track point, it might or it might not be triggered for tracking purposes.

Why mention all of this? Because when you set up a tracking profile, what you are really doing is adding tracking points and locations to the profile object to be used as filters for writing tracked events. Let's work this into the workflow example we've been using throughout the chapter.

Create a new tracking profile

1. Open the WorkflowTracker project in Visual Studio for editing if it's not already open. Select Program.cs in Solution Explorer, and click the View Code toolbar button to edit the C# source code for the main application file. All the code we'll add in this section will be placed in this one file.

2. The code we'll be adding isn't necessarily difficult to understand, but there is quite a bit of it. Therefore, let's add the necessary *using* directives we'll need to compile as well as to keep IntelliSense happy. Add these lines to the *using* directives you find in Program.cs:

```
using System.Data;
using System.Data.SqlClient;
using System.Globalization;
using System.IO;
```

3. As for the code we'll add, we'll begin by locating the *Main* method. Add these lines following the opening brace for the *Main* method. You want to do this before you execute the code that creates your workflow:

```
TrackingProfile profile = CreateProfile();
StoreProfile(profile, ConfigurationManager.
                        ConnectionStrings["TrackingDatabase"].
                        ConnectionString);
```

4. The code we just added calls two methods we need to add to the *Program* class. Scroll down through the *Program* class, and add the *CreateProfile* method you see here:

```
static TrackingProfile CreateProfile()
{
    TrackingProfile profile = new TrackingProfile();

    ActivityTrackingLocation actLoc = new
                        ActivityTrackingLocation(typeof(Activity));
    actLoc.MatchDerivedTypes = true;
    actLoc.ExecutionStatusEvents.Add(ActivityExecutionStatus.Executing);

    ActivityTrackPoint actPt = new ActivityTrackPoint();
    actPt.MatchingLocations.Add(actLoc);
    profile.ActivityTrackPoints.Add(actPt);

    WorkflowTrackingLocation wfLoc = new WorkflowTrackingLocation();
    wfLoc.Events.Add(TrackingWorkflowEvent.Started);
    wfLoc.Events.Add(TrackingWorkflowEvent.Idle);

    WorkflowTrackPoint wfPt = new WorkflowTrackPoint();
    wfPt.MatchingLocation = wfLoc;
    profile.WorkflowTrackPoints.Add(wfPt);

    profile.Version = new Version("1.0.0.0");
    return profile;

}
```

5. Similarly, add the *StoreProfile* method:

```
static void StoreProfile(TrackingProfile profile, string connString)
{
    TrackingProfileSerializer serializer = new TrackingProfileSerializer();
    StringWriter writer = new StringWriter(new StringBuilder(),
                                        CultureInfo.InvariantCulture);
    serializer.Serialize(writer, profile);

    SqlConnection conn = null;
    try
    {
        if (!String.IsNullOrEmpty(connString))
        {
            conn = new SqlConnection(connString);

            string storedProc = "dbo.UpdateTrackingProfile";
```

```
                        SqlCommand cmd = new SqlCommand(storedProc, conn);
                        cmd.CommandType = CommandType.StoredProcedure;

                        SqlParameter parm = new SqlParameter("@TypeFullName",
                                                      SqlDbType.NVarChar, 128);
                        parm.Direction = ParameterDirection.Input;
                        parm.Value = typeof(TrackedWorkflow.Workflow1).ToString();
                        cmd.Parameters.Add(parm);
                        parm = new SqlParameter("@AssemblyFullName",
                                                      SqlDbType.NVarChar, 256);
                        parm.Direction = ParameterDirection.Input;
                        parm.Value =
                              typeof(TrackedWorkflow.Workflow1).Assembly.FullName;
                        cmd.Parameters.Add(parm);
                        parm = new SqlParameter("@Version", SqlDbType.VarChar, 32);
                        parm.Direction = ParameterDirection.Input;
                        parm.Value = "1.0.0.0";
                        cmd.Parameters.Add(parm);
                        parm = new SqlParameter("@TrackingProfileXml",
                                                         SqlDbType.NText);
                        parm.Direction = ParameterDirection.Input;
                        parm.Value = writer.ToString();
                        cmd.Parameters.Add(parm);

                        conn.Open();
                        cmd.ExecuteNonQuery();
                    } // if
                } // try
                catch (Exception ex)
                {
                    if (ex is SqlException)
                    {
                        // Check to see if it's a version error.
                        if (ex.Message.Substring(0,24) == "A version already exists")
                        {
                            // Version already exists...
                            Console.WriteLine("NOTE: a profile with the same version" +
                                            " already exists in the database");
                        } // if
                        else
                        {
                            // Write error message
                            Console.WriteLine("Error writing profile to database: {0}",
                                                            ex.ToString());
                        } // else
                    } // if
                    else
                    {
                        // Write error message
                        Console.WriteLine("Error writing profile to database: {0}",
                                                            ex.ToString());
                    } // else
                } // catch
                finally
                {
```

```
            if (conn != null)
            {
                conn.Close();
            } // if
        } // finally
    }
```

6. If you execute the application at this point, by pressing F5 or Ctrl+F5, the profile created in *CreateProfile* should be built and written to the database. If you look closely at the code shown in step 4, you'll note that only a small handful of activity and workflow events are being tracked. Therefore, we should expect to see far fewer lines of text written to the console window by *ShowActivityTrackingEvents* and *ShowWorkflowTrackingEvents*. And in fact, that is exactly what happens, as you can see in Figure 5-4 (compare this to Figure 5-2):

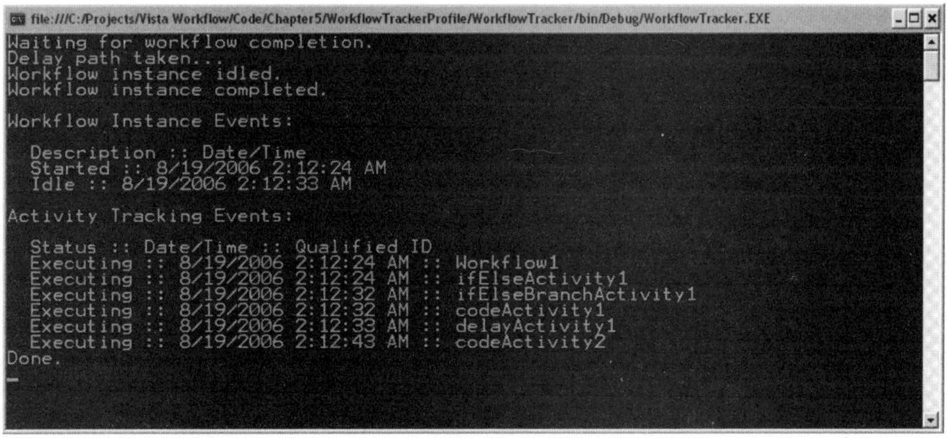

Figure 5-4   WorkflowTracker screen output with tracking data

CreateProfile creates a new *TrackingProfile* and adds both an activity tracking point and a workflow tracking point. Each tracking point has a single tracking location defined that dictates which events are tracked. (Events not listed are excluded by default.) So we should see only *Executing* events from activities and *Started* and *Idle* events from the workflow instance, and indeed, if you examine the screen output shown in the preceding figure, this is the case.

StoreProfile, in turn, serializes the tracking profile to its XML form and then uses typical ADO.NET techniques to record the XML in the tracking database. Because it is considered an error by the tracking database profile update logic to try to update a tracking profile with the same version, the *catch* logic in *StoreProfile* senses this and writes an informational note to the console window. Otherwise, the entire error string is written if there is an exception.

Viewing Tracking Information with WorkflowMonitor

Wouldn't it be nice if someone came up with a ready-made tool we could use to monitor workflow events? It's great to be able to spit out the tracking records as we did earlier in the chapter, but a nice graphical user interface would be a lot better to work with. And in fact, we're in luck! When you loaded WF, you also loaded a set of samples, and included in the samples is an application called *WorkflowMonitor*.

So for the price of a compilation step and some file finagling, we can have a simple yet graphical event tracking monitor application. Here's what we need to do to compile the application.

Compile WorkflowMonitor

1. WorkflowMonitor is part of the workflow samples library that ships with the Windows Software Development Kit (SDK). Copy the WFSamples.zip file from its installed location to \Workflow\Chapter5 and unzip the contents if you've not already done so in another directory. The WFSamples.zip file can be found in the following directory:

   ```
   C:\Program Files\Microsoft SDKs\Windows\v6.0\Samples\WFSamples.zip
   ```

2. Open the WorkflowMonitor.sln file in Visual Studio by selecting File, Open, Project/ Solution and locating the file by using the resulting Open Project dialog box. You'll find the solution file in the following (unzipped) directory:

   ```
   \Workflow\Chapter5\Applications\WorkflowMonitor\CS
   ```

> **Tip**   You must unzip the entire WorkflowMonitor directory before attempting to open the solution in Visual Studio. As soon as the directory is unzipped, you can open the solution by browsing to this directory using Windows Explorer and dragging and dropping the .sln file onto Visual Studio. I prefer this approach and use it when I can.

3. Compile the application by selecting Build WorkflowMonitor from the Build menu.

The application should compile without error, but you won't be able to execute it quite yet. When *SqlTrackingService* writes tracking records into the tracking database, the data type of the workflow object is one of the pieces of information that's recorded. If the type that supports your workflow isn't located in the Global Assembly Cache, WorkflowMonitor won't be able to load the designer view for your workflow object. (WorkflowMonitor is an example of an application that hosts the workflow designer in addition to Visual Studio.) Therefore, you must either place your workflow components, such as *TrackedWorkflow*, into the Global Assembly Cache or place their dynamic-link library (DLL) into the same directory as the WorkflowMonitor's executable file, WorkflowMonitor.exe. For this example, it's easier just to copy the WorkflowMonitor.exe file into the same directory as our workflow executable code.

Execute WorkflowMonitor

1. Copy the WorkflowMonitor executable file (WorkflowMonitor.exe) to the **\Workflow\Chapter5\WorkflowTracker\WorkflowTracker\bin\Debug** subdirectory containing the executable and library file for the WorkflowTracker application that we created to demonstrate *SqlTrackingService*. You should find the WorkflowMonitor.exe executable file in the following directory, assuming you built the debuggable version of the application:

   ```
   \Workflow\Chapter5\Applications\WorkflowMonitor\CS\WorkflowMonitor\bin\Debug\
   ```

2. In Windows Explorer, double-click the WorkflowMonitor.exe file to execute the WorkflowMonitor application.

3. WorkflowMonitor stores configuration information in the WorkflowMonitor.config configuration file, found in *Application.LocalUserAppDataPath*. (If you are running SQL Server Express, you may see an error message when WorkflowMonitor tries to connect to SQL Server; simply click OK.) Because this is likely the first time you've run WorkflowMonitor on your system, this configuration file is nonexistent. WorkflowMonitor senses this and immediately displays its Settings dialog box.

4. The settings you can control are the name of the server that hosts the tracking database, the name of the tracking database itself, the polling period (initially set to five seconds), and whether you want the currently executing workflow selected when WorkflowMonitor initializes (defaulted to not selected). For now, all we really need to do is set the server's name and database name. If you've named things according to the steps I outlined when we created the database, the server's name will be **localhost** (or **.\SQLExpress** if you are using SQL Server Express) and the database name will be **WorkflowTracking**. After you've typed these values, click OK.

> **Note** Be sure to type the actual information for your system if it differs from the values I've used here. Note that WorkflowMonitor builds the connection string using the server and database names you provide in the Settings dialog box. It assumes Windows Integrated Security for the connection, so if you are using SQL Server Authentication, you'll need to edit the code that creates the connection string to include this information. You'll find this code in the DatabaseService.cs file.

5. WorkflowMonitor should then open a connection to the tracking database and read the tracking records it finds there. If it has type information, it will display the designer for the workflows it finds. In this case, the only workflow it should find is *TrackedWorkflow*, but as you create more workflows, more will be displayed. The WorkflowMonitor user interface looks like the following:

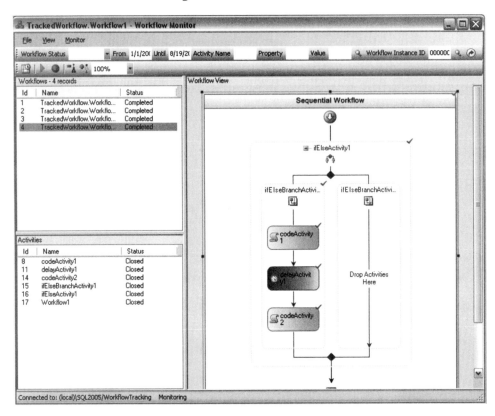

If you want to continue to the next chapter, keep Visual Studio 2005 and the SQL Server Management Studio Express running and turn to Chapter 6. If you've worked through the book to this point without stopping, isn't it about dinnertime?

If you want to stop, exit Visual Studio 2005 now and stick a bookmark in at the beginning of Chapter 6. In Chapter 6, we'll use SQL Server again as we persist and retrieve workflows. The whole point is it'll wait for you!

Chapter 5 Quick Reference

To	Do This
Create the workflow tracking database	After creating a new database for the task, execute the SQL scripts you find in the <%WINDIR%>\Microsoft.NET\Frame-work\v3.0\Windows Workflow Foundation\SQL\EN directory within SQL Server Management Studio Express. You'll need to execute both the Tracking_Schema.sql script and the Tracking_Logic.sql script.
Use the *SqlTrackingService*	After creating an instance of *WorkflowRuntime* but before you call its *StartRuntime* method, add a new instance of *SqlTrackingService* to the runtime services using *WorkflowRuntime.AddService*.
Filter tracked events to limit the number and type of events to be tracked	Create a *TrackingProfile* object (or the equivalent XML), adding included and excluded events as required, and then write the XML stream to the tracking database. Note that *TrackingProfileSerializer* can create the XML stream given a *TrackingProfile* object, and the *UpdateTrackingProfile* stored procedure (in the tracking database) can store the XML in the appropriate table for you.
Monitor your workflows	Build and execute WorkflowMonitor, the source code for which is included with the workflow samples that load when you install Workflow Foundation. Note you'll need to introduce your workflow assemblies to the Global Assembly Cache or copy their DLLs into the same subdirectory as WorkflowMonitor.exe so that WorkflowMonitor can display the designer for the workflows it finds in the tracking database.

Chapter 6

Loading and Unloading Instances

After completing this chapter, you will be able to:

- Understand why and when workflow instances are unloaded and then later reloaded
- Understand why and when workflow instances are persisted
- Set up SQL Server 2005 to work with WF and workflow persistence
- Use the *SqlWorkflowPersistenceService*
- Load and unload instances in your workflow code
- Enable the persistence service to automatically load and unload idled workflow instances

If you take a moment and really consider how you might use Windows Workflow Foundation (WF) and workflow processing in your applications, you'll probably imagine a lot of situations that involve long-running processes. After all, business software essentially simulates and executes business processes, and many of those processes involve people or outside vendors, ordering and shipping, scheduling, and so forth. People aren't capable of responding to automated processes in microseconds, but on loaded business servers, microseconds count. Servers are valuable, busy resources, and having them spin up threads only to have the threads wait minutes, hours, or even days and weeks is unacceptable for many reasons.

So the designers of WF knew they would have to provide a mechanism for taking idle workflows temporarily offline while waiting for some long-running task to complete. They decided to offer Microsoft SQL Server as an optional storage medium because databases are great places to store (and not lose) valuable data. They also created another pluggable service we can easily incorporate into our workflows to support this persistence mechanism. The hows, whys, and whens are what we'll explore in this chapter.

Persisting Workflow Instances

Did you know that at the very core of modern Microsoft Windows operating systems is a very special piece of software that is responsible for allocating time on the computer's processor for the various threads that request it? If a single thread monopolized the processor for an undue period of time, other threads would starve and the system would appear to lock up. So this piece of software, the *task scheduler*, moves threads into and out of the processor's execution stack so that all threads are given execution time.

In a sense, workflows are similar. If you have many, many long-running workflows that all hang around on a given computer competing for processing time and resources, eventually the system chokes on the unprocessed workflows. There is no scalability. In reality, WF is very efficient when maintaining its workflow queue, but you'll likely agree there must be a physical upper limit and that moving idled, long-running workflows out of an actively executing status is a good idea.

Or what happens if a system shuts down suddenly? Workflows are processed exclusively in memory unless we take steps to unload and persist them. So, unless we planned ahead and had contingencies in place, we lose the executing workflow instances. Guaranteed. If those long-running workflows were managing critical processes, could we afford to lose them? In most cases, we could not, or at least we wouldn't willingly allow those processes to be lost without a fight.

The good news is that not only does WF provide you with a way to unload and then reload workflow instances, it also ships with a service, *SqlWorkflowPersistenceService*, that is designed to serialize workflow instances into a SQL Server database. If you have read through the previous chapter, you are probably already familiar and even comfortable with the notion of writing workflow instance information to a database. In this case, the information that is written changes, and the situations in which that information is written and recalled differs from the information described in Chapter 5, but the general concept is essentially the same.

So when are workflow instances unloaded, and if they are unloaded, how do we persist them? Workflow instances are unloaded at some very specific points in their execution. In most cases, this happens for us automatically for just the reason I mentioned—WF cannot leave (or would rather not leave) long-running workflows in memory to needlessly consume resources and processing time. But we also have some control ourselves as well. Here is the list of workflow instance unload points, and where persistence is possible, I note it:

- After an *ActivityExecutionContext* completes and is closed (unloaded). We talked briefly about *ActivityExecutionContext* objects in Chapter 4, "Introduction to Activities and Workflow Types."

- When an *Activity* enters the idle state (optionally unloadable and persistable), assuming you enabled this feature (more on this later in the chapter).

- Once a *TransactionScopeActivity* completes (unloaded). We'll look at this activity in Chapter 15, "Workflows and Transactions."

- Once an *Activity* adorned with the *PersistOnCloseAttribute* completes (unloaded and optionally persistable).

- When you explicitly call *WorkflowInstance.Unload* or *WorkflowInstance.TryUnload* (unloaded and persisted).

You can control when workflow instances are persisted by calling specific methods on the *WorkflowInstance* object or by allowing your workflow to enter an idle state by using a *Delay* activity. In the case of a delay, you'll control automatic persistence by providing a parameter to the persistence service constructor. The workflow instance is persisted until that condition is met and the delay duration has expired.

> **Note** Suspending a workflow instance is not the same as delaying it. Using a *Delay* activity will automatically write the workflow instance to the database (if you're using *SqlWorkflowPersistenceService* and have configured it to do so, as you'll see in the final section of this chapter). Suspension merely withdraws the workflow from actively processing. You then have the option to manually write the workflow to the database using *Unload* or *TryUnload*.

How WF accomplishes this is through the use of *SqlWorkflowPersistenceService* combined with a database created specifically for the task (very much like the one we created for the tracking database in the previous chapter). Both Windows Vista and .NET 3.0 ship with scripts you can use to create the database schema (the tables and views) as well as the logic necessary to perform the persistence (the stored procedures). Let's establish the database first.

Setting Up SQL Server for Persistence

As we did in the last chapter, we'll begin by creating a new database in SQL Server Management Studio Express. We'll run some SQL scripts that ship with the .NET 3.0 components (downloadable as a separate installation or prepackaged with Windows Vista). As with tracking, these scripts will create the database roles, tables and views, and stored procedures necessary to persist workflow instances.

Create a SQL Server 2005 persistence database

1. Open SQL Server Management Studio Express.

> **Note** The set of steps you'll follow here are very similar to the steps you followed in the previous chapter in the procedure "Create a SQL Server 2005 tracking database." The major difference is that the scripts you'll execute here are designed for saving executing workflows rather than tracking their activity.

2. We'll need to again connect to the database engine we want to use, using the SQL Server Connect To Server dialog box:

3. Activate Object Explorer if it is not visible. You can activate it by selecting Object Explorer from the View menu.

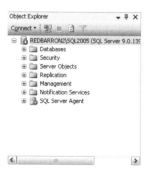

4. Right-click on the Databases node to activate the context menu, and select New Database.

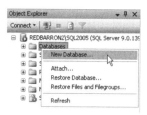

5. The New Database dialog box should now appear. Type **WorkflowStore** in the Database Name field, and click OK.

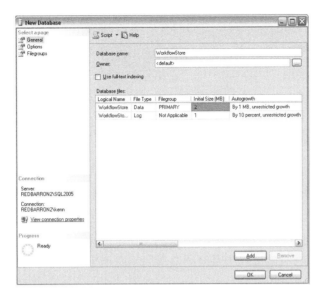

6. If you expand the Databases node in Object Explorer, you should find the new WorkflowStore database has been added.

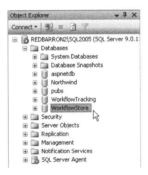

7. Next we'll need to execute the scripts I mentioned that .NET 3.0 provides for persistence, starting with the schema script. As before, the scripts are located in <%WINDIR%>\Microsoft.NET\Framework\v3.0\Windows Workflow Foundation\SQL\EN, where <%WINDIR%> is your Windows directory (typically, C:\Windows). From SQL Server Management Studio's File menu, select Open and then File, which brings up the common Open File dialog box. Using the controls in the Open File dialog box, locate the schema script, *SqlPersistenceService_Schema.sql*. Select that from the available scripts, and click the Open button. Note that you'll need to connect to your database server once again.

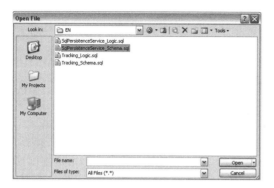

8. SQL Server Management Studio will load the script into a new window, but before we actually run the script, remember we'll need to specify which database we want the script to run against. Of course, we want to use the WorkflowStore database we just created. Therefore, locate the WorkflowStore database in the drop-down list of databases and select it as the target.

9. With the WorkflowStore database designated as the target of the script, execute the script by clicking the Execute button on the toolbar.

10. Repeat steps 7 through 9 to execute the *SqlPersistenceService_Logic.sql* script. This loads the necessary stored procedures into the database.

If everything worked as it should, we now have a database ready for workflow instance storage. It's time to plug *SqlWorkflowPersistenceService* into our workflow processing so that we can use the database we just created.

Introducing the *SqlWorkflowPersistenceService* Service

If it becomes necessary to persist an executing workflow, something must actually perform the persistence action. However, saving and restoring workflow instances is optional—you don't have to shuffle workflow instances off to a durable storage medium (such as a database) if you don't want to. So it probably makes sense that persistence is implemented by a pluggable service, *SqlWorkflowPersistenceService*. *WorkflowInstance* works in concert with

SqlWorkflowPersistenceService if the service is present when the workflow instance is running to perform the save and restore tasks.

On the surface, this all sounds relatively simple. If we need to swap a workflow instance out to the database, we just tell the persistence service to save it for us. But what happens if we're using a single database to persist workflows running in different processes? How do workflow instances actually stop and restart in the middle of their execution?

It's not uncommon for there to be a single database used for storing workflow instances. But each instance might have been executing on different machines and possibly within different processes on any given machine. If a workflow instance is saved and later restored, we must have a way to also restore the system state that was in effect at the time the workflow instance was executing. For example, *SqlWorkflowPersistenceService* stores whether or not the instance was blocked (waiting for something), its execution status (executing, idle, and so on), and various and sundry informational items such as serialized instance data and the owner identifier. All this information is necessary to rehydrate the instance at a later time.

We can control this persistence via the *WorkflowInstance* object through three methods, shown in Table 6-1.

Table 6-1   *WorkflowInstance* Methods, Revisited

Method	Purpose
Load	Loads a previously unloaded (persisted) workflow instance.
TryUnload	Tries to unload (persist) the workflow instance from memory. Unlike calling *Unload*, calling *TryUnload* will not block (hold up execution) if the workflow instance cannot be immediately unloaded.
Unload	Unloads (persists) the workflow instance from memory. Note that this method blocks the currently executing thread that made this unload request until the workflow instance can actually unload. This can be a lengthy operation, depending on the individual workflow task.

As Table 6-1 indicates, we have two methods available for unloading and persisting a workflow instance. Which method you use depends on what you intend for your code to do. *Unload* waits for the workflow instance to become ready to be persisted. If this takes a long time, the thread executing the *Unload* operation also waits a long time. However, *TryUnload* will return immediately when asked to unload an executing workflow instance. But there is no guarantee the workflow instance actually unloaded and persisted to the database. To check for that, you should examine the return value from *TryUnload*. If the value is *true*, the workflow instance did unload and persist itself. If the value is *false*, the workflow instance didn't unload and persist. The advantage of *TryUnload* is that your thread isn't sitting there waiting. The disadvantage, or course, is that you might have to repeatedly use *TryUnload* to force out the executing workflow instance.

Unloading Instances

Although there are specific times WF will unload and persist your workflow instance, in some cases you might want to take control of that yourself. For those situations, *WorkflowInstance.Unload* and *WorkflowInstance.TryUnload* are there to help.

If you call either of these methods without first plugging in the *SqlWorkflowPersistenceService*, WF will throw an exception. Of course, if there is a database error of some kind, you'll also receive an exception. Therefore, it's good practice to wrap these calls in *try/catch* blocks to keep from crashing your entire application. (Note that's not to say you have to *do* anything with the exception...sometimes you may just want to ignore it.)

Let's try it out! In fact, let's build a small graphical user interface that provides us with buttons we can use to force specific application behavior. The application complexity will increase a little, but we'll also be moving toward more realistic applications.

The application we'll build here is still relatively simple-minded. It will have only a few buttons we can click at specific times to force a workflow instance to unload. (In the next section, we'll then load it again.) I'm going to intentionally force a long-running workflow, but unlike the workflows we've seen so far, it won't use a *Delay* activity. The reason for this, as you probably guessed, is simply that *Delay* activities are special and come with persistence abilities of their own. Instead, I want to force our workflow instance to unload rather than have it automatically unload as a *Delay* activity could do. We'll look at *Delay* activities and their abilities in the "Loading and Unloading Instances on Idle" section of this chapter. For this application, I'll ask the workflow thread to sleep for 10 seconds to give us plenty of time to push one of our application's buttons.

Create a new host application

1. As you have in the previous chapters, open Visual Studio to create a new application project. However, instead of creating a console-based application, select instead a Windows-based application. Name it **WorkflowPersister**. Be sure to create the application in **\Workflow\Chapter6**. Follow the steps from Chapter 2 described in "Adding the workflow assembly references", "Hosting the workflow runtime" (add code to the *Main* method following the call to *Application.Run*), "Creating the *WorkflowRuntime* factory object", "Starting the workflow runtime," "Stopping the workflow runtime," "Using the workflow runtime factory object," and "Handling workflow runtime events" procedures. Finally, add an app.config file following steps 1 and 2 from the previous chapter in "Add *SqlTrackingService* to your workflow." (Don't forget to add a reference to *System.Configuration*.)

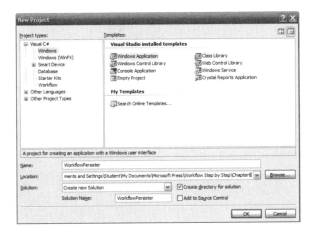

2. Now add the proper connection string to app.config, one that reflects the database we'll be using (remember, the database is called WorkflowStore). Keep in mind that the *connectionString* attribute in the *add* XML element presented here is to be applied as a single line in the app.config file. Printable line length limitations prevent this from being shown as a single line.

```
<connectionStrings>
    <add name="StorageDatabase"
        connectionString="Data Source=(local)\SQLEXPRESS;
            Initial Catalog=WorkflowStore;Integrated Security=True;"/>
</connectionStrings>
```

3. When you created the WorkflowPersister project, Visual Studio displayed the Windows Forms visual designer. The preceding step took you to the code editor, where you modified app.config. Return now to the Windows Forms visual designer by selecting Form1.cs in Solution Explorer and clicking the View Designer toolbar button. In a manner similar to designing workflows, this visual designer allows you to drag and drop Windows controls onto the design surface to customize their properties and hook their events. For now, move the mouse to the Toolbox, select a Button control, and drag it onto the designer's surface.

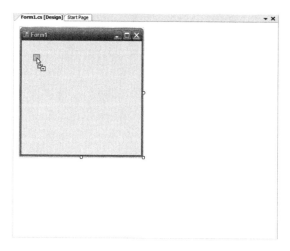

Then drop it to insert the button into your form.

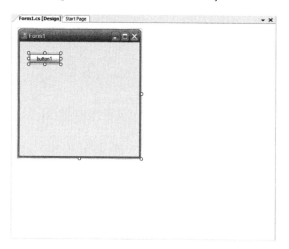

4. We'll want to assign some meaningful text to the button so that we know what we're clicking. (The control text "button1" just isn't descriptive enough!) With the button highlighted (the little squares showing), select the button's *Text* property in the Visual Studio Properties pane and change the text value to **Start Workflow**.

Note   In general it is a good idea to also rename the variable names Visual Studio assigns to the controls. If you have many controls on your form, pretty soon auto-generated names such as "button1" become meaningless from a coding perspective. I won't worry about that here because we'll have few controls to deal with, but in any real-world application you should change the control names to useful values. For this example, leave the variable names as Visual Studio assigned them so that you won't have to translate variable names while typing the code I'm about to present.

5. As you might expect, we'll want to take some action when the button is clicked. To do that, we'll need to inject a button click handler. While in the Properties pane, click the Events toolbar button (the lightning bolt) and double-click the *Click* event to add a click event handler. Visual Studio will automatically switch you to the code view, so return to the designer for the next step. We'll add code to the event handler in a later step.

6. The text we added will most likely be too wide for the button as Visual Studio created it, so we'll want to stretch the button to be a bit wider. To do so, click the button on the designer's surface (if it's not activated already) and drag the rightmost square to the right to stretch the button's width.

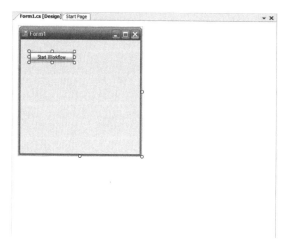

7. Repeat steps 3 through 5 to add two more buttons, one with the text **Unload Workflow** and the other with the text **Load Workflow**. (No need to change the variable names for this simple example.)

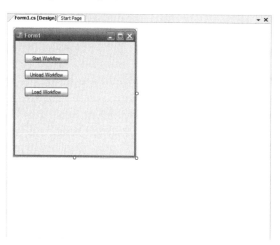

8. Our user interface is now visually established for our workflow testing purposes. Now it's time to code some internal application processes we'll execute in response to application events. We'll need to initialize some things when the application loads, and a great place to do that is in the *Load* event handler for the main application form. Click the title bar of the form in the visual editor to activate the form's properties. Click the Events button (as you did for the three button controls), and double-click the *Load* event to insert a *Load* event handler.

9. Once the load event handler is inserted, Visual Studio will switch you to the code view for the main application form. Because we just added the form's *Load* event handler, we might as well add the initialization code we'll need. Type the following into the *Form1_Load* handler method:

```
_runtime = WorkflowFactory.GetWorkflowRuntime();
_runtime.WorkflowCompleted +=
    new EventHandler<WorkflowCompletedEventArgs>(Runtime_WorkflowCompleted);
_runtime.WorkflowTerminated +=
    new EventHandler<WorkflowTerminatedEventArgs>(Runtime_WorkflowTerminated);
```

We've seen code like this before that creates the workflow runtime and hooks some of the major events we'll be interested in intercepting.

10. Somewhere we need to declare the *_runtime* field, so look for the opening brace for the *Form1* class. After the opening brace, type this:

```
protected WorkflowRuntime _runtime = null;
protected WorkflowInstance _instance = null;
```

11. If you try to compile the application at this point, it won't compile. We'll need to add a reference to the Windows Workflow Foundation assemblies as we've done in previous chapters—that process is the same whether we're building a graphical user interface or a console-based application. So add the workflow assembly references for *System.Workflow.Runtime*, *System.Workflow.ComponentModel*, and *System.Workflow.Activity* and then insert the following *using* declaration at the top of the source file following the other *using* declarations:

```
using System.Workflow.Runtime;
```

12. Although we now have an application that hosts the workflow runtime, it doesn't actually do anything. To make it functional, we'll need to add some code to the button event handlers, starting with *button1_Click*. Scroll through the main application form's source file until you find *button1_Click*, and add this code:

```
button2.Enabled = true;
button1.Enabled = false;
_instance = _runtime.CreateWorkflow(typeof(PersistedWorkflow.Workflow1));
_instance.Start();
```

This code disables the Start Workflow button, enables the Unload Workflow button, and then starts a new workflow instance. (We'll add the workflow that it will execute shortly.)

13. Next, find the Unload Workflow button's handler, *button2_Click*, and add the following code. Here, we're using the *WorkflowInstance.Unload* method to unload the workflow instance and write it to our database. After the workflow instance unloads, we enable the Load Workflow button (the code for which we'll add in the next section). Note that if we sustain an exception while unloading the workflow instance, the Load Workflow button is not enabled. This makes sense...there would be nothing to load if the unload request failed.

```
button2.Enabled = false;
try
{
    _instance.Unload();
    button3.Enabled = true;
} // try
catch (Exception ex)
{
    MessageBox.Show(String.Format("Exception while unloading workflow" +
                            " instance: '{0}'",ex.Message));
} // catch
```

> **Note**   I mentioned this previously in the chapter, but it's an important point. Keep in mind that *WorkflowInstance.Unload* is *synchronous*. That means the thread making the attempt to unload the workflow instance will *block* (wait) and continue to be blocked until the operation has completed (the instance has unloaded or failed to unload). In this case, that's precisely the behavior I want because I don't want to repeatedly ask the instance whether it unloaded. But in some cases, you'll want to use the nonblocking alternative I mentioned, *WorkflowInstance.TryUnload*. Later, when you add the final pieces of code and run this application, as you click Unload Workflow, watch closely and you'll see the application freeze briefly as it waits for the workflow to unload.

14. Now we turn our attention to the workflow event handlers, *Runtime_WorkflowCompleted* and *Runtime_WorkflowTerminated*. Both of these event handlers will actually perform the same action, which is to reset the application in preparation for another workflow instance execution. Add these methods following the click event handler for *button2* (the method containing the code we added in the preceding step):

```
void Runtime_WorkflowCompleted(object sender, WorkflowCompletedEventArgs e){
    WorkflowCompleted();
}

void Runtime_WorkflowTerminated(object sender, WorkflowTerminatedEventArgs e)
{
    WorkflowCompleted();
}
```

15. Of course, we'll now need to create the *WorkflowCompleted* method. If you're familiar with Windows programming, you're probably aware of a limitation that has existed in Windows from the earliest days. That limitation is simply that you cannot change window control state on any thread other than the thread that created the window control. So if you want to change a control's text, for instance, you must assign the control's text on the same thread that created it. Using any other thread will most likely crash your application. So if the code we're about to add seems funny to you, all it's really doing is making sure that we'll enable and disable buttons using only the original, creating, thread. (Event handlers are almost always invoked on different threads.) If we just enabled the buttons in the event handlers themselves, the application might work, but it would more likely crash or hang. Simply copy the code verbatim and place it at the end of the source file, just prior to the closing brace for the *Form1* class, and it should work correctly:

```
private delegate void WorkflowCompletedDelegate();
private void WorkflowCompleted()
{
    if (this.InvokeRequired)
    {
        // Wrong thread, so switch to the UI thread...
        WorkflowCompletedDelegate d = delegate() { WorkflowCompleted(); };
        this.Invoke(d);
    } // if
    else
    {
        button1.Enabled = true;
        button2.Enabled = false;
        button3.Enabled = false;
    } // else
}
```

Tip   To learn more about thread-safe Windows Forms programming, see the "How to: Make Thread-Safe Calls to Windows Forms Controls" article at *http:// msdn2.microsoft.com/en-us/library/ms171728.aspx*.

16. The last thing we'll need to do before creating the workflow we'll execute is modify the *WorkflowFactory* class. If you precisely followed all the steps from Chapter 5 to create and modify *WorkflowFactory* ("Add *SqlTrackingService* to your workflow"), you would actually be creating a factory object that provides the tracking service to the workflow runtime. With some minor adjustments, that same code works here. We'll change the service from *SqlTrackingService* to *SqlWorkflowPersistenceService* and change the *using* statement (from *System.Workflow.Runtime.Tracking* to *System.Workflow.Runtime.Hosting*). Open the WorkflowFactory.cs file for editing.

17. Instead of including the *using* statement for *System.Workflow.Runtime.Tracking*, add the following:

```
using System.Workflow.Runtime.Hosting;
using System.Configuration;
```

18. Finally add the persistence service to the runtime by adding this code following the creation of the workflow runtime object:

```
string conn = ConfigurationManager.
                ConnectionStrings["StorageDatabase"].
                ConnectionString;
_workflowRuntime.AddService(new
                    SqlWorkflowPersistenceService(conn));
```

> **Note**   Because we inserted code to create a workflow instance from the *Persisted-Workflow.Workflow1* type (in step 12), our host application won't compile and execute. We'll take care of that in the following section.

There you have it! A Windows graphical user interface and host application we can use to house our workflow. Speaking of workflow, shouldn't we create one to execute? In fact, that's next.

Create a new unloadable workflow

1. We're again going to add a new sequential workflow library to our existing project as we've done in previous chapters. With the WorkflowPersister application active in Visual Studio, select Add from the File menu. When the secondary menu pops up, select New Project. Add a sequential workflow library project named **PersistedWorkflow** from the resulting New Project dialog box.

2. After the new project is created and added to the application solution, the workflow visual designer will appear. Drag a *Code* activity from the Toolbox and drop it onto the designer's surface. In the Visual Studio Properties panel, set the *Code* activity's *ExecuteCode* property to **PreUnload** and press the Enter key.

3. Visual Studio will automatically take you to the source code file for your workflow, so while there, add this code to the newly inserted *PreUnload* method:

```
_started = DateTime.Now;
System.Diagnostics.Trace.WriteLine(
    String.Format("*** Workflow {0} started: {1}",
                WorkflowInstanceId.ToString(),
                _started.ToString("MM/dd/yyyy hh:mm:ss.fff")));
System.Threading.Thread.Sleep(10000); // 10 seconds
```

4. So that we can calculate the duration of time the workflow took (at least the time between the two *Code* activity executions), I saved the starting time in a field called *_started*. Add that field to your source file just above the constructor:

```
private DateTime _started = DateTime.MinValue;
```

5. Now switch back to the designer view and add a second *Code* activity. To this activity's *ExecuteCode* property add the method name **PostUnload**. The designer should appear as you see here.

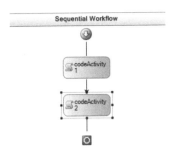

6. As you add the *PostUnload* method to the *Code* activity's *ExecuteCode* property, Visual Studio will again switch you to the source code file for your workflow. There, add the code necessary for *PostUnload*:

```
DateTime ended = DateTime.Now;
TimeSpan duration = ended.Subtract(_started);
System.Diagnostics.Trace.WriteLine(
    String.Format("*** Workflow {0} completed: {1}, duration: {2}",
                  WorkflowInstanceId.ToString(),
                  ended.ToString("MM/dd/yyyy hh:mm:ss.fff"),
                  duration.ToString()));
```

> **Note**   You might have noticed that I'm writing information to the trace output window. Because we have a Windows application rather than a console application, this is appropriate. However, it also means that when you execute the application, to see the trace output you'll need to have a trace window open. The easiest way to do this is to simply run the application in the Visual Studio debugger and look in the Output window that Visual Studio provides. Alternatively, you can run DBMon.exe, found in the Windows SDK: <%Program Files%>\Microsoft SDKs\Windows\v6.0\Bin\DBMon.exe (and remember, "<%Program Files%>" represents the location of the Program Files directory on your system, typically C:\Program Files). DBMon is designed to capture and display trace information from all executing applications on your machine.

7. The final step we need to take is to add a project-level reference to the workflow from our main application, as we've done in previous chapters. Right-click the WorkflowPersister tree control node in Visual Studio's Solution Explorer, and select Add Reference. When the Add Reference dialog box appears, click the Projects tab and select PersistedWorkflow from the list. Click OK.

> **Note**   You might be tempted to run the application at this time, but wait! If you run the application and then click the Start Workflow button but do not click the Unload Workflow button, the application should run without error. But because we've not added the code to reload the persisted workflow instance once unloaded, you shouldn't click the Unload Workflow button until we add the code in the next section.

The intention here is that the workflow will begin execution, at which time the first *Code* acivity puts its thread to sleep for 10 seconds. During that time, you can click the Unload Workflow button to unload the workflow. After the 10 seconds expire, the workflow will be unloaded and persisted to the database. Once that happens, you can take a coffee break, grab a candy bar, or do anything at all—your workflow is stored in the database, waiting to be loaded once again. Let's see how that works.

Loading Instances

WorkflowInstance exhibits the two unload methods—*Unload* and *TryUnload*—but it has only a single *Load* method. It doesn't matter how the workflow instance was stored in the database. Once it is stored, you use *WorkflowInstance.Load* to bring it back into executing status again. We'll now add the appropriate code to our WorkflowPersister application to make this happen.

Load a persisted workflow

1. With the WorkflowPersister application open for editing in Visual Studio, open the source code file for the main application form for editing and locate the *button3_Click* event handler.

2. Add this code to the *button3_Click* event handler:

```
button3.Enabled = false;
try
{
    _instance.Load();
} // try
catch (Exception ex)
{
    MessageBox.Show(String.Format("Exception while loading workflow" +
                                  " instance: '{0}'", ex.Message));
} // catch

button1.Enabled = true;
```

Now let's see if all this actually works. We'll run two test workflows—one we'll let run to completion, and one we'll force to unload. Then we'll compare execution times and look inside the SQL Server database to see what was recorded there.

Test the WorkflowPersister application

1. With the WorkflowPersister application open for editing in Visual Studio, press F5 or select Start Debugging from the Debug menu to execute the application. Fix any compilation errors if there are any. Note that for this test we want to write trace output to the Output window, so if you don't already have the Output window available, be sure to activate it by choosing Output from the Visual Studio View menu.

2. Click the Start Workflow button to create and start a workflow instance. The Start Workflow button should become disabled, while the Unload Workflow button will be enabled. Because we told the workflow thread to sleep for 10 seconds, after 10 seconds has elapsed the Unload Workflow button should disable itself and the Start Workflow button should be re-enabled. In this test, the workflow ran to completion, and the duration of time the workflow executed should total 10 seconds.

3. Click the Start Workflow button again. However, this time click the Unload Workflow button within the 10-second sleep period. The button will be disabled for the duration of the 10-second period, after which the Load Workflow button will be enabled. At this point, your workflow is persisted and will remain unloaded until you reload it.

4. But before you reload the workflow instance, open SQL Server Management Studio Express as we've done in the past and open the WorkflowStore database. Expand the Tables node, and right-click the InstanceState table and select Open Table from the context menu to open the table for editing. There should be one row in the table. This row is your persisted workflow instance!

5. Feel free to look at the table; there is no rush. But when you're ready, go back to your executing instance of WorkflowPersister and click the Load Workflow button. The Load Workflow button will then become disabled, while the Start Workflow button will become enabled.

6. Close the WorkflowPersister application by clicking the X in the upper right corner or pressing Alt+F4. The application will shut down.

7. The Visual Studio Output window should now contain information regarding the two workflows we executed (because we wrote trace information to the window as each workflow instance ran). Activate the Output window by clicking on the Output tab at the bottom of the Visual Studio application window.

> **Note** Of course, Visual Studio allows you to move windows such as Output around and dock them in different locations. If you've docked the Output window in a location other than the bottom of the Visual Studio application window, activate it wherever you docked it.

8. Scroll to the bottom of the output in the Output window, and look for the text we injected. (We delineated this text using three asterisks, ***.) You should see something like the following:

If you look back at the image of the InstanceState table and compare the workflow instance ID you see there with the second workflow instance ID you see in the Visual Studio Output window, you should see the same instance ID—*15aedcfd-ce83-486c-b55d-3f0ee51b5337* in my case. This instance took over 2 minutes to execute (the time it took me to take the screen shot for the image and finally close the test application), whereas the first workflow instance (ID *33d15fce-758c-4461-972f-7a83863cf871*) took precisely 10 seconds, as expected. Your instance IDs and execution times will differ, but the pattern should be the same. Workflow instances you unload and persist into the SQL Server database will run longer than 10 seconds, and the IDs shown in the InstanceState table and Visual Studio Output window should match.

To see the persisted workflow instance database record, open SQL Server Management Studio (Express or otherwise) and expand the WorkflowStore database tree control node (see the section in the previous chapter, "Add *SqlTrackingService* to your workflow," for instructions for opening the database and viewing a table). Open the InstanceState table while the delay is in effect and you should find a persisted workflow record there.

Loading and Unloading Instances on Idle

I mentioned earlier in the chapter that for our test application's workflow we were going to use *System.Threading.Thread.Sleep* instead of using a *Delay* activity to introduce a delay in our workflow processing. I said at the time that I chose to do this because the *Delay* activity had special processing capabilities as far as persistence was concerned. Let's now look briefly at what *Delay* does for us.

If you introduce a *Delay* activity into your workflow, clearly the intention is to suspend processing for some period of time, whether it's an actual time period or a suspension until a specific point in time, such as a date five days in the future.

When a *Delay* activity is executed, assuming the workflow runtime has the *SqlWorkflowPersistenceService* plugged in and is directed to do so, the workflow runtime will automatically persist the workflow instance for you and recall it when the delay period expires. Note that this will occur regardless of whether the system running the workflow runtime is turned off, rebooted, or was even replaced in the interim period. (It *does* assume some system somewhere is running the workflow runtime with the persistence service included, however!) To enable this automatic persistence, you'll add a special constructor parameter to *SqlWorkflowPersistenceService* when you set up your workflow runtime. (The preceding example omitted this and would not have persisted workflows automatically.)

The constructor parameter I'm referring to enables the *SqlWorkflowPersistenceService*'s internal *UnloadOnIdle* method to be called when workflow instances idle. The method isn't normally called. You must explicitly enable it by using an overloaded *SqlWorkflowPersistenceService* constructor. In the example that follows, you'll use a collection of named parameters, because you want to provide only the connection string and the unload on idle flag. There are other constructors that provide even more flexibility (I describe one following this example). Let's now look at an example where the workflow is automatically persisted.

Create a new workflow for on-idle persistence

1. For this example, you'll use a simple console-based application just so that you can quickly get a feel for how on-idle persistence works. As you did in Chapter 2, open Visual Studio and create a new Windows Project, Console Application named **WorkflowIdler**. As with the preceding example, create the application in \Workflow\Chapter6. Follow the steps from Chapter 2 in the Adding the workflow assembly references," "Hosting the workflow runtime," "Creating the *WorkflowRuntime* factory object," "Starting the workflow runtime," "Stopping the workflow runtime," "Using the workflow runtime factory object," and "Handling workflow runtime events" procedures.

2. Modify the *WorkflowFactory* class as you did in steps 16 and 17 of the preceding example, "Create a new host application." However, some additional modifications will be necessary. First, add this *using* statement:

    ```
    using System.Collections.Specialized;
    ```

3. Then, in a manner similar to what you did in step 18 in this chapter's "Create a new host application," add the persistence service after the runtime object itself is created:

    ```
    NameValueCollection parms = new NameValueCollection();
    parms.Add("UnloadOnIdle", "true");
    parms.Add("ConnectionString", ConfigurationManager.
                          ConnectionStrings["StorageDatabase"].
                          ConnectionString);
    _workflowRuntime.AddService(new SqlWorkflowPersistenceService(parms));
    ```

4. Add an application configuration file as with the previous example (the connection string will remain the same). Follow Steps 1 and 2 from the "Add *SqlTrackingService* to your workflow" procedure in Chapter 5 regarding adding the app.config file.

5. Create a separate sequential workflow library project as you did in Chapter 3 to house our new workflow. (See the section in Chapter 3 entitled "Adding a sequential workflow project to the WorkflowHost solution.") Name this workflow library **IdledWorkflow**.

6. Repeat step 2 and then steps 4 through 6 from the previous example, in the section entitled "Create a new unloadable workflow." This places two *Code* Activities in your workflow.

7. Adding the second *Code* Activity in the last step will take you to the Visual Studio code editor. While there, add this code to the *PreUnload* method (you added the *PostUnload* method code in the preceding step):

```
_started = DateTime.Now;
System.Diagnostics.Trace.WriteLine(
    String.Format("*** Workflow {0} started: {1}",
            WorkflowInstanceId.ToString(),
            _started.ToString("MM/dd/yyyy hh:mm:ss.fff")));
```

8. Return to the visual workflow designer and drag a *Delay* Activity onto the surface and drop it between the two *Code* Activities.

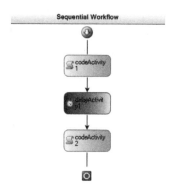

9. Assign the *Delay* Activity's *TimeoutDuration* property to be 30 seconds. This should be enough time to examine the WorkingStore *InstanceState* database table.

10. With the workflow now complete, add a reference to the workflow from the Workflow-Idler application. Right-click the WorkflowIdler tree control node in Visual Studio's Solution Explorer and select Add Reference. When the Add Reference dialog box appears, click the Projects tab. Select IdledWorkflow from the list and click OK.

11. Open Program.cs in the WorkflowIdler project for editing. Locate this line of code:

```
Console.WriteLine("Waiting for workflow completion.");
```

12. Of course, the application *isn't* waiting for workflow completion since no workflow was started. To create a workflow instance, add this code following the line of code you just located:

```
// Create the workflow instance.
WorkflowInstance instance =
    workflowRuntime.CreateWorkflow(typeof(IdledWorkflow.Workflow1));

// Start the workflow instance.
instance.Start();
```

13. Compile the solution by pressing F6. Correct any compilation errors that pop up.

Now, when you execute the WorkflowIdler application, the *Delay* Activity will force the workflow instance to be persisted to the storage database. However, you might wait longer than 30 seconds (up to 2 minutes) for the instance to be reloaded. That's because the workflow runtime periodically checks for persisted workflows in idle states due to delays, but it is not guaranteed that those workflows will wait only for their respective delays. WF polls the database periodically, looking for idled workflows that were persisted waiting for timer events (*Delay* Activity uses a timer). The default polling time is 2 minutes.

> **Note**   The default database polling time can be changed by providing a *TimeSpan* to the *SqlWorkflowPersistenceService* and using the constructor that takes four parameters (the connection string, the unload on idle flag, a *TimeSpan* indicating how long the current instance of the persistence service owns this instance of the workflow, and a *TimeSpan* indicating how often the database should be polled).

If you want to continue to the next chapter, keep Visual Studio 2005 running, and turn to Chapter 7, "Basic Activity Operations." We'll start digging into some of the activities WF provides us with.

If you want to stop, exit Visual Studio 2005 now, save your spot in the book, and close it. Just don't forget all those persisted workflows in your database!

Chapter 6 Quick Reference

To	Do This
Create the workflow persistence database	After creating a new database for the task, execute within SQL Server Management Studio Express the SQL scripts you find in the <%WINDIR%>\Microsoft.NET\Framework\v3.0\Windows Workflow Foundation\SQL\EN directory within SQL Server Management Studio. You'll need to execute both the *SqlWorkflowPersistenceService_Schema.sql* script and the *SqlWorkflowPersistenceService_Logic.sql* script.

To	Do This
Use the *SqlWorkflowPersistenceService*	After creating an instance of WorkflowRuntime but before you call its *StartRuntime* method, add a new instance of *SqlWorkflowPersistenceService* to the runtime services using *WorkflowRuntime.AddService*.
Manually unload and persist a workflow instance	Call *WorkflowInstance.Unload* or *WorkflowInstance.TryUnload*. Keep in mind that the Unload is synchronous and will block your thread until the unload operation is complete or throws an exception.
Manually load a previously persisted workflow instance	Call *WorkflowInstance.Load*.
Automatically unload, persist, and reload a workflow instance	Introduce a *Delay* activity to your workflow processing and start *SqlWorkflowPersistenceService* with the UnloadOnIdle flag set. When the *Delay* activity begins execution, the workflow instance enters the idle state. At that point, *SqlWorkflowPersistenceService* automatically unloads your workflow and serializes it to the database. Later, after the delay period has expired, the instance will be reloaded and re-executed.

Part II
Working with Activities

Chapter 7
Basic Activity Operations

After completing this chapter, you will be able to:

- Know how to use the *Sequence* activity
- Know how to use the *Code* activity
- Know how exceptions are thrown and handled in workflows
- Know how to suspend and terminate your workflow instances from workflow code

Up to this point, we've seen the basics. We've worked a bit with the workflow runtime, which orchestrates the workflow process. We've looked at the workflow instance, which is an executing workflow. And we've dug into a couple of the pluggable services available to us, such as those used for tracking and persistence. "What's next?" you ask.

Now it's time to look at the stars of the show, the activities themselves. Windows Workflow Foundation (WF) ships with a large set of activities you can use from the moment you install WF to bring workflow processing to your applications. And given the wide variety of activities, WF can workflow-enable all sorts of applications, not just those designed to interact with people.

In this chapter, we'll go back and formally introduce a couple of activities we've already seen—*Sequence* and *Code*. But I believe proper error handling is critical in well-designed and well-implemented software, so we'll look at how you throw exceptions using workflow activities, catch exceptions, and even suspend and terminate your workflows. Let's start with the *Sequence* activity.

Using the *Sequence* Activity Object

Actually, it's not entirely correct to say we've seen the *Sequence* activity. The workflow applications we've created have actually used the *SequentialWorkflow* activity, but the general idea is the same—this activity contains other activities that are executed in sequence. This is in contrast to parallel execution, which you might do using the parallel activities we'll see in Chapter 11, "Parallel Activities."

When you execute tasks in a specific order, you're doing things in sequence. This is often necessary. For example, imagine you're making a grilled cheese sandwich for lunch. You find your griddle or frying pan and place it on the stove. You pull a loaf of bread from the pantry and butter one side of two slices. Then you pull the cheese from the refrigerator and place a couple of pieces onto one of the slices of bread, which you've placed butter-side down on the griddle or in the pan. Then you cover the assembly with the second slice of bread, butter-side up. Finally, cook each side until golden brown (and the cheese melts, which is critical). Although you might make a grilled cheese sandwich differently, the point is there is a natural progression of steps to accomplish the task.

In fact, if you find yourself saying things like, "First I do this, then I do that, and finally I do this other thing," the *Sequence* activity is for you. (Conversely, if you find yourself saying, "I can do this while I do that," you'll find Chapter 11 to be helpful as we take a look at parallel activity execution.) Any time you need to make sure steps in your workflow process execute in a specific order, consider placing them in a *Sequence* activity.

The *Sequence* activity is a *composite* activity, which we discussed briefly in Chapter 4, "Introduction to Activities and Workflow Types." It contains other activities and makes sure those activities are executed in order. You can place other composite activities inside a parent *Sequence* activity, including parallel ones. But the child activities are executed one by one, in order, even if those child activities themselves contain parallel execution flows.

Let's build a simple workflow that uses the *Sequence* activity. We'll again call upon the services of our trusty friend, the *Code* activity, which we'll discuss in more detail in the next section, "Using the *Code* Activity." To target specific workflow activity behaviors, we'll generally return to the console-based application. With console-based applications, you typically write less code because you're not maintaining the user interface. (We'll be building other graphical test cases as we progress through the book, however.)

Creating a workflow using the *Sequence* activity

1. To make things easier for you, I've created the initial application for the Sequence sample as well as a completely finished version. The completed version, found in the \Workflow\Chapter7\Sequencer Completed\ directory, is ready to run. Simply open it, examine the code as you follow the steps here, and execute it. However, if you want to type the code and build the workflow I describe here, open the version of the sample in the \Workflow\Chapter7\Sequencer\ directory. To open either sample application, drag its .sln file onto an executing copy of Visual Studio.

2. When Sequencer is opened and ready for editing, add a new sequential workflow library project to the Sequencer solution by clicking File, Add, and then New Project from Visual Studio's menu and then choosing Workflow from the project types and Sequential Workflow Library from the templates list in the Add New Project dialog box. Name it **SequencerFlow**. Visual Studio adds the new library project and opens the workflow visual designer for editing.

3. With the Visual Studio workflow designer showing, drag a *Sequence* activity from the Toolbox and drop it onto the designer's surface.

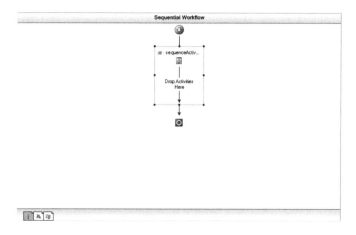

4. Next, drag a *Code* activity from the Toolbox and drop it onto the *Sequence* activity you just placed.

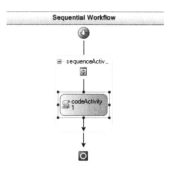

5. In its *ExecuteCode* property, type **DoTaskOne** and press Enter.

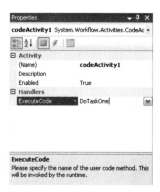

6. Visual Studio automatically brings up the code editor. Locate the *DoTaskOne* method Visual Studio just added, and in that method place this code:

```
Console.WriteLine("Executing Task One...");
```

7. Perform steps 4, 5 and 6 again, twice, adding methods for **DoTaskTwo** and **DoTaskThree**, and changing the *Writeline* text appropriately. The workflow visual designer appears as you see here.

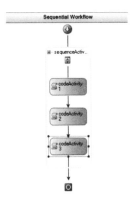

8. Turning to the main application, open the Program.cs file for editing and locate the *Main* method. In the *Main* method, search for the following lines of code:

```
// Print banner.
Console.WriteLine("Waiting for workflow completion.");
```

9. Following the code you found in the preceding step, add this code:

```
WorkflowInstance instance =
    workflowRuntime.CreateWorkflow(typeof(SequencerFlow.Workflow1));

instance.Start();
```

10. Of course, we need to reference the SequencerFlow workflow library from the main application project. Adding a project-level reference as we've done in previous chapters is more than adequate.

11. Compile the application, and correct any errors you find. Press F5 or Ctrl+F5 to run the application. Set a breakpoint or run from a command prompt so you'll be able to see the output. The output is shown here:

As you can see from the graphic from step 11, the tasks were executed in order, as we'd expect. Two things to remember are simply that the *Sequence* activity is a composite activity (a container for other activities) and that it executes the items it contains in sequential order.

Using the *Code* Activity

The other activity we've used often so far in the book is the *Code* activity. The *Code* activity is meant to execute custom code you provide for execution within your workflow. There is a way to call external methods we'll look at in the next chapter.

When you place a *Code* activity in your workflow, the *ExecuteCode* property should be set to the name of the method the workflow runtime will call.

Actually, if you look closely at the code Visual Studio inserted for you when you set the *ExecuteCode* property for the Sequencer application we just completed, it isn't a method that's called as much as it is an actual event handler. For example, here is the method we inserted for *DoTaskOne*:

```
private void DoTaskOne(object sender, EventArgs e)
{
    Console.WriteLine("Executing Task One...");
}
```

As you can see, when the workflow runtime executes your *Code* activity, it fires an event named using the value you provided in the *ExecuteCode* property. The three *Code* activities in the preceding application (Sequencer) demonstrate this. As you can imagine, we'll be making good use of the *Code* activity throughout the remainder of the book.

Using the *Throw* Activity

I mentioned this very early in the book, but I haven't really reinforced this basic concept—workflows model processes. Therefore, we need to be able to model a wide variety of real-world situations, including the case where we need to throw an exception. Suppose that something along the way wasn't quite right, and the situation was not one our software could deal with in any other way than to throw an exception. We could, if we wanted, just throw an exception using the C# *throw* keyword, but using a special activity for this allows us to also use a special activity for handling exceptions, as we'll see in the next section. If we use the C# *throw* keyword, the workflow runtime "swallows" the exception, with no notice given.

This behavior is the reason for the *Throw* activity. When the workflow runtime encounters the *Throw* activity, the workflow runtime fires the *WorkflowTerminated* event if there is no associated fault handler. However, keep in mind that, by then, the workflow instance is terminated and the workflow runtime is halted. It's far too late to make any attempt to correct the exceptional condition at that point. We can only restart the workflow runtime and kick off a new workflow instance. If we want to deal with exceptions earlier in the termination process, we need to use a combination of the *Throw* and *FaultHandler* activities.

> **Note**   The recommended practice is to use the combination of *Throw* and *FaultHandler* rather than *Throw* alone. Using the *Throw* activity by itself is equivalent to using the C# *throw* keyword without an exception handler in traditional application code. In this section, we'll use *Throw* alone to explore what happens. In the next section, we'll combine *Throw* and *FaultHandler* to see how they work together.

Turning our attention to the *Throw* activity, when you drag and drop the *Throw* activity onto the designer, you'll find there are two properties you need to set. The first is the *FaultType* property, where you tell the *Throw* activity what type of exception will be thrown, and the other is the *Fault* property which, if not null at the time the exception is to be thrown, will *be* the actual exception thrown.

The *FaultType* property probably doesn't need a lot of explanation. It simply tells the workflow instance what exception type will be thrown. But logically the mere existence of this property is telling us that we need to provide a *Throw* activity for the specific types of exceptions we want to throw. Exceptions we don't specifically throw (and later handle, if we want) are handled by the workflow runtime and ignored.

But what's the story behind the *Fault* property? It's simply the actual exception the *Throw* activity uses, if set. If null, the *Throw* activity still throws an exception of type *FaultType*, but it is a new exception with no established *Message* (and remember, it's the *Message* property that provides us some description of the error aside from the exception type itself).

> **Note**   Actually, the exception's *Message* property will have a value, but it will be something like the following: "Exception of type 'System.Exception' was thrown." When throwing an exception, the default message (when no message property is set on the exception type) will differ if the exception is constructed using the default constructor. The bottom line is the exception message will depend on the exception and not on anything WF did or didn't do.

If you want the *Throw* activity to throw an exception you establish, with a meaningful *Message*, you need to create an instance of the exception using the *new* operator and assign it to the same property you bound to the *Throw* activity.

Let me state this in a slightly different way. The *Throw* activity, and more specifically its *Fault* property, are bound to a property of the same exception type in an activity of your choosing in your workflow (including the root activity). That is, if you have a *Throw* activity that throws a *NullReferenceException*, you must provide a property on some activity in your workflow that is of type *NullReferenceException* for *Throw* to use. *Throw* then binds to this activity's property so that it can use the same exception you assigned (or should assign) using the *new* operator.

At this point, we should write some code and try this out. Let's build a little workflow that uses a *Throw* activity and see how it works.

Creating a workflow using the *Throw* activity

1. The ErrorThrower sample, like the previous Sequencer sample, comes in two forms. If you want to work with the completed version, open the solution in the \Workflow\Chapter7\ErrorThrower Completed\ directory. If you want to build the workflow yourself, open the solution in the \Workflow\Chapter7\ErrorThrower\ directory. You can open either version by dragging the .sln file onto an executing copy of Visual Studio.

2. Once ErrorThrower is open and ready to edit, add a new sequential workflow library project to the ErrorThrower solution by clicking File, Add, and then New Project from Visual Studio's menu and then choosing Workflow from the project types and Sequential Workflow Library from the templates list in the Add New Project dialog box. Name it **ErrorFlow**. Visual Studio adds the new library project, and opens the workflow visual designer for editing.

3. With the Visual Studio workflow designer showing, drag a *Code* activity from the Toolbox and drop it onto the designer's surface. Assign the value **PreThrow** to its *Execute-Code* property.

4. Next, drag a *Throw* activity from the Toolbox and drop it onto the designer's surface just after (below) the *Code* activity from the preceding step.

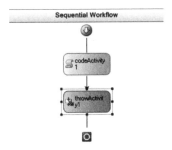

5. With the *Throw* activity in place and selected, look at the Properties for the *Throw* activity. Select the *FaultType* property, and click the browse (...) button. (Three dots used as button text typically mean "browse.")

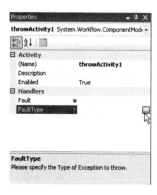

6. This activates the Browse And Select A .NET Type dialog box. Here, you select the type of exception the *Throw* activity will model. We'll model a plain *Exception* here, so with the Type tab active, expand *mscorlib* from the left tree control and select *System*. This fills the right pane with all the exception types in *System* (the primary .NET) namespace. Scroll down until you find *Exception* and select it. The text "System.Exception" is copied to the Type Name edit control. Click OK.

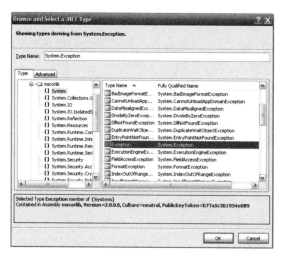

7. We've now established the fact that we'll deal with a *System.Exception* exception type in this *Throw* activity, but we've not set the *Fault* property. Return to the Properties window for the *Throw* activity, select the *Fault* property, and click the browse (...) button for the *Fault* property.

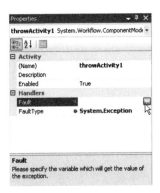

> **Note**   Failing to set the *Fault* property, or even the *FaultType* property, will not result in a compilation error. However, the type will default to *System.Exception* with the message "Property Fault not set."

8. Clicking the *Fault* property's browse button activates the Bind Fault To An Activity's Property dialog box. Because we've added no fault code ourselves, click the Bind To A New Member tab and type **WorkflowException** in the New Member Name edit control. Click OK. This adds the property *WorkflowException* to your root activity.

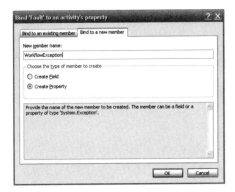

9. Add a second *Code* activity, assigning its *ExecuteCode* property the value of **PostThrow**. The visual designer now looks like this:

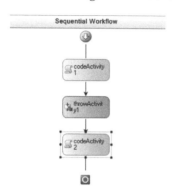

10. Our workflow is now established, so it's time to add some code. After you complete step 9, Visual Studio opens the Workflow1.cs file for editing in the code editor. Scroll down through the code until you find the event handler for *PreThrow*. Add this code:

```
Console.WriteLine("Pre-throwing the exception...");
WorkflowException =
    new Exception("This exception thrown for test and evaluation purposes...");
```

11. Similarly, find the event handler for *PostThrow* and add this code:

```
Console.WriteLine("Post-throwing the exception... (You won't see this output!)");
```

12. The workflow is now complete, so let's now work on the main application. Open the Program.cs file for editing, and locate the *Main* method. In the *Main* method, find this code:

```
// Print banner.
Console.WriteLine("Waiting for workflow completion.");
```

13. Following the banner message you just located, add this code:

```
WorkflowInstance instance =
    workflowRuntime.CreateWorkflow(typeof(ErrorFlow.Workflow1));
instance.Start();
```

14. Now, perhaps not surprisingly, we need to reference the workflow library from the main application project. Add a project-level reference for the ErrorFlow project to the ErrorThrower project as we did previously.

15. Compile the application, and correct any errors you find. Press F5 or Ctrl+F5 to run the application. You should see the following:

If you look closely at the output, you'll see that the *WorkflowTermination* event handler was invoked and presented us with the reason for termination—an exception—which has a *Message* that matches the text in the *Exception* we provided to *WorkflowException* in step 10.

> **Note**   When you add new properties as you did in step 8, those properties are inserted by Visual Studio as dependency properties (see Chapter 4). Adding new fields inserts typical field values (no dependency property constructs). The *Exception* property you added was added as a dependency property.

So now that we've seen how to model exceptions in WF, how do we handle catching them? After all, handling them in the workflow termination event handler often is far too late to be of any value to us. And as you might expect, WF provides us with a handy *FaultHandler* activity we can use. Let's take a look at that now.

Using the *FaultHandler* Activity

If you think about it, having a *Throw* activity is not as useful as having a *Throw* activity combined with some activity designed to handle the exception, and that's the purpose of the *FaultHandler* activity. You use *FaultHandler* in a slightly different way than any of the activities we've seen so far. In fact, it's time to take a little detour and look more closely at the visual designer. Why? Because there is a separate design surface for fault handlers than for workflow activities (and, in fact, there is a third design surface for cancellation processing, which we'll also see at this point).

> **Note**   In Chapter 15, "Workflows and Transactions," we'll look at compensatable activities, including compensated transactions. Handling faults is part of the story. You can also "compensate" for them, which means to take action to mitigate the damage the exception might (or might not) cause.

Quick Tour of the Workflow Visual Designer

At this point in the book, if you've built the example workflows I've presented, you're probably comfortable with the idea of dragging and dropping activities onto the workflow visual designer's surface, wiring up their properties, and compiling and executing basic workflow code. There are a couple of things I've not told you yet, and I withheld their description until now only because we were focusing on different aspects of workflow programming at the time—namely, how we write and execute workflow programs.

However, now that you have some experience writing workflows and using Visual Studio as a workflow authoring tool, let's take a minute and see what else Visual Studio offers in terms of workflow authoring assistance. There are two primary areas I'd like to briefly describe: additional visual designer surfaces and debugging.

Additional Visual Designer Surfaces

If you look back at the first six chapters, in each sample application we dragged items from the Toolbox and dropped them onto the visual designer surface that Visual Studio presented us with. But did you happen to notice the three small buttons in the lower-left corner of the designer's window? I've reproduced them here in Figure 7-1 from the graphic from step 3 of the "Creating a workflow using the *Sequence* activity" procedure at the beginning of this chapter.

Figure 7-1   Visual designer surface selection buttons

The left button activates the default workflow visual editor we've been using so far in the book. The center button activates a view that allows you to write workflow code for cancellation (as shown in Figure 7-2), and the right button activates the fault handlers view (as shown in Figure 7-3).

Figure 7-2   Visual workflow cancellation design surface

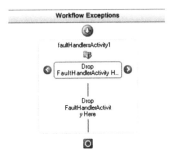

Figure 7-3   Visual workflow fault handler design surface

> **Note**   These are more than just convenience design surfaces. For example, if you tried to drag and drop a *FaultHandler* activity from the Toolbox onto the workflow design surface, you'd find that you can't drop it. You can drop *FaultHandler* activities on the fault handler design surface only.

From time to time, you'll also need to access additional design surfaces through the Smart Tags below some activity names. Looking at Figure 7-4, the Smart Tag is the little rectangle beneath the 'S' in "Sequential." In this case, the same three design surfaces you've seen appear (workflow, cancellation, and fault handlers). But some activities, such as the *EventHandling-Scope* activity (Chapter 10), have even more surfaces you'll need to access.

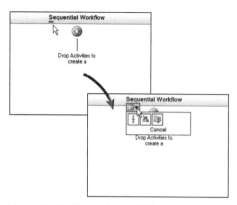

Figure 7-4 Accessing additional design surfaces via a Smart Tag

Not surprisingly, the workflow activities you drop on the cancellation design surface are executed when the workflow instance is canceled. This gives you an opportunity to perform a few cleanup or notification tasks before the workflow instance actually ceases execution.

The fault handler design surface is built to accept many fault handlers. Each fault handler is designed to handle one, and only one, exception type. There can be only one NullReferenceException handler for the activity the fault handler was associated with, for example. Composite activities in general contain fault handlers, allowing child activities to handle faults without forwarding them to the parent activity if desired. Looking back at Figure 7-3, you see two arrow buttons enclosed in blue circles. The fault handler activities are to be dropped between these arrows, and the arrows allow you to scroll to handlers that don't show up in the window because they're scrolled offscreen. The area below the arrow buttons is another workflow design surface for activities associated with exception handling. It's common to drop a *Code* activity here and do whatever cleanup you can, or perform other processing as necessary given the error condition. We'll gain some experience using this design surface after we learn a bit about workflow visual designer debugging.

Visual Designer Debugging

If you've written software for any length of time, you (like me) have come to rely on debuggers. It's a rare program or chunk of code that works the first time without at least some debugging and tweaking. You might have even set a breakpoint here and there in the workflow code we've used in this book. I know I did as I wrote the samples I've presented.

But what you might not realize is that you can also set breakpoints in the workflow visual designer. This allows you to step through your workflow activity by activity (rather than through your source code, line by line).

To set a breakpoint in the workflow visual designer, right-click the activity that will accept the breakpoint and select Breakpoint. Then select Insert Breakpoint from the resulting context menu. I've shown this in Figure 7-5.

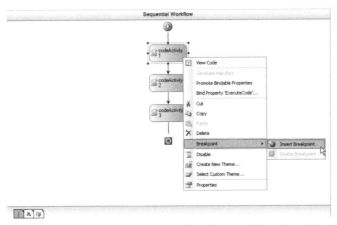

Figure 7-5   Setting a breakpoint using the workflow visual designer

The workflow visual designer then places the familiar red ball within the graphic for the activity, just as it places the red ball next to a line of code you intend to break for debugging. You see this in Figure 7-6. To remove the breakpoint, select Breakpoint and then Delete Breakpoint from the context menu or Toggle Breakpoint (which you can also use to set the breakpoint) from the Debug menu, or even Disable All Breakpoints from the Debug menu.

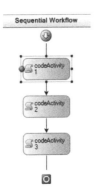

Figure 7-6   An activity in the workflow visual designer with a breakpoint set

Armed with this knowledge, we can now add a *FaultHandler* activity to our workflow.

Modifying our workflow to use the *FaultHandler* activity

1.   With the ErrorThrower application open for editing in Visual Studio, select the Workflow1.cs file in the ErrorFlow project and click the designer button to activate the workflow visual designer. The general workflow is already established, so we won't need to change anything there. (Even though you're working with ErrorThrower, I created a separate completed solution for this section. If you haven't completed the earlier steps in this chapter, you can jump straight to this point by opening the solution in \Workflow\Chapter7\ErrorHandler, or you can follow along with a completed version in \Workflow\Chapter7\ErrorHandler Completed.)

2. Click the View Fault Handlers button to activate the fault handlers visual designer. The View Fault Handlers button is the right button of the three-button group at the lower-left corner of the designer window. The designer should appear as you see here:

3. Select the *FaultHandler* activity from the Toolbox, drag it over the workflow designer's fault handler surface, and drop it between the blue arrows.

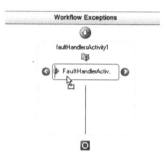

Your designer surface should now look like this:

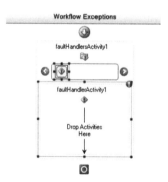

4. As with other activities, we have some properties to set to make this fault handler fully operational. The first property we'll set is the *FaultType* property. Select the *FaultType*

property in Visual Studio's Properties pane, and click the browse button (the button with the three dots) to activate the Browse And Select A .NET Type dialog box.

5. With the Browse And Select A .NET Type dialog box active, select the Type tab if it's not already selected and then expand the mscorlib tree node. From there, select System (for the System assembly) and scroll down the resulting list in the right pane until you find the list item Exception in the Type Name column. Select this by clicking the Exception line in the right pane's *ListView* control. This places the text "System.Exception" in the Type Name edit control. Click OK to accept *System.Exception* as the exception type and dismiss the dialog box. You should find the value *System.Exception* has been assigned to the *FaultType* property.

> **Note**   It's no coincidence that the exception we're asking this *FaultHandler* activity to use is the same as the exception type thrown by the *Throw* activity we used earlier in the chapter. They're a matched set. If you don't have a corresponding fault handler for a *Throw* activity in your workflow, keep in mind that if the exception is thrown at runtime, the *WorkflowTerminated* event is where you'll soon find your workflow executing. If this isn't what you want, add the appropriate *FaultHandler* activity.

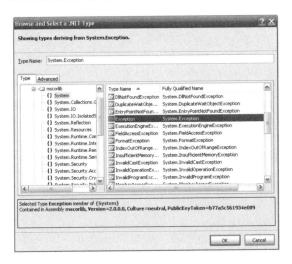

> **Note**   Although you see the *Fault* property in the preceding graphic, it's actually disabled and therefore cannot be set. Ignore it.

6. So far, we've added a *FaultHandler* activity and we've told it what type of exception it will be handling, but we've not actually provided any code to deal with the exception if it's thrown. To do that, drag a *Code* activity from the Toolbox and drop it into the area below where we dropped the *FaultHandler* activity itself. This area, identified by the name *faultHandlerActivity1*, is like a miniature workflow visual designer. So it readily accepts the *Code* activity, and as we've done with other instances of the *Code* activity, assign a value to its *ExecuteCode* property. In this case, type in **OnException** and press Enter.

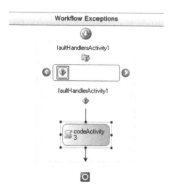

7. Visual Studio then adds the *OnException* event handler to *Workflow1* and opens the code editor for editing. To the *OnException* event handler, add this code:

```
Console.WriteLine(
    "Exception handled within the workflow! The exception was: '{0}'",
    WorkflowException != null ? WorkflowException.Message :
    "Exception property not set, generic exception thrown");
```

> **Note**   And again, it's no coincidence we're using the same *WorkflowException* property we used with the *Throw* activity. If the *WorkflowException* property is null, we're directing *Throw* to simply throw a new instance of *System.Exception*. Otherwise, *WorkflowException* contains the exception to throw.

8.   Now compile and execute the code. You should see this output:

By using the *FaultHandler*, we're able to process the exception (if we want to) and take any required actions.

> **Note**   By throwing and handling exceptions at this level, your workflow instance is still essentially stopped. The advantage is that your workflow can work with the exception rather than throwing it to the workflow runtime to deal with. If you want to continue processing after specific exceptions are thrown (exceptions that you know you can recover from), don't use *Throw* and *FaultHandler* activities to deal with them. Instead, use *try/catch* inside activity code so that the exception never leaks out to the runtime for disposition. If you can't adequately handle the exception internally (using *try/catch*), resort to *Throw* and *FaultHandler*.

Using the *Suspend* Activity

Another housekeeping activity you might find useful under certain conditions is the *Suspend* activity. In fact, a common-use case is to handle a fault using *FaultHandler* and then suspend the activity using *Suspend* to signal human intervention is required.

When you use the *Suspend* activity, you provide the activity with an error string through its *Error* property. This property can be bound to a dependency property (such as the *Throw* activity), a simple class property or field, or even a literal string (which we'll do in the example to follow). When *Suspend* executes, the workflow runtime raises the *WorkflowSuspended* event and provides you with this error string in the event arguments.

Putting a workflow instance into a suspended state means the instance is not currently executing, but neither is it unloaded. It's essentially in a holding pattern, waiting for some action on your part. It's also not considered idle, so automatic persistence doesn't come into play here. Using the *Suspend* activity is relatively simple, as you'll see.

> **Note** In a suspended state, your workflow instance is merely existing. It's a good idea to hook the *WorkflowSuspended* event in your workflow-based applications so that you can take action when workflow instances enter the suspended state. At least then you're notified they've been suspended, and you can take action to remove, resume, or restart them.

Modifying our workflow to use the *Suspend* activity

1. With the ErrorThrower application again open in Visual Studio for editing, select the Workflow1.cs file in the ErrorFlow project and click the designer button to activate the workflow visual designer. (I again created a separate solution that targets this specific section. If you're following along, continue using ErrorThrower. But if you haven't completed the earlier steps in this chapter, you can jump straight to this point by opening the solution in \Workflow\Chapter7\ErrorSuspender, or you can follow along with a completed version in \Workflow\Chapter7\ErrorSuspender Completed.) Because we'll be adding the *Suspend* activity to the *System.Exception* fault handler we just added, select the fault handlers view by clicking the right-hand button at the bottom of the designer's window.

2. From the Toolbox, drag an instance of the *Suspend* activity onto the fault handler's design surface and place it after the *Code* activity, as shown here:

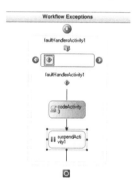

3. With the *Suspend* activity in place, select its *Error* property and type **"This is an example suspension error..."** (including the quotation marks) in the associated property edit control.

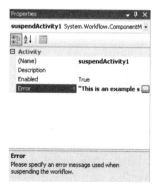

> **Tip**   Typing a literal string, as we've done here, is perfectly acceptable. However, you can also bind this to a string-based dependency property that is more easily altered as your workflow executes. Clicking the browse button (the button with the three dots you see in the graphic) activates the binding dialog box we saw in step 7 of the "Creating a workflow using the *Throw* activity" procedure. Simply follow the same basic steps as you did there.

4. Because we don't have a *WorkflowSuspended* event handler in our main application, we need to edit the Program.cs file from the main application and add it. In the *Main* method, locate code to hook the existing event handlers and add the following:

```
workflowRuntime.WorkflowSuspended +=
    new EventHandler<WorkflowSuspendedEventArgs>(workflowSuspended);
```

5. Because we're using an event handler named *workflowSuspended*, we need to code that:

```
static void workflowSuspended(object sender, WorkflowSuspendedEventArgs e)
{
    Console.WriteLine("Workflow instance suspended, error: '{0}'.",
                                                        e.Error);

    waitHandle.Set();
}
```

6. Compile the application by clicking Build, Build Solution from Visual Studio's main menu and then press F5 or Ctrl+F5 to execute the application (after correcting any compilation errors). The program output should be similar to this:

When you run this application, you should see the console output generated by the *WorkflowSuspended* event handler in our main application. But you can do more than simply write text to the console. You can take any other action appropriate for your process flow. Although you could resume the workflow instance processing from here, it's generally not recommended. For one thing, the entire activity that was processing will be skipped, leaving your workflow instance to resume processing at a later stage in its flow, which probably isn't a good thing (what was skipped, and how do you account for it?). At the very least, however, you can cleanly remove the workflow instance from processing and apply any necessary cleanup code.

As if exceptions and suspended workflow instances aren't enough, you can, if you need to do so, terminate your workflow instance. Let's see how.

Using the *Terminate* Activity

There are times when things get so bad that you have no recourse but to kill off a workflow instance. Perhaps some data came back from an external process in a bad format or was otherwise miscalculated. Or the database server simply disappeared and you can't move forward without it. Or...well, hopefully, you see where this line of reasoning is going.

WF provides us with a ready-made way to terminate our workflow instances through the *Terminate* activity. The *Terminate* activity is used in precisely the same way as the *Suspend* activity, and in fact its properties are identical. The difference is that when *Terminate* executes, all hope for your workflow instance continuing execution is lost.

When *Terminate* executes, the workflow runtime fires the *WorkflowTerminated* event, just as if there were an unhandled exception. To tell the two situations apart is difficult when processing the *WorkflowTerminated* event. All you can really do is examine the *WorkflowTerminatedEventArgs* and look at the *Exception* property. If the workflow instance was terminated using the *Terminate* activity, the exception type will be *System.Workflow.ComponentModel.WorkflowTerminatedException* rather than some other (probably more common) exception type.

Let's see how we use *Terminate* activity in our workflow code.

Modifying our workflow to use the *Terminate* activity

1. We're again going to work with the ErrorThrower application in Visual Studio. (If you haven't completed the earlier steps in this chapter, you can jump straight to this point by opening the solution in \Workflow\Chapter7\ErrorTerminator, or you can follow along with a completed version in \Workflow\Chapter7\ErrorTerminator Completed.) Once again, select the Workflow1.cs file in the ErrorFlow project and click the designer button to activate the workflow visual designer. We first need to remove the *Suspend* activity we added in the preceding section. Simply select it with a single mouse click, and press the Delete key.

2. From the Toolbox, drag an instance of the *Terminate* activity onto the fault handler's design surface and place it after the *Code* activity after first deleting the *Suspend* activity you placed there previously.

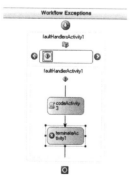

3. With the *Terminate* activity in place, select its *Error* property and type "**This is an example termination error...**" (again with quotes) in the associated property edit control.

> **Note** The tip I provided in the preceding section holds true here as well. You can use a literal string, as we're doing here, or you can bind the string to an activity field, property, or dependency property.

4. Compile the application by choosing Build Solution from Visual Studio's Build menu. After correcting any compilation errors, press F5 or Ctrl+F5 to run it. If all goes as expected, you'll see something like the following:

Terminate, like *Suspend*, is a fairly simple activity, but a powerful one. You won't often need it, but when things go so badly for your workflow that you can't continue, *Terminate* is the best tool in the Toolbox.

If you want to continue to the next chapter, keep Visual Studio 2005 running and turn to Chapter 8. If you suspended a workflow instance somewhere along the way in this chapter, resume it! (Just kidding...)

If you want to stop, exit Visual Studio 2005 now, save your spot in the book, and close it. *Terminate* seems like a good alternative at this point...

Chapter 7 Quick Reference

To	Do This
Use the *Sequence* activity	*SequenceActivity* is a composite activity, and as such it acts as a drop site for other activities. Simply drag and drop an instance of the *Sequence* activity onto the workflow visual designer. Then drag and drop other activities onto *Sequence-Activity* as necessary to complete your workflow. Those activities will be executed in the order they appear in the designer, from top to bottom.
Use the *Code* activity	With the visual workflow designer visible and active, drag an instance of the *Code* activity onto the surface and drop it into the workflow process as appropriate. Then provide an *ExecuteCode* method name in the Properties window. Populate that method with the code you want to execute.
Use the *Throw* activity	With the visual workflow designer visible and active, drag an instance of the *Throw* activity onto the surface and drop it into the workflow process as appropriate. Then assign the *Fault* and *FaultType* properties to provide the *Throw* activity with the exception to throw as well as the type of exception it should expect.
Use the *FaultHandler* activity	With the visual workflow designer visible and active, and with the Fault Handlers view showing, drag an instance of the *FaultHandler* activity onto the surface and drop it into the workflow process as appropriate. Then assign the *FaultType* property to assign the type of exception it will handle.
Use the *Suspend* activity	With the visual workflow designer visible and active, drag an instance of the *Suspend* activity onto the surface and drop it into the workflow process as appropriate. Then assign the *Error* property to assign the error string value it will report to the workflow runtime via the *WorkflowSuspended* event.
Use the *Terminate* activity	With the visual workflow designer visible and active, drag an instance of the *Terminate* activity onto the surface and drop it into the workflow process as appropriate. Then assign the *Error* property to assign the error string value it will report to the workflow runtime via the *WorkflowTerminated* event.

Chapter 8
Calling External Methods and Workflows

After completing this chapter, you will be able to:

- Build and call local data services that are external to your workflow
- Understand how interfaces are used to communicate between the host process and your workflow
- Use external methods designed to transfer data between you workflow and host application
- Invoke additional workflows from within an executing workflow

As I was writing the preceding chapters, I kept thinking to myself, "I can't wait to get to the part where we return real data to the host application!" Why? Because as interesting as workflow is, there is only so much you can do to demonstrate activities and workflows without returning something realistic to the executing application. Theoretically, there might be an infinite number of interesting workflow examples and demonstrations I could write that only processed initialization data (such as the postal code example you saw in Chapter 1, "Introducing Microsoft Windows Workflow Foundation"). But things become far more interesting, and to be honest, far more realistic when we kick off a workflow that seeks and processes data from external sources and returns that data in some processed form to our application.

So why not just crack open an object and start sending data into an executing workflow, or from an executing workflow to the host application? Actually, you can do this with existing technology outside Windows Workflow Foundation (WF) using some form of marshaled communications, such as .NET Remoting or an XML Web service. *Marshaling*, sometimes also called *serialization*, is a process whereby data is converted from its original form into a form suitable for transmission between different processes and even between different computers.

Why mention marshaling? Because your workflow is executing on a different thread than your host process, and passing data between threads without proper marshaling is a recipe for disaster for reasons beyond the scope of this chapter. In fact, your workflow could be in a persisted state at the time you tried to send it data. It's not on a different thread...it's not even executing.

But wouldn't a .NET Remoting connection or an XML Web service be considered excessive if we just want to pass data between our workflow and the host process that's controlling it? Absolutely! And this is the premise of this chapter—how we can establish *local* communications. We'll be setting up the systems necessary to satisfy the thread data-marshaling requirements without calling into play (heavier-duty) technologies that are meant more for computer-to-computer or process-to-process data transfers.

Building an *ExternalDataService* Service

When a workflow communicates with its host application, and specifically when it sends and receives data, the workflow does so using queues and messages. How this is accomplished is internal to WF, and this is not necessarily a bad thing. Although it might be nice to know the specific mechanics that are used, the bottom line is we have applications to write and software to deliver. So the more WF does for us, the more we can focus on our application-specific tasks. But it's important to understand the big picture so that the sections to follow make more sense.

Workflow Intraprocess Communication

To simplify the communications task, WF uses an *abstraction layer* to buffer the workflow from the host. An abstraction layer is like a black box. You feed input to the box, it performs some magical task, and information flows out the other side. Of course, there isn't anything magical about it, but it's still a useful way to describe it. We don't know how it does the job—it simply does the job.

In this case, the black box is known as the *local communication service*. Like any service in WF terms, it's another pluggable service. The difference is *you* write part of the service in this case rather than using a prebuilt WF service. Why? Because the data you pass between your host application and your workflow is specific to your application. Moreover, you can create various data-transfer methods, allowing your host application to send data to and receive data from the workflow using a variety of methods you design.

> **Note**   Something you'll need to watch for here is the sharing of collections or objects. Since the host application and workflow runtime execute within the same AppDomain, reference-type objects and collections are passed by reference rather than by value. This means that both the host application and the workflow instance could access and use the same objects at the same time, opening the possibility for multithreading bugs and concurrent data access issues. If your workflow and application design call for objects to be transferred and the possibility exists that both workflow and host application would use the objects concurrently, you should consider passing a copy of the object or collection, perhaps by implementing *ICloneable*, or consider serializing the object or collection yourself and transferring the serialized version.

I like to think of this local service we write as more of a connector. You write the service, plug it into the workflow, and open connections to send your data. The data might be strings, *DataSet* objects, or even custom objects you design—anything that is serializable. Although I won't show it in this chapter, the communication can be bidirectional. (Here, I'll merely pass data from the workflow back to the executing application.) Using a tool, we'll generate activities designed to send and receive data from the workflow's perspective. From the host application's perspective, receiving data amounts to an event, while sending data is simply a method call on the service object.

> **Note**   We'll return to the concept of bidirectional data transfer after looking at a few more activities in later chapters. The workflow activity to receive data from the host application is based on the *HandleExternalEvent* activity, which we'll look at in Chapter 10, "Event Activities." We also need to dig deeper into the concept of correlation, which we'll do in Chapter 17, "Host Communication." For now, we'll simply return complex data to the host once the workflow instance has completed its task.

Although we need to do more than just this, ultimately we need to add the *ExternalDataService* to our workflow runtime. *ExternalDataService* is a pluggable service that facilitates transferring serializable data between workflow instances and the host application. The service code we'll write in the upcoming sections will do that and more. To see what's in store for us, let's look at the overall development process.

Designing and Implementing Workflow Intraprocess Communication

We begin by deciding what data will be transferred. Will it be a *DataSet*? An intrinsic object, such as an integer or string? Or will it be a custom object we design ourselves? Whatever it is, we'll then design an interface that the *ExternalDataService* can bind to. This interface will contain methods we design, and they can be designed to send and receive data from both the workflow instance's and the host's perspective. The data we're transferring will be passed back and forth using the methods in this interface.

We'll then need to write some code—our part of the external data service—which represents the connection or *bridging* code the host and workflow will use to interact with the WF-provided *ExternalDataService*. If we were dealing with an XML Web service, Visual Studio could automatically create proxy code for us. But there is no such tool for workflow, so we need to devise this bridging code ourselves. The "bridge" we'll use here actually consists of two classes: a *connector* class and a *service* class. You can name them anything you like, and my name assignments are not necessarily what WF might call them (I don't believe WF has a name for them!), but I prefer to think of them in this fashion. The connector class manages the data conduit itself (maintains state), while the service class is used directly by the host and workflow to exchange data.

With the interface we created in hand, we'll execute a tool, *wca.exe*, which is typically located in your Program Files\Microsoft SDKs\Windows\v6.0\Bin directory. The tool is called the *Workflow Communications Activity* generator utility and given an interface it will generate two activities you can use to bind the interface to your workflow instance: one for sending data, the *invoker*; and one for receiving data, the *sink*. Once they are created and massaged a bit, you can actually drag and drop them from the Visual Studio Toolbox onto the workflow visual designer and work with them the same as any other workflow activity. While we don't have a tool to build the connection bridging code I mentioned previously, this tool definitely helps on the workflow side.

> **Tip** From a project perspective, I tend to collect the host application code in one project or a group of related projects (dependent assemblies), the interface and connection bridging code in a second project, and the workflow code in a third project. This allows me to easily reference the interface and bridge classes from both the host application and the workflow, while neatly segregating functionality between assemblies.

We then have the pieces we need to wire up the communications between our workflow and our host application. The entire process, while executing, is facilitated by *ExternalDataService*, but it'll use code we create. Let's take a quick look at this chapter's primary sample application (as it's far more complex than any we've seen so far) and then begin creating the workflow external data communication code we'll require.

The Motor Vehicle Data-Checking Application

The sample application for this chapter is a Windows Forms application that provides a user interface for gathering motor vehicle data for specified drivers (very loosely based on an application I actually wrote). The application itself is significant enough that I won't record each and every detail of its creation. Instead, you should use the sample code provided for this chapter as a starting point. I will, however, show how to tie in the workflow components. And if you were wondering, the application will use fictitious drivers and data, so all you with excessive numbers of traffic violations can maintain your anonymity!

The main user interface form appears as you see in Figure 8-1. The drop-down list control contains the names of three drivers, the selected name of which is sent to a new instance of a workflow designed to retrieve the driver's motor vehicle information and return a completed *DataSet*. The *DataSet* is then bound to the list view controls you see—one for vehicle information and one for violation information, if any.

Figure 8-1   The MVDataChecker primary user interface

When you click the Retrieve MV Data button, you initiate a new workflow instance. The user interface disables the retrieve button as well as the driver drop-down list control and displays a "searching" notice, which you see in Figure 8-2. The picture control you see at the bottom of the form is an animated image file. The application simply shows or hides the label and picture box control as required.

Figure 8-2   The MVDataChecker "searching" user interface

When the workflow instance has completed its work, it uses an activity we'll create to fire an event the host application intercepts, which tells the host application that data is available. Because Windows Forms *ListView* controls don't bind directly to *DataTable* objects, we'll iterate through the tabular data and insert the rows in the view ourselves after retrieving the data from the workflow. Completed *ListView* controls are shown in Figure 8-3.

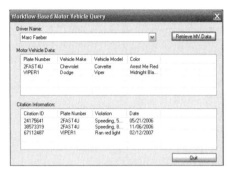

Figure 8-3   The MVDataChecker user interface with retrieved data

At this point in the application's execution, you might decide to retrieve another driver's information or quit the application. If you quit the application while a search is progressing, the actively executing workflow instance is aborted.

With that brief tour of the application complete, let's look at the code we need to write to make all this work, starting with the interface we need to provide to WF so that it can raise that "data available" event I mentioned.

Creating Service Interfaces

The service interface is entirely yours to create, and it should be based on the data you want to communicate between your workflow instance and your host application. For this sample application, imagine you need to design a workflow to retrieve driver information from various sources and that you want the information collated into a single data structure—a *DataSet* with multiple *DataTables*, one table for vehicle identification information and one table for driver traffic violations. In reality, you'd retrieve this data from some source, or from a set of different sources, but we'll simply use imaginary data to keep things more focused on the workflow itself. In the host application, we'll display the (bogus) data in a pair of *ListView* controls.

You'll pass in to the workflow instance the name of the driver, which the workflow instance uses to look up the driver and vehicle information. With the data in hand, the workflow instance notifies the host application that data is ready, and the host application reads and displays the information.

So we really need just a single method in our interface: *MVDataUpdate*. We know we want to send a *DataSet*, so we'll pass a *DataSet* into *MVDataUpdate* as a method parameter.

Creating a workflow data communication interface

1. The sample application, MVDataChecker, comes in two forms: incomplete and complete. The \Workflow\Chapter8\MVDataChecker\ directory I mentioned contains the incomplete application so that you fill in the missing code as you follow the steps I outline throughout the chapter. However, the completed solution in the \Workflow\Chapter8\MVDataChecker Completed\ directory contains the fully operational application you can use as well. Feel free to compare the two, work back and forth, or use the completed application as a pattern if you like. To open either solution, drag the .sln file onto an executing copy of Visual Studio.

2. There should be three projects contained within this solution. In the Visual Studio Solution Explorer, expand the MVDataService project and open the IMVDataService.cs file for editing.

3. Locate the namespace definition. After the opening brace for the *MVDataService* namespace, add this code and then save the file:

```
public interface IMVDataService
{
    void MVDataUpdate (DataSet mvData);
}
```

That's it! Well, that's all you need to do to create an interface. However, we need to add an attribute to make this interface suitable for use with WF. Let's look at that next.

Using the *ExternalDataExchange* Attribute

Although we have an interface, *IMVDataService*, we haven't yet done enough to provide this interface to WF and have WF actually use the interface for data communications. To do that, we need to add the *ExternalDataExchange* attribute.

> **Note**   Later we'll also add attributes associated with *correlation*. We'll look at correlation attributes in greater detail in Chapter 17, "Correlation and Local Host Communication," but for now, just think of correlation as a way to keep different data requests sorted out. I mention it here because your data communication interface is where you specify correlated data values.

The *ExternalDataExchange* attribute is simply a marker that WF uses to identify interfaces suitable for local communications service use. Remember the *wca.exe* tool I mentioned? Both it and Visual Studio use this attribute to identify this interface as one your workflow instance can use. Let's add that attribute now, along with the correlation attributes we need.

> **Note** Don't let the phrase "marker attribute" fool you into believing the *ExternalDataEx-change* attribute isn't a critical component. It most certainly is. The workflow runtime looks for this attribute when attempting to make external data transfers. Without it, data transfers between workflow and host are not possible.

Creating a workflow data communication interface

● Open Visual Studio if it isn't already open, and with the IMVDataService.cs file open for editing, add the following line of code just prior to the interface definition:

```
[ExternalDataExchange]
```

The complete *IMVDataService* interface should look like the code you see in Listing 8-1. Don't worry about compiling the applications at this point. We'll need to add more code before it will compile without error.

Listing 8-1 IMVDataService.cs completed

```
using System;
using System.Collections.Generic;
using System.Text;
using System.Workflow.Activities;
using System.Workflow.Runtime;
using System.Data;

namespace MVDataService
{
    [ExternalDataExchange]
    public interface IMVDataService
    {
        void MVDataUpdate(DataSet mvData);
    }
}
```

Using *ExternalDataEventArgs*

Earlier I mentioned that, to the host application, communications from the executing workflow appear as events. The host application can't know beforehand precisely when the workflow instance will have data, and polling for data is terribly inefficient. So WF uses the asynchronous model that .NET itself uses and fires events when data is available. The host application hooks those events and reads the data.

Because we want to send information to the recipient of our event, we need to create a customized event argument class. If you've created a custom event argument class in your previous work, you probably used *System.EventArgs* as the base class.

WF external data events, however, require a different argument base class if only to carry the instance ID of the workflow instance issuing the event. The base class we use for external data events is *ExternalDataEventArgs*, which itself derives from *System.EventArgs*, so we're on familiar ground. In addition, there are two other requirements: we must provide a base constructor that accepts the instance ID (a Guid), which in turn passes the instance ID to the base constructor, and we must mark our argument class as serializable using the *Serializable* attribute. Let's now build the external data event argument class we need.

Creating a workflow data event argument class

1. With the MVDataService project still open in Visual Studio, locate the MVDataAvailableArgs.cs file and open it for editing.

2. You should find only the using directives and the namespace definition in the file, so after the opening brace for the namespace definition, add the following lines of code:

```
[Serializable]
public class MVDataAvailableArgs : ExternalDataEventArgs
{

}
```

3. Finally, we need to add the required constructor to provide the base class with the workflow instance ID:

```
public MVDataAvailableArgs(Guid instanceId)
    : base(instanceId)
{
}
```

The complete event argument class is shown in Listing 8-2.

Listing 8-2   MVDataAvailableArgs.cs completed

```
using System;
using System.Collections.Generic;
using System.Text;
using System.Workflow.Activities;
using System.Workflow.Runtime;

namespace MVDataService
{
    [Serializable]
    public class MVDataAvailableArgs : ExternalDataEventArgs
    {
        public MVDataAvailableArgs(Guid instanceId)
            : base(instanceId)
        {
        }
    }
}
```

Creating External Data Services

Now we come to a more difficult section, that being our task to create the bridging code for the external data service. The host must have some code it can use to access the data that the workflow instance is trying to communicate. We will use a tool to build activities for the workflow to use (that's in the next section), but no tool exists for the host side of the communications connection.

Here, we'll build a slightly simplified version of a full connection-bridging architecture. This version supports only workflow-to-host communication. (We'll build a general-purpose bidirectional bridge you can reuse when we get to Chapter 17.) The connection bridge we'll build is divided into two parts: the *connector*, which implements the interface we developed earlier, and the *service*, which among other things is responsible for raising the "data available" event as well as providing a "read" method to pull the data from the workflow.

Tip   This is code *you* provide, not WF. The approach I take when writing local data exchange services may differ from code you would write. This is fine. The only requirement is that the local data-exchange services implement the communications interface and provide a mechanism for retrieving the data to be exchanged.

Why this complexity? Unlike traditional .NET objects, workflow instances are executing within the confines of the workflow runtime. So events into and out of the workflow instance are brokered by the workflow runtime. The workflow runtime *must* do this because your host application could be trying to send data to a workflow instance that has been persisted and removed from active execution.

Returning to our bridge, the connection class maintains a field the workflow will fill with returned data. For the sample application we're building here, we don't allow concurrent workflow instances, but that's merely at the convenience of this sample application. Nothing prevents us from executing concurrent workflow instances in general, as we'll see in Chapter 17.

Naturally, each workflow instance would likely return different data, at least if it was passed a different driver than another workflow instance. It's the connection class's responsibility to implement the host side of the interface we developed, as well as to keep the data straight. When the host asks for data, the connection class makes sure the correct *DataSet* is returned given the workflow instance ID it was given.

The service class handles a few tasks for us. First, it registers the *ExternalDataService* with the workflow runtime so that we can communicate between host and workflow instances. It maintains a singleton copy of the connection class and binds itself to that class as the service provider. The service class also serves as a factory object to make sure we have one and only one connection class. And it provides the "read" method we'll use to pull the data from the workflow instance. (If we implemented a bidirectional interface, the service class would also provide for the "write" method.) Let's build these classes now.

Creating the bridge connector class

1. With the MVDataService project open in Visual Studio, locate the MVDataConnector.cs file and open it for editing.

2. You should find only the using directives and the namespace definition in the file. So after the opening brace for the namespace definition, add the following lines of code:

```
public sealed class MVDataConnector : IMVDataService
{
    private DataSet _dataValue = null;
    private static WorkflowMVDataService _service = null;
    private static object _syncLock = new object();

}
```

The *_dataValue* field retains the data generated by the workflow instance. The *_service* field holds the singleton instance of the data service object. And the *_syncLock* object is used merely for thread synchronization while assigning values in static methods.

3. Following the fields, we add a static property to access the singleton service object. Here is the code to add:

```
public static WorkflowMVDataService MVDataService
{
    get { return _service; }
    set
    {
        if (value != null)
        {
```

```
                        lock (_syncLock)
                        {
                            // Re-verify the service isn't null
                            // now that we're locked...
                            if (value != null)
                            {
                                _service = value;
                            } // if
                            else
                            {
                                throw new InvalidOperationException(
                                    "You must provide a service instance.");
                            } // else
                        } // lock
                    } // if
                    else
                    {
                        throw new InvalidOperationException(
                            "You must provide a service instance.");
                    } // else
                }
            }
```

4. Mirroring the accessor property for the service, we need to add a property to access the data. Add this code following the code you added in the preceding step:

```
public DataSet MVData
{
    get { return _dataValue; }
}
```

5. Because the connector class derives from *IMVDataService*, we must implement *MVDataUpdate*:

```
public void MVDataUpdate(DataSet mvData)
{
    // Assign the field for later recall
    _dataValue = mvData;

    // Raise the event to trigger host read
    _service.RaiseMVDataUpdateEvent();
}
```

The workflow uses this method to store the *DataSet* in the data value field. It raises the event to let the host know data is available. The full bridge connector class is shown in Listing 8-3. Note that we're not ready to compile the entire application just yet. We still have a bit more code to add.

Listing 8-3   MVDataconnector.cs completed

```
using System;
using System.Collections.Generic;
using System.Text;
using System.Workflow.Activities;
using System.Workflow.Runtime;
using System.Data;
```

```
namespace MVDataService
{
    public sealed class MVDataConnector : IMVDataService
    {
        private DataSet _dataValue = null;
        private static WorkflowMVDataService _service = null;
        private static object _syncLock = new object();

        public static WorkflowMVDataService MVDataService
        {
            get { return _service; }
            set
            {
                if (value != null)
                {
                    lock (_syncLock)
                    {
                        // Re-verify the service isn't null
                        // now that we're locked...
                        if (value != null)
                        {
                            _service = value;
                        } // if
                        else
                        {
                            throw new InvalidOperationException(
                                "You must provide a service instance.");
                        } // else
                    } // lock
                } // if
                else
                {
                    throw new InvalidOperationException(
                      "You must provide a service instance.");
                } // else
            }
        }

        public DataSet MVData
        {
            get { return _dataValue; }
        }

        // Workflow to host communication method
        public void MVDataUpdate(DataSet mvData)
        {
            // Assign the field for later recall
            _dataValue = mvData;

            // Raise the event to trigger host read
            _service.RaiseMVDataUpdateEvent();
        }
    }
}
```

Creating the bridge service class

1. With the MVDataService project again open in Visual Studio, locate the WorkflowMVDataService.cs file and open it for editing.

2. As with the *MVDataConnector* class, we need to add the class definition and fields. So copy the following code into the WorkflowMVDataService.cs file following the opening namespace brace:

```
public class WorkflowMVDataService
{
    static WorkflowRuntime _workflowRuntime = null;
    static ExternalDataExchangeService _dataExchangeService = null;
    static MVDataConnector _dataConnector = null;
    static object _syncLock = new object();

    public event EventHandler<MVDataAvailableArgs> MVDataUpdate;

    private Guid _instanceID = Guid.Empty;

}
```

3. The *_instanceID* field needs to be accessible from outside the class, so add the following property:

```
public Guid InstanceID
{
    get { return _instanceID; }
    set { _instanceID = value; }
}
```

4. We now add a static factory method we'll use to create instances of this class. We do this so that all the important housekeeping is accomplished as we create instances of this bridge service. For example, we need to make sure the *ExternalDataService* service is plugged into the workflow runtime. We'll also add the bridge connector class we just created as a pluggable service so that the workflow has access to the data connection class. Therefore, add this method following the property we added in step 3:

```
public static WorkflowMVDataService CreateDataService(Guid instanceID,
                                        WorkflowRuntime workflowRuntime)
{
    lock (_syncLock)
    {
        // If we're just starting, save a copy of the workflow
        // runtime reference.
        if (_workflowRuntime == null)
        {
            // Save instance of the workflow runtime.
            _workflowRuntime = workflowRuntime;
        } // if
```

```
    // If we're just starting, plug in ExternalDataExchange service.
    if (_dataExchangeService == null)
    {
        // Data exchange service not registered, so create an
        // instance and register.
        _dataExchangeService = new ExternalDataExchangeService();
        _workflowRuntime.AddService(_dataExchangeService);
    } // if

    // Check to see if we have already added this data
    // exchange service.
    MVDataConnector dataConnector = (MVDataConnector)workflowRuntime.
                            GetService(typeof(MVDataConnector));
    if (dataConnector == null)
    {
        // First time through, so create the connector and
        // register as a service with the workflow runtime.
        _dataConnector = new MVDataConnector();
        _dataExchangeService.AddService(_dataConnector);
    } // if
    else
    {
        // Use the retrieved data connector.
        _dataConnector = dataConnector;
    } // else

    // Pull the service instance we registered with the
    // connection object.
    WorkflowMVDataService workflowDataService =
                                MVDataConnector.MVDataService;
    if (workflowDataService == null)
    {
        // First time through, so create the data service and
        // hand it to the connector.
        workflowDataService = new WorkflowMVDataService(instanceID);
        MVDataConnector.MVDataService = workflowDataService;
    } // if
    else
    {
        // The data service is static and already registered with
        // the workflow runtime. The instance ID present when it
        // was registered is invalid for this iteration and must be
        // updated.
        workflowDataService.InstanceID = instanceID;
    } // else

    return workflowDataService;
  } // lock
}
```

5. The connection object we created in the preceding section ("Creating the bridge connector class") keeps an instance of the bridge object we created in step 4. We now will add a static helper method to return the bridge service instance. Although this might seem more than is necessary now, later when we address correlation it'll become apparent why we did things this way:

```
public static WorkflowMVDataService
                    GetRegisteredWorkflowDataService(Guid instanceID)
{
    lock (_syncLock)
    {
        WorkflowMVDataService workflowDataService =
                                MVDataConnector.MVDataService;

        if (workflowDataService == null)
        {
            throw new Exception("Error configuring data service..." +
                            "service cannot be null.");
        } // if

        return workflowDataService;
    } // lock
}
```

6. Next we add our (private) constructor and destructor. As with the bridge connection class, we need to make sure we break the circular references we're building between the bridge connection object and the bridge service object. Here are the lines of code you need:

```
private WorkflowMVDataService(Guid instanceID)
{
    _instanceID = instanceID;
    MVDataConnector.MVDataService = this;
}

~WorkflowMVDataService()
{
    // Clean up
    _workflowRuntime = null;
    _dataExchangeService = null;
    _dataConnector = null;
}
```

7. Although we've added some important things to the bridge service class, not the least of which is the introduction of the *ExternalDataService* to the workflow runtime, we still have to add code that represents a major functional aspect—the ability to read and return the data to the host application. The bridge connection object actually maintains the connection state (the data), but the host uses this service to gain access to that data. Here is the read method we add:

```
public DataSet Read()
{
    return _dataConnector.MVData;
}
```

8. The final functional block we'll add to our bridge service is a method to raise the "motor vehicle data update" event. The workflow uses this method to fire a notification to the host that data is available for pickup:

```
public void RaiseMVDataUpdateEvent()
{
    if (_workflowRuntime == null)
        _workflowRuntime = new WorkflowRuntime();

    // Load persisted workflow instances.
    _workflowRuntime.GetWorkflow(_instanceID);
    if (MVDataUpdate != null)
    {
        MVDataUpdate(this, new MVDataAvailableArgs(_instanceID));
    } // if
}
```

The full bridge service is shown in Listing 8-4.

Listing 8-4   WorkflowMVDataService.cs completed

```
using System;
using System.Collections.Generic;
using System.Text;
using System.Workflow.Activities;
using System.Workflow.Runtime;
using System.Data;

namespace MVDataService
{
    public class WorkflowMVDataService
    {
        static WorkflowRuntime _workflowRuntime = null;
        static ExternalDataExchangeService _dataExchangeService = null;
        static MVDataConnector _dataConnector = null;
        static object _syncLock = new object();

        public event EventHandler<MVDataAvailableArgs> MVDataUpdate;

        private Guid _instanceID = Guid.Empty;

        public Guid InstanceID
        {
            get { return _instanceID; }
            set { _instanceID = value; }
        }

        public static WorkflowMVDataService CreateDataService(
                Guid instanceID, WorkflowRuntime workflowRuntime)
        {
            lock (_syncLock)
            {
                // If we're just starting, save a copy of the workflow
                // runtime reference.
                if (_workflowRuntime == null)
```

```
    {
        // Save instance of the workflow runtime.
        _workflowRuntime = workflowRuntime;
    } // if

    // If we're just starting, plug in ExternalDataExchange
    // service.
    if (_dataExchangeService == null)
    {
        // Data exchange service not registered, so create an
        // instance and register.
        _dataExchangeService =
                    new ExternalDataExchangeService();
        _workflowRuntime.AddService(_dataExchangeService);
    } // if

    // Check to see if we have already added this data exchange
    // service.
    MVDataConnector dataConnector =
            (MVDataConnector)workflowRuntime.
                GetService(typeof(MVDataConnector));
    if (dataConnector == null)
    {
        // First time through, so create the connector and
        // register as a service with the workflow runtime.
        _dataConnector = new MVDataConnector();
        _dataExchangeService.AddService(_dataConnector);
    } // if
    else
    {
        // Use the retrieved data connector.
        _dataConnector = dataConnector;
    } // else

    // Pull the service instance we registered with the
    // connection object.
    WorkflowMVDataService workflowDataService =
                            MVDataConnector.MVDataService;
    if (workflowDataService == null)
    {
        // First time through, so create the data service and
        // hand it to the connector.
        workflowDataService =
                    new WorkflowMVDataService(instanceID);
        MVDataConnector.MVDataService = workflowDataService;
    } // if
    else
    {
        // The data service is static and already registered
        // with the workflow runtime. The instance ID present
        // when  was registered is invalid for this iteration
        // and must be updated.
        workflowDataService.InstanceID = instanceID;
    } // else
```

```
                return workflowDataService;
        } // lock
    }

    public static WorkflowMVDataService
                GetRegisteredWorkflowDataService(Guid instanceID)
    {
        lock (_syncLock)
        {
            WorkflowMVDataService workflowDataService =
                                    MVDataConnector.MVDataService;

            if (workflowDataService == null)
            {
                throw new Exception("Error configuring data " +
                            "service...service cannot be null.");
            } // if

            return workflowDataService;
        } // lock
    }

    private WorkflowMVDataService(Guid instanceID)
    {
        _instanceID = instanceID;
        MVDataConnector.MVDataService = this;
    }

    ~WorkflowMVDataService()
    {
        // Clean up
        _workflowRuntime = null;
        _dataExchangeService = null;
        _dataConnector = null;
    }

    public DataSet Read()
    {
        return _dataConnector.MVData;
    }

    public void RaiseMVDataUpdateEvent()
    {
        if (_workflowRuntime == null)
            _workflowRuntime = new WorkflowRuntime();

        // Load persisted workflow instances.
        _workflowRuntime.GetWorkflow(_instanceID);
        if (MVDataUpdate != null)
        {
            MVDataUpdate(this, new MVDataAvailableArgs(_instanceID));
        } // if
    }
}
}
```

The *CallExternalMethod* Activity

All of the code you've seen so far in this chapter has been to support a specific WF activity—the *CallExternalMethod* activity. The *CallExternalMethod* activity is designed to accept an interface and a method supported by that interface, and to call that method. The question is, who implements the method?

You might think your host application does, but that's not quite correct. If you look back at the preceding section "Creating the bridge connector class," you actually find the method there. The data connector, which is tied to the *ExternalDataService*, implements the method. The data service, in turn, converts the method invocation into an event to which the host application subscribes.

It's possible to use the *CallExternalMethod* activity directly, and you can even bypass some of the service code you just inserted into your application. However, bypassing the service code poses a couple of problems for you. Your host application and workflow instance are tied together, one for one. Using the data service as done here is moderately better, but when you combine the data service and correlation, then you can have many application instances accessing data from many workflow instances. This is not possible when bypassing the data service you created.

As for using the *CallExternalMethod* activity directly, it's often preferable to create custom activities to call the external method for you. While they're not fully custom activities, written from scratch, there is a tool you can use that consumes your data exchange interface and builds activities derived from *CallExternalMethod* that are more suitably named and have their properties already configured (interface and method name). Let's see how that tool is used next.

Creating and Using Custom External Data Service Activities

Looking back, we just wrote more code than we've written in the entire book so far. The reason for this is WF can't know beforehand what information our workflows will trade with our host applications, so some work is clearly necessary to fill in that gap.

However, WF knows all about workflow activities, and happily there is a tool we can use to interpret our data-transfer interface, marked with the *ExternalDataExchange* attribute, and automatically generate WF activities.

The application we're building in this chapter sends data from the workflow to the host application, which is to say the data transfer is unidirectional. I did this intentionally because there is more to learn before we have all the knowledge required to understand full bidirectional data transfers. The *Workflow Communication Activity* generator utility we'll use is fully capable of creating activities to send and receive host data. We'll just "throw away" part of its output for this particular application because we don't require it. (In fact, the activity it would generate is malformed because our interface did not specify host-to-workflow communications, which we'll save for Chapter 10.)

With all this in mind, let's execute *wca.exe* and create an activity we can use for sending data to our host application.

Creating the communication activities

1. So that *wca.exe* can generate the activity code we desire, we need to make sure it has an interface to model the activities against. Therefore, make sure the MVDataService project builds without error and produces the MVDataService assembly (hosted by MVDataService.dll). (Right-click the project in Solution Explorer and select Build. Don't try to build the entire solution.) Correct any build errors before proceeding.

2. Click the Start button and then the Run menu item to activate the Run dialog box.

3. Type **cmd** in the Open combo box control, and click OK. This activates the Windows Command Shell.

4. Change directories so that we can directly access the *MVDataService* assembly in the book's downloaded sample code. Typically, the command to type would be as follows:

   ```
   cd "\Workflow\Chapter8\MVDataChecker\MVDataService\bin\Debug"
   ```

   However, your specific directory might vary. Remember also that the "Workflow" directory represents the actual directory where the code is to be found rather than being an actual directory name in its own right.

5. The *wca.exe* tool was installed by default into the Windows SDK subdirectory under Program Files. (Of course, if you didn't install it into the default directory, you need to use the directory into which you did install the Windows SDK.) To execute the tool, type the following text at the command-line prompt (including the double quotes):

   ```
   "C:\Program Files\Microsoft SDKs\Windows\v6.0\Bin\Wca.exe" MVDataService.dll
   ```

Press the Enter key. The tool's output should be similar to the following:

6. Type **dir** at the command prompt to see the files *wca.exe* created.

7. The file IMVDataService.Sinks.cs is unnecessary and can be ignored or even deleted since the file contains only directives and no code. (There were no events defined in our communications interface.) We'll use this file when we work through Chapter 10. The other generated file, IMVDataService.Invokes.cs, is a file we want to keep. It contains the source code for a new activity we can use in our workflow to send data to the host application. Therefore, we'll rename the file to something more useful. Type **ren IMVDataService.Invokes.cs MVDataUpdate.cs** at the command prompt, and press Enter to rename the file.

8. Because the file we just renamed is a workflow activity, we need to move it from the current directory into the MVWorkflow directory for compilation and use. At the command prompt, type **move MVDataUpdate.cs ..\..\..\MVWorkflow** and press Enter.

9. Returning to Visual Studio, we need to add the newly created MVDataUpdate.cs file to our workflow project. In the Visual Studio Solution Explorer, right-click the MVWorkflow project's tree node to activate the context menu. From there, click Add and then Existing Item to activate the Add Existing Item dialog box. Select the MVDataUpdate.cs file from the list and click the Add button. The file is now added to the MVWorkflow solution.

10. Compile the MVWorkflow project by pressing Shift+F6 or by selecting Build MVWorkflow from the Visual Studio Build menu, and fix any compilation errors that might have occurred. After you have a successful compilation, check to be sure the *MVDataUpdate* activity was added to the Visual Studio ToolBox. To check, open Workflow1.cs in the visual designer by selecting Workflow1.cs in the Solution Explorer window and clicking the View Designer toolbar button. Once Workflow1.cs is open in the visual designer, open the ToolBox and look for the *MVDataUpdate* activity. (It would typically appear at the top of the ToolBox.)

> **Note**   If for some reason MVDataUpdate wasn't added to the Visual Studio ToolBox, close the solution and then reopen it. Closing and then opening the MVDataChecker solution after the MVWorkflow assembly has been successfully created causes the *MVDataUpdate* activity to be automatically installed into the Visual Studio Toolbox.

We now have a ready-made activity we can use to send data to our host application. The activity's base class is *CallExternalMethod*, and it's designed to trigger calls outside the workflow's execution environment. Let's drop this activity into a workflow and see it in action.

Adding and configuring the communication workflow activity

1. We need to open and edit our workflow process. From the Visual Studio Solution Explorer, select Workflow1.cs in the MVWorkflow project and click the View Designer toolbar button to load it into the workflow visual designer. The workflow comes pre-loaded with two activities: a *Delay* activity that is used to simulate the latency involved in making the data request and a *Code* activity that creates and populates a *DataSet* based on the name of the driver in question.

2. Open the Visual Studio Toolbox, and locate the *MVDataUpdate* activity.

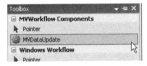

3. Drag the activity to the workflow visual designer's surface, and drop it after the *Code* activity so that it's executed sequentially after the *Code* activity.

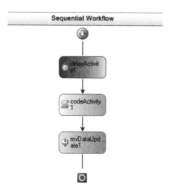

4. Our workflow is complete from the workflow visual designer's perspective. It's time now to write a small amount of code to hook things up. So select Workflow1.cs in the MVWorkflow project, and click the View Code toolbar button. Look for the *GenerateMVData* method in the *Workflow1* class. This method is the method *codeActivity1* executes, and here you see the calls to the helper methods *GenerateVehicleTable* and *GenerateViolationTable* to create and fill the *DataSet* to return. (In reality, you would make a call to some external service for driver information, but we're simulating that.) Following the creation of the *DataSet*, we need to add the following lines of code to return the *DataSet* to the host:

```
// Assign the DataSet we just created as the host data
mvDataUpdate1.mvData = ds;
```

With the assignment of the *DataSet* we're returning, we've completed the development of our workflow, as well as the tools we need to ship the *DataSet* to the host application. But what does our host application need to do to receive the data? Let's find out.

Receiving Workflow Data Within the Host Application

Let's now turn to our main application. The basic workflow housekeeping we've seen so far in the book has already been added to the sample simply because we've seen it before and the chapter would expand tenfold if we created the application from scratch. I'd rather concentrate on the workflow aspects we're examining in this chapter. So the workflow factory creates an instance of the workflow runtime, and we even kick off a workflow instance when the Retrieve MV Data button is clicked. What we'll do now is modify the application to use the bridging classes we created in the "Creating External Data Services" section in this chapter.

> **Note**   Feel free to look the application code over, however. Although this is a simplified example, this application is still a full-fledged Windows Forms application and shows how workflow is handled and multithreaded operations are performed (such as when updating controls).

To marry the *DataSet* the workflow will return to our user interface, we need to register our workflow instance with the connector class in our bridge code (so that we receive the correct *DataSet*). We also need to hook the *MVDataUpdate* event so that our application knows when to retrieve the data. To facilitate this, we'll add a little code to the event handler for the Retrieve MV Data button, as well as add a new event handler for *MVDataUpdate*.

> **Note**   If you're not familiar with *anonymous methods*, now is a good time to briefly review them! We'll be using one shortly. See http://msdn2.microsoft.com/en-us/library/0yw3tz5k.aspx for assistance.

Adding the workflow external data service to our host application

1. In the Visual Studio Solution Explorer, open the code for Form1.cs in the code editor. Select Form1.cs and click the View Code toolbar button to do so.

2. Scroll down through the source code until you find the *cmdRetrieve_Click* method. There is already code in this method to initiate a workflow instance in response to the button click, but we need to insert some code between where we create the workflow instance and where we start its operation. Following the call to *_workflowRuntime.CreateWorkflow*, add the following lines of code. (If you are cutting and pasting the code, make sure you type the equal sign (=) in the last line of code below, then use the Tab key so that Visual Studio will create a stub for the event handler for you.)

```
// Hook returned data event.
MVDataService.WorkflowMVDataService dataService =
        MVDataService.WorkflowMVDataService.CreateDataService(
                                _workflowInstance.InstanceId,
                                _workflowRuntime);
dataService.MVDataUpdate +=
            new EventHandler<MVDataService.MVDataAvailableArgs>(
                                dataService_MVDataUpdate);
```

3. The code we just added references the *WorkflowMVDataService MVDataUpdate* event by adding a new event handler. In the *Form1* class, add the following event handling code to the *dataService_MVDataUpdate* event handler Visual Studio just created, replacing the existing "not implemented" exception. (Note the anonymous method to be sure the *ListView* controls are updated on the proper thread.)

```
IAsyncResult result = this.BeginInvoke(
    new EventHandler(
        delegate
        {
            // Retrieve connection. Note we could simply cast the
            // sender as our data service, but we'll instead be sure
            // to retrieve the data meant for this particular
            // workflow instance.
            MVDataService.WorkflowMVDataService dataService =
                MVDataService.WorkflowMVDataService.
                GetRegisteredWorkflowDataService(e.InstanceId);

            // Read the motor vehicle data.
            DataSet ds = dataService.Read();

            // Bind the vehicles list to the vehicles table.
            ListViewItem lvi = null;
            foreach (DataRow row in ds.Tables["Vehicles"].Rows)
            {
                // Create the string array
                string[] items = new string[4];
                items[0] = (string)row["Plate"];
                items[1] = (string)row["Make"];
                items[2] = (string)row["Model"];
                items[3] = (string)row["Color"];

                // Create the list item
                lvi = new ListViewItem(items);

                // Add to the list
                lvVehicles.Items.Add(lvi);
            } // foreach

            // Bind the violations list to the violations table.
            foreach (DataRow row in ds.Tables["Violations"].Rows)
            {
                // Create the string array
                string[] items = new string[4];
                items[0] = (string)row["ID"];
                items[1] = (string)row["Plate"];
                items[2] = (string)row["Violation"];
                items[3] =
                    ((DateTime)row["Date"]).ToString("MM/dd/yyyy");

                // Create the list item
                lvi = new ListViewItem(items);

                // Add to the list
                lvViolations.Items.Add(lvi);
            } // foreach
        } // delegate
    ), null, null
); // BeginInvoke
this.EndInvoke(result);

// Reset for next request.
WorkflowCompleted();
```

That's it! The application is now complete. Press F6 to compile, and F5 to execute the application. When you click the Retrieve MV Data button, the selected driver's name is issued to the workflow instance. When the *DataSet* is built, the workflow instance fires the *MVDataUpdate* event. The host application code intercepts that event, retrieves the data, and binds it to the *ListView* controls.

A critical thing to note in the code for that last step is that we called *WorkflowMVDataService*'s static *GetRegisteredWorkflowDataService* method to retrieve the data service containing the *DataSet*. We then used the data service's *Read* method to pull the *DataSet* into our host application's execution environment so that we could perform the data binding.

Invoking External Workflows with *InvokeWorkflow*

Here is a question for you: if you have an executing workflow, can that workflow execute a second workflow?

The answer is yes! There is an activity, *InvokeWorkflow*, that's used to start a secondary workflow. Let's briefly take a look at this activity by way of an example. We'll create a new sample console application that starts a workflow that merely writes a message to the console. After writing this message, the workflow instance starts a second workflow instance that also writes a message, graphically showing us that both workflows executed.

Invoking a secondary workflow

1. Although we could build a fancy demonstration application, we'll revert to using a simple console application as we've done in previous chapters. As you've done throughout the book, decide whether you want to follow along using a solution that's completed or whether you want to create the workflow as you go using a started but incomplete application. The completed version of WorkflowInvoker is in the \Workflow\Chapter8\WorkflowInvoker Completed\ directory, while the incomplete version is in the \Workflow\Chapter8\WorkflowInvoker\ directory. Whichever version you choose, simply drag the .sln file onto an executing copy of Visual Studio and it will load the solution for editing.

2. After Visual Studio has loaded the WorkflowInvoker solution for editing, add a new sequential workflow library project to the WorkflowInvoker solution by clicking File, Add, and then New Project from the Visual Studio menu and then choosing the Workflow project type and Sequential Workflow Library template in the Add New Project dialog box. Name it **Workflow1**. Visual Studio adds the new library project and opens the workflow visual designer for editing. Be sure to save the new workflow project in the \Workflow\Chapter8\WorkflowInvoker directory.

3. Next, drag a *Code* activity from the Toolbox and drop it onto the workflow design surface. In its *ExecuteCode* property, type **SayHello** and press Enter.

4. Visual Studio then automatically brings up the code editor. Locate the *SayHello* method Visual Studio just added, and within that method place the following code:

```
// Output text to the console.
Console.WriteLine("Hello from Workflow1!");
```

5. We now need to add a second workflow to execute, so repeat step 2 but substitute the name **Workflow2** for the name of the project. Repeat steps 3 and 4, but replace the message "Hello from Workflow1!" to "Hello from Workflow2!" Rename the workflow source file from workflow1.cs to workflow2.cs to avoid confusing the workflows later.

6. We want the first workflow to invoke the second one, but to do that, we need to add a reference to the second workflow. Before we can do that, we need to build Workflow1. Pressing F6 or selecting Build Solution from Visual Studio's Build menu builds everything.

7. Returning to the Visual Studio Solution Explorer, select the Workflow1 project and add a project-level reference to the Workflow2 project.

8. Return to the workflow graphical designer for *Workflow1*, and open the Toolbox again. This time, however, drag an instance of the *InvokeWorkflow* activity onto your sequential workflow's design surface.

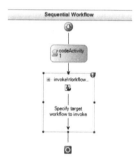

9. Looking at the properties for this new activity, we see there is a *TargetWorkflow* property we need to set. Click the *TargetWorkflow* property once to activate it, and then click its browse (...) button (the button with the three dots).

10. This activates the Browse And Select A .NET Type dialog box. Select *Workflow2* in the left pane, which displays the *Workflow2* type in the right pane. Select the *Workflow1* type (*Workflow2.Workflow1* is the fully qualified name) in the right pane and click OK.

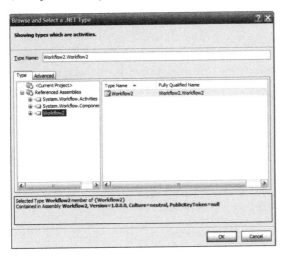

11. Visual Studio then examines the *Workflow2* workflow and displays its graphical representation inside the *InvokeWorkflow* activity in the visual workflow designer.

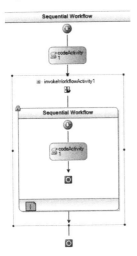

12. The workflow implementations are now complete, so we can add them as references to the main WorkflowInvoker application. From Solution Explorer, right-click the WorkflowInvoker project and select Add Reference. When the Add Reference dialog box appears, click the Projects tab. Select both Workflow1 and Workflow 2 from the list and click OK.

13. Next add the code to create and start the instance. Locate this line of code in Program.cs:

```
Console.WriteLine("Waiting for workflow completion.");
```

14. Add this code following the line of code you just located:

```
// Create the workflow instance.
WorkflowInstance instance =
    workflowRuntime.CreateWorkflow(typeof(Workflow1.Workflow1));

// Start the workflow instance.
instance.Start();
```

15. We'll now add a small amount of code to the host application simply to tell us when each workflow completes. Insert the following code in the event handler for *WorkflowCompleted*:

```
if (e.WorkflowDefinition is Workflow1.Workflow1)
    Console.WriteLine("Workflow 1 completed.");
else
    Console.WriteLine("Workflow 2 completed.");
waitHandle.Set();
```

The first workflow to complete sets the *AutoResetEvent* we're using to force the application to wait for workflow completion. We could add code to force the application to wait for both workflows, but for demonstration purposes this should suffice. If you compile and execute the WorkflowInvoker application, you'll see console output similar to what you see in Figure 8-4. If the output messages appear in a slightly different order, don't be alarmed. This is the nature of multithreaded programming...

Figure 8-4 The WorkflowInvoker application console output

If you want to continue to the next chapter, keep Visual Studio 2005 running and turn to Chapter 9, "Logic Flow Activities." It's one thing to crunch numbers, but we also need tools to make decisions, and that's the next topic.

If you want to stop, exit Visual Studio 2005 now, save your spot in the book, and watch your favorite movie on DVD. Be sure to fast-forward through any boring parts.

Chapter 8 Quick Reference

To	Do This
Design workflow/host data transfers	Create an interface with methods designed to pass the data back and forth. Be sure to add the *ExternalDataExchange* attribute, as well as the correlation attributes, as we did in the sample application.
Create the "data available" event arguments	Derive an event argument class from *ExternalDataEventArgs*, and anoint it with information you need to pass back and forth.
Create the external data service	This is a somewhat complex task in that you must write a lot of code yourself to manage the data (which can come from any number of workflow instances). But in general, you create a class (the *connector*) that manages the data (and is plugged into the workflow runtime because it manages workflow state) and another class (the *service*) that the host application (or invoking workflow) uses to hook the "data available" event and read (or write) the data.
Create the communications-based activities	With your interface in hand, run *wca.exe*. The *wca.exe* tool creates a pair of activities for you: one to send data to the external (workflow) process and one to receive data. In this chapter, we looked only at sending data, but in Chapter 17 we'll revisit this topic and build a bidirectional interface.
Receive data in your host application (or calling workflow)	Using the service class you created, hook the "data available" event and call the services "read" method.
Invoke secondary workflows	Add an instance of *InvokeWorkflow* to your workflow process, and provide the data type of the workflow to be invoked. Note you have to add a reference to the secondary workflow to accomplish this.

Chapter 9
Logic Flow Activities

After completing this chapter, you will be able to:

- Explain how to execute conditional expressions using the *IfElse* activity
- Show how the *While* activity can be used to execute loops
- Understand how the *Replicator* activity simulates a *for* loop, as well as how it's used

We're starting to piece together some of the critical components we'll need to build real-world workflows. We've seen how to execute code, both within and outside our workflow instances, and we know how to handle exceptions, suspend processing, and even terminate our workflow if things get out of hand. But certainly a major component for any computational system is the ability to make decisions based on runtime conditions. In this chapter, we begin to address workflow activities that require us to tackle if/else scenarios as well as basic looping.

Conditions and Condition Processing

By now, it probably won't surprise you to find that Windows Workflow Foundation (WF) provides activities for logical process control flow based on runtime conditions. After all, if WF provides activities to both raise and catch exceptions, why not have activities to ask questions regarding executing workflow conditions and make decisions based on those findings?

The activities we'll examine in this chapter include the *IfElse* activity, the *While* activity, and the *Replicator* activity. The *IfElse* activity is designed to test a condition and execute a different workflow path depending on the result of the test. (We actually used this activity in Chapter 1, "Introducing Microsoft Windows Workflow Foundation," when we asked whether or not a given postal code was valid when tested against a regular expression.) The *While* activity, perhaps not too surprisingly, is used to perform a *while* loop. A *for* loop, however, is accomplished using something known as the *Replicator* activity. Let's start by looking at this chapter's sample application.

 Note The conditional processing you'll do in this chapter is based on the *CodeCondition*, which means you'll write C# code to process the conditional expression. In Chapter 12, "Policy And Rules," you'll use the *RuleCondition* which uses WF rules-based processing for conditional expression evaluation. Both are equally valid. I simply chose to include *RuleCondition*, in the same chapter I discuss rules-based processing in general.

The Questioner Application

This chapter's sample application is a Windows Forms application that asks you three questions, the text for which you can modify. (The question text is stored in the application's settings property bag.) You can also indicate whether the questions are dependent or independent. You'll pass the questions and dependency status into the workflow as it begins execution.

Dependent questions will continue to be asked only if the previous questions were answered in the affirmative. For example, if you're asked, "Have you seen the document in question?" and you have not, it makes little sense to ask, "Do you approve this document?" If the questions are dependent, the first negative response returns negative for the given response as well as for all remaining question responses.

Independent questions will always be asked regardless of preceding responses. The question, "Do you like ice cream?" is unrelated to "Is it raining outside at this time?" Whether you do or do not like ice cream, the answer to that question is independent of the weather outside. Independent questions continue to be asked whether you provide a negative response to an earlier question or not.

The user interface appears as you see in Figure 9-1. If you modify the text for any of the three questions, the new question text will automatically be stored in your application settings property bag. (The same is true of the question type.) The questions are intended to generate yes/no responses so that the workflow can pass the responses back to the host application as an array of Boolean values.

Figure 9-1   The Questioner primary user interface

When you click the Execute button, the questions appear in order as message boxes with Yes and No buttons. Once the workflow has processed all the questions, it returns a Boolean array to the host application. The host application will examine the array for user-interface display purposes.

While the workflow is executing, the responses appear as blue balls (as you see in Figure 9-1). When the workflow task has completed, affirmative responses are shown as green balls and negative responses are shown as red balls. If all responses were affirmative, the "final answer" image appears as a green ball. However, if any of the three questions resulted in a negative response, the final answer appears as an "8 ball." You can see the application in action in Figure 9-2.

Figure 9-2   The Questioner application user interface during execution

The intention is for us to use this application for testing the three activities in this chapter. The first Questioner iteration will use *IfElse* activity workflow activities to decide what course of action to take (affirm or negate a response, and continue based on the dependency setting if a given response was negative). The second iteration will use the *While* activity to ask questions while questions remain to be asked. And the final iteration will use the *Replicator* activity to simulate a *for* loop to ask the questions. For each of these application iterations, we'll use the technique shown in the previous chapter to return the responses to the host application.

With that in mind, let's look at using the *IfElse* activity.

Using the *IfElse* Activity

The *IfElse* activity is designed to simulate an if-then-else conditional expression, and in fact you've used this activity in previous chapters (notably in Chapter 1, where the workflow decided whether a given postal code was valid).

The *IfElse* activity requires you to provide a conditional expression, which is actually implemented as an event handler. The event arguments, of type *ConditionalEventArgs*, have a Boolean *Result* property you set to indicate the results of the conditional expression you build into the event handler.

Depending on the *Result* value, the *IfElse* activity directs workflow execution to one of two branches. Visually, in the Microsoft Visual Studio workflow visual designer, *true* executes the path shown on the left and *false* executes the path to the right. Both branches are containers for other activities, allowing you to insert whatever workflow activities are required to process the information or application flow given the Boolean conditional value. Let's drag and drop a few of these into our sample application and give them a try.

> **Note**   As you'll probably agree after working through this section, the *IfElse* activity probably isn't the best activity you could use to model this workflow. You'll find activities better suited for this particular workflow later in the chapter. (In fact, this was intentional on my part.)

Creating the QuestionFlow workflow using the *IfElse* Activity

1. Open Visual Studio, and open the Questioner application's solution from the book samples. You'll find the solution in \Workflow\Chapter 9\IfElse Questioner. Simply click File, then Open, and then finally Project/Solution. Using the resulting Open Project dialog box, browse your computer's file system until you find Questioner.sln and click Open.

2. Scanning Visual Studio Solution Explorer, you should see a solution layout similar to the one from the previous chapter. The main application files are located in the Questioner project, while the host communication service files are located in the QuestionService project. So that you can concentrate on the workflow aspects of this application, I have already created the service interface, *IQuestionService*, and executed the *wca.exe* tool to create the necessary communication activity, *SendReponseDataToHost*. To begin, locate the QuestionFlow project and open the Workflow1.cs file for editing in the Visual Studio workflow visual designer. Select Workflow1.cs in Solution Explorer, and then click the View Designer toolbar button as you have in previous chapters.

3. When *Workflow1* is ready for editing in the workflow visual designer, drag an *IfElse* activity from the Toolbox to the designer's surface and drop it. This inserts an *IfElse* activity item into your workflow.

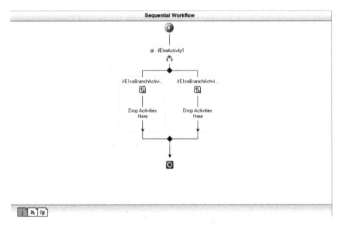

4. The exclamation mark (!) you see, outlined by the red circle, tells you that more information is required to compile your workflow. In fact, what's missing is the conditional expression itself! Select the left branch of *ifElseActivity1* to bring the activity's properties into the Visual Studio Properties pane. Select *Condition* to activate the drop-down list, and from the list select Code Condition.

> **Note**   You actually have two choices for conditional expressions: code and rules-based. We'll use the code-based conditional expression here, saving the rules-based technique for Chapter 12, "Policy Activities."

5. Expand the resulting *Condition* property, type in the value **AskQuestion1**, and press Enter. Visual Studio inserts the *AskQuestion1* event handler for you and switches to code view. For now, return to the workflow visual designer so that you can drag more activities into your workflow.

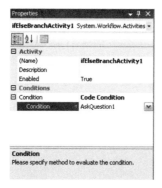

6. With the Visual Studio workflow visual designer active, drag a *CodeActivity* onto the designer's surface and drop it into the right-hand branch of *IfElseActivity1*.

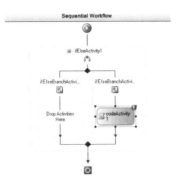

7. Assign the code activity's *ExecuteCode* property the value of **NegateQ1**. When Visual
   Studio inserts the *NegateQ1* event handler and switches to the code editor, again return
   to the workflow visual designer to drag one more activity onto the designer's surface.

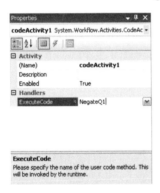

8. Repeat steps 6 and 7, but this time drop the code activity into the left branch of
   IfElseActivity1.

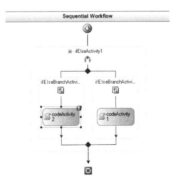

Assign its *ExecuteCode* property the value **AffirmQ1**. However, when Visual Studio
inserts the *AffirmQ1* event handler, do not switch back to the workflow visual designer.
Instead, it's time to add some code.

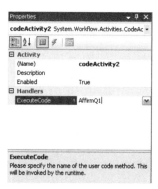

9. We now need to add some properties to the workflow class that we can assign as parameters when we start our workflow processing. Following the *Workflow1* constructor, add the following lines of code to contain the three questions the workflow will ask:

```
private string[] _questions = null;

public string[] Questions
{
    get { return _questions; }
    set { _questions = value; }
}
```

10. We also need to add the *Dependent* property, which is used to tell whether the questions are or are not independent of one other. After the code you inserted in the preceding step, add the following:

```
private bool _dependent = true;

public bool Dependent
{
    get { return _dependent; }
    set { _dependent = value; }
}
```

11. The question responses, as Boolean values, need to be stored somewhere until returned to the host application. Therefore, following the *Dependent* property you just inserted, add this field:

```
private bool[] _response = null;
```

12. The *_response* field is uninitialized, so locate the *Workflow1* constructor and add this code after the *InitializeComponent* method invocation:

```
// Initialize return vector.
_response = new bool[3];
_response[0] = false;
_response[1] = false;
_response[2] = false;
```

13. Now scan down the code file until you find the *AskQuestion1* event handler Visual Studio added for you. To this event handler, add the following lines of code:

```
// Ask the question!
DialogResult result = MessageBox.Show(Questions[0], "Questioner:",
            MessageBoxButtons.YesNo, MessageBoxIcon.Question);
e.Result = (result == DialogResult.Yes);
```

14. To the *NegateQ1* event handler, add this code:

```
// Negate answer.
_response[0] = false;

if (Dependent)
{
    // Negate remaining answers.
    _response[1] = false;
    _response[2] = false;
}
```

15. Next, locate the *AffirmQ1* event handler and add this code:

```
// Affirm answer.
_response[0] = true;
```

16. You have just added the workflow components designed to ask the first question. However, two more questions remain. For the second question, repeat steps 3 through 8 to add the *IfElse* activity to the workflow, substituting references to question 1 with references to question 2. Doing this inserts the event handlers *AskQuestion2*, *NegateQ2*, and *AffirmQ2*. The workflow visual designer will appear as follows:

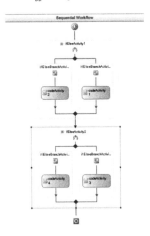

17. Now find the *AskQuestion2* event handler and add the following lines of code:

```
if (_response[0] == false && Dependent)
{
    // No need to ask!
    e.Result = false;
}
else
{
    // Ask the question!
    DialogResult result = MessageBox.Show(Questions[1], "Questioner:",
                    MessageBoxButtons.YesNo, MessageBoxIcon.Question);
    e.Result = (result == DialogResult.Yes);
}
```

18. To the *NegateQ2* event handler, add this code:

```
// Negate answer
_response[1] = false;

if (Dependent)
{
    // Negate remaining answer
    _response[2] = false;
}
```

19. And, to the *AffirmQ2* event handler, add this code:

```
// Affirm answer.
_response[1] = true;
```

20. Repeat steps 3 through 8 once again to add the third question, substituting references to the first question with references to the third question. Doing this creates the *AskQuestion3*, *NegateQ3*, and *AffirmQ3* event handlers. At this point, the workflow visual designer should appear like so:

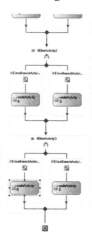

21. Locate the *AskQuestion3* event handler and insert these lines of code:

```
if (_response[1] == false && Dependent)
{
    // No need to ask!
    e.Result = false;
}
else
{
    // Ask the question!
    DialogResult result = MessageBox.Show(Questions[2], "Questioner:",
                    MessageBoxButtons.YesNo, MessageBoxIcon.Question);
    e.Result = (result == DialogResult.Yes);
}
```

22. Modify *NegateQ3* event handler by adding this code:

```
// Negate answer.
_response[2] = false;
```

23. To the *AffirmQ3* event handler, add the following:

```
// Affirm answer
_response[2] = true;
```

24. Now return to the workflow visual designer. If you move the mouse pointer to the Toolbox and allow the Toolbox to open, you should find a custom activity called *SendResponseDataToHost*. (Note that if the *SendResponseDataToHost* activity isn't in the Toolbox, compile the project and then look again.)

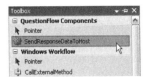

25. Drag an instance of *SendResponseDataToHost* onto the workflow visual designer, and drop it after the third question's *IfElse* activity, *ifElseActivity3*.

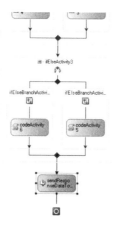

26. Because the data to be returned is simply an array of value types (Boolean values), the process is slightly different than in the previous chapter. Instead of adding a dependency property to contain the Boolean array, the *SendResponseDataToHost* activity contains the data as a field. The user interface to create the field differs from the user interface you saw in Chapter 7 (in step 8 of the "Creating a workflow using the *Throw* activity" procedure). Select the *responses* property in the Visual Studio Properties pane, and click the browse (...) button.

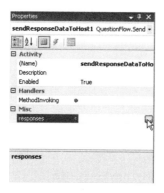

This activates the Boolean Collection Editor dialog box.

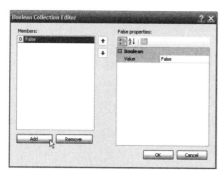

27. Click the Add button three times, leaving the default values as *False*, and then click OK. Visual Studio adds a three-element Boolean array to your code for you in the Workflow1.designer.cs file.

> **Tip**   In step 28 to follow, you'll add a *CodeActivity* to assign the *_response* field you added to *Workflow1* (in step 11) to the Boolean array we just created for this instance of *SendResponseDataToHost*. You could, however, use *SendResponseDataToHost*'s *response* property directly now that we've created it. I elected to do things this way only because it made more sense (from an illustrative standpoint) to show how to add and work with *IfElse* activity objects before dealing with the host communication activity.

28. We need to tie the response array we're using for our question responses to the value the *SendResponseDataToHost* activity will use (the property we created in steps 26 and 27). Therefore, drag a *CodeActivity* onto the workflow visual designer and drop it between the third *IfElse* activity, *ifElseActivity3,* and the *SendResponseDataToHost* activity, *sendResponseDataToHost1.*

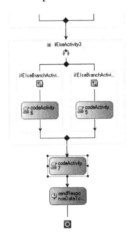

29. Enter the code activity's *ExecuteCode* property as **CopyResponse**.

30. When Visual Studio inserts the *CopyResponse* event handler and activates the code editor, insert this code:

```
// Assign outgoing data.
sendResponseDataToHost1.responses = _response;
```

31. Compile the entire solution by pressing F6, and correct any compilation errors.

The host application file has already been created, and the appropriate code has been inserted to execute the workflow as created here. Simply press F5 to execute the application. Does changing the question *Dependency* property have any effect when asking questions and providing negative responses?

Using the *While* Activity

If you look back at the preceding section, you'll note at least two things. First, you certainly did gain some experience using *IfElse* activities. And second, it took 31 separate steps to create the workflow process. There are some programmatical constructs that lend themselves nicely to if-then-else processing, but this particular application would be better suited to questions that were asked in a looping construct. And that's what we'll look at next. You'll replace the workflow you just created with another that uses a *while* loop.

The WF *While* activity uses a similar approach to the *IfElse* activity when processing conditional expressions. It fires an event to request permission to continue with the loop, and it uses *ConditionalEventArgs* to return your decision (again using the *Result* property).

However, unlike using the *IfElse* activity, when you are using the *While* activity, setting *Result* to *true* causes the loop to continue. Setting *Result* to *false* breaks the loop. Let's see how switching the conditional processing from if-then-else to a *while* loop simplifies our workflow.

Creating the QuestionFlow workflow using the *While* Activity

1. Open Visual Studio, and again open the Questioner application's solution from the book examples. In this case, you'll find the solution in \Workflow\Chapter 9\While Questioner. Click File, then Open, and then finally Project/Solution. Using the Open Project dialog box, again browse your computer's file system until you find Questioner.sln and then click Open.

2. As with the preceding section, the application is essentially complete, including the creation of the *SendResponseDataToHost* activity. What remains to be completed is the workflow processing itself. Look at the Solution Explorer pane and find the Workflow1.cs file in the QuestionFlow project. Select it in the tree control, and click the View Designer toolbar button to load it into the Visual Studio workflow visual designer.

3. When *Workflow1* is ready for editing in the workflow visual designer, drag an instance of the *While* activity from the Toolbox to the designer's surface and drop it, inserting a *While* activity item into your workflow.

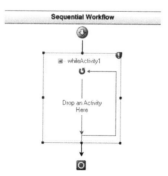

4. In a manner similar to the *IfElse* activity, select the *Condition* property for the *whileActivity1* activity to activate its drop-down list. From the drop-down list, select Code Condition.

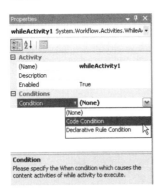

5. Expand the *Condition* property, type **TestComplete**, and press Enter to add the *TestComplete* event handler to your workflow code. After Visual Studio inserts the event handler and switches the user interface to the code editor, return to the workflow visual designer.

6. With the workflow visual designer active, drag an instance of *CodeActivity* and drop it in the center of *whileActivity1*. Assign the value **AskQuestion** to the *ExecuteCode* property, and return to the workflow visual editor when the *AskQuestion* event handler has been added.

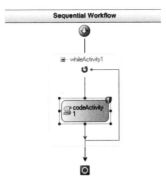

7. So that we can return the Boolean array of question responses back to the host application, follow steps 24 and 25 of the preceding section to insert an instance of *SendResponseDataToHost*. (As before, compile the application first if the *SendResponseDataToHost* activity doesn't show up in the Toolbar.) Drop the *SendResponseDataToHost* activity below *whileActivity1* so that it's executed after the *while* loop.

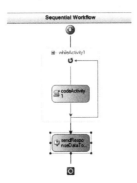

8. We also need to repeat steps 9 through 12 from the preceding section to insert the *Questions* and *Dependent* properties, as well as to create and initialize the *_response* array.

9. Following the declaration of the *_response* array, add this code to contain our loop counter:

```
private Int32 _qNum = 0;
```

10. Next let's add the condition test code we'll need to continue or terminate loop processing. Scan through the code until you find the *TestComplete* event handler, and add the following:

```
// Check for completion.
if (_qNum >= Questions.Length)
{
    // Assign outgoing data.
    sendResponseDataToHost1.responses = _response;
```

```
        // Done, so exit loop.
        e.Result = false;
    }
    else
    {
        // Not done, so continue loop.
        e.Result = true;
    }
```

11. The last bit of code we require is the code to actually ask the questions. In the Workflow1.cs file, you should find the *AskQuestion* event handler. Add the following code to the *AskQuestion* event handler. If the question's response is no and the *Dependent* property is *true*, all remaining questions are negated and the loop counter is advanced such that the next completion test (in *TestComplete*) will cause the *while* loop to terminate.

```
// Ask the question!
DialogResult result = MessageBox.Show(Questions[_qNum], "Questioner:",
                    MessageBoxButtons.YesNo, MessageBoxIcon.Question);
_response[_qNum] = (result == DialogResult.Yes);

// Check response versus dependency
if (!_response[_qNum] && Dependent)
{
    // Negate remaining questions
    while (_qNum < Questions.Length)
    {
        // Negate this question
        _response[_qNum] = false;

        // Next question
        ++_qNum;
    } // while
} // if
else
{
    // Set up for next iteration
    ++_qNum;
} // else
```

12. Repeat steps 28 through 30 of the preceding section to tie in a *Code* activity you will use to assign the return value array. (Drop the *Code* activity between the *While1* activity and the *SendResponseDataToHost1* activity.)

13. Compile the solution by pressing F6. If you find that any compilation errors are present, correct them and recompile.

If you take a moment to compare the screen shot from step 7 in this section to the image from step 28 in the preceding section, it's easy to see that using the *While* activity (at least for this scenario) simplifies the workflow processing tremendously. The entire workflow wouldn't even fit in the graphic for the preceding section's image for step 28!

If there is a workflow-equivalent *while* loop, could there also be a workflow-equivalent *for* loop? In fact, there is. It's the *Replicator* activity, and it happens to be the next topic of discussion.

Using the *Replicator* Activity

It would be incorrect to say that the *Replicator* activity is equivalent to a *for* loop in C# processing terms. The C# Language Specification 1.2 tells us the *for* loop in C# looks like the following:

```
for ( for-initializer ; for-condition ; for-iterator ) embedded-statement
```

embedded-statement is executed until the *for-condition* evaluates to *true* (if omitted, it's assumed to be *true*), beginning with *for-initializer* and executing *for-iterator* for every iteration. There is *nothing* mentioned regarding replication in any of the C# *for* statement components. With replication, we envision a cookie-cutter software factory that stamps out exact replicas of the original code. C# *for* loops don't operate in this fashion.

In fact, the cookie-cutter concept isn't terribly far off the mark when looking at WF's equivalent *for* loop activity. If you're familiar with ASP.NET, you might have used the *Repeater* control (a favorite of mine). The ASP.NET *Repeater* control accepts an item template (and alternatively, an alternating item template) and replicates it as many times as required, depending on the number of items in the data object to which it is bound.

The *Replicator* activity is similar to the ASP.NET *Repeater* control in that it binds to an *IList*-based data source and replicates its embedded (single) child activity, with one child activity instance per element in the *IList*-based data source. Yet the *Replicator* activity is similar to a C# *for* statement in some respects because it allows a loop initialization event (similar to *for-initializer*), a loop completion event (such as when *for-iterator* is compared with *for-condition*), and a loop continuation event (similar to *for-condition*). It provides events to indicate the creation of a replicated (*embedded-statement*) child activity, so that you can individualize the data binding, and it fires an event for child activity completion so that you can perform any cleanup or housekeeping tasks on a per–child activity instance basis.

In a nutshell, the *Replicator* activity accepts—and requires—a single child activity, which can be a container activity (such as the *Sequence* activity), and it fires an initialization event to kick things off. During the initialization event, you can bind an *IList*-based collection to the *Replicator* activity's *InitialChildData* property.

The *Replicator* activity then replicates the child activity you provided to match the number of items in your *IList*-based collection. These child activity instances can then be executed sequentially or in parallel (by setting the *ExecutionType* property). The *UntilCondition* event fires before each child activity is executed, and you tell the *Replicator* activity to continue execution by setting the *ConditionalEventArgs Result* property to *false* (*true* terminates the loop) when handling *UntilCondition*. Table 9-1 outlines the *Replicator* activity properties we need to be concerned with, while Table 9-2 lists the events we need to handle when using the *Replicator* activity in our workflows.

Table 9-1 *Replicator* **Activity Properties**

Method	Purpose
ExecutionType	Gets or sets the *ExecutionType* (the enumeration) for the *Replicator* activity. The *ExecutionType* enumeration contains the values *Parallel* and *Sequence*.
InitialChildData	Gets or sets a list of child activity data. This property is similar to the data-binding properties found in other .NET technologies, and in fact the object assigned to this property must be based on *IList*. The *Replicator* activity creates child activity instances for each of the items in the *IList*-based collection assigned to this property.

Table 9-2 *Replicator* **Activity Events**

Method	Purpose
ChildCompletedEvent	Fired when the child activity instance of the *Replicator* activity has completed. This is fired once for each replicated activity.
ChildInitializedEvent	Fired when the child activity instance of the *Replicator* activity has initialized. This is fired once for each replicated activity.
CompletedEvent	Fired when the *Replicator* activity has completed (that is, when all replicated instances of the child activity have completed their execution).
InitializedEvent	Fired when the *Replicator* activity begins to execute. This event is fired just once, prior to any child activity execution.
UntilCondition	Although listed in much of the WF documentation as a property, *UntilCondition* represents an event handler in much the same way the *ExecuteCode* property represents an event handler to execute the code associated with a *CodeActivity*. This event is fired prior to the execution of each child activity instance. The *Conditional-EventArgs* event arguments control the continued execution of the loop. Assigning *Result* a value of *false* allows the next child activity to execute. Assigning *Result* a *true* value causes the *Replicator* activity to stop the execution of all subsequent child activities.

Although Tables 9-1 and 9-2 are useful in describing the properties and events the *Replicator* activity exhibits, I think a diagram is also helpful to show the timing. Figure 9-3 provides you with a basic flowchart showing which events are fired and at what point. (I can hardly believe I worked so hard to learn Unified Modeling Language only to provide you with a *flowchart!*)

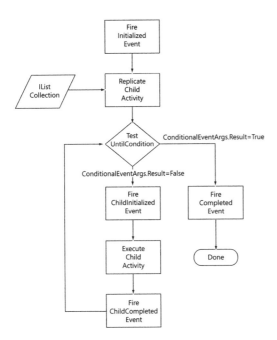

Figure 9-3   The Replicator activity event sequencing flowchart

The *IList*-based collection you see in Figure 9-3 is assigned to the *InitialChildData* property, either before or during the processing of the *Initialized* event. The flowchart also doesn't illustrate the fact that the replicated child activities (one for each element in the *IList*-based collection in *InitialChildData*) can be executed sequentially or in parallel, depending on the *ExecutionType* property setting.

How do you actually use the *Replicator* activity? From the description so far, it sounds a great deal more complicated than it really is. In fact, the mechanics aren't very different than for other activities. Drag an instance onto the workflow visual designer, assign values for the various event handlers, and drag a single child activity into the center of the *Replicator* activity. This single child activity, like the *Replicator* activity itself, can be a container (such as a *Sequence* activity), so more than one activity can in fact be executed. With these tables and figures in mind, let's rebuild the Questioner application using the *Replicator* activity.

Creating the QuestionFlow workflow using the *Replicator* Activity

1. If you've not already done so, open Visual Studio and open the Questioner application's solution from the \Workflow\Chapter 9\Replicator Questioner. Click File, then Open, and then finally Project/Solution. Using the Open Project dialog box, browse until you find Questioner.sln and click Open.

2. As with both preceding sections, the application is once again essentially complete so that you can concentrate on the workflow aspects. Select the Workflow1.cs file in Solution Explorer's tree control, and click the View Designer toolbar button to load it into the Visual Studio workflow visual designer.

3. When *Workflow1* is ready for editing in the workflow visual designer, drag an instance of *Replicator* from the Toolbox to the designer's surface and drop it. This, of course, inserts an instance of the *Replicator* activity into your workflow.

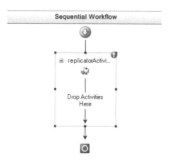

4. In the Visual Studio Properties pane, select the *Initialized* property and enter **InitializeLoop**. Visual Studio inserts the event handler in your code and shifts you to the code editor. Return to the workflow visual designer so that you can continue setting properties.

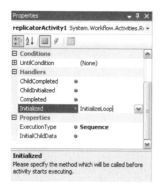

5. For the *Completed* property, enter **LoopCompleted** to add the *LoopCompleted* event handler to your workflow code. Again return to the workflow visual designer.

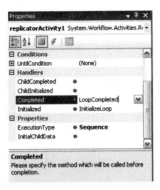

6. In the text area for the *ChildInitialized* property, enter **PrepareQuestion**. The *PrepareQuestion* event handler will be added to *Workflow1*'s code base. Return to the workflow visual designer.

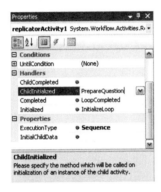

7. Next establish the *ChildCompleted* event handler by entering **QuestionAsked** next to the *ChildCompleted* property. Return to the workflow visual designer.

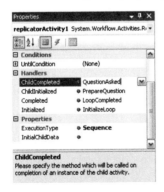

8. So that the loop terminates after asking all the questions (or when the questions are dependent and the user responded negatively), add an event handler by selecting the *UntilCondition* property and opening the selection list. Select Code Condition.

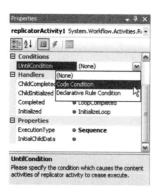

9. For the *UntilCondition*'s *Condition* property, enter **TestContinue**. Once again return to the workflow visual designer.

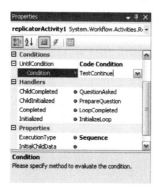

10. The *Replicator* activity *replicatorActivity1* requires a single child activity. Therefore, from the Toolbox drag a *Code* activity and drop it into *replicatorActivity1*. Designate its *ExecuteCode* property to be **AskQuestion**.

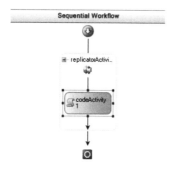

11. For the final task in the workflow visual designer, drag an instance of *SendResponseDataToHost* onto the designer's surface and drop it below *replicatorActivity1*. Follow steps 24 through 30 in the "Creating the QuestionFlow workflow using the *IfElse* activity" procedure shown earlier to properly configure this activity. (As before, you might need to compile the application for the *SendResponseDataToHost* activity to show up in the Toolbox.)

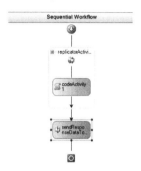

12. At this point the code file for *Workflow1* should be open for editing. If not, select it in Solution Explorer and click the View Code toolbar button.

13. Because we modified the various *replicatorActivity1* properties, Visual Studio added several event handlers. It's time to complete those as well as provide the other supporting code the workflow will require. To start, follow steps 9 through 12 in the "Creating the QuestionFlow workflow using the *IfElse* Activity" procedure to add the basic properties the workflow will require to begin processing questions.

14. The *Replicator* activity requires an *IList*-based collection of items on which to base the replication of its child activity. We have an array of questions we can use because the basic array type is based on *IList*. However, if we simply hand the replicated activity the question text, how will we return the result? There is no direct tie between the question text and the question number. Without that, we can't assign the Boolean return value within the returned array. Therefore, we'll change the rules slightly and create a new array—an array of integers that represent element offsets—into the question text array. It's this integer array we'll hand to the *Replicator* activity. The replicated child activity, then, will have access to the question number it is to ask, giving it an index into both the question text array and the Boolean response array. To do this, add the following code after the declaration of the *_response* array:

```
private Int32[] _qNums = null;
```

> **Note** The *Replicator* activity's *ExecutionType* defaults to *Sequence*, and it's a good thing too. This technique wouldn't work if the questions were asked in parallel. (The questions could potentially be asked out of sequence.)

15. The *_qNums* array is clearly uninitialized and must be initialized somewhere to be useful. The best place to do this is at the point the questions are provided to the workflow. Locate the code for the *Questions* property, and modify the *set* accessor so it looks like the following:

```
public string[] Questions
{
    get { return _questions; }
    set
    {
        // Save question values
        _questions = value;

        // Create new question number array
        _qNums = new Int32[_questions.Length];
        for (Int32 i = 0; i < _questions.Length; i++)
        {
            // Assign this question number to the array
            _qNums[i] = i;
        } // for
    }
}
```

16. To demonstrate the use of all the *Replicator* activity events, add the following lines of code after the declaration of the *_qNums* array:

```
private Int32 _currentQuestion = -1;

private bool _currentQuestionResponse = false;
```

17. With the supporting code in place, scan the code file for the *InitializeLoop* event handler and add this code to initialize *InitialChildData*:

```
replicatorActivity1.InitialChildData = _qNums;
```

> **Note** You could have assigned *InitialChildData* directly through the workflow visual designer if there was a *Workflow1* property to bind to. However, because the *Replicator* activity is using an internally generated array (*_qNums*), you have to assign *InitialChildData* in the *InitializeLoop* event handler as shown here.

18. To the *LoopCompleted* event handler, add this line of code to return the question responses:

```
sendResponseDataToHost1.responses = _response;
```

19. Now we turn our attention to the child *Code* activity that will execute as many times as we have questions to ask. Before one of the questions is asked, the *Replicator* activity will fire the *ChildInitialized* event. We'll handle that event and extract from the event arguments the question number we're to ask. Later, when the *CodeActivity* executes, it'll ask the currently active question as assigned here. Therefore, add the following code to the *PrepareQuestion* method (the event handler for the *ChildInitialized* event):

```
_currentQuestion = (Int32)e.InstanceData;
```

20. We need to take a similar approach when storing the response from the child *Code* activity. Locate the *QuestionAsked* event handler (which handles the *Replicator* activity *ChildCompleted* event), and add this code:

```
_response[_currentQuestion] = _currentQuestionResponse;
```

21. Editing the *Replicator* activity's *UntilCondition* is next. Look for the *TestContinue* method, and add the code you see here. It's in *TestContinue* that the *Dependent* property is examined. If there are no more questions, the loop terminates. But if the questions are marked as dependent and the most recent response is negative, all remaining questions are marked as having negative responses and the loop terminates.

```
if (_currentQuestion >= 0)
{
    // Check dependency.
    if (!_response[_currentQuestion] && Dependent)
    {
        // Negate remaining questions.
        for (Int32 i = _currentQuestion + 1; i < Questions.Length; i++)
        {
            // Negate this question.
            _response[i] = false;
        } // for

        // Stop processing.
        e.Result = true;
    } // if
    else
    {
        // Check for complete loop.
        if (_currentQuestion == _qNums[Questions.Length - 1])
        {
            // Done.
            e.Result = true;
        } // if
        else
        {
```

```
                    // Continue processing.
                    e.Result = false;
                } // else
            } // else
        } // if
```

22. Somewhere along the way, you might expect the workflow would finally ask a question, and the time is now for that code to be inserted. Scan the code file to find the *AskQuestion* method Visual Studio added for you, and add this code:

```
// Ask the question!
DialogResult result = MessageBox.Show(Questions[_currentQuestion],
    "Questioner:", MessageBoxButtons.YesNo, MessageBoxIcon.Question);
_currentQuestionResponse = (result == DialogResult.Yes);
```

23. Compile the entire solution by pressing F6, and correct any errors that crop up.

If you press F5 to run the application and compare its behavior to the previous iterations, you should find that it functions exactly the same as the two earlier versions, at least at the user-interface level.

If you want to continue to the next chapter, keep Visual Studio 2005 running and turn to Chapter 10, "Event Activities." Pat yourself on the back...you're just about halfway through the book!

If you want to stop, exit Visual Studio 2005 now, save your spot in the book, and close it. The next chapter should be a good one...we'll deal with events and event handling.

Chapter 9 Quick Reference

To	Do This
Process if-then-else conditional branching scenarios	Drop an instance of the *IfElse* activity into your workflow process, and assign a condition event handler as well as "true" and "false" branch activities.
Process workflow activities while a given condition is true	Consider the *While* activity, and if it's appropriate, drop it into your workflow. Be sure to assign a conditional handler. Remember that assigning the *ConditionalEventArgs Result* property a *false* value exits the loop.
Replicate activities to be processed in a for-next scenario	Insert an instance of the *Replicator* activity into your workflow, keeping in mind that its single child activity can be a container activity (allowing you to process more than one activity in the looping construct). Note that you must provide an *IList*-based collection of items for the *Replicator* activity to use to replicate the child activity. There will be one child activity instance for each item in the *IList*-based collection.

Chapter 10
Event Activities

After completing this chapter, you will be able to:

- Create specific event handlers using the *HandleExternalEvent* activity
- Add delays to your workflow using the *Delay* activity
- Incorporate event-driven activities into your workflow using the *EventDriven* activity
- Use the *Listen* activity to gather event handlers
- Understand how the *EventHandlingScope* activity allows for concurrent activity execution while listening for events

With Chapter 8, "Calling External Methods and Workflows," you saw how a workflow communicates with its host application using the *CallExternalMethod* activity. When the workflow calls an external method, using a local communication service you provide, the host application receives an event. The host then processes the data and takes any appropriate actions.

The converse process involves the host application raising events to be handled by the workflow (although workflow event handling can be used for a far wider array of tasks than just host communication). In Chapter 8, I mentioned we'd revisit host/workflow communication after describing the activities that workflows used to handle events, and in this chapter we'll do just that.

Unlike other chapters so far, where I describe an individual workflow activity and then provide a small application designed to show that activity in action, this chapter will describe multiple activities and then present a single sample application. Why? Because the activities I describe here are all related and depend on one another. I can't show one and not show the others. The *Listen* activity is a container in which you find *EventDriven* activities. Inside an *EventDriven* activity, you'd expect to find a single *HandleExternalEvent* activity. And so forth. So I'll describe the activities themselves but build a single application toward the end of the chapter. The "Host to Workflow" section should tie it all together. Let's start with the workhorse *HandleExternalEvent* activity.

Using the *HandleExternalEvent* Activity

No matter where in your workflow you handle an event, and no matter in what composite activity your workflow execution finds itself when it's active and executing, when an event comes your workflow's way the *HandleExternalEvent* activity is the workflow activity that ultimately deals with the event. To me, of all the powerful features .NET itself brings to the table, .NET's ability to fire and handle events is one of the most powerful. Having your workflows process events is similarly powerful.

The *HandleExternalEvent* activity is designed to respond to workflow events based on the *IEventActivity* interface, which has three primary members: the *QueueName* property and the *Subscribe* and *Unsubscribe* methods. *QueueName* identifies the workflow queue that is waiting for the event, while the *Subscribe* and *Unsubscribe* methods are used to tell the workflow runtime that your event handler will (or will not) be accepting instances of the particular event.

The *HandleExternalEvent* activity is itself designed to be used with the *CallExternalMethod* activity (which you worked with in Chapter 8). Whereas the workflow can use the *CallExternalMethod* activity to send data to the host application, *HandleExternalEvent* is used by the workflow when data is sent from the host while the workflow is executing.

> **Note**   Keep in mind that using external data exchange isn't the only opportunity your host application has to send data to the workflow. You can always provide initialization data when you create your workflow instances. However, it is the only mechanism available for direct, local communication with your host application once the workflow is executing (in lieu of other, more indirect, means such as with File Transfer Protocol—FTP—or a Web service invocation).

Tables 10-1 and 10-2 depict some of the major properties and methods you'll work with when using the *HandleExternalEvent* activity. Note these are in addition to the methods and properties exposed by all activities (shown in Chapter 4, "Introduction to Activities and Workflow Types," in Tables 4-1 and 4-2). The properties and methods I show here are certainly not all the properties and methods available to you through this activity, but they are the ones you will commonly use.

Table 10-1   Often-Used *HandleExternalEvent* Activity Properties

Property	Purpose
CorrelationToken	Gets or sets a binding to a correlation token. We'll deal with correlation in Chapter 17, "Correlation and Local Host Communication."
EventName	The event the activity will handle. Note that if this is not set, the activity will not listen for events and host communication will not be possible. Oddly, you won't receive a validation error for omitting this property value.
InterfaceType	Gets or sets the type of the interface used for communication. The interface must be decorated with the *ExternalDataExchange* attribute. (As you might recall from Chapter 8, this is the same interface you provide to the *CallExternalMethod* activity.)

Table 10-2   Often-Used *HandleExternalEvent* Activity Method

Method	Purpose
OnInvoked	This protected method is useful for binding values found in the event arguments to fields or dependency properties within your workflow. Overriding this method (or handling the event that it fires) is your primary mechanism for retrieving the data from the event argument as the data comes in from the host. Generally, you create a custom event argument with the data embedded in the argument object itself.

In practice, although you can use the *HandleExternalEvent* activity directly from the Microsoft Visual Studio Toolbox, it's more common to use the *wca.exe* tool you saw in Chapter 8 to create classes derived from *HandleExternalEvent* that are customized for the communications interface you are using. For example, if in your interface you defined an event named *SendDataToHost*, *wca.exe* would create a new activity called *SendDataToHost* (derived from *HandleExternalEvent*) and assign for you the *EventName* and *InterfaceType*, as well as assign data bindings as specified by the event arguments you create to use with your *SendDataToHost* event. I'll provide an example of this later in the chapter.

Using *HandleExternalEvent* is easy to do. Simply place an instance of this activity in your workflow, assign the interface and event name, provide an event handler for the *Invoked* event if you'd like, and then execute your workflow. If you use *wca.exe*, you are provided with activities derived from *HandleExternalEvent* that you can drop directly into your workflow, adding bindings in the Properties window to bind the data in the event arguments with locally defined fields or dependency properties.

With a *HandleExternalEvent* activity in your workflow, all processing through the sequential flow stops while waiting for the event. In a sense, placing this activity in your workflow acts like an *AutoResetEvent* in .NET Framework programming terms. Unlike *AutoResetEvent*, the processing thread doesn't suspend (workflow queue processing is what is suspended), but it controls the flow of your workflow in much the same way *AutoResetEvent* holds processing until the event is set. It's like a door or gate that allows workflow processing to continue through its sequential path only if the event is triggered.

Using the *Delay* Activity

We've seen and used the *Delay* activity a few times so far in the book, but I've saved a more formal description until this point. Why? As it happens, the *Delay* activity implements the *IEventActivity* interface. Because of this, it's also classified as a Windows Workflow Foundation (WF) event-based activity.

The premise is simple: hand *Delay* a *TimeSpan* object, and it will delay for that duration of time. After the time duration expires, it will fire an event. You can initialize the time duration by setting a property (*TimeoutDuration*) in the Visual Studio visual workflow designer, or you can set it programmatically. There is also an event handler (*InitializeTimeoutDuration*) you can provide that is called upon when the *Delay* activity is initialized and is requesting duration information.

> **Tip**   A delay event is a close relative of a timer event. A delay fires once and is then done, while a timer fires events when the delay duration expires until the timer is shut down. WF doesn't have a built-in timer activity, but you can create one by combining the *Delay* activity with the *While* activity in very much the same way this chapter's sample application does.

HandleExternalEvent and *Delay* are *basic activities*, as opposed to *composite activities*. That is, *HandleExternalEvent* and *Delay* each perform a single function and are not containers for other activities. A common use for these activities is, as you might expect, to trigger a sequence of activities based on a single event. How would you dictate what this sequence of events might be? By using another WF activity—the *EventDriven* activity.

Using the *EventDriven* Activity

EventDriven acts like a sequential activity in that it is a composite activity that executes its contained activities in a sequential manner. That's not to say you can't insert a *Parallel* activity in the container, but activities inserted prior to and after the *Parallel* activity will be executed in sequential order. The only rule for contained activities is that the very first activity in the execution path must be an activity that handles *IEventActivity*. (*HandleExternalEvent* and *Delay* are the two WF activities that qualify.) Aside from the properties and methods the *Activity* base class provides, *EventDriven* has no other methods or properties of use. (It's simply a container.)

Unlike a sequential activity, however, *EventDriven* will not allow the contained activities to execute until the event fires and is handled by the first activity. (Remember, the first activity must handle *IEventActivity*.)

EventDriven has a second rule. The parent (containing) activity must be either *Listen*, *State*, or *StateMachineWorkflow*. You can't just drop an instance of *EventDriven* anywhere in your workflow. It has to be dropped into one of these three containers. We'll cover the *State* and *StateMachineWorkflow* activities in Chapter 14, "State-Based Workflows." But now is a great time to look at the *Listen* activity.

Using the *Listen* Activity

If saying *EventDriven* acts like a sequential activity is a reasonable statement, it's also fair to say the *Listen* activity acts like a parallel activity. *Listen* is a container for two or more *EventDriven* activities. Which of the two (or more) *EventDriven* activity paths is selected depends entirely on which one receives an event first. Once one handles an event, however, *none* of the other, parallel, *EventDriven* activity paths will be executed. Those activities cease waiting for their respective events, and the sequential execution path continues down the *EventDriven* activity that handled the event. As with the *EventDriven* activity, there are no interesting properties or methods outside those exposed by the *Activity* base class.

Note there must be a minimum of two *EventDriven* activity objects contained within the *Listen* activity, and only *EventDriven* activity objects can be placed directly in a *Listen* activity. Furthermore, *Listen* cannot be used within a state machine–based workflow. Why are these rules in place?

If WF were to allow zero or one event-driven child activities, the usefulness of the *Listen* activity is dubious. You would be better served to use an *EventDriven* activity directly. If you had zero event-driven child activities, you're not even processing events!

Banning *Listen* from state machine–based workflows might seem like an odd rule, but only until you consider the possibility of cycles. A *cycle* in state machine terms is a series of events that depend on one another to fire. In a sense, this is similar to the concept of deadlocking in multithreaded programming systems. If Event A depends on Event B firing, but Event B is waiting for Event A to fire, we have a cycle. Banning parallel event handlers is one measure the WF designers have taken to reduce the potential for such cycles in state machine–based workflows.

Using the *EventHandlingScope* Activity

Looking back at the activities we've seen so far, we have a basic activity that handles events, a delay activity that fires events, a composite activity that enables sequential flow, and a parallel flow composite activity. Would you believe there is an event-related activity that combines both sequential and parallel behavior? There is—the *EventHandlingScope* activity.

EventHandlingScope is a composite activity that is designed to contain an *EventHandlers* activity (which is, itself, a container for *IEventActivity* objects) as well as a single other non-event-based composite activity, such as *Sequence* or *Parallel*. The non-event-based composite activity continues to execute until all the events contained in the *EventHandlers* activity are handled. After all the events have fired and been handled, control passes out of the *EventHandlingScope* activity to the next activity in the workflow.

Host-to-Workflow Communication

Having introduced the activities in WF that deal with events, I can now fulfill my promise to show you the other half of the workflow/host communication scheme. From Chapter 8, you might recall that the *CallExternalMethod* activity is used by the workflow instance to send information to the host process. The "external method" that's called is actually a method you provide that is exposed by a local communications service you write. The service then takes the information destined for the host and fires an event. The event signals the availability of data, and the host can take measures to read the data from the service (which cached the data after receiving it from the workflow).

The reverse process, where the host sends data to an already-executing workflow, also involves the local communication service as well as events and the handlers responsible for dealing with those events. When you design the interface to be used for communication between host and workflow (as shown in the "Creating Service Interfaces" section in Chapter 8), the methods you add to the interface are for the workflow to use to send data to the host. Adding events to your interface allows the host to send data to the workflow *after* it has begun executing.

The sample application for this chapter will use each of the activities I've described. An *EventHandlingScope* activity will handle a "stop processing" event. While waiting for that event, a *Sequence* activity will contain a workflow process that simulates updating stock-market values. As quotes are updated, the new values are passed to the host for inclusion in the user interface (shown in Figure 10-1). The application, eBroker, doesn't actually check the current stock value for each stock "ticker symbol," which is the three- to four-character nickname representing the company that issued the stock. It calculates new values using a simple *Monte Carlo simulation*. A Monte Carlo simulation is a simulation using random numbers, similar to rolling dice to decide an outcome. The intention is to see how workflows and hosts communicate. Although it's not a minor detail, actually checking current stock-market values is a detail I'll omit for this sample.

Figure 10-1   The eBroker primary user interface

The eBroker application is able to let the workflow know that new stocks are to be checked or that existing stocks should be removed from consideration. In this case, you can add or remove stock values from the simulation using the Add and Remove buttons. Clicking Add pops up the dialog box you see in Figure 10-2. When you complete the dialog box and click OK, the new watched stock is added to the watched stock list.

Figure 10-2   Adding a new watched stock

Selecting a symbol in the ticker symbol list enables the Remove button. Clicking the Remove button removes the item from the watched stock list. The removal action is shown in Figure 10-3. The stocks you are monitoring are stored in the application's Settings file (in XML form). The next time you execute eBroker, it will "remember" your stocks and begin checking anew.

Figure 10-3   Removing an existing watched stock

In Figure 10-2, you see that the application needs to know how many shares you currently have so that it can calculate the total value of the shares you own. These figures are used to calculate the current market value. If you later want to adjust the number of shares (by buying and selling stock), select the stock in the market value list and click either Buy! or Sell! The dialog box you see in Figure 10-4 will request the number of shares you want to buy or sell, and the workflow will be notified.

Figure 10-4   Dialog box requesting number of shares to buy or sell

The Add dialog box in Figure 10-2 also requests buy and sell "trigger" amounts. The workflow contains business logic that uses these values to notify you when not you should buy or sell shares in any of the companies you are currently monitoring. If the stock price exceeds the sell trigger value, a red flag is displayed in the market list. If the stock price drops below the buy trigger value, a green flag appears. You can buy and sell shares at any time...the flags are just visual indicators. You see a couple of flags in Figure 10-5.

Figure 10-5 The eBroker user interface indicating buy/sell recommendations

> **Note** *DO NOT* think for a microsecond that the simulation I've provided here in any way truly simulates any stock market or company on the planet. The simulation is completely fabricated for demonstration purposes only.

Each of these four buttons (Add, Remove, Buy! and Sell!) fires an event to the workflow, providing the appropriate content, which includes the watched stock to add or remove and the number of shares to buy or sell (so that the total market value is accurate). There is a fifth event, *Stop*, that is used to stop the simulation from executing. This event is fired by the Quit button.

Much of the application has been written for you, allowing you to concentrate on the workflow-related aspects. Here is the bigger picture. First, you'll complete the interface the workflow and host will use for communication. Then you'll use *wca.exe* to create activities based on the *CallExternalMethod* activity and the *HandleExternalEvent* activity. With these in hand, you'll lay out the actual workflow, using each of the activities you've seen in this chapter. You'll see how the local communication service glues the host application and workflow communication process together. And finally, you'll briefly examine and add code to the eBroker user interface source file to direct it to interact with the workflow. Let's get started!

Creating the Communication Interface

We need a single method, *MarketUpdate*, to return market information to the user interface, as well as five events. The events—*AddTicker*, *RemoveTicker*, *BuyStock*, *SellStock*, and *Stop*—are used to drive the workflow. The single method and five events are plugged into an interface, which we'll build first. Everything related to the local communications service hinges on this interface.

Creating a workflow data communication interface

1. Open Visual Studio, and open the eBroker application's solution from the book samples. You'll find the solution in \Workflow\Chapter10\. Click File, Open, and then finally

Project/Solution. Using the resulting Open Project dialog box, browse your computer's file system until you find this chapter's sample and open its solution file.

> **Note**   As with the most sample applications in this book, the eBroker sample application comes in two forms: incomplete and complete. You can follow along and add code to the incomplete version, or you can open the complete version and verify that the code I mention here is in place.

2. You will find that three projects have been added to the solution. In Visual Studio Solution Explorer, expand the eBrokerService project and open the IWFBroker.cs file for editing.

3. Locate the namespace definition. After the opening brace for the *eBrokerService* namespace, add this code and then save the file:

```
[ExternalDataExchange]
public interface IWFBroker
{
    void MarketUpdate(string xmlMarketValues);

    event EventHandler<TickerActionEventArgs> AddTicker;
    event EventHandler<TickerActionEventArgs> RemoveTicker;
    event EventHandler<SharesActionEventArgs> BuyStock;
    event EventHandler<SharesActionEventArgs> SellStock;
    event EventHandler<StopActionEventArgs> Stop;
}
```

4. Compile the project by pressing Shift+F6 or by selecting Build eBrokerService from the main Visual Studio Build menu. Correct compilation errors, if any.

Don't forget the *ExternalDataExchange* attribute. Without it you cannot successfully transfer information between workflow and host using the data transfer mechanism I describe here.

Before you create the communication activities (using *wca.exe*), take a moment to open and glance through the event arguments you see in the eBrokerService project. *MarketUpdateEventArgs* is really no more than a strongly typed version of *System.Workflow.ExternalDataEventArgs*, as is *StopActionEventArgs*. These event argument classes convey no data. However, *TickerActionEventArgs* and *SharesActionEventArgs* both convey information to the workflow. *TickerActionEventArgs* carries XML representing the stock to add or remove, while *SharesActionEventArgs* carries the ticker symbol as a primary key, as well as the number of shares to buy or sell.

> **Tip**   Designing the event arguments is important because the event arguments carry data from the host to the workflow. Moreover, *wca.exe* examines the event arguments and builds bindings into the derived classes that allow you to access the data from the event arguments as if the data were intrinsic to the derived activity. Put another way, if the event argument has a property named *OrderNumber*, the class that *wca.exe* builds would have a property named *OrderNumber*. Its value would come from the underlying event's event argument and would be assigned automatically for you.

Now let's use *wca.exe* to create the communication activities.

Creating the communication activities

1. To begin, click the Start button and then the Run button to activate the Run dialog box. Windows Vista users who have not installed the Run command on the Start button can run the command prompt by selecting the All Programs button from the Start menu. When the programs appear, select Accessories and then Command Prompt.

2. Type **cmd** in the Open combo box control, and click OK. This activates the Command Shell.

3. Change directories so that you can directly access the eBrokerService assembly in the book's downloaded sample code. Typically, the command to type is as follows: **cd "\Workflow\Chapter10\eBroker\eBrokerService\bin\Debug"**. However, your specific directory might vary.

4. As you did in Chapter 8, type the following at the command-line prompt (including the double quotes): **"<%Program Files%>\Microsoft SDKs\Windows\v6.0 \Bin\Wca.exe" /n:eBrokerFlow eBrokerService.dll**. (Note that **<%Program Files%>** represents the location of your Program Files directory, typically **"C:\Program Files"**.) Press the Enter key.

5. *wca.exe* loads the assembly it finds in eBrokerService.dll and scans the interfaces it locates for one decorated with the *ExternalDataExchange* attribute, which in this case is *IWFBroker*. The methods are parsed out and turned into classes derived from the *CallExternalMethod* activity and stored in the file named IWFBroker.Invokes.cs. The events are similarly turned into classes derived from the *HandleExternalEvent* activity and placed in IWFBroker.Sinks.cs. Rename the "invokes" file by typing this command on the command line: **ren IWFBroker.Invokes.cs ExternalMethodActivities.cs**.

6. Rename the "sinks" file by typing the following at the command-line prompt: **ren IWFBroker.Sinks.cs ExternalEventHandlers.cs**.

7. Move both files from the current directory into the workflow project's directory using this command: **move External*.cs ..\..\..\eBrokerFlow**.

8. Now return to Visual Studio and add the newly created files to the eBrokerFlow workflow project. Right-click the eBrokerFlow project name in Solution Explorer and select Add, then Existing Item. From the resulting Add Existing Item dialog box, select the files to add and then click Add. Be sure to add both ExternalMethodActivities.cs and ExternalEventHandlers.cs to the project.

9. Compile the eBrokerFlow project by pressing Shift+F6, and fix any compilation errors that might have occurred. Once you have a successful compilation, verify that Visual Studio placed the custom activities (in the C# files you just loaded) into the Toolbox. To do this, open Workflow1.cs for editing in the visual designer by selecting the file and then clicking the View Designer toolbar button in Solution Explorer. With the workflow

loaded into the visual workflow designer, open the Toolbox and look for the custom events. You should find *AddTicker*, *BuyStock*, and so forth loaded at the head of the Toolbox tool list.

> **Note**   As a reminder, if after compiling the workflow solution the new activities don't appear in the Toolbox, closing and then opening the eBroker solution will force them to load. You'll need them in the next section.

Creating the broker workflow

1. In the eBrokerFlow project, if you didn't already open Workflow1.cs for editing in the visual designer, do so now. Select the file in Solution Explorer and click the View Designer button on the toolbar.

2. To begin the workflow, insert a *Code* activity that will be used to assign the desired time duration to a *Delay* activity (which you'll insert later), as well as to initialize some internal data structures. Drag an instance of the *Code* activity onto the visual workflow designer's surface. Once you've done this, type **Initialize** into the *ExecuteCode* property to create the *Initialize* event handler in the workflow code. After Visual Studio inserts the event handler, return to the workflow visual designer to continue adding activities.

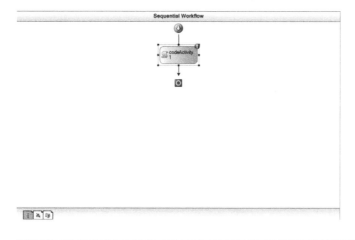

> **Note**   Although the user interface doesn't allow you to change this, there is a setting for a delay in the workflow that governs the *Delay* activity in this step. This delay represents the time elapsed between successive stock value queries. In reality, you'd not check more often than every 15 or 20 minutes, if that often. But to see the values actually shift and change, the delay between the simulated stock-market value checks is set to 7 seconds. The delay value is stored in Settings.

3. Next drag an instance of *EventHandlingScope* onto the visual workflow designer's surface and drop it.

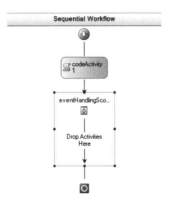

4. Remember that you need to provide an event handler as well as a child activity for *EventHandlingScope* to execute while it waits for the event. Let's set up the event handler first. To access the event handlers, move the mouse pointer to the tiny rectangular icon below the first *e* in *eventHandlingScope1*. (The rectangle is known as a "Smart Tag.")

The Smart Tag is transformed into a larger, darker rectangle with a down arrow.

Click the down arrow to activate a small window with four icons: View EventHandling-Scope, View Cancel Handler, View Fault Handlers, and View Event Handlers.

Click the rightmost icon to activate the Event Handlers view. The user interface you see is a lot like the user interface associated with fault handlers that you saw in Chapter 7, "Basic Activity Operations."

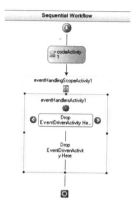

Drag an instance of the *EventDriven* activity onto the visual workflow designer's surface and drop it into the center rectangle (where you see the text "Drop Event Driven Activity Here").

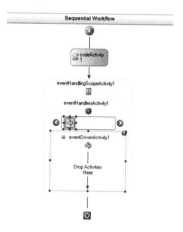

5. Now return to the Toolbox and look for the *Stop* activity in the eBrokerFlow Components section. Drag an instance of this activity onto the visual workflow designer's surface, and drop it into the *EventDriven* activity you added in the preceding step. If you want to wait for multiple events, you can drag and drop them at this time. In our case, only the *Stop* event is desired.

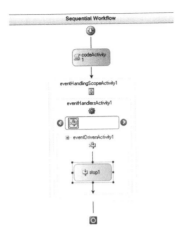

6. You've just added the event that the *EventHandlingScope* activity will wait for to cease execution (conveniently named "Stop"). Next you need to add the child activity that *EventHandlingScope* will execute while waiting for the *Stop* activity to fire. To do this, you need to return to *eventHandlingScopeActivity1*'s event handling scope view by repeating the first part of step 4. However, instead of selecting the right icon, select the left icon.

7. Once you click the leftmost icon ("View EventHandlingScope") and are presented with the *EventHandlingScope* activity's container-based user interface, drag an instance of the *While* activity onto the visual workflow designer's surface and drop it in the center of your *EventHandlingScope* activity.

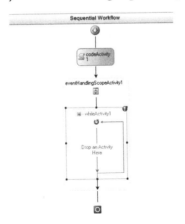

8. Assign its *Condition* property to be a Code Condition, rather than a Declarative Rule Condition, and assign the event handler the name **TestContinue**. Once Visual Studio

adds the *TestContinue* event handler, return to the visual workflow designer to add more activities.

9. The *While* activity accepts only a single child activity, so drop an instance of the *Sequence* activity into the *While* activity you just placed in your workflow.

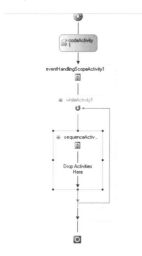

10. You need a *Code* activity at this point to perform the Monte Carlo stock-value simulation, so drag an instance of *Code* onto the designer's surface and drop it into the *Sequence* activity you added in the preceding step. Use the Properties window to rename it **updateMarket**.

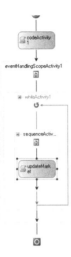

11. Assign the *updateMarket Code* activity's *ExecuteCode* property to be *UpdateMarketValues*. After Visual Studio adds the method and switches you to the code editor, return to the visual workflow designer to continue laying out your workflow.

12. With the results of the simulation complete (after you add the code to actually perform the simulation), you need to communicate the potentially revised values to the host application. To do this, move the mouse pointer to the Toolbox and find the *MarketUpdate* activity you created from *IWFBroker* and drag it onto the designer's surface. Drop it into the *Sequence* activity following the *Code* activity you placed in the preceding step.

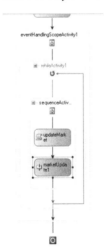

13. The *MarketUpdate* activity needs to send a small XML snippet to the host. To do that, it must bind to the field or property that, at the time, contains the XML it will forward. To do this, select the *xmlMarketValues* property in the Visual Studio Properties pane and click the Browse (...) button to activate the Bind 'xmlMarketValues' To An Activity's Property dialog box. Click the Bind To A New Member tab, click Create Property, and

type **Updates** in the New Member Name field. Click OK. Visual Studio then adds the dependency property *Updates*.

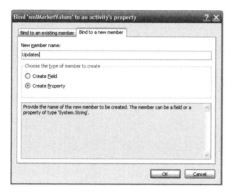

14. So that you can handle the events coming from the host, drag an instance of the *Listen* activity onto the designer's surface and drop it into the *Sequence* activity.

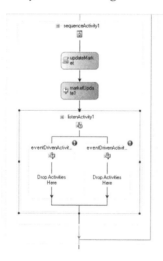

15. If you recall, the *IWFBroker* interface specified five events. One of them, *Stop*, you've already used, leaving four more to handle. The *Listen* activity presents only two *EventDriven* activity containers by default, but adding more is easy. Simply drag and drop three more *EventDriven* activity instances into the *Listen* activity you placed in the preceding step. Why add three more and not just two? Because the fifth *EventDriven* activity contains a *Delay* activity that acts as a timer. When the delay expires, the *Listen* activity releases the workflow thread. The *While* activity then tests the condition, which later will always be set to return *true*, leaving the *While* loop to loop forever. The market values are updated and communicated to the host. The *Listen* activity then waits for another round of host events.

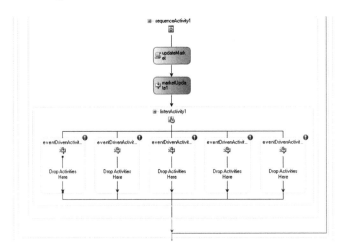

16. Into the rightmost *EventDriven* activity, drag and drop a *Delay* activity. Name it **updateDelay** using the Properties pane.

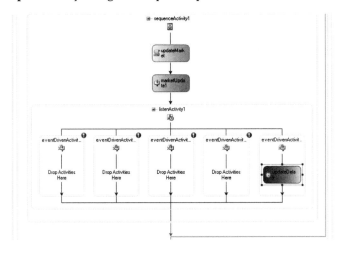

17. Next drag an instance of *SellStock*, from eBrokerFlow, onto the designer's surface, and drop it into the next rightmost *EventDriven* activity.

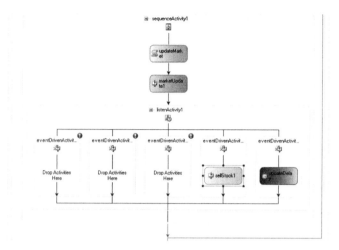

18. Select the *NumberOfShares* property in the Visual Studio Properties pane, and click the browse (...) button to again activate the Bind 'NumberOfShares' To An Activity's Property dialog box. Click the Bind To A New Member tab, click Create Field, and type **_sharesToSell** in the New Member Name field. Click OK. Visual Studio then adds the field *_sharesToSell*.

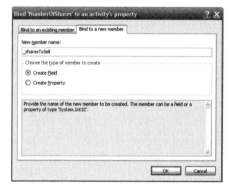

Note   I chose to create *_sharesToSell* as a field instead of as a dependency property simply because the field is never accessed outside the *Workflow1* class. The XML-based market values are provided to the host, however, and should be exposed to outside access.

19. The *Symbol* property must also be bound. Follow the same procedure as in the preceding step, but name the field *_tickerToSell*.

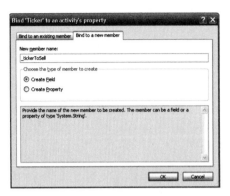

20. To actually perform the stock sale, drag an instance of the *Code* activity and drop it below the *SellStock* event handler. Into its *ExecuteCode* property, type **SellStock**. Once the code for *SellStock* is added, return to the visual workflow designer.

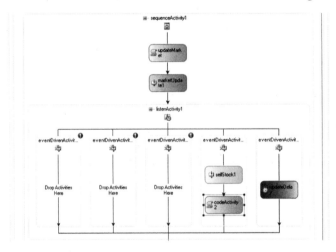

21. Now let's buy some stock. Drag a *BuyStock* event handling activity (again from eBrokerFlow) onto the designer's surface, and drop it into the middle *EventDriven* activity.

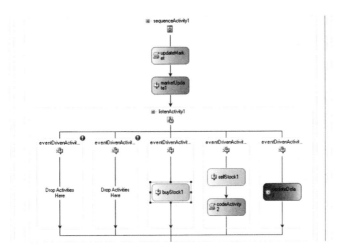

22. Bind the *BuyStock* activity's *NumberOfShares* property to a new field, *_sharesToBuy*, using the method outlined in step 18. Bind its *Symbol* property to a new field, *_tickerToBuy*, as you did in step 19.

23. Just as you needed a *Code* activity to sell stock, so will you need a *Code* activity to buy stock. Repeat step 20 and add a new *Code* activity, naming its *ExecuteCode* method **BuyStock**.

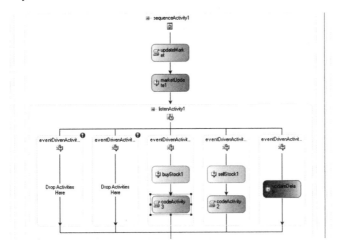

24. Repeat steps 17 through 20 two more times, adding the *RemoveTicker* and *AddTicker* events to the *Listen* activity. The *RemoveTicker* activity should have its *TickerXML* property bound to a new **_tickerToRemove** field, while the *Code* activity for the *RemoveTicker* event should have its *ExecuteCode* property assigned to be **RemoveTicker**. Similarly, *AddTicker* should have its *TickerXML* property bound to *_tickerToAdd*, with the

associated *Code* activity's *ExecuteCode* property assigned to be **AddTicker**. The completed *Listen* activity appears as you see here.

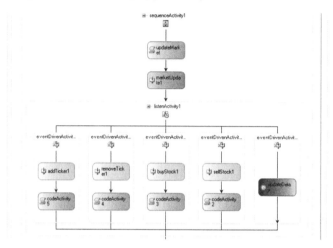

25. Compile your workflow by pressing Shift+F6, and correct any errors before adding code. The visual aspects of the workflow development are now complete.

26. Open the Workflow1.cs file for editing within Visual Studio.

27. Visual Studio added quite a bit of code for you, so first locate the Workflow1 constructor and insert this code following the constructor. The code you are inserting you probably recognize as initialization code. When the workflow is started, you'll pass the workflow a dictionary of watched stock items contained in a collection of *Tickers* items keyed by the stock ticker symbol, such as "CONT." You also need to provide the polling interval, which is the amount of time the workflow waits before rechecking the stock-market values.

```
private Dictionary<string, eBrokerService.Ticker> _items =
    new Dictionary<string, eBrokerService.Ticker>();

private string _tickersXML = null;

public string TickersXML
{
    get { return _tickersXML; }
    set { _tickersXML = value; }
}

private TimeSpan _interval = TimeSpan.FromSeconds(7);

public TimeSpan PollInterval
{
    get { return _interval; }
    set { _interval = value; }
}
```

28. Next locate the *Initialize* event handler Visual Studio created for you when you added the first *Code* activity (step 2). Insert this code:

```
// Establish the market update timeout
updateDelay.TimeoutDuration = PollInterval;

// Stuff the known ticker values into the dictionary
// for later recall when updating market conditions.
eBrokerService.Tickers tickers = null;
using (StringReader rdr = new StringReader(TickersXML))
{
    XmlSerializer serializer =
        new XmlSerializer(typeof(eBrokerService.Tickers));
    tickers = (eBrokerService.Tickers)serializer.Deserialize(rdr);
} // using
foreach (eBrokerService.Ticker ticker in tickers.Items)
{
    // Add the ticker to the dictionary
    _items.Add(ticker.Symbol, ticker);
} // foreach
```

> **Tip**   I assigned the *Delay* activity's *TimeoutDuration* in this initialization method for convenience. Don't forget, though, that you could also use the *Delay* activity's *InitializeTimeoutDuration* method to make this assignment.

29. Scrolling down through the code file, find the *TestContinue* event handler the *While* activity uses to decide if it should continue looping. Insert the following code to have the *While* activity loop forever (don't worry...it will actually stop looping eventually!):

```
// Continue forever...
e.Result = true;
```

30. The next code block to insert is a lengthy one, as it forms the Monte Carlo simulation used to update the stock-market values. Find the *UpdateMarketValues* event handler associated with the *Code* activity named *updateMarket* (shown in step 10), and insert this code:

```
// Iterate over each item in the dictionary and decide
// what its current value should be. Normally we'd call
// some external service with each of our watch values,
// but for demo purposes we'll just use random values.
Random rand = new Random(DateTime.Now.Millisecond);
eBrokerService.UpdateCollection updates =
    new eBrokerService.UpdateCollection();
foreach (string key in _items.Keys)
{
    // Locate the item
    eBrokerService.Ticker item = _items[key];

    // If we're starting out, we have no current value,
    // so place the value at half the distance between the
    // buy and sell triggers.
    if (item.LastPrice <= 0.0m)
```

```csharp
{
    // Assign a price...
    decimal delta = (item.SellTrigger - item.BuyTrigger) / 2.0m;

    // The last price must be a positive value, so add
    // the delta to the smaller value.
    if (delta >= 0.0m)
    {
        // Add delta to buy trigger value
        item.LastPrice = item.BuyTrigger + delta;
    } // if
    else
    {
        // Reverse it and add to the sell trigger
        // value
        item.LastPrice = item.SellTrigger + delta;
    } // else
} // if

// Set up the simulation
decimal newPrice = item.LastPrice;
decimal onePercent = item.LastPrice * 0.1m;
Int32 multiplier = 0; // no change

// We'll now roll some dice. First roll: does the
// market value change? 0-79, no. 80-99, yes.
if (rand.Next(0, 99) >= 80)
{
    // Yes, update the price. Next roll: will the
    // value increase or decrease? 0-49, increase.
    // 50-99, decrease
    multiplier = 1;
    if (rand.Next(0, 99) >= 50)
    {
        // Decrease the price.
        multiplier = -1;
    } // if

    // Next roll, by how much? We'll calculate it
    // as a percentage of the current share value.
    // 0-74, .1% change. 75-89, .2% change. 90-97,
    // .3% change. And 98-99, .4% change.
    Int32 roll = rand.Next(0, 99);
    if (roll < 75)
    {
        // 1% change
        newPrice = item.LastPrice + (onePercent * multiplier * 0.1m);
    } // if
    else if (roll < 90)
    {
        // 2% change
        newPrice = item.LastPrice + (onePercent * multiplier * 0.2m);
    } // else if
    else if (roll < 98)
    {
```

```
                // 3% change
                newPrice = item.LastPrice + (onePercent * multiplier * 0.3m);
            } // else if
            else
            {
                // 4% change
                newPrice = item.LastPrice + (onePercent * multiplier * 0.4m);
            } // else if
        } // if
        else
        {
            // No change in price
            newPrice = item.LastPrice;
        } // else

        // Now create the update for this ticker.
        eBrokerService.Update update = new eBrokerService.Update();
        update.Symbol = item.Symbol;
        update.LastPrice = item.LastPrice;
        update.NewPrice = newPrice;
        update.Trend = multiplier > 0 ? "Up" :
            (multiplier == 0 ? "Firm" : "Down");
        update.Action = newPrice > item.SellTrigger ? "Sell" :
            (newPrice < item.BuyTrigger ? "Buy" : "Hold");
        update.TotalValue = newPrice * item.NumberOfShares;
        updates.Add(update);

        // Update the data store.
        item.LastPrice = newPrice;
} // foreach

// Serialize the data.
StringBuilder sb = new StringBuilder();
using (StringWriter wtr = new StringWriter(sb))
{
    XmlSerializer serializer =
        new XmlSerializer(typeof(eBrokerService.UpdateCollection));
    serializer.Serialize(wtr, updates);
} // using

// Ship the data back...
Updates = sb.ToString();
```

Essentially, for each update loop there is a 20 percent chance the stock value will change. If the stock value is to change, half the time it increases and half the time it decreases. It will change value by 1 percent of its current per-share price 75 percent of the time, have a 2 percent change 15 percent of the time, have a 3 percent change 7 percent of the time, and have a 4 percent change 3 percent of the time. For each loop, all watched stocks to be monitored are updated even if there is no change. The data to be sent back to the host for display is an XML string containing the ticker symbols, their current price and their calculated total value based on the number of shares purchased, the trend (up or down), and whether there is a buy or sell recommendation. The buy or sell recommendation triggers the appropriate flag (red or green), which you saw in Figure 10-5.

31. Now it's time to add code to the external event handlers, starting with *SellStock*. Locate the *SellStock* event handler, and add the following:

```
// Reduce the number of shares for the given ticker.
try
{
    // Find this ticker.
    eBrokerService.Ticker item = _items[_tickerToSell];
    if (item != null)
    {
        // Reduce the number of shares.
        item.NumberOfShares = item.NumberOfShares - _sharesToSell >= 0 ?
            item.NumberOfShares - _sharesToSell : 0;
    } // if
} // try
catch
{
    // Do nothing...we just won't have sold any.
} // catch
```

32. Scroll down once again to find the *BuyStock* event handler, and add this code:

```
// Increase the number of shares for the given ticker.
try
{
    // Find this ticker.
    eBrokerService.Ticker item = _items[_tickerToBuy];
    if (item != null)
    {
        // Increase the number of shares.
        item.NumberOfShares += _sharesToBuy;
    } // if
} // try
catch
{
    // Do nothing...we just won't have purchased any.
} // catch
```

33. *RemoveTicker* is next. Search the code file for *RemoveTicker*, and insert the following:

```
// Remove the given ticker from the watch.
try
{
    // Deserialize
    eBrokerService.Ticker ticker = null;
    using (StringReader rdr = new StringReader(_tickerToRemove))
    {
        XmlSerializer serializer =
            new XmlSerializer(typeof(eBrokerService.Ticker));
        ticker = (eBrokerService.Ticker)serializer.Deserialize(rdr);
    } // using

    // Find this ticker.
    if (_items.ContainsKey(ticker.Symbol))
    {
        // Remove it.
```

```
        _items.Remove(ticker.Symbol);
    } // if
} // try
catch
{
    // Do nothing...we just won't have removed it.
} // catch
```

34. Finally, modify *AddTicker* by inserting this code:

```
try
{
    // Deserialize
    eBrokerService.Ticker ticker = null;
    using (StringReader rdr = new StringReader(_tickerToAdd))
    {
        XmlSerializer serializer =
            new XmlSerializer(typeof(eBrokerService.Ticker));
        ticker = (eBrokerService.Ticker)serializer.Deserialize(rdr);
    } // using

    // Add the item if not already existing.
    if (!_items.ContainsKey(ticker.Symbol))
    {
        // Add it.
        _items.Add(ticker.Symbol, ticker);
    } // if
} // try
catch
{
    // Do nothing...we just won't have added it.
} // catch
```

35. If you press Shift+F6, the workflow project should compile without error.

With the workflow complete, we now need to turn our attention to the local communication service and host integration. Because we covered both of these topics in some detail in Chapter 8, I won't revisit them in their entirety here. If you open the associated files for this example, you will see code similar to what you saw in Chapter 8.

> **Note**   I mentioned the following in Chapter 8, but it's an important issue and your aware-ness of this issue should be reinforced: If you share objects or collections of objects between workflow and host application, you run the risk of introducing multithreaded data access problems since the workflow and host application will share references to the same objects. If this is an issue for your application, consider cloning the objects as they're moved between workflow and host (by implementing *ICloneable* within your data class), or use serialization techniques. For this application, I chose XML serialization.

However, I would like to touch on some of the code in the connector class, *BrokerDataConnector*. The *IWFBroker* interface is different from the sample interface we saw in Chapter 8 because of the events *IWFBroker* contains. Because the connector class must implement the interface (*Broker-DataConnector* implements *IWFBroker*, in this case), the connector must also deal with the events. However, the event implementations are nothing special, as Listing 10-1 shows you. If you look down toward the end of the listing, you'll see typical event implementations much like event implementations you might have written yourself.

Listing 10-1 BrokerDataConnector.cs completed

```csharp
using System;
using System.Collections.Generic;
using System.Text;
using System.Threading;
using System.Workflow.Activities;
using System.Workflow.Runtime;
using System.Data;

namespace eBrokerService
{
    public sealed class BrokerDataConnector : IWFBroker
    {
        private string _dataValue = null;
        private static WorkflowBrokerDataService _service = null;
        private static object _syncLock = new object();

        public static WorkflowBrokerDataService BrokerDataService
        {
            get { return _service; }
            set
            {
                if (_service == null)
                {
                    lock (_syncLock)
                    {
                        // Re-verify the service isn't null
                        // now that we're locked...
                        if (_service == null)
                        {
                            _service = value;
                        } // if
                        else
                        {
                            throw new InvalidOperationException(
                                "You must provide a service instance.");
                        } // else
                    } // lock
                } // if
                else
                {
                    throw new InvalidOperationException(
                        "You must provide a service instance.");
                } // else
            }
        }

        public string MarketData
        {
            get { return _dataValue; }
```

```
}

// Workflow to host communication method
public void MarketUpdate(string xmlMarketValues)
{
    // Assign the field for later recall
    _dataValue = xmlMarketValues;

    // Raise the event to trigger host read
    _service.RaiseMarketUpdatedEvent();
}

// Host to workflow events
public event EventHandler<TickerActionEventArgs> AddTicker;
public event EventHandler<TickerActionEventArgs> RemoveTicker;
public event EventHandler<SharesActionEventArgs> BuyStock;
public event EventHandler<SharesActionEventArgs> SellStock;
public event EventHandler<StopActionEventArgs> Stop;

public void RaiseAddTicker(Guid instanceID, string tickerXML)
{
    if (AddTicker != null)
    {
        // Fire event
        AddTicker(null,
            new TickerActionEventArgs(instanceID, tickerXML));
    } // if
}

public void RaiseRemoveTicker(Guid instanceID, string tickerXML)
{
    if (RemoveTicker != null)
    {
        // Fire event
        RemoveTicker(null,
            new TickerActionEventArgs(instanceID, tickerXML));
    } // if
}

public void RaiseBuyStock(Guid instanceID,
                          string symbol,
                          Int32 numShares)
{
    if (BuyStock != null)
    {
        // Fire event
        BuyStock(null,
            new SharesActionEventArgs(instanceID,
                                      symbol,
                                      numShares));
    } // if
}
```

```
        public void RaiseSellStock(Guid instanceID,
                                   string symbol,
                                   Int32 numShares)
        {
            if (SellStock != null)
            {
                // Fire event
                SellStock(null,
                    new SharesActionEventArgs(instanceID,
                                              symbol,
                                              numShares));
            } // if
        }

        public void RaiseStop(Guid instanceID)
        {
            if (Stop != null)
            {
                // Fire event
                Stop(null, new StopActionEventArgs(instanceID));
            } // if
        }
    }
}
```

The workflow executes the connector's *MarketUpdate* method, while the host executes the "raise" methods to fire the various events based on user inputs. Chapter 8 describes the mechanism the workflow uses to invoke the *MarketUpdate* method. To see the host invoke an event designed to ripple down to the workflow—which might or might not carry data in the event arguments—look at this code snippet. This code is used by the Quit button to exit the application.

```
private void cmdQuit_Click(object sender, EventArgs e)
{
    // Stop the processing
    // Remove from workflow
    eBrokerService.BrokerDataConnector dataConnector =
        (eBrokerService.BrokerDataConnector)_workflowRuntime.GetService(
        typeof(eBrokerService.BrokerDataConnector));
    dataConnector.RaiseStop(_workflowInstance.InstanceId);

    // Just quit...
    Application.Exit();
}
```

To fire the events that carry data to the workflow, you first retrieve the connector using the workflow runtime's *GetService* method. Note the service is cast to its appropriate type so that the "raise" methods are known and available. Once the service is retrieved, you simply call the appropriate "raise" method, sending in the information necessary to create the appropriate event arguments.

If you want to continue to the next chapter, keep Visual Studio 2005 running and turn to Chapter 11, "Parallel Activities." In Chapter 11, we take a look at parallel processing activities. If you've always wanted to multitask, this chapter's for you!

If you want to stop, exit Visual Studio 2005 now, save your spot in the book, and close it. Take a break. Just fire an *OpenBook* event when you're ready and we'll get started again.

Chapter 10 Quick Reference

To	Do This
Handle an external event, such as from the host application	Drop an instance of the *HandleExternalEvent* activity into your workflow. If you prefer, you can use *wca.exe* to build classes derived from *HandleExternalEvent* that have basic settings and properties assigned for you (via code that *wca.exe* injects as it creates the new classes).
Introduce a delay in your workflow	Drag and drop an instance of the *Delay* activity into your workflow, and set its *TimeoutDuration* value to the length of time you want to delay.
Use an event to drive workflow execution	The *EventDriven* activity is made just for this situation. When (or if) the event triggers the event handling activity you place in the *EventDriven* activity, activities that follow are executed. If the event is never fired, the trailing activities will never execute.
Handle multiple events simultaneously	Use the *Listen* activity. *Listen* gathers event handlers (two or more) and allows the code from the first event handled to drive the workflow execution path. If the event never fires, that particular path is never executed. Keep in mind the first event to fire dictates the workflow execution path. Other events, once the first event fires, are subsequently ignored.
Handle events while processing another child activity	Consider using the *EventhandlingScope* activity. *EventHandlingScope* waits for all the events to fire before exiting the activity. Meanwhile, a single child activity can execute freely. Remember that all events must fire to cause *EventHandlingScope* to release the thread to process other activities in the workflow.
Communicate data between the host process and the workflow	Create a local communication service based on an interface you design. This interface should exhibit events. The host raises the events, with the data to be transferred within custom event arguments. Event handlers in the workflow read the data from the event arguments and execute code accordingly.

Chapter 11
Parallel Activities

After completing this chapter, you will be able to:

■ Understand how *Parallel* activities execute in the workflow environment, and know how they're used

■ Synchronize data access and critical code sections within parallel execution paths

■ Use the *ConditionedActivityGroup* activity to execute activities in parallel based on conditional expressions that are evaluated before each parallel execution

Up until this point in the book, we've dealt exclusively with sequential processes. Activity A executes and transfers execution context to Activity B, and so forth. We've not looked at parallel execution paths and the complexities that typically come with that. In this chapter, we'll look at parallel activity processing and see how to synchronize access to shared information across parallel execution paths.

Using the *Parallel* Activity

Whenever I go to the grocery store for something I've run out of, it seems like there is usually only one checkout line operating. All the customers have to pass through this single line to pay for their goods. Of course, there are 14 other cash registers in this store, but nobody is there to staff them. On those rare occasions when two or more checkout lines are open, however, people and groceries move through more quickly because they're processed in parallel.

In a sense, you can do the same thing with workflow activities. There are times when you cannot perform specific activities out of order, or worse, in random order. In those cases, you must select a *Sequence* activity to house your workflow. But at other times, you might be able to lay out workflow processes that can execute at the same time (or at nearly the same time, as we'll see). For those cases, the *Parallel* activity is the choice.

The *Parallel* activity is a composite activity, but it can support *Sequence* activities only as children. (Of course, feel free to place whatever activities into the *Sequence* activities you want.) A minimum of two *Sequence* activities is required.

The child *Sequence* activities do not execute using separate threads, so the *Parallel* activity isn't a multithreaded activity. Instead, the child *Sequence* activities execute on a single thread. Windows Workflow Foundation (WF) processes an individual activity executing in one *Parallel* activity execution path until it completes before switching execution to an activity in the next parallel execution path. That is, as one activity in one branch finishes, another activity in another branch is scheduled for execution. What is not guaranteed is the order in which parallel activities are actually executed.

The effect of this is that parallel execution paths do not execute concurrently, so they're not truly executing in parallel in the multithreaded sense. (This is called *cooperative multithreading* and was last seen by Windows software developers in Windows 3.11, although it is also popular in many control systems in use today.) However, they are executed *as if* they were operating concurrently, and you should think of them as such. Execution can, and does, switch back and forth between the activities within the parallel paths. Viewing the *Parallel* activity as truly parallel is the wisest course—treat parallel activities as you would treat any multithreaded process.

> **Note**   If you need to impose order between the parallel execution paths, consider using the *SynchronizationScope* activity. I'll show you how later in this chapter.

A good question to ask at this point is "What about *Delay* activities?" As you know, *Delay* activities stop execution in a sequential workflow for the duration of their *TimeoutDuration*. Does this stop the *Parallel* activity from processing? No. The delay does cause that particular sequential workflow path to be stopped, but the other parallel paths continue processing normally.

Given all the multithreading warnings I've issued, you might think using the *Parallel* activity is challenging. In fact, though, it's very easy to use. It appears a lot like the *Listen* activity (discussed in Chapter 10, "Event Activities") in the visual workflow designer. Instead of *EventDriven* activities, you will find *Sequence* activities; otherwise, the visual representation is similar. Let's create a simple example to show the *Parallel* activity in action.

Creating a new workflow application with parallel execution

1. To quickly demonstrate the *Parallel* activity, this example uses a Windows console-based application. I took the liberty of creating for you two versions of a sample application to experiment with the *Parallel* activity: a completed version and an incomplete version. Both are found in \Workflow\Chapter11\. The ParallelHelloWorld application is incomplete, but it requires only the workflow definition. The ParallelHelloWorld completed version is ready to run. If you'd like to follow the steps I've outlined here, open the incomplete version. If you'd rather follow along but not type in code or drag activities, open the completed version. To open either version, drag the .sln file onto Visual Studio and it will open it for you.

2. After Visual Studio has opened the ParallelHelloWorld solution, look for and open the *Workflow1* workflow for editing in the visual workflow designer. Select Workflow1.cs in Solution Explorer, and click the View Designer button. The visual workflow designer appears, and you can begin adding activities.

3. Open the Toolbox, and drag an instance of the *Parallel* activity onto the designer's surface and drop it.

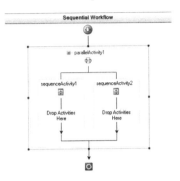

4. When instances of the *Parallel* activity are dropped onto the visual workflow designer's surface, they're automatically populated with a pair of *Sequence* activities. Drag a *Code* activity into the left-hand *Sequence* activity and drop it. In the Properties pane, give it the name **msg1** and type **Message1** into its *ExecuteCode* property.

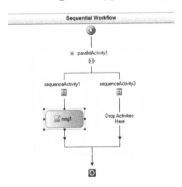

> **Note**   Although you can never have less than two parallel execution paths in a
> *Parallel* activity, nothing prevents you from having more. If you need three or more
> parallel execution paths, simply drag additional copies of the *Sequence* activity onto the
> designer's surface and drop them into the *Parallel* activity.

5. Visual Studio shifts you to the code editor, where you can provide an implementation for *Message1*. Type this into the *Message1* event handler and then return to the visual workflow designer:

```
Console.WriteLine("Hello,");
```

6. Drag and drop a second *Code* activity into the left *Sequence* activity. Drop it following the *msg1 Code* activity. Name it **msg2**, and type **Message2** into its *ExecuteCode* property.

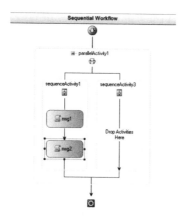

7. When Visual Studio transfers you to the code editor, type this code into the *Message2* event handler and switch back to the visual workflow designer:

```
Console.WriteLine(" World!");
```

8. Now drag a *Code* activity and drop it into the right *Sequence* activity. Name it **msg3**, and type **Message3** into its *ExecuteCode* property.

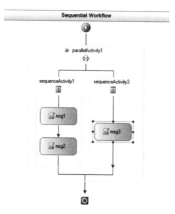

9. As you did for the preceding two *Code* activities, place this code in the *Message3* event handler:

```
Console.WriteLine("The quick brown fox");
```

10. Return to the visual workflow designer, and drag a fourth instance of the *Code* activity and drop it in the right *Sequence* activity, below the *Code* activity you added in the previous step. Its name should be **msg4**, with **Message4** as its *ExecuteCode* property value.

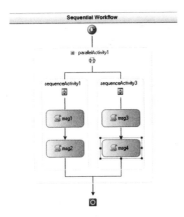

11. In the resulting *Message4* event handler, place this code:

```
Console.WriteLine(" jumps over the lazy dog.");
```

12. With the workflow now complete, add a reference to the workflow from the ParallelHelloWorld application. Right-click the ParallelHelloWorld tree control node in Visual Studio's Solution Explorer, and select Add Reference. When the Add Reference dialog box appears, click the Projects tab. Select ParallelFlow from the list and click OK.

13. Open Program.cs in the ParallelHelloWorld project for editing and then look for this line of code:

```
Console.WriteLine("Waiting for workflow completion.");
```

14. To create a workflow instance, add this code following the line of code you just located:

```
// Create the workflow instance.
WorkflowInstance instance =
    workflowRuntime.CreateWorkflow(typeof(ParallelFlow.Workflow1));

// Start the workflow instance.
instance.Start();
```

15. Compile the solution by pressing F6. Correct any compilation errors that might be present.

16. Execute the application by pressing F5 (or Ctrl+F5). Note you might have to set a breakpoint in Program.cs (the *Main* method) to see the output.

As you see from the last graphic, the messages are jumbled. If the left *Sequence* activity had run to completion without interruption, the output would have read "Hello," followed by "World!" The quote, created by Western Union to test teletype machines because it uses all 26 letters of the Latin alphabet, would read "The quick brown fox jumps over the lazy dog" if the right *Sequence* activity had not been interrupted. This is good, however. The jumbled order of the messages from the *Code* activities indicates parallel activity execution.

If you look closely, you'll see that the individual *Code* activities ran to completion before the execution context was passed to another *Code* activity. You might also note that execution started with the left *Sequence* activity and proceeded to the right *Sequence* activity. The current implementation of the *Parallel* activity is akin to pseudorandom number generation. If you use the same seed value, the random numbers are actually not random. They're generated in a predictable way. In the case of the *Parallel* activity, execution always proceeds in this manner, from left to right, top to bottom. It is also (currently) predictable.

However, *do not* incorporate this behavior into your business logic. As I mentioned earlier, you should consider the Parallel activity to be truly parallel. You *must* assume the parallel execution paths are executed in random order. It is likely that individual activities will always complete before swapping execution context. If WF were to break that contract, internal activity code not designed for multithreaded operations would break. Not good.

A natural question arises. How do you coordinate parallel execution paths, and why? This is an excellent question, and one that leads us to the next topic—synchronization.

Using the *SynchronizationScope* Activity

Anyone who has ever written multithreaded applications knows that thread synchronization is a critical topic. The task scheduler, which is used by modern Windows operating systems to control thread execution on the CPU, can pull an executing thread out at any time, even in the middle of critical operations if you're not careful. I myself had a multithreading bug in the early sample applications for this book. (Many thanks to Scott Seely for catching this lazy programmer in the act!)

There are many multithreaded tools available to you when writing Windows-based applications—the mutex, the kernel event, critical sections, semaphores, and more. But in the end, two things must be controlled: completion of critical code without a thread context switch, and access to shared memory (such as variables containing volatile information).

> **Note**   The word *volatile* used in this sense is intentional. It means the data changes and is not guaranteed to remain any particular value for any length of time.

WF provides for both situations through the use of the *SynchronizationScope* activity. In contrast to what you would do with traditional multithreaded programming, you won't need to use many different tools (requiring you to understand when and how each tool is used). Instead, this one activity is designed to handle both cases: completion of critical code sections and access to volatile memory.

When you place an instance of *SynchronizationScope* in your workflow, WF guarantees that all activities inside this composite activity will run to completion before the execution context switches to another parallel path. What this means is you can access volatile memory *and* complete critical code sequences all within *SynchronizationScope*.

The mechanism *SynchronizationScope* uses is similar to a *mutex*. (In fact, the implementation of this could be a critical section or a lock because the synchronization effect won't span AppDomains, but there is no way to know for sure without seeing the implementation within WF.) In traditional Windows programming, a mutex is an object that provides for mutual exclusion. In a sense, it's like a token, or the key to the gas station restroom. That is, when one thread requests the mutex, access to the mutex is granted only if another thread isn't already using it. If another thread is already using the mutex, the second thread blocks (waits) until the first thread has completed its work and releases the mutex.

Mutex objects are typically "named." The name of the mutex is nothing more than a string, and the string can contain any text you like. However, threads accessing the same mutex *must* use the *same* string.

SynchronizationScope has a similar feature, which is supported by its *SynchronizationHandles* property. *SynchronizationHandles* is really a collection of strings, each designated to identify other *SynchronizationScope* objects to synchronize with. Although you won't receive an error from Visual Studio if you don't assign at least one synchronization handle, *SynchronizationScope* won't work unless you do. As with a mutex, all *SynchronizationScope* activities that are to be synchronized must use the same synchronization string value.

We'll dive into an example of this in a few sentences, but before we do, look back at the output from the preceding sample application. (See step 16 in the preceding section.) See the jumbled messages? This is a direct result of allowing an execution context switch while processing individual parallel execution paths. Let's apply *SynchronizationScope* to the preceding sample application and force the messages to be output in the proper order. Strictly speaking, we'll force critical sections of code to run to completion before the execution context switch, but I'll also introduce volatile memory just to show that working as well.

Creating a new workflow application with synchronized parallel execution

1. In this example, you'll again use a Windows console-based application, one that is very similar to the preceding example. As before, I've created both a completed and an incomplete version of the sample, SynchronizedHelloWorld. You'll find both versions in the \Workflow\Chapter11\ directory. If you want to follow along with the book but not edit code, open the completed version, SynchronizedHelloWorld Completed. Or, if you'd rather, open the incomplete version, SynchronizedHelloWorld, and follow the steps as I have them here. To open either solution, drag its respective .sln file onto an executing copy of Visual Studio.

2. After Visual Studio has added the SynchronizedFlow project and opened the *Workflow1* workflow for editing in the visual workflow designer, drag an instance of the *Parallel* activity onto the designer's surface and drop it.

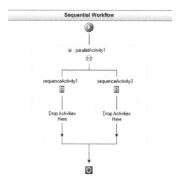

3. Now drag an instance of *SynchronizationScope* onto the designer's surface and drop it into the left *Sequence* activity.

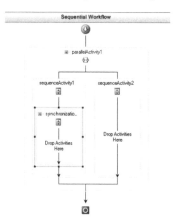

4. For the *SynchronizationScope* activity you just placed in your workflow, assign the
    SynchronizationHandles property to be **SyncLock**.

> **Note**   The text you place in the *SynchronizationHandles* property isn't important. What
> is important is that all *SynchronizationScope* activities that are to be synchronized use
> the same handle (string) value.

5. Drag a *Code* activity into the *SynchronizationScope* activity and drop it. In the Properties
    pane, give it the name **msg1** and type **Message1** into its *ExecuteCode* property.

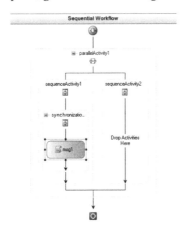

6. Visual Studio shifts you to the code editor, where you can provide an implementation for
    Message1. Place this code into the *Message1* event handler:

```
_msg = "Hello,";
PrintMessage();
```

7. While you're in the code editor, you need to add the _msg field and the *PrintMessage* method. Scroll through the Workflow1 source code until you find the constructor. After the constructor, add this code:

```
private string _msg = String.Empty;

private void PrintMessage()
{
    // Print the message to the screen
    Console.Write(_msg);
}
```

8. Drag and drop a second *Code* activity into the *SynchronizationScope* activity, dropping it after the *msg1 Code* activity. Name it **msg2**, and type **Message2** into its *ExecuteCode* property.

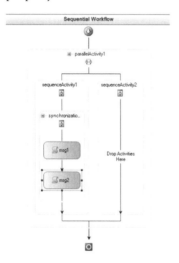

9. When Visual Studio transfers you to the code editor, type this code into the *Message2* event handler:

```
_msg = " World!\n";
PrintMessage();
```

10. Drag an instance of *SynchronizationScope* into the right *Sequence* activity and drop it.

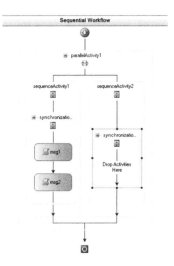

11. So that this *SynchronizationScope* activity synchronizes with the one you inserted in step 4, type **SyncLock** into this *SynchronizationScope* activity's *SynchronizationHandles* property.

12. Now drag a *Code* activity and drop it into the *SynchronizationScope* activity you just inserted. Name it **msg3**, and type **Message3** into *ExecuteCode*.

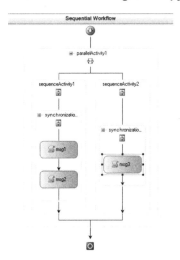

13. Type this code in the *Message3* event handler:

```
_msg = "The quick brown fox";
PrintMessage();
```

14. To top it off, drag a fourth instance of the *Code* activity and drop it in the *Synchronization-Scope* activity in the right *Sequence* activity . Name it **msg4**, and type **Message4** into the text control for its *ExecuteCode* property.

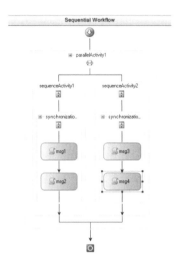

15. In the resulting *Message4* event handler, place this code:

```
_msg = " jumps over the lazy dog.\n";
PrintMessage();
```

16. With the fourth *Code* activity in place, the workflow is now complete. Add a reference to the workflow from the SynchronizedHelloWorld application in the same way you added the project-level reference in step 12 of the preceding procedure, "Creating a new workflow application with parallel execution."

17. Open Program.cs in the SynchronizedHelloWorld project for editing and then look for this line of code:

```
Console.WriteLine("Waiting for workflow completion.");
```

18. Add this code following the line of code you just located to create a workflow instance:

```
// Create the workflow instance.
WorkflowInstance instance =
    workflowRuntime.CreateWorkflow(typeof(SynchronizedFlow.Workflow1));

// Start the workflow instance.
instance.Start();
```

19. Compile the solution by pressing F6. Correct any compilation errors you find.

20. Execute the application by pressing F5 or Ctrl+F5 if debugging. If you don't run the application from within an open command window, you might have to set a breakpoint in *Main* to see the output. If your output still shows the two messages mixed together, check to make sure you've entered the same string value in the *SynchronizationHandles* property for both *SynchronizationScope* activities (steps 4 and 11 above).

The final activity we'll cover in this chapter is a bit different from any other activity you've seen, or will see, as delivered out of the box from WF. It's called the *ConditionedActivityGroup* activity, and it has both a parallel and a looping behavior. Let's check it out.

Using the *ConditionedActivityGroup* (CAG) Activity

In a nutshell, the *ConditionedActivityGroup* activity, or CAG as it's often called, is a composite activity that allows you to take a role in scheduling parallel child activities for execution. The CAG, as a whole, runs until a condition you specify becomes true or until all child activities report they have no more work if you do not apply this condition. The condition I refer to is known as the CAG's *until condition*.

Child activities are executed in parallel, and they execute only when conditions for each individual child activity are met. This is known as the *when condition* for the child activity. If none of the child *when* conditions are met, no child activities execute and the CAG activity terminates unless you force it to continue by means of its *until* condition. If one or more child *when* conditions are met, those child activities execute in parallel. The other child activities whose *when* conditions have not been met remain in an idle state. You can establish child activity execution by judiciously selecting child *when* conditions.

The CAG begins execution by evaluating its *until* condition. If that test indicates execution is to continue, each child activity's *when* condition is evaluated. Child activity *when* conditions that affirm execution cause their associated child activities to be scheduled to run. If more than one activity is scheduled for execution, the order of execution will be determined by the order in which they are placed into the parent CAG.

After each child activity completes execution, the CAG's *until* condition is reevaluated, as are the child activity *when* conditions. This is because an executing activity, once complete, could affect the execution order of other child activities or even the CAG as a whole.

Using the CAG in the visual workflow designer is a bit different as well. Its designer user interface mimics that of the fault handler insertion interface for other activities. (See Figure 11-1.) You drag individual child activities onto the CAG's design surface and drop them between the arrow icons, in the rectangle just above the word *Editing* as shown in Figure 11-1. As you drop child activities into this rectangle, their designer images appear in the window below. In Figure 11-1, you see an activity named *setLevel1*, which comes from the sample application you'll build shortly.

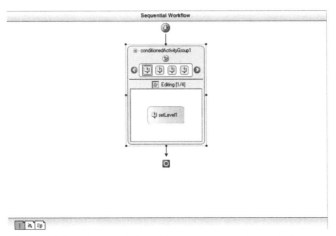

Figure 11-1   The *ConditionedActivityGroup* activity designer user interface

The child activities, when dropped into the CAG, are either in a *preview* mode or in an *editing* mode. Figure 11-1 shows the editing mode. In editing mode, you can set the properties for the child activity, for example to add a *when* condition. When in preview mode, you can view only the child activity's designer image. The properties that appear will be for the CAG itself. To toggle betwen editing and preview mode, click the small square button to the left of the word *Editing* in Figure 11-1, or double-click the child activity in the main CAG window.

Only individual activities can be placed into the CAG as child activities. If one of the child activities in your workflow process model needs to execute more than one function, such as when handling an event and then executing a *Code* activity in response, you should wrap those in a *Sequence* activity and drop the *Sequence* activity into the CAG as a direct child activity.

When might an activity such as the CAG be used? I think it's one of those activities that you will rarely use, but when it fits your process model, it makes things a lot easier for you.

For example, imagine a workflow process that monitors levels of some chemical or material. If when filling the tank you fill it too full, the workflow would automatically release some of the material to an overflow tank. As the tank empties, the workflow monitors the level and sends an alert if the level falls below a specific value. Otherwise, the workflow continues to monitor the tank level but takes no overt action.

Translating this to the CAG, the CAG itself runs until you decide monitoring isn't necessary. One child activity would issue an alert if the tank became too empty, while another would activate the overflow tank if the material level exceeded the specified maximum value. You could do the same thing with nested *IfElse* activities housed in a *While* activity, but the CAG is a perfect fit in this case. (One could argue that using the CAG activity is a more elegant solution as well.)

To demonstrate the CAG, I've created the very application I mentioned. TankMonitor uses a workflow to monitor the fluid levels in a simulated tank, which uses a simple animated control. The empty tank is shown in Figure 11-2.

Figure 11-2   The TankMonitor user interface with an empty tank

Figure 11-3 shows a half-full tank. And Figure 11-4 illustrates a tank with too much fluid. To change the tank's level, simply move the track bar control up and down. As you do, the label below the tank provides you with any alert status. The alert label is entirely controlled by the responses from the workflow, not directly by the movement of the track bar control.

Figure 11-3   The TankMonitor user interface with a half-filled tank

Figure 11-4   The TankMonitor user interface with a tank with too much fluid

Let's see how a workflow using the CAG could perform the tank monitor task I imagined.

Using the *ConditionedActivityGroup* activity in your workflow

1. In the \Workflow\Chapter11 directory, you will find an application called TankMonitor. Actually, there are two versions for TankMonitor, just as there were two applications for the parallel and synchronization scope sample applications—one is incomplete, Tank-Monitor, and one is completed and ready to run, TankMonitor Completed. If you'd like to follow the steps to build the workflow, open the TankMonitor application for editing. If not, open the completed version to follow along if you'd like. To open either solution, drag the .sln file onto an executing instance of Visual Studio.

2. Once Visual Studio opens the solution you selected for editing, open the Workflow1.cs file for editing in the visual workflow designer by selecting the Workflow1.cs file and then clicking the View Designer button from the Visual Studio's Solution Explorer tool-bar. If you're using the completed solution, the workflow is prebuilt and you should read along. However, if you opened the incomplete version, perform the remaining steps in this section to build the workflow and executable application.

3. Drag an instance of the *ConditionedActivityGroup* activity onto the visual workflow designer and drop it.

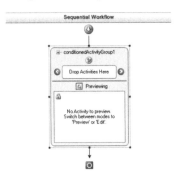

4. The properties for *conditionedActivityGroup1* appear in Visual Studio's Properties window. Select the *UntilCondition* property to activate the down arrow. Click the down arrow to display the selection list, and choose Code Condition.

5. Type **CheckContinue** into the *Condition* property, after first clicking the plus sign (+) to expand the *UntilCondition* property. Once Visual Studio adds the event handler and switches you to the code editor, return to the visual workflow designer.

6. Build the solution (press F6) so that the custom activities in the project will appear in the Toolbox. Now drag your first child activity and drop it into the CAG. From the Visual Studio Toolbox, drag a copy of the custom *SetLevel* activity onto the visual workflow designer surface and drop it into the CAG activity, to the right of the < button in the rectangular area. The *setLevel1* activity appears in the main CAG window.

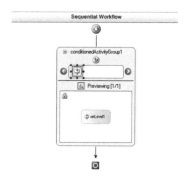

> **Note**   The lock icon in the main CAG window indicates that the child activity is in preview mode. (This is also indicated by the text above the main CAG window.) Although you can edit *setLevel1*'s properties by entering edit mode, you can also work with *setLevel1*'s properties when in preview mode by clicking the *setLevel1*'s activity icon in the rectangular window to the right of the < button.

7. Let's enter the CAG's edit mode. Click the tiny square button next to the word *Preview*. This button is a toggle button, so selecting it again directs the CAG to enter preview mode.

8. With the CAG in edit mode, you can work with a child activity's properties by selecting the activity in the main CAG window (the familiar rounded-corner shaded rectangle

with the activity's name inscribed within). Click the rounded corner rectangle to activate *setLevel1*'s properties.

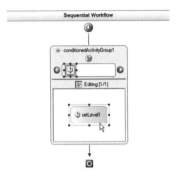

9. Select *setLevel1*'s *WhenCondition* property to activate its down arrow, and then select Code Condition from the selection list.

10. Expand the *WhenCondition* property, and enter **AlwaysExecute** into the *Condition* property's text box. Visual Studio again adds the method for you and switches you to the code editor. Return to the visual workflow designer so that you can establish more *setLevel1* activity properties.

11. Type **OnSetLevel** into *setLevel1*'s *Invoked* property and press Enter. Visual Studio adds the *OnSetLevel* event handler to the *Workflow1* code base and switches you to the code editor. Return to the visual workflow designer once again.

12. The last *setLevel1* property you need to work with is the *Level* property. Select the *Level* property to enable the browse (...) button, and then click the browse button. This activates the Bind 'Level' To An Activity's Property dialog box. Click the Bind To A New Member tab, and type **TankLevel** in the New Member Name field. After first making sure Create Property is selected, click OK.

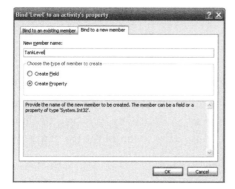

13. You're now ready to place another child activity into the CAG. Drag a copy of the custom *Stop* activity from the Toolbox, and drop it into the rectangular window to the right of the <, dropping it to the right of the *setLevel1* activity.

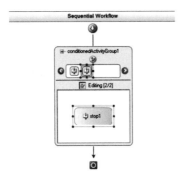

14. The properties for *stop1* are now available for editing in the Properties window. Select its *WhenCondition* to activate the down arrow, and select Code Condition from the selection list.

15. Click the + next to *WhenCondition* to show the *Condition* property. In this case, you can share conditional evaluation with the *setLevel1* activity, so select the *Condition* property to enable its down arrow and select *AlwaysExecute* from the list of available conditional evaluation methods.

16. Next select *stop1*'s *Invoked* property, and enter **OnStop** into its text input box. Of course, this adds the *OnStop* method. Simply return to the visual workflow editor once the method is added.

17. The *Stop* activity is now fully configured, so let's add a third child activity to the CAG. This time, drag an instance of the *UnderfillAlert* custom activity onto the designer's surface and drop it into the CAG to the right of the *stop1* activity.

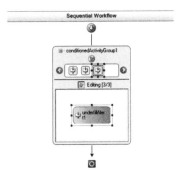

18. Turning to *underfillAlert1*'s properties, click its *WhenCondition* to activate the down arrow and select Code Condition from the list.

19. Expand the *WhenCondition* by clicking the +, and enter **CheckEmpty** into the *Condition* edit field. This adds the *CheckEmpty* method to your workflow code. Return again to the visual workflow designer.

20. Next you need to bind *underfillAlert1*'s *level* property to the *TankLevel* property you created in step 12. To do that, click the *level* property to activate the browse (...) button. Click the browse button, which will activate the Bind 'level' To An Activity's Property dialog box. This time, however, the property to which you want to bind exists, so simply select *TankLevel* from the list of available properties and click OK.

21. *underfillAlert1* is now fully configured, so it's time to add the last activity for this sample application to the CAG. Drag a copy of the custom *OverfillRelease* activity onto the designer's surface, and drop it into the CAG to the right of the other activities already present.

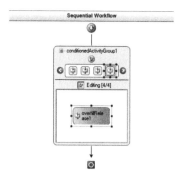

22. Once again, you need to apply a *WhenCondition*, so click *overfillRelease1*'s *WhenCondition* property and select Code Condition from the list.

23. Expand the + next to *WhenCondition* to show the *Condition* property. Into the *Condition* property, enter **CheckOverfill**. This adds the *CheckOverfill* method and switches you to the code editor, so return to the visual workflow designer.

24. Now bind *overfillRelease1*'s *level* property to the *TankLevel* property as you did for *underfillAlert* in step 20. Click the *level* property to activate the browse (...) button. Click the browse button to activate the Bind 'level' To An Activity's Property dialog box. Select *TankLevel* from the list of available properties, and click OK.

25. The workflow is complete from a visual editing perspective, so switch to the code editor for Workflow1.cs so that you can now add code. To do that, select Workflow1.cs in the Solution Explorer window and click the View Code button on the toolbar.

26. With the code editor active and the code for Workflow1.cs displayed, scan the source file for the *Workflow1* constructor. After the constructor, add the following code. You need to establish the minimum and maximum tank levels when you start the workflow:

```
private bool _stop = false;
private Int32 _min = -1;
private Int32 _max = -1;
private bool _notificationIssued = false;

public Int32 TankMinimum
{
    get { return _min; }
    set { _min = value; }
}

public Int32 TankMaximum
{
    get { return _max; }
    set { _max = value; }
}
```

27. The next method you should see is the *CheckContinue* method you added as the *Until-Condition* for the CAG. The method is really an event handler, and the *Conditional-EventArgs* contain a *Result* property you should set to continue or cease CAG processing. Setting *Result* to *true* stops processing, while setting *Result* to *false* continues processing. Add this single line of code to *CheckContinue* (_stop is a flag set in the *OnStop* event handler):

```
e.Result = _stop;
```

28. Two of the CAG activities, *setLevel1* and *stop1*, should always run, and the method bound to their *WhenCondition* is next for editing. Add this single line of code to *AlwaysExecute*:

```
e.Result = true;
```

29. Continuing to scroll down the code file, you should come to the *OnSetLevel* method that's invoked when the *SetLevel* event is handled. The actual tank level is automatically set for you by WF because you bound *setlevel1*'s *Level* property to the *TankLevel* dependency property. The code you'll add here resets any alert notifications, allowing the over-fill or underfill activities to make their notifications if the new tank level is out of bounds:

```
_notificationIssued = false;
```

30. When the *Stop* event fires, the intention is to trip the *UntilCondition* of the CAG and have it stop processing. Scrolling further down the Workflow1.cs file, find the *OnStop* method and add the following two lines of code:

```
// Set the stop flag
_stop = true;
```

31. Next locate the *CheckEmpty* method that *underfillAlert1* will use for its *WhenCondition*. Although you want the condition to be evaluated each time the CAG evaluates its child activities' *WhenConditions*, you don't want notifications constantly sent to the user interface. This consumes excessive CPU cycles. (Trust me on that one.) Instead, you want notification to be issued one time only, per single tank level change. The following code does that for you. Add these lines of code to *CheckEmpty*:

```
// If too empty, execute
e.Result = false;
if (TankLevel <= TankMinimum)
{
    e.Result = !_notificationIssued;
    _notificationIssued = e.Result;
} // if
```

32. *overfillRelease1* also needs its *WhenCondition* evaluated, so find the *CheckOverfill* method and add similar notification code:

```
// If too full, execute
e.Result = false;
if (TankLevel >= TankMaximum)
{
    e.Result = !_notificationIssued;
    _notificationIssued = e.Result;
} // if
```

33. Save all open files, and compile the solution by pressing F6 or selecting Build Solution from Visual Studio's Build menu.

34. To execute the application, press F5 if you built a debug version or Shift+F5 if you built a release version. Slide the trackbar up and down, which simulates the filling and emptying of the tank, and watch the label below the tank change as you exceed or fall below the boundary conditions for the tank.

Note   As I was creating the TankMonitor application, it occurred to me how very much like a state-based workflow the CAG became as I added event handlers. If when creating your sequential workflows you find a touch of state-based processing would be useful in a particular process, the CAG might be an excellent choice for a quick and simple alternative to creating and invoking a separate state-based workflow.

Believe it or not, at this point you've seen enough workflow processing to tackle a great many of the workflow-related tasks you might be asked to implement. The chapters that remain tackle topics that will deepen your understanding of WF.

If you want to continue to the next chapter, keep Visual Studio 2005 running and turn to Chapter 12, "Policy and Rules." There, we'll learn how to apply rules to workflow processing.

If you want to stop, exit Visual Studio 2005 now, save your spot in the book, and close it. Who wants to follow rules anyway? (Of course, I'm smiling when I say that...)

Chapter 11 Quick Reference

To	Do This
Perform workflow activities in parallel	Drop an instance of the *Parallel* activity into your workflow, and place activities in the parallel branches (within the provided *Sequence* activities).
Synchronize workflow activities, either to lock access to volatile memory or to make sure specific activities complete before your workflow sustains an execution context switch	Wrap the activities you want to synchronize within *SynchronizationScope* activities. Provide identical *SynchronizationHandle* values for all *SynchronizationScope* activities that are to be synchronized.
To execute activities in parallel based on conditional evaluations	Consider using a *ConditionedActivityGroup* activity, or CAG. Each activity is evaluated for execution through its *WhenCondition* before each time the parallel paths are executed. The CAG as a whole can also be conditionally executed using its *UntilCondition*.

Chapter 12
Policy and Rules

After completing this chapter, you will be able to:

- Know how policy and rules are handled in workflow processing
- Understand forward chaining and how this affects rules-based workflow processing
- Build rules for workflow processing
- Use rules in conjunction with the *Policy* activity

Most of us, I'm sure, are very comfortable writing *imperative* code. Imperative code is C# code that implements business processes through programmatic constructs—for example, reading a database table, adding the values from some columns in that table, and then writing the total into another database table.

In this chapter, however, we'll dig into *rules*, which are mechanisms for controlling workflow execution but are considered *declarative*. Declarative code, in general, is code you create that isn't compiled into assemblies but rather interpreted as the application executes. Many of the new freatures in ASP.NET 2.0 are declarative, including data binding and improved templated controls. They allow you to write ASP.NET applications without writing C# code to perform data-binding or other complex control rendering tasks.

Windows Workflow Foundation (WF) has a declarative capability as well, though for binding rules and policy instead of data. You don't declare your rules using HTML or ASP.NET constructs, of course, but the concepts involved are similar.

But what is a rule? What is policy?

Policy and Rules

When I write a program that involves data or a process, I'm taking my understanding of the data or process and putting it into code for a computer to execute. For example, consider this logic to handle a checking account: "If the value in the *AvailableBalance* column is less than some requested value, throw a new *OverdraftException*." This seems simple enough...here is some pseudocode that models this behavior:

```
IF (requestedValue > AvailableBalance) THEN
    throw new OverdraftException("Insufficient funds.")
```

But what if the banking customer has overdraft protection by accessing a secondary account if the primary account has insufficient funds? What if the customer doesn't have overdraft protection but instead has an automatic line of credit for overdraft coverage? If the customer has both...which one do we use?

As you can imagine, the code to check for all these individual cases can grow to be both complex and spaghettilike. Worse, it's not very portable to other processes, and it likely will be difficult to maintain.

Breaking this example down a little further, however, we see that it's not just that we have data to process but also relationships between the data. In code, we're applying procedural processing methods to processes that are based on relationships, and that often translates to many nested *if* statements, *switch* statements, and loops. If you've ever written code that employs many *if* statements to check for all sorts of conditions before proceeding, you've probably wondered whether there isn't a better way.

And, at least in WF, there is a better way. We can build declarative rules and use a *rules engine* to process them. Declarative rules describe relationships and are well suited to applying priorities to potential decisions.

WF ships with a rules engine. The rules engine accepts XML-encoded rules and applies those rules to methods and fields in your workflow. With WF, you can combine both imperative (procedural) code and declarative rules to form a total solution.

Rules processing in WF is found in two primary locations—conditional processing and policy. You'll find that conditional processing is a part of the *IfElse* activity, *While* activity, *Replicator* activity, and *ConditionedActivityGroup* activity. If you refer back to Chapter 9, "Logic Flow Activities," and Chapter 11, "Parallel Activities," where these activities were described and demonstrated, in each case I used a Code Condition to evaluate the processing flow. Of course, the implementation of a Code Condition is an event handler in your workflow processing class (bound by a *CodeCondition* class WF provides). However, in this chapter, you'll begin to use the Rule Condition instead. Policy has not played a part in this book so far, but we'll address policy in this chapter when I introduce the *Policy* activity.

> **Note**   An entire book—no, an entire *series* of books—could be dedicated to WF and rules-based processing. I can't possibly cover everything in one chapter. But an achievable goal is to introduce several key concepts that might be new to you and to provide some WF-based applications that demonstrate specific aspects of rules-based processing. If you find this topic of interest, I heartily recommend some quality time with Google (*www.google.com*). A large number of Web sites have articles and information about implementing business processes in workflow-based systems.

In WF, a *rule* is represented by a condition, which returns a Boolean value, coupled with one or more actions. The WF style of rules layout follows an *if-then-else* style. The rules engine evaluates the condition and then directs workflow execution based on the result of the conditional processing. In a sense, rules are analogous to scripted code, with the rules engine serving as the script execution environment. The advantage to using rules over imperative code is that rules can be easily changed, allowing parts of your business process to more easily adapt to changing conditions.

Policies in WF terms are collections of rules contained in a *RuleSet*. This facilitates something known as *forward chaining*, which is a fancy term for reevaluating rules later based on state changes caused by a rule being processed currently.

Implementing Rules

Rules are based on XML, with that XML being compiled as a resource when your workflow is built in Microsoft Visual Studio. Many WF-based classes understand specific aspects of working with rules, all based in *System.Workflow.Activities.Rules*. These classes work together with the XML to execute the scripted rules, ultimately resulting in a true or false conditional statement your workflow logic uses to direct process flow.

Working with rules in Visual Studio is performed through two main user interfaces. For simple rules editing, such as for conditional evaluation in the flow-based activities (which is discussed in Chapters 9 and 11), you edit the rule using a user interface that allows you to build your rule as text. Within your rule, you combine scripted relational operators (shown in Table 12-1), arithmetic operators (shown in Table 12-2), logical operators (shown in Table 12-3), keywords (shown in Table 12-4), and fields, properties, and methods in your workflow to evaluate the conditional expression for the flow-based activity.

To reference fields or properties in your workflow, you type *this* followed by a dot into the editor. After the dot is typed, a list appears that provides you with fields and properties from your workflow that you can to select to work with. (Of course, you can always type in the field or property name directly.) If the field or property represents a class, you can nest calls into that class by using more dots, as in *this.Customer.Name.*

You can call methods as well, including static methods. To call a static method, type the class name followed by the method name just as you would in imperative code.

Table 12-1   Rule Relational Operators

Operator	Purpose
== *or* =	Tests for equality
> *or* >=	Tests for greater (>) or for greater than or equal to (>=)
< *or* <=	Tests for less than (<) or for less than or equal to (<=)

Table 12-2   Rule Arithmetic Operators

Operator	Purpose
+	Add
–	Subtract
*	Multiply
/	Divide
MOD	Modulus

Table 12-3   Rule Logical Operators

Operator	Purpose
AND or &&	Logical AND
OR or ||	Logical OR
NOT or !	Inversion
&	Bitwise AND
|	Bitwise OR

Table 12-4   Rule Keywords

Operator	Purpose
IF	Initiates conditional test
THEN	Flow path taken if the conditional test evaluates to *true*
ELSE	Flow path taken if the conditional test evaluates to *false*
HALT	Terminates rule processing, and returns control to the owning activity. This is *not* equivalent to using the *Terminate* activity, however. Workflow processing does not cease. Only the processing of this particular condition ceases.
Update	Informs the rules engine that a particular field or property value has been modified (which facilitates dependency checking for forward chaining, to be discussed later in the chapter).

For policy, you use a special editor to edit your *RuleSet* (shown in Figure 12-1). Here, multiple sets of rules can be edited and combined. You specify rule priority, how rules are reevaluated if conditions change, and the specific forward chaining mechanism you want applied. You assign the priority value that a rule receives as well as its forward chaining behavior through the Visual Studio Rule Set Editor user interface when you create the rule.

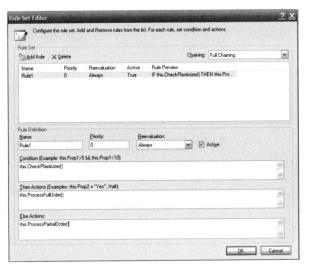

Figure 12-1   The Rule Set Editor user interface

Rule Attributes

When your workflow's methods are called by rules, there might be dependencies the rules engine is unaware of. Rules become *dependent* when they share workflow fields and properties (workflow state). Sometimes that dependency is obvious, but sometimes it's not. For example, imagine that a customer purchasing a certain number of items is granted free shipping, but a handling charge is still assessed. Consider these rules:

```
IF this.PurchasedQuantity >= this.DiscountQuantity THEN this.DiscountShipping(1.0)
```

And

```
IF this.HandlingCost > 0 THEN
    this.OrderCost = this.OrderCost + this.HandlingCost
```

The first rule states that if the number of purchased items exceeds a threshold value, the shipping cost is waived (100 percent of the shipping cost is discounted, and note we're calling a method to set this value). The second rule, which is executed in a completely different part of the workflow, adds the handling cost to the order total. If the shipping is discounted, normally the handling is as well, but the two rules are separate. If the call to *DiscountShipping* writes a value to the *HandlingCost* property, and that write causes the second rule to execute later in the process, you should let the rules engine know there is a dependency. You do that using special rules-based workflow attributes, which are listed in Table 12-5. The following code shows one of these attributes in action:

```
[RuleWrite("HandlingCost")]
public void DiscountShipping(decimal percentageDiscount)
{
    ...
    // Code here to update handling cost
    ...
}
```

These attributes come into play when dealing with forward chaining.

Table 12-5   Rules-Based Attributes

Attribute	Purpose
RuleRead	The default. This attribute tells the rules engine that the method reads workflow instance properties and fields but does not update their values.
RuleWrite	This attribute tells the rules engine that the workflow method updates the value of a potentially dependent field or property.
RuleInvoke	This attribute tells the rules engine that the method this attribute decorates calls one or more other methods that might also update potentially dependent fields or properties.

The *Update* Statement

Table 12-4 listed the rules-based keywords you have at your disposal. They're relatively self-explanatory, with the exception of *Update*. As with the rules-based attributes, we'll talk more about *Update* when we get to forward chaining, but the idea is to inform the rules engine that your rule is explicitly updating a field or property so that other dependent rules are made aware of the change. *Update* doesn't actually modify the field or property—it informs the rules engine that the field or property changed.

Update takes a single string value, which represents the name of the field or property, and it uses that to notify the rules engine that dependent rules might require reevaluation. Although best practices dictate that use of the rules-based attributes is preferred, there are times when *Update* is appropriate. A good example of this is when you're modifying a property on a workflow assembly you didn't write (one that doesn't have rules-based attributes, and one for which you can't update the source code to include the necessary attributes).

Probably the best way to begin to understand how rules can be used in workflow processing is to write some code and try them out. We'll start with rule conditions, which are in contrast to the code conditions we used in Chapter 9.

Rule Conditions

The WF activities that evaluate conditional expressions include the *IfElse* activity, *While* activity, *Replicator* activity, and *ConditionedActivityGroup* activity. Each of these activities requires you to make a true/false decision. In Chapter 9, we used the Code Condition property setting, which caused Visual Studio to inject an event handler into our workflow code. The event arguments, which are of type *ConditionalEventArgs*, contained a *Result* property that we set to *true* or *false*, depending on our decision.

However, for each of these conditional decisions, we could have used a Rule Condition instead. Rule Conditions are rules that evaluate to true or false. "The number of purchased items exceeds the free shipping threshold," for example. To clarify this a bit, here is a sample application that uses a Rule Condition.

Create a new workflow application with Rule Condition conditional evaluation

1. The RuleQuestioner sample application comes in two forms, as the samples have in previous chapters. The completed form, found in the \Workflow\Chapter12\RuleQuestioner Completed\ directory, is great for opening and following along with the text without having to actually type anything. It runs as is. The version to open for editing if you want to follow along is found in the \Workflow\Chapter12\RuleQuestioner directory. This version of the application is started for you, but you have the opportunity to type code and create the workflow. To open either solution, drag its respective .sln file onto an executing copy of Visual Studio.

2. With the solution open and ready for editing, create a separate sequential workflow library project as you did in Chapter 3, "Workflow Instances," in the "Adding a sequential workflow project to the WorkflowHost solution" procedure. Name this workflow library **RuleFlow** and save it in the \Workflow\Chapter12\RuleQuestioner directory.

3. After Visual Studio has added the RuleFlow project, it will open the *Workflow1* workflow for editing in the visual workflow designer. Open the Toolbox, and drag an instance of the *Code* activity onto the designer's surface and drop it. For its *ExecuteCode* property value, type **AskQuestion**.

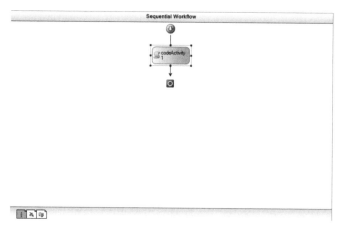

4. Visual Studio creates the *AskQuestion* method and switches you to the code editor. In the *AskQuestion* method, type this code:

```
// Ask a question
DialogResult res = MessageBox.Show("Is today Tuesday?", "RuleFlow",
                    MessageBoxButtons.YesNo, MessageBoxIcon.Question);
_bAnswer = res == DialogResult.Yes;
```

5. Look for the *Workflow1* constructor, and following the constructor, add this code:

```
private bool _bAnswer = false;
```

6. Scroll further up and locate the *using* statements. At the end of the existing list, append this line:

```
using System.Windows.Forms;
```

7. Because *MessageBox* is supported by *System.Windows.Forms*, which is not an assembly automatically referenced by Visual Studio when you create a sequential workflow project, you need to add a reference. Right-click the References tree node in the RuleFlow project in Solution Explorer, and select Add Reference from the context menu. Click the .NET tab, and locate *System.Windows.Forms* in the list. Select it and then click OK.

8. Now switch back to the visual workflow designer. Once there, drag an *IfElse* activity onto the visual workflow designer's surface and drop it below the *Code* activity you just placed. The red exclamation mark indicates additional work is required, which in this case means we need to add the condition that triggers the workflow to take the left path ("true") or right path ("false").

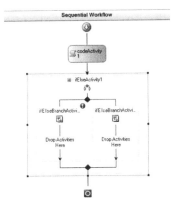

9. In the visual workflow designer, select the left branch, *ifElseBranchActivity1*. This activates its properties in Visual Studio's Properties pane.

10. Select the *Condition* property, and click the down arrow to display the selection list of available conditional processing options. Choose the Declarative Rule Condition option.

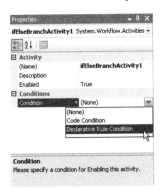

11. Expand the *Condition* property by clicking the plus sign (+) next to the property name. Once the property expands, click the *ConditionName* property to activate the Browse (...) button. Click it.

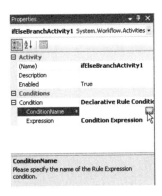

12. This activates the Select Condition dialog box. Click the New button.

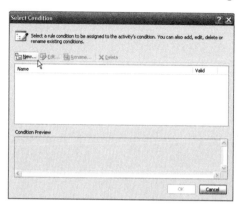

13. This activates the Rule Condition Editor dialog box. In the Condition field, type **System.DateTime.Now.DayOfWeek == System.DayOfWeek.Tuesday** and then click OK.

14. Click OK to dismiss the Select Condition dialog box. Note there is now a condition named *Condition1* in the condition list.

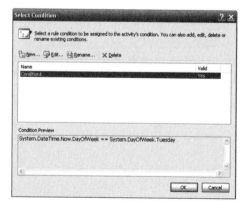

15. At this point, the *IfElse* activity has a condition to process, but it doesn't execute any code! Therefore, drag a *Code* activity onto the designer's surface and drop it into the left branch. For its *ExecuteCode* property, enter **ShowTuesday**.

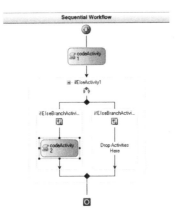

16. Visual Studio shifts you to the code editor, where you can provide an implementation for *ShowTuesday*. Type this into the *ShowTuesday* event handler and then return to the visual workflow designer:

```
string msg = _bAnswer ?
     "The workflow agrees, it is Tuesday!" :
          "Sorry, but today IS Tuesday!";
MessageBox.Show(msg);
```

17. Drag and drop a second *Code* activity into the right *IfElse* activity branch. Enter **ShowNotTuesday** into its *ExecuteCode* property.

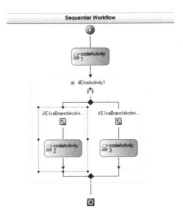

18. When Visual Studio transfers you to the code editor, type this code into the *ShowNotTuesday* event handler and switch back to the visual workflow designer:

```
string msg = !_bAnswer ?
     "The workflow agrees, it is not Tuesday!" :
          "Sorry, but today is NOT Tuesday!";
MessageBox.Show(msg);
```

19. With the workflow now complete, add a reference to the workflow from the RuleQuestioner application. Right-click the RuleQuestioner tree control node in Visual Studio's Solution Explorer, and select Add Reference. When the Add Reference dialog box appears, click the Projects tab. Select RuleFlow from the list and click OK.

20. Open Program.cs in the RuleQuestioner project for editing and then look for this line of code:

```
// Print banner.
Console.WriteLine("Waiting for workflow completion.");
```

21. To create a workflow instance, add this code following the line of code you just located:

```
// Create the workflow instance.
WorkflowInstance instance =
    workflowRuntime.CreateWorkflow(typeof(RuleFlow.Workflow1));

// Start the workflow instance.
instance.Start();
```

22. Compile the solution by pressing F6 or by selecting Build Solution from the main Visual Studio Build menu. Correct any compilation errors that might be present.

23. Execute the application by pressing F5 (or Ctrl+F5).

If you look closely at step 13, the rule we added has nothing to do with whether the user told the workflow that today is or is not Tuesday. The rule checked the actual day of the week. It *could* have taken the user's input into account. (I would have added *this._bAnswer* to the rule to access the Boolean value.)

You also might wonder why this is better than using a code condition. Actually, it's not that one is better than the other (code condition over rule condition). The effect is the same. What changed is the decision that was made was made using stored rule material, which at run time could be replaced with different rule material. It's a powerful concept. It becomes even more powerful when more than one rule is involved, which is the case with *policy*. But before we get to policy, we need to look at *forward chaining*.

Forward Chaining

If you've ever watched cars being assembled, you can't help but be amazed. They're actually quite complex, and the assembly process is necessarily even more complex. Wrapped up in the assembly process is the concept of an option. Cars have optional components. Maybe some have satellite radio, or others come with Global Positioning System receivers so that the driver never becomes lost. Not all cars on the assembly line have every option.

So when a car comes down the line that does have more options than others, the assembly process often changes. Some options require different wiring harnesses very early in their assembly. Or they require stronger batteries or different engine components.

The point is that the assembly process changes on a *per-car* basis. At each assembly station, the line workers (or robots) are told what pieces to assemble. The process that informs them could easily be envisioned as a workflow process using a rules-based approach. Moreover, decisions made early affect how decisions will be made later. Some options aren't compatible with others, so the assembly process must change as the cars move down the line.

This is the essence of forward chaining. Rules are indelibly linked together, or chained, such that one rule's decision affects how rules down the line are evaluated. When we have more than one rule to deal with, as we will when working with policy, we'll need to be concerned with rule dependencies and how we want to handle forward chaining.

> **Note**   The phrase "dependencies between rules" really means that two or more rules share a common workflow field or property. If no rule shares access to a workflow field or property with another rule, there is no dependency between these two rules. If there is a dependency, the problem will be informing the rules engine that dependencies exist, as there are situations that could mask their existence. (We'll look at those in this section.)

As I mentioned earlier in the chapter, rules are collected together in a *RuleSet*. Rules within a *RuleSet* can be assigned priorities, and you can specify whether or not they're active at a particular point in time (akin to an enabled property). When more than one rule is present, the rules are processed in the following manner:

1. The list of active rules is derived.

2. The highest priority rule (or set of rules) is found.

3. The rule (or rules) is evaluated, and its then or else actions are executed as necessary.

4. If a rule updates a workflow field or property used by a previous, higher-priority rule in the list, that previous rule is reevaluated and its actions are re-executed as necessary.

5. The process continues until all rules in the *RuleSet* have been evaluated, or reevaluated, as required.

Rules can be forward-chained as a result of three situations: implicit chaining, attributed chaining, or explicit chaining. That is, rules can be linked and share dependencies because the workflow runtime ascertained there was a need (implicit chaining), you applied one of the rules-based attributes to a method (attributed chaining), or you used the *Update* statement (explicit chaining). Let's look briefly at each.

Implicit Chaining

Implicit chaining comes about when fields and properties are updated by a rule when those fields or properties are clearly read by other rules. For example, consider these rules:

```
IF this.OrderQuantity > 500 THEN this.Discount = 0.1
```

And

```
IF this.Discount > 0 && this.Customer == "Contoso"
THEN this.ShippingCost = 0
```

The first rule applies a discount if the ordered quantity is greater than 500 units. The second rule states that if the company is Contoso, the shipping is free if there is also a discount. The second rule might need to be reevaluated and executed again if the first rule comes into play.

Attributed Chaining

Because methods in your workflow can modify fields and properties without the rules engine being aware of it, WF provides the rules-based attributes I mentioned previously in the chapter. Looking at the preceding example, with the rules rewritten slightly, attributed chaining might look like this:

```
IF this.OrderQuantity > 500 THEN this.SetDiscount(0.1)
```

And

```
IF this.Discount > 0 && this.Customer == "Contoso"
THEN this.ShippingCost = 0
```

Here, the first rule calls a method in the workflow class, *SetDiscount*, which updates the *Discount* property. The rules engine cannot know *SetDiscount* will change the value of *Discount*, so when writing the *SetDiscount* method, you should use the *RuleWrite* (or *RuleInvoke*) attribute:

```
[RuleWrite("Discount")]]
private void SetDiscount(decimal discountValue)
{
    ...
}
```

The *RuleWrite* attribute informs the rule engine that a call to *SetDiscount* results in the *Discount* property being updated. Because this then forms a dependency, the rules will be reevaluated if the *SetDiscount* method is called.

Explicit Chaining

The final type of forward chaining is explicit, which is to say your rule uses the *Update* statement to inform the rules engine that the value of a field or property has changed. The effect of *Update* is the same as if the *RuleWrite* attribute were applied. When calling a workflow method, the rules engine cannot know whether or not the method made updates to a field or property that the rules depend on. However, you do know. In that case, you call the workflow method followed by an *Update* statement to inform the rules engine of the dependency (and the change to the underlying data on which the rules engine bases decisions).

This might sound odd, but it has value. If you write your own workflows, you should use the rules-based attributes. However, as workflow-based software grows in popularity and people begin using third-party workflows, they might find the rules-based attributes haven't been applied to the various workflow methods. In that case, they should use the *Update* statement to maintain the correct workflow state and keep the rules engine in sync. The rules-based attributes state changes declaratively, while the *Update* statement is imperative. You need an imperative solution when working with precompiled third party software.

Returning to the preceding example, assume the *SetDiscount* method did not have the *RuleWrite* attribute applied. The two rules would then look like this:

```
IF this.OrderQuantity > 500 THEN this.SetDiscount(0.1)
 Update(this.Discount)
```

And

```
IF this.Discount > 0 && this.Customer == "Contoso"
THEN this.ShippingCost = 0
```

Armed with this information, the rules engine is aware that the *Discount* property has been updated and will reevaluate the application of the rules accordingly.

Controlling Forward Chaining

You might think that once you initiate rules-based workflow execution you give up control and allow the rules engine to make all the decisions. Although in most cases this is precisely what you want, you do have some control over how rule dependencies and forward chaining are handled.

Table 12-6 contains the three types of forward chaining control you have.

Table 12-6   Forward Chaining Control Actions

Action	Purpose
Full Chaining	The default. This action allows the rules engine to process and reevaluate rules as it deems necessary.
Explicit Chaining	When applied, this control action limits forward chaining behavior to rules that include the *Update* statement.
Sequential	This effectively turns forward chaining off. No dependencies are evaluated, and rules are applied in order, once per rule.

Full chaining allows the rules engine to process rules as it was designed to do, including implicit and attributed reevaluations as required.

Explicit chaining deactivates implicit and attributed forward chaining, and it places the burden of notifying the rules engine of dependencies squarely on your shoulders, using explicit forward chaining. Where the *Update* statement is used, you have total control over rule dependencies and reevaluation. Where the *Update* statement is omitted, the rules engine makes no attempt to ascertain whether dependencies exist, so rules will not be reevaluated even if dependencies actually exist. The effect of this is you have total control over forward chaining, at the cost of added *Update* statements in your rules. You might do this to increase performance (because the rules engine doesn't make what might amount to unnecessary rules reevaluations), or you might have to do this to eliminate cyclical dependencies in your rules.

Sequential chaining effectively turns all forward chaining off. Rules are evaluated from top to bottom in a single pass. If there are dependencies, those dependencies are completely ignored.

> **Tip** The judicious use of priority can often control forward chaining quite effectively as well. Higher-priority rules execute first, so updating fields and properties within higher-priority rules establishes the values that lower-priority rules will use before the lower-priority rules execute. As you recall, you establish the priority in the same Visual Studio user interface you use to create the rule.

Controlling Rule Reevaluation

You also have control over how rules are reevaluated. Table 12-7 lists the modes. An important thing to keep in mind is that the rule reevaluation modes are applied at the individual rule level. On a rule-by-rule basis, you can specify the reevaluation behavior for that particular rule.

Table 12-7   Rule Reevaluation Modes

Mode	Purpose
Always	The default. This mode allows the rules engine to reevaluate rules as necessary.
Never	When applied, this mode indicates the rule should be evaluated only once (never reevaluated).

By always allowing rules to be reevaluated, the rules engine makes decisions that might change the end result of the rules processing based on interim changes in state. As dependent field and property values are modified, the rules engine can re-execute rules as necessary to take those changes into account.

However, sometimes you might not want this to happen, in which case you select *Never* as your rule reevaluation mode. Why would you select this reevaluation mode? Well, one example might include the following:

```
IF this.Handling < 5.0 && this.OrderQuantity > 500 THEN this.Handling = 0
```

This rule says, "If the handling charge is less than $5.00 and the order quantity is greater than 500 units, then don't charge for handling at all." But what happens when the rule criteria are met and the handling charge is set to 0? Well, the dependent property *Handling* has been updated, so the rule is reapplied! If you guessed that the rule represents an infinite loop, you guessed correctly. Therefore, applying a reevaluation mode of *Never* makes sense—once the handling cost is 0, why evaluate the rule again? Although there might be other ways to write this particular rule to prevent an infinite loop, the point is you have this reevaluation mode as a tool in your workflow authoring toolkit.

Using the *Policy* Activity

Forward chaining is a situation that arises when more than one rule is to be processed. For Rule Condition situations, this is never the case—there is only one rule. In fact, it's not even a complete rule but rather a Boolean expression. However, the *Policy* activity changes all that. With the *Policy* activity, you *do* have the opportunity to combine multiple rules and you might (or might not) see the effects of forward chaining.

When you use a *Policy* activity, rules are aggregated into a collection, and this collection is maintained by the WF *RuleSet* object. When you drag and drop an instance of the *Policy* activity into your workflow, you'll need to create a *RuleSet* object and insert your rules, applying forward chaining control and rule reevaluation modes as necessary. Visual Studio is there to help with a user interface designed for authoring collections of rules, just as there is one for adding a single Rule Condition.

To demonstrate the *Policy* activity, let's revisit the scenario I outlined in the "Selecting a Workflow Type" section in Chapter 4. I won't implement all the rules mentioned there, but I'll implement enough to demonstrate the *Policy* activity in action. The basic set of rules is as follows:

1. When you receive an order, check the nominal amount of plasticizer you should have on hand. If you think you have enough, try to fulfill the complete order. If not, prepare to fill a partial order.

2. If you're filling a partial order, check to see whether the company accepts partial orders or requires you to wait until you can produce a full order.

3. If you're filling a complete order, check the actual level of plasticizer in the tank (some might have evaporated). If there is enough plasticizer to complete the full order, process the full order.

4. If there isn't enough plasticizer to complete the order, process a partial order. (See the second rule.)

I realize any competent plastics company would know the true level of plasticizer in its tank, but this is still a good example because there are many conditions in effect. If an order comes in and we know we can't fill it, we see whether we can ship a partial order (which we might or might not be able to do based on agreements with the customer). We could always try to process orders we know we can fill, but what happens when the amount of plasticizer we think we have differs from the amount we actually have, and this difference causes a partial shipment? It's this scenario I'm interested in demonstrating because it shows the rules evaluation process in action.

Imagine we're the plastics manufacturer and we have two major customers, Tailspin Toys and Wingtip Toys. Tailspin Toys has told us they accept partial shipments, but Wingtip requires the full order to be delivered. Our workflow will use a *Policy* activity to apply the rules I outlined to these customers, their orders, and the amount of raw material we have on hand, which might or might not be enough to complete their order. Let's see this activity in action.

Create a new workflow application with the *Policy* activity

1. The PlasticPolicy application is again provided to you in two varieties: completed and incomplete. You can use the completed version, so simply follow along, and you'll find it in the \Workflow\Chapter12\PlasticPolicy Completed\directory. The incomplete version will require you to work through the steps I've outlined here, and you can find it in the \Workflow\Chapter12\PlasticPolicy\ folder. To open either solution, just drag its .sln file onto an executing copy of Visual Studio.

2. Once Visual Studio has loaded the PlasticPolicy solution and made it available for editing, create a separate sequential workflow library project as you did in Chapter 3, in the "Adding a sequential workflow project to the WorkflowHost solution" procedure. Name this workflow library **PlasticFlow** and save it in the \Workflow\Chapter12\ PlasticPolicy directory.

3. After Visual Studio has added the PlasticFlow project, Visual Studio opens the *Workflow1* workflow for editing in the visual workflow designer. Open the Toolbox, and drag an instance of the *Policy* activity onto the designer's surface and drop it.

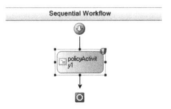

4. Before you actually create the rules to go with the *Policy* activity you just inserted into your workflow, you need to add some initialization code and helper methods. To begin, open Workflow1.cs in the code editor by selecting it in the Solution Explorer tree control and clicking the View Code toolbar button. Prior to the constructor, type in this code:

```
private enum Shipping { Hold, Partial };
private decimal _plasticizer = 14592.7m;
private decimal _plasticizerActual = 12879.2m;
private decimal _plasticizerRatio = 27.4m; // plasticizer for one item
private Dictionary<string, Shipping> _shipping = null;

// Results storage
private bool _shipPartial = false;
```

```
private Int32 _shipQty = 0;

// Order amount
private Int32 _orderQty = 0;
public Int32 OrderQuantity
{
    get { return _orderQty; }
    set
    {
        // Can't be less than zero
        if (value < 0) _orderQty = 0;
        else _orderQty = value;
    }
}

// Customer
private string _customer = String.Empty;
public string Customer
{
    get { return _customer; }
    set { _customer = value; }
}
```

5. Scroll up in the source file, and add this *using* statement to the list of other *using* statements:

```
using System.Collections.Generic;
```

6. Then scroll down, and again look for the *Workflow1* constructor. Within the constructor, add this code following the call to *InitializeComponent*:

```
// Establish shipping for known customers
this._shipping = new Dictionary<string, Shipping>();
this._shipping.Add("Tailspin", Shipping.Partial);
this._shipping.Add("Tailspin Toys", Shipping.Partial);
this._shipping.Add("Wingtip", Shipping.Hold);
this._shipping.Add("Wingtip Toys", Shipping.Hold);
```

7. Following the constructor, add these helper methods:

```
private bool CheckPlasticizer()
{
    // Check to see that we have enough plasticizer.
    return _plasticizer - (OrderQuantity * _plasticizerRatio) > 0.0m;
}

private bool CheckActualPlasticizer()
{
    // Check to see that we have enough plasticizer.
    return _plasticizerActual - (OrderQuantity * _plasticizerRatio) > 0.0m;
}

[RuleWrite("_shipQty")]
private void ProcessFullOrder()
{
```

```
        // Set shipping quantity equal to the ordered quantity.
        _shipQty = OrderQuantity;
    }

    [RuleWrite("_shipQty")]
    private void ProcessPartialOrder()
    {
        // We can ship only as much as we can make...
        _shipQty = (Int32)Math.Floor(_plasticizerActual / _plasticizerRatio);
    }
```

8. So that you can see the output from the rules processing, activate the visual workflow designer and click the background of the main sequential workflow. This activates the Properties pane for the main workflow activity. In the Properties pane, click the Events toolbar button (the button with the lightning bolt image). In the editable field for the *Completed* event, enter **ProcessingComplete**. This adds an event handler for the *WorkflowComplete* event to your workflow code and switches you to the code editor for the *Workflow1* class.

9. Locate the *ProcessingComplete* method Visual Studio just added, and insert this code:

```
Console.WriteLine("Order for {0} {1} be completed.", _customer,
        OrderQuantity == _shipQty ? "can" : "cannot");
Console.WriteLine("Order will be {0}", OrderQuantity == _shipQty ?
        "processed and shipped" : _shipPartial ?
        "partially shipped" : "held");
```

10. Now switch back to the visual workflow designer. It's time to add some rules. To begin, select the *policyActivity1* object to activate its Properties pane. Click the *RuleSetReference* edit control to activate the browse (...) button.

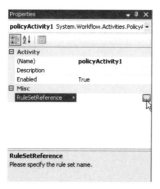

11. Click the browse button to activate the Select Rule Set dialog box. Once the Select Rule Set dialog box is active, click its New button.

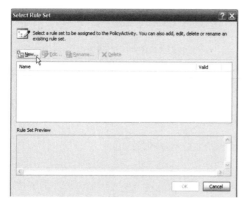

12. Clicking the New button activates the Rule Set Editor dialog box. Click Add Rule to add a new rule and activate the dialog box controls.

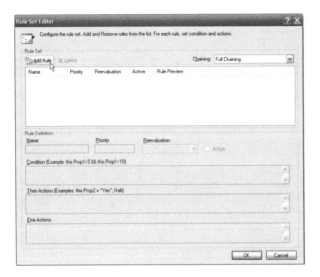

13. You are going to add the first of three rules. Each rule you add comes in three parts: Condition, Then Actions, and Else Actions (the last of which is optional). In the Condition field, type **this.CheckPlasticizer( )**. (Note that it's a method call, so the parentheses are required.) In the Then Actions field, type **this.ProcessFullOrder( )**. And finally, in the Else Actions field, type **this.ProcessPartialOrder( )**.

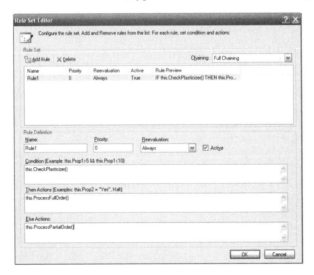

14. Click Add Rule again, which adds a second rule to the rule set. To this rule's Condition field, type **this.CheckActualPlasticizer( )**. In the Then Actions field, type **this.ProcessFullOrder( )**. In the Else Actions field, type **this.ProcessPartialOrder( )**.

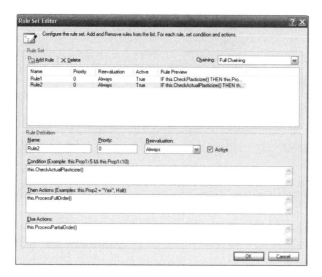

15. To insert a third rule, click Add Rule again. In the third rule's Condition field, add
    **this._shipping[this._customer] == PlasticFlow.Workflow1.Shipping.Hold &&
    this._shipQty != this.OrderQuantity**. In the Then Actions field, type **this._shipPartial
    = False**. And in the Else Actions field, add **this._shipPartial = True**.

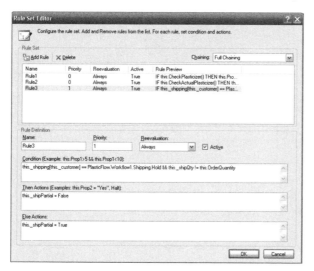

16. Click OK to dismiss the Rule Set Editor dialog box. Note there is now a rule named
    RuleSet1 in the rule list. Click OK to dismiss the Select Rule Set dialog box.

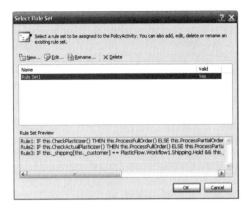

17. Your workflow is now complete. Although it might seem odd to have an entire workflow reside in a single activity, in reality you've told your workflow what to do by the rules you provided. In any case, add a reference to the workflow from the PlasticPolicy application. Right-click the PlasticPolicy tree control node in Visual Studio's Solution Explorer, and select Add Reference. When the Add Reference dialog box appears, click the Projects tab and select PlasticFlow from the list. Click OK.

18. Open Program.cs in the PlasticPolicy project for editing, and then look for the *Main* method. Following the opening brace for *Main*, add this code:

```
// Parse the command line arguments
string company = String.Empty;
Int32 quantity = -1;
try
{
    // Try to parse the command line args...
    GetArgs(ref company, ref quantity, args);
} // try
catch
{
    // Just exit...
    return;
} // catch
```

19. Then find this line of code a bit further down in *Main*:

```
// Print banner.
Console.WriteLine("Waiting for workflow completion.");
```

20. Add this code following the line of code you just located:

```
// Create the argument.
Dictionary<string, object> parms = new Dictionary<string, object>();
parms.Add("Customer", company);
parms.Add("OrderQuantity", quantity);

// Create the workflow instance.
WorkflowInstance instance =
    workflowRuntime.CreateWorkflow(typeof(PlasticFlow.Workflow1), parms);

// Start the workflow instance.
instance.Start();
```

21. In step 18, you added code that calls a method to interpret the command-line parameters. You need to add that method now. Scroll to the end of the Program.cs source file, and add this method:

```
static void GetArgs(ref string company, ref Int32 quantity, string[] args)
{
    // Preset quantity...
    quantity = -1;

    try
    {
        // Parse the arguments...we must have both a company
        // and a quantity.
        for (Int32 i = 0; i < args.Length; i++)
        {
            // Check this argument...must have at least
            // two characters, "/c" or "/q" or even "/?".
            if (args[i].Length < 2)
                throw new Exception();

            if (args[i].ToLower()[1] == 'c')
            {
                // Company... The company name will be
                // located in character position 3 to
                // the end of the string.
                company = args[i].Substring(3);
            } // if
            else if (args[i].ToLower()[1] == 'q')
            {
                // Quantity... The quantity will be
                // located in character position 3 to
                // the end of the string. Note Parse
                // will throw an exception if the user
                // didn't give us an integer.
                quantity = Int32.Parse(args[i].Substring(3));
            } // else if
            else
            {
                // "/?" or unrecognized.
                throw new Exception();
            } // else
        } // for

        // Make sure we have both a company and a
        // quantity value.
        if (String.IsNullOrEmpty(company) || quantity == -1)
            throw new Exception();
    } // try
    catch
    {
        // Display usage
        Console.WriteLine("\nPlasticPolicy.exe -");
        Console.WriteLine("\tTests Windows Workflow Foundation " +
                        "rules-based processing\n");
        Console.WriteLine("PlasticPolicy.exe /c: /q:\n");
        Console.WriteLine("\t- Required Arguments -\n");
        Console.WriteLine("/c:<company>\n\tCompany placing order\n");
```

```
            Console.WriteLine("/q:<quantity>\n\tOrder quantity\n");
            throw;
        } // catch
    }
}
```

22. Compile the solution by pressing F6, and correct any compilation errors that might occur.

We'll now use this sample application and execute four scenarios. The first scenario is one of the trickier scenarios for the rules engine to handle: Tailspin Toys is ordering 500 units. This is a significant number because the assumed plasticizer amount is 14,592.7 (a totally fabricated number for this example), while the actual amount of plasticizer in the tank is 12,879.2 (a number I totally made up!). Because it takes 27.4 units of plasticizer to create a single item (another value I made up, represented by _plasticizerRatio_ in *Workflow1*), the order falls into that range where on the surface the order can be completed but in reality there isn't enough plasticizer. That is, we believe there is enough plasticizer to create 532 items (14,592.7 divided by 27.4), but looking at the actual level in the tank, we can create only 470 items (12,879.2 divided by 27.4). In the end, we must create a partial shipment.

And indeed, if you run the application, providing "Tailspin Toys" as the company name and "500" as the quantity (command line: **PlasticPolicy.exe /c:"Tailspin Toys" /q:500**), you see the output shown in Figure 12-2. Moreover, Tailspin is known to accept partial shipments, and the workflow indicated that as well.

Note Because the PlasticPolicy application accepts command-line parameters, you need either to provide the parameters using the Visual Studio project settings and run the application in debug mode or to open a command window and browse to the directory containing PlasticPolicy.exe and execute the application from there at the command prompt.

Figure 12-2 Tailspin Toys partial shipment

But will the workflow execute correctly if Tailspin ordered, say, 200 items? Let's find out. Run the program again with this command line: **PlasticPolicy.exe /c:"Tailspin Toys" /q:200**. The results are shown in Figure 12-3.

Figure 12-3   Tailspin full and complete shipment

Tailspin is registered as accepting partial shipments. Wingtip Toys, however, wants orders held until its entire order can be filled. Does the workflow handle Wingtip as well? Moreover, what if Wingtip's order fell into that range where we thought we had enough plasticizer but in reality didn't? To find out, try this command: **PlasticPolicy.exe /c:"Wingtip Toys" /q:500**. As Figure 12-4 shows, we find out we can only partially complete Wingtip's order. On top of that, when we accessed our customer preference records, we elected to withhold Wingtip's order for the moment.

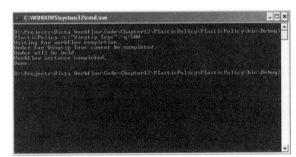

Figure 12-4   Wingtip Toys partial shipment

To test a final scenario, one where we can meet Wingtip's needs regardless of the actual level of plasticizer, at the command prompt type the following command: **PlasticPolicy.exe /c:"Wingtip Toys" /q:200**. Wingtip Toys now has ordered 200 items, and indeed, as Figure 12-5 indicates we can completely fill Wingtip's order.

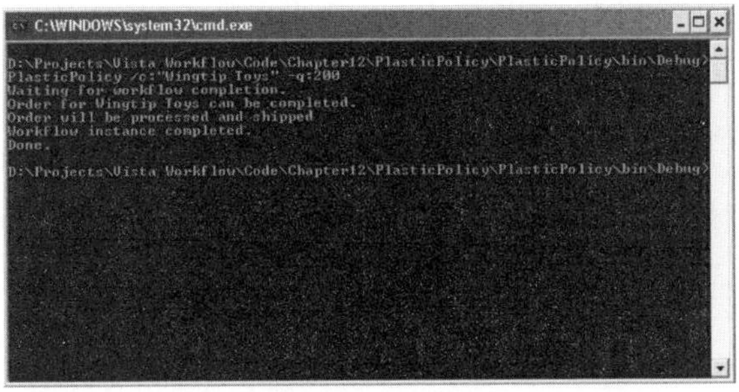

Figure 12-5   Wingtip Toys full and complete shipment

The power in a rules-based approach lies in the way rules are processed. Imagine this plastic policy example being built using several nested *IfElse* activities coupled with, perhaps, a *ConditionedActivityGroup* activity and built imperatively using the visual workflow designer. (The *ConditionedActivityGroup* activity would be there to account for the rule reevaluation when we check the plasticizer level in the tank.) The imperative model just doesn't work well in this case, especially considering many nested *IfElse* activities and priority.

However, a rules-based approach does simplify the processing model. Many nested activities are rolled into one. Moreover, because the rules are resources, you can swap them out and replace them with different rules more easily than you can (generally) deploy a new set of assemblies. You might find that real-world workflows are combinations of imperative and rules-based approaches. The true goal is to select the proper tool given the situational bounds within which your workflow must work.

If you want to continue to the next chapter, keep Visual Studio 2005 running and turn to Chapter 13, "Crafting Custom Activities." You'll see there how to create your own activities.

If you want to stop, exit Visual Studio 2005 now, save your spot in the book, and close it. When I finish a chapter, it's a high-priority rule of mine to grab a snack. Custom activities will wait!

Chapter 12 Quick Reference

To	Do This
Use a Rule Condition instead of a Code Condition	In the *Condition* property for the given conditional activity, select Declarative Rule Condition and provide the rule.
Use policy in your workflow	Drag and drop an instance of the *Policy* activity into your workflow, and edit the *RuleSet* according to your processing needs.
Indicate dependencies between rules	Dependencies between rules amount to fields and properties (workflow state) that are shared between rules. To indicate dependencies that might not be automatically understood by the rules engine, use any of the rules-based attributes (*RuleRead*, *RuleWrite*, and *RuleInvoke*) or use the *Update* statement explicitly.
Deactivate forward chaining	Set the forward chaining action to *Sequential*. Each rule will be processed once in the order it is stored.
Take control of forward chaining from the WF rules engine	Set the forward chaining action to *Explicit Chaining*, and use the *Update* statement where fields and property values are modified.
Control how individual rules are reevaluated	Set the rule reevaluation mode (found in the *RuleSet* editor) to either *Always* or *Never*. *Always* allows the rules engine to reevaluate the rule as necessary. *Never* allows the rule to be processed only once and never reevaluated.

Chapter 13
Crafting Custom Activities

After completing this chapter, you will be able to:

■ Understand what components are necessary to create a fully functional custom workflow activity

■ Create a basic custom workflow activity

■ Apply validation rules to a basic custom workflow activity

■ Integrate a basic custom workflow activity into the Microsoft Visual Studio visual workflow designer and Toolbox

As deep and functional as Windows Workflow Foundation (WF) is, it can't possibly encompass everything you might want to achieve with your workflows. Even though WF is still very new to the development community, many freely distributed custom activities are already available, and you can be sure commercial-grade activities eventually will follow.

In this chapter, you'll get a look inside WF by creating a new workflow activity, one that retrieves a file from a remote File Transfer Protocol (FTP) server. You'll see what pieces are necessary, as well as what parts are nice to have when building your own activity. You'll also dig a little into how activities interact with the workflow runtime.

 Note It won't be possible to explore every nuance of custom activity development in a single chapter. There are simply too many details. However, the good news is it's easy to get a fully functional activity working without knowing every detail. Where there is more detail, I'll provide links to more information.

More About Activities

In Chapter 4, "Introduction to Activities and Workflow Types," we took an initial look at activities and discussed topics such as the *ActivityExecutionContext*, which is used to contain information about executing activities the workflow runtime needs to access from time to time. We'll dig into WF activities a little deeper here.

Activity Virtual Methods

The first thing to know when creating custom activities is what the base class provides you by way of virtual methods and properties. Table 13-1 shows the commonly overridden methods for *Activity*. (There are no virtual properties.)

Table 13-1   Commonly Overridden *Activity* Virtual Methods

Method	Purpose
Cancel	Invoked when the workflow is canceled.
Compensate	This method isn't actually implemented by the *Activity* base class but rather required by the *ICompensatableActivity* interface from which many activities derive. Therefore, for all intents and purposes it is an *Activity* method. You'll implement this method to compensate for failed transactions.
Execute	The main activity worker method, *Execute*, is used to perform the work that the activity was designed to perform.
HandleFault	Called when internal activity code throws an unhandled exception. Note there is no way to restart the activity once this method is invoked.
Initialize	Called when the activity is initialized.
OnActivityExecutionContextLoad	Called when the activity is handed an *ActivityExecutionContext* for processing.
OnActivityExecutionContextUnload	Called when the activity has finished its workflow process. The current execution context is being shifted to another activity.
Uninitialize	Called when the activity is to be uninitialized.

If you need to handle some specific processing once your activity has been loaded into the workflow runtime but before it is executing, a great place to do that is in the *Initialize* method. You would perform similar out-processing in the *Uninitialize* method.

The *OnActivityExecutionContextLoad* and *OnActivityExecutionContextUnload* methods signify the activity loading into the workflow runtime and the activity's removal from it, respectively. Before *OnActivityExecutionContextLoad* is called, and after *OnActivityExecutionContextUnload* is called, the activity is in an unloaded state from a WF perspective. It might be serialized into a queue, stored in a database, or even on disk waiting to be loaded. But it does not exist in the workflow runtime before or after these methods are called.

Cancel, *HandleFault*, and *Compensate* are all called when the obvious conditions arise (canceling, faulting, and compensating). Their primary purpose is to perform any additional work you want to perform (logging, for example), although *Compensate* is where you truly implement your transaction compensation. (See Chapter 15, "Workflows and Transactions.") Keep in mind that at the point these methods are called, it's too late. You can't revive a transaction by the time your activity is asked to compensate for failure, and you can't undo an unhandled exception or stop a cancel request. All you can do is perform cleanup or other processing as required, and in the case of *Compensate*, actually provide the compensation function for the failed transaction.

Execute is probably the most overridden *Activity* virtual method, if only because this is the method you override to perform the work that the activity was created to perform.

Activity Components

Although it's certainly true that you'll need to write the custom activity code itself, fully developed WF activities carry with them additional code to support non-workflow-related behavior, mostly to provide a richer developer experience in the visual workflow designer. For example, you might want to provide a validator object that checks for inappropriate activity configurations and fires back error messages to that effect. Or you might need to provide a *ToolboxItem* or *ToolboxBitmap* to better integrate with the Visual Studio Toolbox. And believe it or not, you can actually adjust the way your activity looks when dropped into the visual workflow designer through modifications to the activity theme, with which you work using a specialized designer class. The sample activity in this chapter implements all these things to demonstrate their purpose and impact.

Execution Contexts

As you might recall, there are two types of activities: basic (single-purpose) and composite (containers). You might think that the major difference between them is that one is a lone activity and the other contains embedded activities. And this is certainly one of the major differences.

But there are other important differences as well, not the least of which is how an activity works with an execution context. Activity execution contexts, introduced in Chapter 4, are simply a way for WF to keep track of important things, such as from which workflow queue a given activity is working. But it also provides a mechanism for activity control and a way for WF to enforce rules between activities when they're executing. An interesting aspect of activity execution contexts is that the context your workflow instance starts with might not be the context being used inside your custom activity. Activity execution contexts can be cloned and passed to child activities, which always happens for iterative activities.

But for our purposes here, probably the most important things to remember when creating custom activities, at least with respect to activity execution context, are that the execution context maintains the current execution status and that when you override the virtual methods you find in *System.Workflow.Activity*, only certain status values are valid. Table 13-2 shows which execution status values apply to the overridden *System.Workflow.Activity* methods. *Compensate* is somewhat of an exception because it's not a *System.Workflow.Activity* virtual method. Rather, it's the lone method resident in *ICompensatableActivity*, which is implemented by activities. However, the rule regarding the returned status value still applies to *Compensate*. Returning any invalid status value (returning *ActivityExecutionStatus.Faulting* from *Execute*, for example) results in the runtime throwing an *InvalidOperationException*.

Table 13-2   Valid Execution States

Overridden Method	Valid Return Execution States
Cancel	*ActivityExecutionStatus.Canceling* and *ActivityExecutionStatus.Closed*
Compensate	*ActivityExecutionStatus.Compensating* and *ActivityExecutionStatus.Closed*
Execute	*ActivityExecutionStatus.Executing* and *ActivityExecutionStatus.Closed*
HandleFault	*ActivityExecutionStatus.Faulting* and *ActivityExecutionStatus.Closed*
Initialize	*ActivityExecutionStatus.Initialized*. Unlike the other status values, at the time the workflow activity is initialized there is nothing to close, so returning *ActivityExecutionStatus.Closed* is not an option.

Generally, you'll want to handle the task at hand for each of these virtual methods and return *ActivityExecutionStatus.Closed*. Returning the other valid status indicates further action is required by either the workflow runtime or an enclosing activity. For example, if your activity has child activities that haven't completed when your main activity's *Execute* method is complete, the main activity's *Execute* method should return *ActivityExecutionStatus.Executing*. Otherwise, it should return *ActivityExecutionStatus.Closed*.

Activity Lifetime

So when are the methods executed by the workflow runtime? The order in which the methods in Table 13-1 are executed is as follows:

1. *OnActivityExecutionContextLoad*

2. *Initialize*

3. *Execute*

4. *Uninitialize*

5. *OnActivityExecutionContextUnload*

6. *Dispose*

OnActivityExecutionContextLoad and *OnActivityExecutionContextUnload* define the activity's lifetime from the workflow runtime's point of view. *OnActivityExecutionContextLoad* is called just after an activity is loaded into the runtime's memory, while *OnActivityExecution-ContextUnload* is called just before an activity is dropped from the runtime.

> **Note**   Activities are generally created from a deserialization process rather than from the workflow runtime calling their constructors directly. Therefore, if you need to allocate resources when the activity is created, *OnActivityContextLoad* is the best place to do so, rather than from within a constructor.

Although *OnActivityExecutionContextLoad* and *OnActivityExecutionContextUnload* denote the activity's creation from a memory perspective, *Initialize* and *Uninitialize* identify the activity's execution lifetime within the workflow runtime. When the workflow runtime calls the *Initialize* method, your activity is ready to go. When *Uninitialize* is executed, your activity has finished from a workflow runtime point of view and is ready to be shifted out of memory. *Dispose*, the archetypical .NET object destruction method, is useful for deallocating static resources.

Of course, the workflow can't always control the execution of some of the methods. *Compensate*, for example, is called only when a compensatable transaction fails. These remaining methods will nondeterministically be called while *Execute* is in effect.

Creating an FTP Activity

To demonstrate some of what I've described so far in the chapter, I decided to create an activity many of us writing business process software will (hopefully) find useful—an FTP activity. This activity, *FtpGetFileActivity*, retrieves files from a remote FTP server using the built-in .NET Web-based FTP classes. It is possible to use those same classes for writing files to remote FTP resources, but I leave that activity for you to create as an exercise.

> **Note**   I'll work under the assumption that you have a known (and correctly configured) FTP site to work with. For the purposes of discussion here, I'll use the well-known Internet Protocol (IP) address 127.0.0.1 as the server's IP address. (Of course, this represents *localhost*.) Feel free to replace this IP address with any valid FTP server address or host name you prefer. It is beyond the scope of this chapter to address FTP security issues and server configuration. If you are using Internet Information Server (IIS) and need more information regarding FTP configuration, see *http://msdn2.microsoft.com/en-us/library/6ws081sa.aspx* for assistance.

To host the FTP activity, I created a sample application I called FileGrabber. (Its user interface is shown in Figure 13-1.) With it, you can provide an FTP user account and password as well as the FTP resource you want to retrieve. The resource I'll be downloading is an image file of the Saturn V rocket moving into position for launch, and I've provided the image on the book's CD for you to place on your FTP server as well. Assuming your FTP server was your local machine, the URL for the image is *ftp://127.0.0.1/SaturnV.jpg*. If you don't use my image file, you'll need to modify the file in the URL to match whatever file you have available on your local server, or use any valid URL from which you can download files.

Figure 13-1   The FileGrabber user interface

As you might already know, not all FTP sites require an FTP user account and password for access. Some allow anonymous access, using "anonymous" as the user name and your e-mail address as the password. The FTP activity is configured such that if you don't provide either or both, the user name defaults to *anonymous* while the password defaults to *someone@example.com*.

Because this sample application is a Windows Forms application, we don't want to have the application appear to lock up while the workflow is retrieving the file. After all, the workflow instance is executing on a different thread, so our user interface should be able to remain responsive. However, we will disable some controls while allowing others to remain active. A status control will be displayed for the duration of time the file transfer is taking place. Once the file has been downloaded, the status control will be hidden. If the user tries to quit the application while a file transfer is in progress, we'll confirm the user's decision before canceling the workflow instance and exiting the application. The application user interface state during file download is shown in Figure 13-2.

Figure 13-2   The FileGrabber user interface while downloading a file

The FileGrabber application has been written to save you some time. The only thing missing is a little bit of code to configure the workflow and kick it off. However, the FTP activity itself is nonexistent, as is the workflow that will execute the activity. Let's create the FTP activity first. As we progress through the chapter, we'll add more to the activity, finally dropping it into a workflow that FileGrabber can execute to download a file.

Creating a new FTP workflow activity

1. The FileGrabber application in its initial form can be found in the \Workflow\Chapter13\FileGrabber directory. As you might expect, you'll find two different versions there—an incomplete version and a completed version. If you're interested in following along but don't want to perform the steps outlined here, open the solution file for the completed version. (It will be in the FileGrabber Completed directory.) The steps you'll follow here take you through building the FTP activity and workflow, so if you're

interested in working through the steps, open the incomplete version. To open either solution, drag the .sln file onto a copy of Visual Studio, which will then open the solution for you.

2. The FileGrabber solution contains a single project (for the Windows Forms application). We'll now add a second project, which we'll use to build our FTP activity. To do so, right-click the solution name in Visual Studio's Solution Explorer window and select Add and then New Project. Expand the Visual C# tree control node and select Windows. Then select the Class Library template. In the Name field, type **FtpActivity** and click OK. A new project, named FtpActivity, is added to your solution.

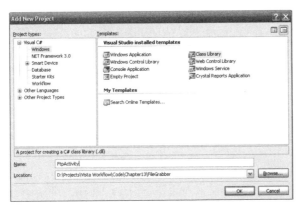

3. Once the new FtpActivity project has been added, Visual Studio automatically opens the Class1.cs file it created in that project. First, do some housekeeping. Rename the file from "Class1.cs" to "FtpGetFileActivity.cs" by right-clicking on the Class1.cs file in Solution Explorer and selecting Rename. Type **FtpGetFileActivity.cs** in the filename edit control. When Visual Studio asks you to rename references to Class1, click Yes. This additionally renames the class from *Class1* to *FtpGetFileActivity* for you, which is a handy feature Visual Studio offers.

4. Of course, we're building a WF activity. However, without adding references to WF, we won't get far. While we're adding WF references, we'll add other references for ancillary tasks we'll perform in this chapter. So right-click on the FtpActivity project in Solution Explorer, and select Add Reference. When the Add Reference dialog box appears, select all the following assemblies from the .NET tab's list and then click OK:

   a. *System.Drawing*

   b. *System.Windows.Forms*

   c. *System.Workflow.Activities*

   d. *System.Workflow.ComponentModel*

   e. *System.Workflow.Runtime*

5. Now we can add the *using* statements we'll need. Following the list of *using* statements Visual Studio inserted for you when the source file was created, add these:

```
using System.IO;
using System.Net;
using System.ComponentModel;
using System.ComponentModel.Design;
using System.Workflow.ComponentModel;
using System.Workflow.ComponentModel.Compiler;
using System.Workflow.ComponentModel.Design;
using System.Workflow.Activities;
using System.Drawing;
```

6. Because we're building an activity, we need to derive *FtpGetFileActivity* from the appropriate base class. Change the current class definition to the following:

```
public sealed class FtpGetFileActivity :
                    System.Workflow.ComponentModel.Activity
```

> **Note** Because you're creating a basic activity, the FTP activity derives from *System.Workflow.ComponentModel.Activity*. However, if you were creating a composite activity, it would derive from *System.Workflow.ComponentModel.CompositeActivity*.

7. For this example, the *FtpGetFileActivity* will expose three properties: *FtpUrl*, *FtpUser*, and *FtpPassword*. Activity properties are nearly always dependency properties, so we'll add three dependency properties, starting with the *FtpUrl*. Type this code into the *FtpGetFileActivity* class following the class's opening brace (at this point the class contains no other code):

```
public static DependencyProperty FtpUrlProperty =
        DependencyProperty.Register("FtpUrl", typeof(System.String),
            typeof(FtpGetFileActivity));

[Description ("Please provide the full URL for the file to download.")]
[DesignerSerializationVisibility(DesignerSerializationVisibility.Visible)]
[ValidationOption(ValidationOption.Required)]
[Browsable(true)]
[Category("FTP Parameters")]
public string FtpUrl
{
    get
    {
        return ((string)
            (base.GetValue(FtpGetFileActivity.FtpUrlProperty)));
    }
    set
    {
        Uri tempUri = null;
        if (Uri.TryCreate(value, UriKind.Absolute, out tempUri))
        {
            if (tempUri.Scheme == Uri.UriSchemeFtp)
            {
                base.SetValue(FtpGetFileActivity.FtpUrlProperty,
```

```
            tempUri.AbsoluteUri);
        }
    }
    else
    {
        // Not a valid FTP URI...
        throw new ArgumentException("The value assigned to the" +
            " FtpUrl property is not a valid FTP URI.");
    };
    }
}
```

> **Note**   It is beyond the scope of this chapter to fully describe all the designer
> attributes and how they allow the *FtpGetFileActivity* to be hosted within the visual work-
> flow designer. However, having said that, the *Description* attribute provides verbal feed-
> back in the Visual Studio Properties pane when the given property is selected. The
> *DesignerSerializationVisibility* attribute dictates how the property will be encoded
> when the designer inserts code. (In this case, the property itself will be encoded.)
> The *Browsable* attribute tells Visual Studio to show this property in the editor. And the
> *Category* attribute dictates where in the property grid the property will be shown (in
> this case, a custom category). The *ValidationOption* attribute is WF-specific and tells the
> visual workflow designer whether this property's validation is optional or not optional.
> (In this case, the FTP URL is not optional.) We'll need this attribute later when we add
> a custom activity validator. *http://msdn2.microsoft.com/en-us/library/a19191fh.aspx*
> provides you with an overview of the designer attributes and their use as well as links
> to even more information.

8. Next add the code for the *FtpUser* property. Place this code following the *FtpUrl* code
   you inserted in the preceding step:

```
public static DependencyProperty FtpUserProperty =
            DependencyProperty.Register("FtpUser", typeof(System.String),
            typeof(FtpGetFileActivity));

[Description("Please provide the FTP user account name.")]
[DesignerSerializationVisibility(DesignerSerializationVisibility.Visible)]
[ValidationOption(ValidationOption.Optional)]
[Browsable(true)]
[Category("FTP Parameters")]
public string FtpUser
{
    get
    {
        return ((string)(
            base.GetValue(FtpGetFileActivity.FtpUserProperty)));
    }
    set
    {
        base.SetValue(FtpGetFileActivity.FtpUserProperty, value);
    }
}
```

9. Now place the final property, *FtpPassword*, following the *FtpUser* code you just inserted:

```
public static DependencyProperty FtpPasswordProperty =
        DependencyProperty.Register("FtpPassword", typeof(System.String),
        typeof(FtpGetFileActivity));

[Description("Please provide the FTP user account password.")]
[DesignerSerializationVisibility(DesignerSerializationVisibility.Visible)]
[ValidationOption(ValidationOption.Optional)]
[Browsable(true)]
[Category("FTP Parameters")]
public string FtpPassword
{
    get
    {
        return ((string)(
            base.GetValue(FtpGetFileActivity.FtpPasswordProperty)));
    }
    set
    {
        base.SetValue(FtpGetFileActivity.FtpPasswordProperty, value);
    }
}
```

10. As you may know, some FTP servers allow for anonymous access. While many require users to be registered with the server, other FTP sites are configured for public access. In the case of public access, the user name is traditionally *anonymous*, with the user's e-mail address used as the password (presumably for tracking purposes). We'll require the *FtpGetFileActivity* to have an FTP URL, but the user name and password will be optional from the application's perspective. However, from an FTP perspective, we have to provide something. Therefore, we'll add these constant strings now for later use when we insert the code for FTP authentication. Therefore, following the *FtpPassword* property you just inserted, add these constant strings:

```
private const string AnonymousUser = "anonymous";
private const string AnonymousPassword = "someone@example.com";
```

11. Depending upon what you want your custom activity to do, you'll typically override one or several of the virtual methods the base *Activity* class exposes. While it's not strictly required, you'll probably want to at least override *Execute* because that's where the work will be accomplished. Following the constant strings you inserted into *FtpGetFileActivity*'s source file, add this code to override *Execute*:

```
protected override ActivityExecutionStatus Execute(
                    ActivityExecutionContext executionContext)
{
    // Retrieve the file.
    GetFile();

    // Work complete, so close.
    return ActivityExecutionStatus.Closed;
}
```

12.   *Execute* invokes the *GetFile* method, so add that following *Execute*:

```
private void GetFile()
{
    // Create the URI. We check the validity again
    // even though we checked it in the property
    // setter since binding may have taken place.
    // Binding shoots the new value directly to the
    // dependency property, skipping our local
    // getter/setter logic. Note that if the URL
    // is very malformed, the URI constructor will
    // throw an exception.
    Uri requestUri = new Uri(FtpUrl);
    if (requestUri.Scheme != Uri.UriSchemeFtp)
    {
        // Not a valid FTP URI...
        throw new ArgumentException("The value assigned to the" +
            "FtpUrl property is not a valid FTP URI.");
    } // if

    string fileName =
        Path.GetFileName(requestUri.AbsolutePath);

    if (String.IsNullOrEmpty(fileName))
    {
        // No file to retrieve.
        return;
    } // if

    Stream bitStream = null;
    FileStream fileStream = null;
    StreamReader reader = null;
    try
    {
        // Open the connection
        FtpWebRequest request =
            (FtpWebRequest)WebRequest.Create(requestUri);

        // Establish the authentication credentials.
        if (!String.IsNullOrEmpty(FtpUser))
        {
            request.Credentials =
                new NetworkCredential(FtpUser, FtpPassword);
        } // if
        else
        {
            request.Credentials =
                new NetworkCredential(AnonymousUser,
                !String.IsNullOrEmpty(FtpPassword) ?
                FtpPassword : AnonymousPassword);
        } // else
```

```
            // Make the request and retrieve response stream.
            FtpWebResponse response =
                (FtpWebResponse)request.GetResponse();
            bitStream = response.GetResponseStream();

            // Create the local file.
            fileStream = File.Create(fileName);

            // Read the stream, dumping bits into local file.
            byte[] buffer = new byte[1024];
            Int32 bytesRead = 0;
            while ((bytesRead = bitStream.Read(buffer, 0, buffer.Length)) > 0)
            {
                fileStream.Write(buffer, 0, bytesRead);
            } // while
        } // try
        finally
        {
            // Close the response stream.
            if (reader != null) reader.Close();
            else if (bitStream != null) bitStream.Close();

            // Close the file
            if (fileStream != null) fileStream.Close();
        } // finally
    }
```

> **Note**   I admit it...if I can find code to do what I need rather than write it from scratch, I'll do that every time. (In fact, a graduate school professor once told me that was a major tenet of software engineering.) Most of this code I reused from a Microsoft sample. I mention this in case you want to build the converse activity, one that sends files to the FTP server or perhaps even deletes them. (Code for these actions is given in the Microsoft sample as well.) You can find the sample at *http://msdn2.microsoft.com/en-us/library/system.net.ftpwebrequest.aspx*.

13. Press Shift+F6, or select Build FtpActivity from Visual Studio's Build menu to build the FtpActivity project. You shouldn't have any compilation errors, but if you do, correct them at this time.

The FTP activity as it stands so far is shown in Listing 13-1. Believe it or not, at this point you have the makings of a functional FTP activity. Additional work needs to be done to make the activity more correctly fit into the visual workflow designer, but if you wanted you could use this activity as is in your workflows.

Listing 13-1   FtpActivity.cs completed

```
using System;
using System.Collections.Generic;
using System.Text;
using System.IO;
using System.Net;
using System.ComponentModel;
using System.ComponentModel.Design;
using System.Workflow.ComponentModel;
using System.Workflow.ComponentModel.Compiler;
using System.Workflow.ComponentModel.Design;
using System.Workflow.Activities;
using System.Drawing;

namespace FtpActivity
{
    public sealed class FtpGetFileActivity :
                            System.Workflow.ComponentModel.Activity
    {
        public static DependencyProperty FtpUrlProperty =
            DependencyProperty.Register("FtpUrl", typeof(System.String),
            typeof(FtpGetFileActivity));

        [Description("Please provide the full URL for the file to " +
                                                    "download.")]
        [DesignerSerializationVisibility(
                            DesignerSerializationVisibility.Visible)]
        [ValidationOption(ValidationOption.Required)]
        [Browsable(true)]
        [Category("FTP Parameters")]
        public string FtpUrl
        {
            get
            {
                return ((string)(
                    base.GetValue(FtpGetFileActivity.FtpUrlProperty)));
            }
            set
            {
                Uri tempUri = null;
                if (Uri.TryCreate(value, UriKind.Absolute, out tempUri))
                {
                    if (tempUri.Scheme == Uri.UriSchemeFtp)
                    {
                        base.SetValue(FtpGetFileActivity.FtpUrlProperty,
                            tempUri.AbsoluteUri);
                    } // if
                } // if
                else
                {
                    // Not a valid FTP URI...
                    throw new ArgumentException("The value assigned to" +
                        " the FtpUrl property is not a valid FTP URI.");
                } // else
```

```csharp
        }
    }

    public static DependencyProperty FtpUserProperty =
        DependencyProperty.Register("FtpUser", typeof(System.String),
        typeof(FtpGetFileActivity));

    [Description("Please provide the FTP user account name.")]
    [DesignerSerializationVisibility(
                        DesignerSerializationVisibility.Visible)]
    [ValidationOption(ValidationOption.Optional)]
    [Browsable(true)]
    [Category("FTP Parameters")]
    public string FtpUser
    {
        get
        {
            return ((string)(
                base.GetValue(FtpGetFileActivity.FtpUserProperty)));
        }
        set
        {
            base.SetValue(FtpGetFileActivity.FtpUserProperty, value);
        }
    }

    public static DependencyProperty FtpPasswordProperty =
        DependencyProperty.Register("FtpPassword", typeof(System.String),
        typeof(FtpGetFileActivity));

    [Description("Please provide the FTP user account password.")]
    [DesignerSerializationVisibility(
                        DesignerSerializationVisibility.Visible)]
    [ValidationOption(ValidationOption.Optional)]
    [Browsable(true)]
    [Category("FTP Parameters")]
    public string FtpPassword
    {
        get
        {
            return ((string)(
                base.GetValue(FtpGetFileActivity.FtpPasswordProperty)));
        }
        set
        {
            base.SetValue(FtpGetFileActivity.FtpPasswordProperty,
                                                    value);
        }
    }

    private const string AnonymousUser = "anonymous";
    private const string AnonymousPassword = "someone@example.com";

    protected override ActivityExecutionStatus Execute(
        ActivityExecutionContext executionContext)
```

```
{
    // Retrieve the file.
    GetFile();

    // Work complete, so close.
    return ActivityExecutionStatus.Closed;
}

private void GetFile()
{
    // Create the URI. We check the validity again
    // even though we checked it in the property
    // setter since binding may have taken place.
    // Binding shoots the new value directly to the
    // dependency property, skipping our local
    // getter/setter logic. Note that if the URL
    // is very malformed, the URI constructor will
    // throw an exception.
    Uri requestUri = new Uri(FtpUrl);
    if (requestUri.Scheme != Uri.UriSchemeFtp)
    {
        // Not a valid FTP URI...
        throw new ArgumentException("The value assigned to the" +
            "FtpUrl property is not a valid FTP URI.");
    } // if

    string fileName =
        Path.GetFileName(requestUri.AbsolutePath);

    if (String.IsNullOrEmpty(fileName))
    {
        // No file to retrieve.
        return;
    } // if

    Stream bitStream = null;
    FileStream fileStream = null;
    StreamReader reader = null;
    try
    {
        // Open the connection.
        FtpWebRequest request =
            (FtpWebRequest)WebRequest.Create(requestUri);

        // Establish the authentication credentials.
        if (!String.IsNullOrEmpty(FtpUser))
        {
            request.Credentials =
                new NetworkCredential(FtpUser, FtpPassword);
        } // if
        else
        {
            request.Credentials =
                new NetworkCredential(AnonymousUser,
                !String.IsNullOrEmpty(FtpPassword) ?
```

```
                    FtpPassword : AnonymousPassword);
        } // else

        // Make the request and retrieve response stream.
        FtpWebResponse response =
            (FtpWebResponse)request.GetResponse();
        bitStream = response.GetResponseStream();

        // Create the local file.
        fileStream = File.Create(fileName);

        // Read the stream, dumping bits into local file.
        byte[] buffer = new byte[1024];
        Int32 bytesRead = 0;
        while ((bytesRead = bitStream.Read(buffer, 0,
                                        buffer.Length)) > 0)
        {
            fileStream.Write(buffer, 0, bytesRead);
        } // while
    } // try
    finally
    {
        // Close the response stream.
        if (reader != null) reader.Close();
        else if (bitStream != null) bitStream.Close();

        // Close the file.
        if (fileStream != null) fileStream.Close();
    } // finally
    }
  }
}
```

One of the more important things that's left to be done is to create a custom validator. Although you could use the FTP activity as it exists now, it's not completely wired into the visual workflow designer at this point. What it's missing is property validation. Let's see what's involved with adding a validator.

Creating a Custom *ActivityValidator*

By now, I'm sure you've seen the small red circle containing an exclamation mark that appears in activities that have unfinished configurations in the visual workflow designer. A *Code* activity that has nothing established for its *ExecuteCode* property will display this indicator, for example. What causes this?

The answer is that an activity validator forces this behavior. A validator examines the properties of its associated activity and inserts errors into an error collection if any properties are missing or invalid. The validator is asked to reevaluate the rules it applies to the activity properties when the state of the designer changes (that is, when new activities are added or properties change) and when the workflow is compiled.

The validator can choose to ignore property configurations, or it can mark them as warnings or outright errors. The FTP activity has three properties, one of which is critical (the URL). The other two can be left untouched, which will cause authentication with the default (anonymous) user. As we complete our validator, we'll mark the lack of a URL (or lack of a binding to a URL property in the main workflow activity) as an error. If the user name or password is omitted we'll generate warnings stating that the anonymous login will be used.

Creating a validator for the *FtpGetFileActivity* workflow activity

1. Activity validators in WF are just classes, so we'll begin by adding a new class to the FtpActivity project. Right-click the FtpActivity project in Visual Studio's Solution Explorer window, select Add, and then select Class. When the Add New Item dialog box appears, type **FtpGetFileActivityValidator.cs** in the Name field and click the dialog box's Add button.

2. Add the following *using* statement to the list of preexisting *using* statements:

```
using System.Workflow.ComponentModel.Compiler;
```

3. When the new *FtpGetFileActivityValidator* class is created, it's created as a private class. Moreover, WF activity validators must use *ActivityValidator* as a base class. Visual Studio opens the source file for editing, so change the class definition to the following by adding the public keyword as well as the *ActivityValidator* as the base:

```
public class FtpGetFileActivityValidator : ActivityValidator
```

4. To actually perform validation yourself, you must override the *Validate* method. Here, you'll examine the properties, and if they're lacking, you'll add an error to an errors collection the designer maintains. Here is the completed *Validate* override you need to add to the *FtpGetFileActivityValidator* class:

```
public override ValidationErrorCollection
    Validate(ValidationManager manager, object obj)
{
    FtpGetFileActivity fget = obj as FtpGetFileActivity;

    if (null == fget)
        throw new InvalidOperationException();

    ValidationErrorCollection errors = base.Validate(manager, obj);

    if (null != fget.Parent)
    {
        // Now actually validate the activity...
        if (String.IsNullOrEmpty(fget.FtpUrl) &&
            fget.GetBinding(FtpGetFileActivity.FtpUrlProperty) == null)
        {
            ValidationError err =
                new ValidationError("Note you must specify a URL " +
```

```
                                "(including filename) for the FTP server.",
                                100, false);
                    errors.Add(err);
                } // if
                Uri tempUri = null;
                if (Uri.TryCreate(fget.FtpUrl, UriKind.Absolute, out tempUri))
                {
                    if (tempUri.Scheme != Uri.UriSchemeFtp)
                    {
                        ValidationError err =
                            new ValidationError("The FTP URL must be set to an" +
                                    " FTP endpoint.", 101, false);
                        errors.Add(err);
                    } // if
                } // if
                else if (!String.IsNullOrEmpty(fget.FtpUrl))
                {
                    ValidationError err =
                        new ValidationError("The FTP URL must be a valid FTP URI.",
                                102, false);
                    errors.Add(err);
                } // else if
                if (String.IsNullOrEmpty(fget.FtpUser) &&
                    fget.GetBinding(FtpGetFileActivity.FtpUserProperty) == null)
                {
                    ValidationError err =
                        new ValidationError("The 'anonymous' user account will " +
                            "be used for logging in to the FTP server.", 200, true);
                    errors.Add(err);
                } // if
                if (String.IsNullOrEmpty(fget.FtpPassword) &&
                    fget.GetBinding(FtpGetFileActivity.FtpPasswordProperty) == null)
                {
                    ValidationError err =
                        new ValidationError("The default anonymous password " +
                                "'someone@example.com' will be used for logging " +
                                "in to the FTP server.", 300, true);
                    errors.Add(err);
                } // if
            }
            return errors;
        }
```

5. The *FtpGetFileActivityValidator* class is now complete, but we've not actually told WF to perform validation. To do that, return to the *FtpGetFileActivity* class and add the following attribute prior to the class definition:

   ```
   [ActivityValidator(typeof(FtpGetFileActivityValidator))]
   ```

6. Press Shift+F6, or select Build FtpActivity from Visual Studio's Build menu to build the FtpActivity project, correcting any errors that might result.

The completed validator is shown in Listing 13-2. Now, when you drop the *FtpGetFileActivity* into your workflow, if you forget to assign the URL or you don't create a binding that provides the URL, the workflow won't compile. Also, you'll receive warnings if you don't provide a user name or password, or at least bind these properties using the Properties pane in Visual Studio.

Listing 13-2   FtpGetFileActivityValidator.cs completed

```
using System;
using System.Collections.Generic;
using System.Text;
using System.Workflow.ComponentModel.Compiler;

namespace FtpActivity
{
    public class FtpGetFileActivityValidator : ActivityValidator
    {
        public override ValidationErrorCollection
            Validate(ValidationManager manager, object obj)
        {
            FtpGetFileActivity fget = obj as FtpGetFileActivity;

            if (null == fget)
                throw new InvalidOperationException();

            ValidationErrorCollection errors = base.Validate(manager, obj);

            if (null != fget.Parent)
            {
                // Now actually validate the activity...
                if (String.IsNullOrEmpty(fget.FtpUrl) &&
                    fget.GetBinding(FtpGetFileActivity.FtpUrlProperty) ==
                                                                  null)
                {
                    ValidationError err =
                        new ValidationError("Note you must specify a " +
                            "URL (including filename) for the FTP server.",
                            100, false);
                    errors.Add(err);
                } // if
                Uri tempUri = null;
                if (Uri.TryCreate(fget.FtpUrl, UriKind.Absolute,
                    out tempUri))
                {
                    if (tempUri.Scheme != Uri.UriSchemeFtp)
                    {
                        ValidationError err =
                            new ValidationError("The FTP URL must be" +
                                " set to an FTP endpoint.", 101, false);
                        errors.Add(err);
                    } // if
                } // if
                else if (!String.IsNullOrEmpty(fget.FtpUrl))
                {
                    ValidationError err =
                        new ValidationError("The FTP URL must be a valid" +
                            " FTP URI.", 102, false);
                    errors.Add(err);
                } // else if
                if (String.IsNullOrEmpty(fget.FtpUser) &&
                    fget.GetBinding(FtpGetFileActivity.FtpUserProperty) ==
```

```
                                                                  null)
         {
             ValidationError err =
                 new ValidationError("The 'anonymous' user " +
                     "account will be used for logging in to the " +
                     "FTP server.", 200, true);
             errors.Add(err);
         } // if
         if (String.IsNullOrEmpty(fget.FtpPassword) &&
             fget.GetBinding(FtpGetFileActivity.FtpPasswordProperty)
                                                        == null)
         {
             ValidationError err =
                 new ValidationError("The default anonymous " +
                     "password 'someone@example.com' will be used " +
                     "for logging in to the FTP server.", 300, true);
             errors.Add(err);
         } // if
     }
     return errors;
   }
  }
}
```

Providing a Toolbox Bitmap

The next thing we'll do to our activity is give it a Toolbox bitmap. This isn't truly a WF task. This capability is built into .NET, to be primarily used for Visual Studio designer support. It also isn't hard to do.

Assigning a Toolbox bitmap to the *FtpGetFileActivity* workflow activity

1. To assign a bitmap, you must first have a bitmap. In the Chapter13 directory of the book's sample code, you will find a bitmap file named FtpImage. I find the easiest thing to do is to drag the FtpImage from a Windows Explorer window and drop it onto the FtpActivity's project tree control node in Visual Studio's Solution Explorer window. This both copies the file into your project directory and adds it to the project.

2. With the bitmap included in the project, you now must compile it into your assembly as a resource. Select the FtpImage file in the FtpActivity project in Solution Explorer to activate its properties. Change the Build Action property from Compile to Embedded Resource.

3. As with the validator, it isn't enough just having a bitmap compiled into your activity's assembly. You must also tell Visual Studio the activity has an associated Toolbox bitmap. And as before, you tell Visual Studio using an attribute. Add this attribute to the *FtpGetFileActivity* class definition (just before the *ActivityValidator* you added in the preceding section):

```
[ToolboxBitmap(typeof(FtpGetFileActivity), "FtpImage")]
```

> **Note** *ToolboxBitmapAttribute* isn't specific to WF. It's available to any control. See *http://msdn2.microsoft.com/en-us/library/4wk1wc0a(VS.80).aspx* for more information.

4. Press Shift+F6, or select Build FtpActivity from Visual Studio's Build menu to build the FtpActivity project once again. You shouldn't have any errors, but if you do, correct them now.

If you created a sequential workflow right now and dropped this activity into that workflow, it would appear rather unremarkable. The default appearance is a black-bordered rounded rectangle with white fill. Want to do better? Here's how.

Tailoring Activity Appearance in the Visual Workflow Designer

The visual workflow designer is actually based on the general-purpose Visual Studio designer. And since .NET 1.0, components in the .NET Framework exist to help you integrate your custom objects into the general-purpose designer. One of those components is the *Designer* attribute, which links in code to be executed within the visual designer for controlling such things as object display and behavior.

WF extends that concept by providing a mechanism for visual activity representation through a *theme*. A theme is really nothing more than a designer class that contains many properties you can set to control how your activity is drawn. You can control the colors used for rendering, the border line style and color, and so forth.

You also have the ability to control behavior in the visual designer. For example, you can add items to the context menu that appears when the activity is clicked with the right mouse button. Both the theming and the behavioral actions are dictated by a class you write that derives from *ActivityDesigner* or *CompositeActivityDesigner* (for composite activities). For our example, we'll create a special designer class called *FtpGetFileActivityDesigner*.

Adding a visual designer to the *FtpGetFileActivity* workflow activity

1. Here you'll start in the same manner you did for the last section—creating a new class. Right-click the FtpActivity project and select Add from the menu. From the secondary menu, choose Class. When the Add New Item dialog box appears, type **FtpGetFileActivityDesigner.cs** into the Name field and click Add.

2. Insert the following using statements into the source file, placing them after the existing using statements:

```
using System.ComponentModel;
using System.ComponentModel.Design;
using System.Drawing;
using System.Drawing.Drawing2D;
using System.Workflow.Activities;
using System.Workflow.ComponentModel.Design;
```

3. Because the designer class you're creating is derived from *ActivityDesigner*, you need to modify the class definition. Replace what Visual Studio created for you with the following:

```
public class FtpGetFileActivityDesigner : ActivityDesigner
```

> **Note** Again, because this is a basic activity, the designer you're creating derives from *ActivityDesigner*. However, if this activity were a composite activity, you would use *CompositeActivityDesigner* as the base class.

4. *ActivityDesigner* provides several virtual properties and methods you can override to inject behaviors into the visual designer. The *Verbs* property, for example, allows you to add context menu selections. (The context menu is the menu you see when you right-click the activity in the designer.) Being rather simple, the FTP activity won't need special support from a behavioral perspective, but it would be nice to tweak the visual aspects. To do that, first add this attribute prior to the *FtpGetFileActivityDesigner* class definition:

```
[ActivityDesignerThemeAttribute(typeof(FtpGetFileActivityDesignerTheme))]
```

5. The attribute you just added specifies a designer theme class that contains drawing property assignments. Let's create that class now. Look for the closing brace of the *FtpGetFileActivityDesigner* class. Following that brace, add this internal class:

```
internal sealed class FtpGetFileActivityDesignerTheme :
                                        ActivityDesignerTheme
{
    public FtpGetFileActivityDesignerTheme(WorkflowTheme theme)
        : base(theme)
    {
        this.BorderColor = Color.Black;
        this.BorderStyle = DashStyle.Solid;
        this.BackColorStart = Color.Silver;
        this.BackColorEnd = Color.LightBlue;
        this.BackgroundStyle = LinearGradientMode.Horizontal;
    }
}
```

> **Note** Composite activities also have their own designer theme class: *CompositeDesignerTheme*. That's because composite activities need to render child activities, and you might want tighter control over that visual presentation.

6. As with the validator and the Toolbox bitmap, you need to add an attribute to the *FtpGetFileActivity* class to tell the visual workflow designer that you have *ActivityDesigner*-based information for displaying your activity:

```
[Designer(typeof(FtpGetFileActivityDesigner), typeof(IDesigner))]
```

7. Compile the project (by pressing Shift+F6 or selecting Build FtpActivity from Visual Studio's Build menu), and correct any compilation errors you encounter.

The complete *FtpGetFileActivityDesigner* file is shown in Listing 13-3. Although we could have done more in the designer class itself if there were designer behavior we required, in this case the designer class exists merely to inject the theme. The activity will be rendered in the visual workflow designer using a horizontal gradient coloration (silver to light blue), contained by a solid black border.

Listing 13-3   FtpGetFileActivityDesigner.cs completed

```
using System;
using System.Collections.Generic;
using System.Text;
using System.ComponentModel;
using System.ComponentModel.Design;
using System.Drawing;
using System.Drawing.Drawing2D;
using System.Workflow.Activities;
using System.Workflow.ComponentModel.Design;

namespace FtpActivity
{
    [ActivityDesignerThemeAttribute(typeof(FtpGetFileActivityDesignerTheme))]
    public class FtpGetFileActivityDesigner : ActivityDesigner
    {
    }

    internal sealed class FtpGetFileActivityDesignerTheme :
                                                ActivityDesignerTheme
    {
        public FtpGetFileActivityDesignerTheme(WorkflowTheme theme)
            : base(theme)
        {
            this.BorderColor = Color.Black;
            this.BorderStyle = DashStyle.Solid;
            this.BackColorStart = Color.Silver;
            this.BackColorEnd = Color.LightBlue;
            this.BackgroundStyle = LinearGradientMode.Horizontal;
        }
    }
}
```

There is one detail remaining—the name the *FtpGetFileActivity* icon will display when it's loaded into the Toolbox.

Integrating Custom Activities into the Toolbox

As you know, *ToolboxBitmapAttribute* displays an icon that is associated with your activity when your activity is installed in the Visual Studio Toolbox. But as it happens, there is more you can do than just show a bitmap.

Composite activities, for example, often create child activities that are necessary for the proper operation of the parent composite activity. A good example is the *IfElse* activity. When you drop an instance of the *IfElse* activity into your workflow, it automatically is populated with a left and right branch activity. I won't show how that is done here because we're building a basic activity. However, I'll provide a link at the end of this section to more information, as well as sample code for building composite activities and prepopulating them with child activities.

So if we're not adding child activities, what else might we need to accomplish to integrate our activity into the Toolbox? For one thing, given no other direction, Visual Studio will load your activity into the Toolbox and use the class name as the display name. Because the other WF activities don't use their class names as display names, we'll override the default behavior and provide a display name more like the de facto standard WF itself has established (not using class names as display names). Although that's all we'll tweak here, other things you can modify include providing a description, your company name, and a version.

 You can also provide filtering so that your activity appears only for workflow-based use, but the base class *ActivityToolboxItem* you'll be using shortly provides this behavior for you.

Adding Toolbox integration to the *FtpGetFileActivity* workflow activity

1. As with the previous couple of sections, you start by creating a new class. Right-click the FtpActivity project, select Add, and then select Class. After the Add New Item dialog box appears, type **FtpGetFileActivityToolboxItem.cs** into the Name field. Click Add to add the class to your project.

2. Insert the following using statements into the source file, placing them after the existing using statements:

    ```
    using System.Workflow.ComponentModel.Design;
    using System.Runtime.Serialization;
    ```

3. The class you're creating must derive from *ActivityToolboxItem*. Therefore, you need to modify the class definition Visual Studio created for you. Replace what you find with the following:

    ```
    class FtpGetFileActivityToolboxItem : ActivityToolboxItem
    ```

4. The *FtpGetFileActivityToolboxItem* class must be marked as serializable, so add the *Serializable* attribute just before the class definition:

    ```
    [Serializable]
    ```

5. Now you add the meat of the class. You need three constructors: a default constructor, a typed constructor, and a serialization constructor. Each constructor will call *InitializeComponent* to assign the display name:

    ```
    public FtpGetFileActivityToolboxItem()
    {
        // Initialize
        InitializeComponent();
    }

    public FtpGetFileActivityToolboxItem(Type type)
        : base(type)
    ```

```
    {
        // Initialize
        InitializeComponent();
    }

    private FtpGetFileActivityToolboxItem(SerializationInfo info, StreamingContext
    context)
    {
        // Call base method to deserialize.
        Deserialize(info, context);

        // Initialize
        InitializeComponent();
    }

    protected void InitializeComponent()
    {
        // Assign the display name
        this.DisplayName = "FTP File Get";
    }
```

> **Note**   There is a virtual method *Initialize* you could override to assign the display name. However, that method isn't universally called. Providing our own *InitializeComponent* method is the best way to make sure the display name is assigned for all cases.

6. To make sure the *ToolboxItem* you just created is used by the FTP activity, add this attribute to the list of attributes you've already added to *FtpGetFileActivity*:

```
[ToolboxItem(typeof(FtpGetFileActivityToolboxItem))]
```

7. Compile the FtpActivity project by pressing Shift+F6 or by selecting the build command from Visual Studio's Build menu. As always, correct any compilation errors you find.

With that last step, your custom activity is complete. However, the FileGrabber application is incomplete. You need to add a workflow that uses *FtpGetFileActivity*, as well as adding the necessary code to the FileGrabber application itself to invoke the workflow. Let's build the workflow first.

Adding a workflow to use the *FtpGetFileActivity* workflow activity

1. To add a new workflow, as you've done throughout the book, simply right-click the FileGrabber solution and select Add. From the submenu, choose New Project.

2. When the New Project dialog box pops up, expand the Visual C# tree control node in the Project Types panel and select Workflow. From the resulting workflow templates collection in the Templates pane, select Sequential Workflow Library. Type **GrabberFlow** in the Name field, and click OK.

3. Visual Studio adds the new sequential workflow library and opens the visual workflow designer, allowing you to begin editing your workflow. Open the Visual Studio Toolbox. You should find *FtpGetFileActivity* there.

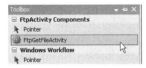

> **Note**   You might be wondering where the nice little FTP bitmap went (to be replaced by the blue gear icon), as well as why the display text you added in the *FtpGetFileActiv- ityToolboxItem* class didn't appear in the Toolbox. This is because the *FtpGetFileActivity* is supported by an assembly in the current solution. I'll describe the solution to this after you complete the workflow.

4. Drag an instance of *FtpGetFileActivity* onto the designer's surface, and drop it in the center.

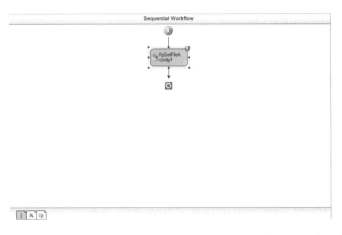

5. The red dot with the exclamation mark is an indication that there are validation errors present. And, in fact, if you place the mouse over the down arrow and click once, you'll see the particular validation failure. Does it look familiar? It should...it's the validation error you inserted when you created the activity validation class in an earlier section.

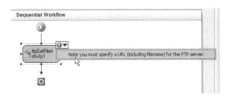

6. The main FileGrabber application is capable of passing in to your workflow the user name, the password, and the file's URL. Therefore, you need to provide properties in your main workflow for each of these values. Here is a great way to do just that—have Visual Studio add them for you. If you select the FTP activity and then look at its prop- erties in the Properties pane, you'll see the three properties you added to the activity: *FtpUrl*, *FtpUser*, and *FtpPassword*. So that you clear the error condition first, select the *FtpUrl* property to activate the browse (...) button. Click the browse button.

7. This activates the Bind 'FtpUrl' To An Activity's Property dialog box. Click the Bind To A New Member tab, and type **FtpUrl** in the New Member name field, making sure Create Property is selected. Click OK. (Notice that the red dot with the exclamation mark is now gone.)

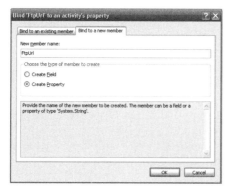

8. Follow the same procedure (steps 6 and 7) to add a new *FtpUser* property as well as a new *FtpPassword* property. The Properties pane shows bindings for all three properties when you've finished.

9. Compile your workflow by pressing Shift+F6 or selecting Build GrabberFlow from the Visual Studio Build menu. If there are any errors, correct those now.

I mentioned in step 3 that I'd describe how to load the *FtpGetFileActivity* into the Toolbox to show that the metadata you added in the previous sections is actually there. Here's what you do.

Loading the *FtpGetFileActivity* workflow activity into the Toolbox

1. For this to work, you must have a workflow in the visual workflow designer. (The Toolbox filters inappropriate components.) The GrabberFlow workflow should still be loaded in the visual workflow designer, but if it's not, reload it and open the Toolbox. Right-click on the Toolbox content (not the header) to activate the context menu, and select Choose Items.

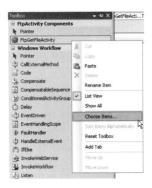

2. This activates the Choose Toolbox Items dialog box. Click the Activities tab and then the Browse button.

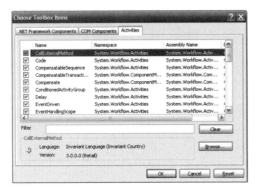

3. Clicking Browse activates a common file dialog box. Using the navigation tools, browse to the location in your local file system where you compiled the FtpActivity project, typically \Workflow\Chapter13\FileGrabber\FtpActivity\bin\Debug\ (or Release, depending on the build mode you selected). Select the FtpActivity.dll file, and click Open. Then click OK to dismiss the Choose Toolbox Items dialog box.

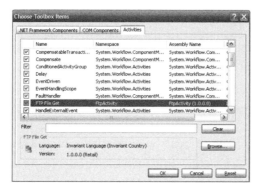

4. This loads the *FtpGetFileActivity* into the Toolbox, and you should see the custom icon and display text you added previously.

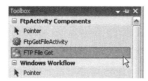

Our last task is to add the code we need to kick off the workflow from the main application.

Executing the *FtpGetFileActivity* workflow

1. Open the file Form1.cs in the code editor. To do so, click the Form1.cs file in the FileGrabber project and click the View Code toolbar button.

2. All the code you'll need has been added for you with the exception of the code required to actually start a workflow instance. That code will be placed in the *Get_Click* event handler. Scroll down through the source file until you find the *Get_Click* event handler. Following the code you find there (to disable the user interface controls), add this code:

    ```
    // Process the request, starting by creating the parameters.
    Dictionary<string, object> parms = new Dictionary<string, object>();
    parms.Add("FtpUrl", tbFtpUrl.Text);
    parms.Add("FtpUser", tbUsername.Text);
    parms.Add("FtpPassword", tbPassword.Text);

    // Create instance.
    _workflowInstance = _workflowRuntime.CreateWorkflow(typeof(GrabberFlow.Workflow1),
    parms);

    // Start instance.
    _workflowInstance.Start();
    ```

3. Because you're using the workflow from the *GrabberFlow* namespace, you need to reference the workflow assembly. Simply right-click the FileGrabber project in Solution Explorer and select Add Reference from the context menu. When the Add Reference dialog box appears, click the Projects tab and select the GrabberFlow project from the list. Click OK.

4. Execute FileGrabber by pressing F5 (or Ctrl+F5) or by selecting Start Debugging or Start Without Debugging from Visual Studio's Debug menu. If you provide a valid file's FTP URL, is the file downloaded? (Note the file will be downloaded and placed in the same directory as the application's executable file.)

In this chapter, we created a basic activity. The steps necessary for creating a composite activity are similar if slightly more involved. (The *ToolboxItem* class you build has some additional code to facilitate adding contained activities, for example.) If you'd like to read more about composite activity creation, you'll find more at *http://msdn.microsoft.com/library/default.asp?url=/library/en-us/dnlong/html/parallelif.asp.*

If you want to continue to the next chapter, keep Visual Studio 2005 running and turn to Chapter 14, "State-Based Workflows." You'll find out more about the fascinating topic of state machine workflows there.

If you want to stop, exit Visual Studio 2005 now, save your spot in the book, and close it. Although state-based workflows are fascinating, they'll wait. Take a break and come back when you're ready.

Chapter 13 Quick Reference

To	Do This
Create a custom WF activity	Create a new class library project, and derive the new activity class from *Activity* (or *CompositeActivity* if you're building a composite activity).
Validate the activity properties	Provide a custom activity validator. Note validation can ignore activity state, return warnings, or elect to fail compilation by returning errors for specific conditions. Don't forget you need to add the *ActivityValidator* attribute to your main activity class.
Add a Toolbox bitmap	Insert an appropriate bitmap into your activity project. Set its Build Action property to Embedded Resource. Finally, add the *ToolboxBitmapAttribute* to your activity to actually load it.
Tailor the appearance of your activity in the visual workflow designer	Provide a designer class, derived from either *ActivityDesigner* or *CompositeActivityDesigner*. To tailor the visual appearance in the visual workflow editor, also provide a theme class. You also need to add the *Designer* attribute to your main activity class.
Customize the display name for your activity when it's loaded into the Toolbox	Create a new *ToolboxItem* class derived from *ActivityToolboxItem* (good for both basic and composite activities). You need to also use the *ToolboxItemAttribute* in your main activity class.

Part III
Workflow Processing

In this part:

Chapter 14
State-Based Workflows

After completing this chapter, you will be able to:

- Understand the notional concept of a state machine and how it is modeled in workflow processing
- Create state-based workflows
- Apply initial and terminal state conditions
- Incorporate code to transition from state to state

In Chapter 4, "Introduction to Activities and Workflow Types," where I described the types of workflows you can create using Windows Workflow Foundation (WF), I mentioned the state-based workflow. State-based workflows model something known as the *finite state machine*. State-based workflows shine when the workflow requires much interaction with outside events. As events fire and are handled by the workflow, the workflow can transition from state to state as required.

WF provides a rich development experience for creating state-based workflows, and much of what you've seen in the book so far applies to state-based workflows. For example, when a state is transitioned into, you can, if you want, execute a few sequential activities, make conditional decisions (using rules or code), or iterate through some data points using an iterative activity structure. The only real difference is how the activities are queued for execution. In a sequential or parallel workflow, they're queued as they come up. But in a state-based workflow, activities are queued as states are transitioned into and out of. Events generally drive those transitions, but this is not a universal rule. Let's take another look at the conceptual state machine and relate those concepts to WF activities you can use to model your workflows.

The State Machine Concept

State machines are meant to model discrete points within your processing logic, the transitions to which are controlled by events. For example, you load your washing machine, close the door, and push the start button. Pushing the start button initiates a state machine that runs your laundry through the various cleaning cycles until the cycles are complete.

State machines have known starting points and known termination or end points. The states in between should be controlled by events expected to occur while the machine is at a specific state. Sometimes events throw state machines into invalid states, which are conditions not unlike sustaining unhandled exceptions in your applications. The entire process either comes to a sudden halt or crashes entirely. Either way, transitioning to invalid states is something you want to monitor closely, at least in digital electronic systems. (WF is a bit more forgiving because you control when states are transitioned to by using an activity designed for the task—no transitional activity, no transition.)

Chapter 4 covered the essential concepts involved with state machines in general. For a quick refresher, see the section "The *State* Activity." Let's instead find out how activities designed to be used within state-based workflows are used.

Using the *State* Activity

Perhaps not too surprisingly, the *State* activity models a state in your state-based workflow. It's a composite activity, but it's limited to accepting only certain types of activities as children: the *EventDriven* activity, the *StateInitialization* activity, the *StateFinalization* activity, and other *State* activities. The *EventDriven* activity waits for the events that will cause a transition to another state, while *StateInitialization* and *StateFinalization* are activities guaranteed to execute when a state is transitioned into and out of, respectively. It might seem odd to be able to drop a secondary *State* activity into an existing *State* activity, but the intent is to provide the capability for embedding child state machines within parent state machines.

There is also a restriction regarding the number of valid activities your state can contain. Only a single instance of *StateInitialization* and *StateFinalization* is allowed. You can have one of each, but not more than one of each. Neither is required.

However, nothing says you can't have one or more instances of child *EventDriven* and *State* activities. In fact, it's common to find multiple *EventDriven* activities, because each event might cause a transition to a different state. For example, a "disapprove" event might transition to the final state, while an "approve" event might transition to a state designed to request more approval. As for *State* activities, clearly more than one should be allowed if you are to create embedded state-based workflows. *State*-based workflows with a single state model a simple sequential workflow, so in that case you should probably use a sequential workflow directly.

In any case, to use the *State* activity, simply drag an instance from the Toolbox onto the visual workflow designer. The only requirement is the workflow itself must be a state-based workflow rather than sequential. Then decide what child activities your state should maintain, and drag and drop them as required, keeping in mind the four types of activities you can insert.

Using the *SetState* Activity

In a purely electronic system, one made using electrical components (your computer's processor, for example), the fact that an event fires is enough to transition from one state to another. The presence of an electrical voltage or voltages sets in motion everything that's required for a state change.

WF is not an electronic system, even if it is executed on your system's processor. What this means to you is that firing an event your design specifies as the signal for a state change is *not* enough to transition to the other state. Instead, you must insert another activity—*SetState*.

The *SetState* activity, interestingly enough, isn't one of the activities you can drop into the *State* activity directly. Why is this? Because the *State* activity knows that something must trigger a state change. If you could drop *SetState* directly into *State*, when that state was entered it would immediately be transitioned out of. The state is then meaningless.

Instead, you drop an instance of *SetState* into two of the other three valid *State* child activities. Although it's more common to find *SetState* in *EventDriven* activities (changing to a new state as a result of an event), you will from time to time find it useful to drop *SetState* into *StateInitialization*. I do this in this chapter's sample application when the initial state merely sets things up for the remaining states. You cannot drop an instance of *SetState* into *StateFinalization*. *StateFinalization* is invoked when the particular state is being transitioned out of, so a previous instance of *SetState* would have already executed. It's too late to change your mind when *StateFinalization* is executing.

So aside from dropping an instance of *SetState* into your state's *EventDriven* or *StateInitialization* activities, how does it actually cause a transition to a different state? The answer is simply that *SetState*'s *TargetStateName* property should be set to the name of the state to be transitioned to.

 Tip   The visual workflow designer in Microsoft Visual Studio makes setting the *TargetStateName* easier by keeping track of all the states in your workflow and then presenting them to you in a drop-down list when you click on the *TargetStateName* property. For this reason, it's often better to drop all the states you'll require into your workflow before "wiring them up" using instances of *SetState*.

When the workflow runtime encounters a *SetState* activity when executing your workflow, it searches for the *State* activity bearing the same name as specified in the *TargetStateName* property. That state is then queued for execution. In the visual workflow designer, this is represented by an arrow traveling from the *SetState* activity to the state it indicates.

Using the *StateInitialization* Activity

When a state is transitioned into, you have the opportunity to initialize things related to that state through the *StateInitialization* activity. Although *StateInitialization* is not a required activity in your state, if an instance is present, WF guarantees that *StateInitialization* will be invoked before any other activity in your state.

StateInitialization derives from the *Sequence* activity, so nearly any activity you want to place in this composite activity is available to you and will be executed in sequential order. Certain activities are not allowed, such as any activity based on *IEventActivity*. To handle events in your state, you must use the *EventDriven* activity.

StateInitialization is also executed in a nonblocking manner. This approach is necessary because your state needs to be able to listen for events. If *StateInitialization* were a blocking activity, the thread executing the initialization code would be tied up and unable to listen for events. Note, however, that the event, although it has been received, will not be acted upon until *StateInitialization* completes. After all, critical initialization code might need to be executed prior to actually handling the event.

Using *StateInitialization*, and indeed any of the child activities in a given *State* activity, requires you to interact with the visual workflow designer in a slightly different way than you have so far in this book. If you drag and drop an instance of *StateInitialization* into a *State* activity, you'll find you can't then drop child activities directly into *StateInitialization*. (This is true for the *EventDriven* and *StateFinalization* activities as well.) To drop child activities into *StateInitialization*, you must first double-click the instance of *StateInitialization* you just dropped to activate the sequential workflow editor you've used in previous chapters. To return to the state-based workflow editor, you'll find hyperlink-style buttons in the upper-left corner of the workflow designer that will return you to a view of the particular state you're editing or the entire workflow.

Using the *StateFinalization* Activity

The *StateFinalization* activity is a mirror image of the *StateInitialization* activity and is used in a similar way. Where the *StateInitialization* activity is executed when the state itself begins execution, *StateFinalization* executes just prior to transitioning out of the state. Like *StateInitialization*, the *StateFinalization* activity is based on the *Sequence* activity. *StateFinalization* also limits the types of activities it can contain—*IEventActivity* activities are disallowed, as are *State* and *SetState*.

Creating a State-Based Workflow Application

If you recall the sample state machine I presented in Chapter 4, Figure 14-1 will look familiar. Yes, it's the (simplified) vending machine state diagram. I thought it might be interesting to build this state diagram into a true WF state-based workflow and then drive it using a user interface that, given my feeble artistic abilities, models a crude soft drink ("soda") vending machine.

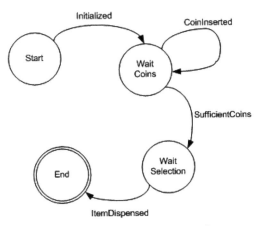

Figure 14-1   The SodaMachine state diagram

Given no user interaction, the soda machine application appears as you see in Figure 14-2. A bottle of soda costs $1.25. While you insert coins, the soda buttons on the left are inactive. However, when you insert enough money, the soda buttons are enabled and you can make a selection. This simplified model doesn't deal with such things as refunds and making change, but feel free to modify the application if you wish.

> **Note**   For the sake of simplicity, I did not internationalize the sample application. It simulates a vending machine that accepts United States currency only. However, keep in mind the salient point here is the workflow, not the monetary unit used.

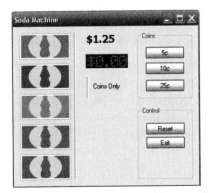

Figure 14-2   The SodaMachine user interface in its initial state

However, you can't actually insert coins into a Windows Forms application, so I provided buttons for 5¢, 10¢, and 25¢. Sorry, coins only. When you click one of the coin buttons for the first time, a new state-based workflow instance is started, one that implements the workflow shown in Figure 14-1. Figure 14-3 shows you the soda machine after several coins have been added. The state-based workflow keeps track of the coinage received and reports the total back to the application, which displays it in the simulated liquid crystal diode (LCD) display.

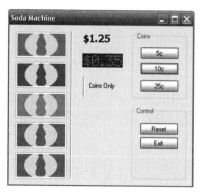

Figure 14-3   The SodaMachine user interface as coins are added

When sufficient coins have been inserted, the workflow notifies the application that the user can now make a selection, as shown in Figure 14-4. The application, in turn, enables the individual soda buttons, located on the left of the user interface.

Figure 14-4   The SodaMachine user interface allowing soda selection

When one of the soda buttons on the left has been clicked, as the darkened button in Figure 14-5 indicates, a label appears that says "Soda!" This is my way of simulating the bottle of soda dropping from the machine for the customer to retrieve. To reset the entire process, click the Reset button. This doesn't affect the workflow but rather resets the user interface buttons. The user interface now appears as it did in Figure 14-2, and you can start the process all over again.

Figure 14-5   The SodaMachine user interface once a selection has been made

A great deal of the application has been created for you. If you wade through the sample Soda-Machine code, you'll find I used the *CallExternalMethod* activity (from Chapter 8, "Workflow Data Transfer") and the *HandleExternalEvent* activity (from Chapter 10, "Event Activities"). These are great tools for interacting with your workflow from your application. What's left to create is the workflow itself, and here's how.

Building a state-based workflow

1. The SodaMachine application in its initial form can be found in the \Work-flow\Chapter14\SodaMachine directory. As I've done in the past for the more complex sample applications, I placed two different versions in the Chapter14 directory—an incomplete version and a completed version. If you're interested in following along but don't want to perform the steps outlined here, open the solution file for the completed version. (It will be in the SodaMachine Completed directory.) The steps you'll follow here take you through building the state-based workflow. If you're interested in working through the steps, open the incomplete version instead. To open either solution, drag the .sln file onto a copy of Visual Studio to open the solution for editing and compilation. (If you decide to compile and execute the completed version directly, compile it twice before executing it. Internal project-level dependencies must be resolved after the first successful compilation.)

2. With the SodaMachine solution open in Visual Studio, press F6 or select Build Solution from Visual Studio's Build menu. The projects have various dependencies, and compiling the solution generates assemblies that dependent projects can reference.

3. Find the Workflow1.cs file in the SodaFlow project, within Visual Studio's Solution Explorer window. (You might need to expand tree control nodes to find it.) When the file is in view in the tree control, select it with a single mouse click and then click the View Designer toolbar button. This brings the workflow into the visual workflow designer for editing.

> **Note** I have already created the basic workflow project because the application uses *CallExternalMethod* and *HandleExternalEvent* activities using the techniques you saw in Chapters 8 and 10. There wasn't any need to rehash the steps necessary to create the custom activities, as you would need to do if you created the workflow project from scratch. (If you were starting from scratch you'd add a new workflow library project using the State Machine Workflow Library template.)

4. The workflow consists of a single *State* activity. Select the activity, *stateActivity1*, and change its name to **StartState**. You will find its *Name* property in Visual Studio's Properties pane when the activity is selected in the visual workflow designer.

5. When the workflow was created, Visual Studio inserted this original *State* activity for you. But it also established this activity as the initial, or "start," activity. When you renamed the activity in the preceding step, the workflow lost this linkage. To reestablish this activity as the start activity, click once anywhere in the visual workflow designer's surface except for the *State* activity to activate the properties for the workflow as a whole. In the Properties pane, you should see an *InitialStateName* property. Change that from *stateActivity1* to **StartState**. Note you can either type this value into the property itself or use the drop-down list and select StartState.

6. Let's now drop the remaining *State* activities onto the visual workflow designer's surface. As you recall, this facilitates assigning target states when working with *SetState*. From the Visual Studio Toolbox, drag an instance of the *State* activity onto the designer's surface and drop it next to the *StartState* activity. Change its name to **WaitCoinsState**.

7. Drop another *State* activity onto the visual workflow designer's surface, and name it **WaitSelectionState**.

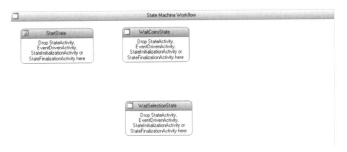

8. Drop the final *State* activity onto the visual workflow designer's surface, and change its name to **EndState**.

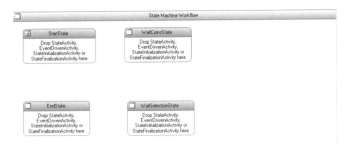

9. Just as you reassigned the starting state, so too will you need to tell WF what the ending state will be. Click the visual workflow designer's surface outside any *State* activity to enable the workflow properties. Assign the *CompletedStateName* property to be **End-State**. Visual Studio then clears *EndState*'s contents and changes the icon in the upper-left corner. As before, you can type **EndState** or select it from the drop-down list.

10. With the state activities in place, let's now add details. Starting with *StartState*, drag an instance of the *StateInitialization* activity from the Toolbox and drop it into *StartState*.

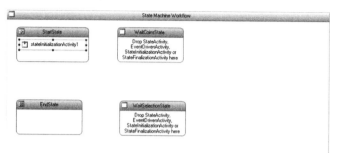

11. Double-click the activity you just inserted, *stateInitialization1*, to enter the sequential workflow editor.

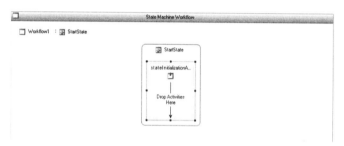

12. Drag a copy of the *Code* activity from the Toolbox, and drop it into the state initialization activity. Assign its *ExecuteCode* method to be **ResetTotal**. Visual Studio then adds the *ResetTotal* method for you and switches you to the code editor. Rather than add code at this point, return to the visual workflow designer.

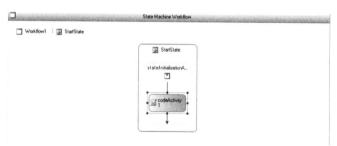

13. Next drag an instance of *SetState* onto the designer's surface, and drop it just below the *Code* activity you just inserted.

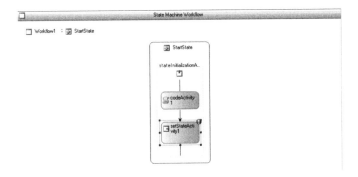

14. Assign the *SetState*'s *TargetStateName* property to be **WaitCoinsState**.

15. To return to the visual workflow designer's state editor view, click the Workflow1
   hyperlink-style button in the upper-left corner.

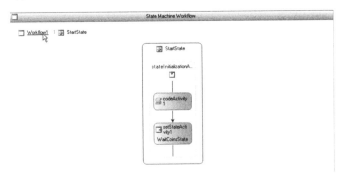

The state editor should now indicate that *StartState* transitions to *WaitCoinsState*.

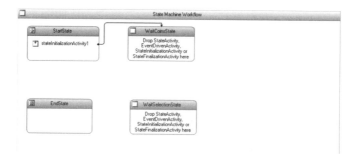

16. *StartState* is now complete. Next we'll turn to *WaitCoinsState*. To begin, drag a copy of the *EventDriven* activity onto the designer's surface and drop it into *WaitCoinsState*. Name it **CoinInserted** by changing its *Name* property in the Visual Studio Properties pane (you must press Enter for the change to take place).

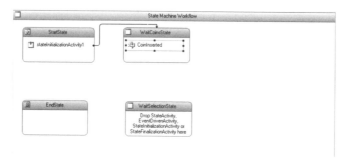

17. Double-click the *CoinInserted EventDriven* activity to enable the sequential workflow editor.

18. Now drag an instance of the *CoinInserted* custom activity from the Toolbox and drop it onto the *EventDriven* activity's surface. Note that if you haven't yet compiled the entire solution, the *CoinInserted* event doesn't appear in the Toolbox. You might have to remove the EventDriven activity to successfully compile if you skipped step 2.

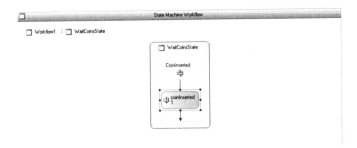

19. With the *ExternalEventHandler coinInserted1* activity selected in the visual workflow designer, click the *CoinValue* property in the Properties pane to activate the browse (...) button, and then click the browse button. This brings up the Bind 'CoinValue' To An Activity's Property dialog box. Click the Bind To A New Member tab, and type **LastCoin-Dropped** in the New Member Name field. The Create Property option should be selected, but if it isn't, select it so that you create a new dependency property. Click OK.

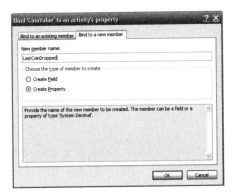

20. Now we need to make a decision—did the user just drop enough money to enable soda selection? To do this, drag an instance of the *IfElse* activity onto the visual workflow designer's surface and drop it into the *CoinInserted EventDriven* activity, following the *coinInserted1* event handler.

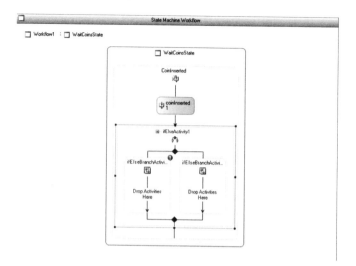

21. Select the left branch of *ifElseActivity1* to display its properties in the Properties pane. For its *Condition* property, select Code Condition. Expand the Condition node and in the child Condition property, type **TestTotal**. When Visual Studio adds the new method and switches you to the code editor, return to the visual workflow designer.

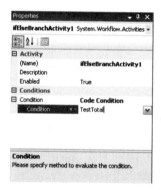

22. *TestTotal* will eventually check the total amount of money inserted into the soda machine. (We'll finish the workflow in the visual workflow designer before adding code because there are properties we need that have not yet been created.) If enough money has been inserted, we need to transition to the *WaitSelectionState*. Therefore, drag a copy of *SetState* into the left *IfElse* activity branch, *ifElseBranchActivity1*, and drop it. Assign its *TargetStateName* to be **WaitSelectionState**.

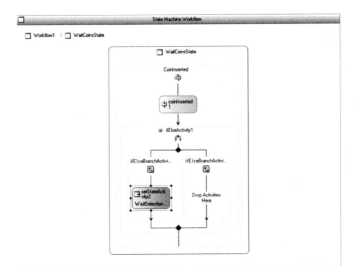

23. If *TestTotal* decides there isn't enough money to purchase a soda, the workflow needs to communicate the total amount of money inserted into the soda machine so far. To do this, drag an instance of *UpdateTotal* from the Toolbox and drop it into the right *IfElse* activity branch. *UpdateTotal* is a customized instance of *CallExternalMethod* I created for the job.

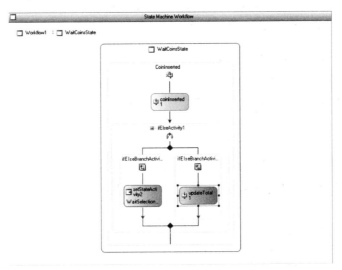

24. *UpdateTotal* requires a total value to communicate, so select its *total* property and click the browse (...) button to activate the bindings dialog box once again. When the bindings dialog box appears, select the Bind To A New Member tab and type **Total** into the New Member Name field, again making sure the Create Property option is selected. Click OK.

25. Click the Workflow1 hyperlink-style button in the upper-left corner to return to the state designer view. Drag an instance of *StateFinalization* onto the visual workflow designer's surface, and drop it into *WaitCoinsState*.

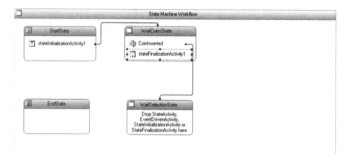

26. Double-click the *stateFinalizationActivity1* activity you just inserted to reactivate the sequential designer view.

27. From the Toolbox, drag an instance of *ReadyToDispense* and drop it into *stateFinalizationActivity1*. *ReadyToDispense* is also a customized *CallExternalMethod* activity.

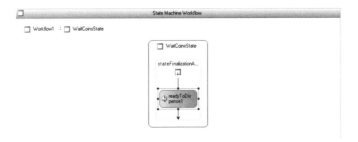

28. *ReadyToDispense1*, the activity you just inserted, will return the final total to the main application. To do that, it needs to access the *Total* property you inserted in step 24. Looking at *readyToDispense1*'s properties, click the *finalTotal* property, and then click the browse (...) button in the *finalTotal* property. Clicking the browse button activates the binding dialog box, but this time bind to an existing member. Select the *Total* property from the list and click OK.

29. Click the Workflow1 hyperlink-style button to return to the state designer view. There, select the *EventDriven* activity from the Toolbox and drag it onto the designer's surface, dropping it into the *WaitSelectionState* activity. Name it **ItemSelected**.

30. Double-click the *ItemSelected EventDriven* activity to enter the sequential designer view.

31. Drag a copy of the custom *ExternalEventHandler* activity *ItemSelected*, and drop it into the *ItemSelected EventDriven* activity.

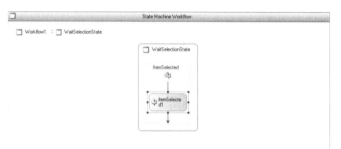

32. After the user makes a selection, the main application fires the *ItemSelected* event. When that happens, we want to transition to *EndState*. To do that, of course, we need to insert a copy of the *SetState* activity. So drag an instance of *SetState* from the Toolbox and drop it into the *ItemSelected EventDriven* activity following the *itemSelected1* event handler. Assign its *TargetStateName* to be **EndState**.

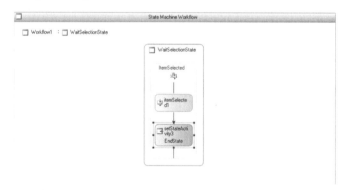

33. Click the Workflow1 hyperlink-style button to return to the state designer view.

34. The workflow is complete from a visual workflow designer's point of view, but we still have some code to write. Select Workflow1.cs in Visual Studio's Solution Explorer, and click the View Code toolbar button to open the file for editing in the code editor.

35. Scan the Workflow1.cs source file, and locate the *ResetTotal* method you added in step 12. Insert the following code in the *ResetTotal* method:

```
// Start with no total.
Total = 0.0m;
```

36. Finally, locate the *TestTotal* method you added in step 21. To that method, add this code:

```
// Add the last coin dropped to the total and check
// to see if the total exceeds 1.25.
Total += LastCoinDropped;
e.Result = Total >= 1.25m;
```

37. Compile the entire solution by pressing F6 or by selecting Build Solution from Visual Studio's Build menu. Correct any compilation errors.

Now you can run the application by pressing F5 or Ctrl+F5. Click a coin button. Does the total update in the LCD display? When you insert enough money, can you select a soda?

> **Note** If the application crashes with an *InvalidOperationException*, it's most likely due to the references not being fully updated by the first complete solution compilation. Simply recompile the entire application (repeat step 37) and run the application again. It should run cleanly.

If you want to continue to the next chapter, keep Visual Studio 2005 running and turn to Chapter 15, "Workflows and Transactions." In Chapter 15, you'll take your first steps into the fascinating world of workflow transactional processing.

If you want to stop, exit Visual Studio 2005 now, save your spot in the book, and close it. Who needs transactions anyway? Actually, we all do, but we'll wait for you.

Chapter 14 Quick Reference

To	Do This
Add new states to your state-based workflow	Drag as many copies of the *State* activity onto the visual workflow designer's surface as you require. Remember it's easier to wire the states together (using the *SetState* activity) with the states in place. However, this is not a requirement.
Receive events within your workflow's states	Drag instances of *EventDriven* into your *State* activity, and assign event handlers to each event. *EventDriven* can accept only a single event, so you might need to drop multiple copies of the *EventDriven* activity into your *State* activity—one for each discrete event you need to accept.
Transition between states	Drag an instance of *SetState* activity into your state's *EventDriven* activity or *StateInitialization* activity. Assign the *TargetStateName* to the name of the state you want to transition to.
Initialize your state as it is transitioned into	Drag a copy of the *StateInitialization* activity into your *State* activity, and drop the necessary activities into *StateInitialization* as required for your initialization process. *StateInitialization* is a composite, sequential activity, but it will allow for events to be accepted by your state event handlers (even if the processing of those events is deferred until the initialization work is complete). Note that only a single instance of *StateInitialization* is allowed per *State* activity.
Execute code as your state is transitioned out of	Drag an instance of *StateFinalization* onto the visual workflow designer's surface, and drop it into your *State* activity. Like *StateInitialization*, the *StateFinalization* activity is a composite, sequential activity, and only one per *State* activity is allowed.

Chapter 15
Workflows and Transactions

After completing this chapter, you will be able to:

- Understand the classical transaction model and where that model does and does not fit

- Know where classical transactions do not fit and when compensated transactions are appropriate

- See how transactions are rolled back or compensated

- See how to modify the default order of compensation

If you write software, sooner or later you'll need to understand transactional processing. *Transactional processing* in this sense means writing software that records information to a *durable resource*, such as a database, Microsoft Message Queue (which uses a database under the covers), Windows Vista with transacted file system and Registry access, or even some other software system that supports transactional processing. Durable resources retain the written information no matter what happens to them once the data has been recorded.

Transactions are critical to any business process because, by using transactions, you can be sure the data contained within your application is consistent. If the business process sustains an error yet still persists any data, the erroneous data most likely will propagate throughout the system, leaving you to question which data is good and which data is bad. Imagine ordering this book from an online merchant, only to find the merchant "had a little accident" with your credit card transaction and charged you 100 times the face value of the book instead of their discounted price. Transactional processing isn't a laughable or avoidable subject when errors such as this can happen.

Understanding Transactions

Transactional processing, at its very core, is all about managing your application's state. By *state*, I really mean the condition of all the application's data. An application is in a determinate state when all of its data is consistent. If you insert a new customer record into your database and that update requires two insertions (one to add a normalized row to tie the address to your customer and one to record the actual address information), adding the normalized row but failing to insert the address itself places your application in an indeterminate state. What will happen later when someone tries to retrieve that address? The system says the address should be there, but the actual address record is missing. Your application data is now inconsistent.

To be sure both updates are successful, a *transaction* comes into play. A transaction itself is a single unit of work that either completely succeeds or completely fails. That's not to say you can't update two different database tables. It just means that both table updates are considered a single unit of work, and both must be updated or else neither one is. If either or both updates fail, ideally you want the system to return to its state just prior to your attempt to update the tables. Your application should move forward with no evidence that there had been an incomplete attempt to modify the tables, and more important, you don't want to have data from the unsuccessful update in one table but not in the other.

> **Note**   Entire volumes have been written about transactions and transactional processing. Although I'll describe the concepts in sufficient depth to explain how Microsoft Windows Workflow Foundation (WF) supports transactions, I cannot possibly cover transactional processing in great depth in this book. If you haven't reviewed general transactional support in .NET 2.0, you should do so. WF transactions model .NET 2.0 transactional support very closely, and you might find the information in the following article helpful to understanding WF transactional support: *msdn2.microsoft.com/en-us/library/ms973865.aspx*.

Traditionally, transactions have come in a single form—that of the *XA*, or *two-phase commit*, style of transaction. However, with the advent of Internet-based communication and the need to commit long-running transactions, a newer style of transaction was introduced known as the *compensated* transaction. WF supports both styles. We'll first discuss the classical transaction, and then after noting the conditions that make this type of transaction a poor architectural choice, we'll discuss the compensated transaction.

Classic (XA) Transactions

The first system known to have implemented transactional processing was an airline reservation system. Reservations that required multiple flights could not progress if any of the individual flights could not be booked. The architects of that system knew this and designed a transactional approach that today we know as the. X/Open Distributed Transaction Processing Model, known as *XA*. (See *en.wikipedia.org/wiki/X/Open_XA*.)

An XA transaction involves the XA protocol, which is the two-phase commit I mentioned earlier, and three entities: the application, resource, and transactional manager. The application is, well, your application. The resource is a software system that is designed to join in XA-style transactions, which is to say it *enlists* (joins) in the transaction and understands how to participate in the two phases of committing data as well as provides for durability (discussed shortly). The transactional manager oversees the entire transactional process.

So what is a two-phase commit? In the end, imagine your application needs to write data to, say, a database. If that write is performed under the guise of a transaction, the database holds the data to be written until the transactional manager issues a *prepare* instruction. At that point, the database responds with a *vote*. If the vote is to go ahead and commit (write) the data into a table, the transaction manager proceeds to the next participating resource, if any.

If all resources vote to commit the data, the transactional manager issues a *commit* instruction and each resource writes the data into its internal data store. Only then is the data destined for your table actually inserted into the database.

If any one resource has a problem and votes not to commit the data, the transactional manager issues a *rollback* instruction. All resources participating in the transaction must then destroy the information related to the transaction, and nothing is permanently recorded.

Once the data has been committed, the XA protocol guarantees that the result of the transaction is permanent. If data was inserted, it is there for your application to use. If information was deleted, it has been deleted permanently. Your application, then, can move forward comfortable in the knowledge that all is well with the data. The data is consistent, and the application is in a determinate state.

ACID Properties

When we speak of XA transactions, it's hard not to mention the ACID acronym—Atomic, Consistent, Isolated, and Durable (*en.wikipedia.org/wiki/ACID*). All XA-style transactions, to non-volatile resources, must exhibit these properties or the transaction is architecturally invalid.

By *atomic*, we mean the resource enlisted in the transaction supports the two-phase commit protocol. The data to be transacted is either completely transacted (updated, deleted, or whatever) or none of it is. If the transaction fails, the resource returns to the state just prior to the attempt to transact the data.

Consistency means the data maintains integrity. For databases, this typically means the data doesn't violate any constraints, but for other resources maintaining integrity might have different or additional connotations. If the data violates any rules or constraints, which ultimately would result in an indeterminate application state, the resource must vote to roll back the transaction to prevent inconsistent data from being permanently recorded in the system.

Isolation is the transactional property that causes the system to be unable to access data while a transaction is ongoing. In a database, attempting to write to a previously locked row, or perhaps reading from a row with uncommitted data, is disallowed. Data is available only when it has been committed, or in the case of the read operation, when you explicitly allow uncommitted reads (often called "dirty reads").

Durable resources guarantee that when the data is committed it will always be available in a nonvolatile manner. If the data is committed and the power to the database server is cut off one millisecond later, when the database server is back online that data will be in the database, ready for your application to use. This is much more difficult to do in practice than it sounds, and it is one of the primary reasons architects use a database for persistent data storage rather than simple data files, such as XML, for critical data. (Admittedly, Windows Vista might change things a bit with its transacted file system, but hopefully you see my point.)

Long-Running Transactions and Application State

Keep in mind that the entire premise of the XA-style transaction is that your application will retain its original state if the transaction rolls back. But consider this: What happens to your application if a transaction takes an inordinate amount of time to commit?

Before I answer that, imagine your online purchasing system received an order from a customer, but the credit card validation process got hung up. Clearly your process is running within a transaction because you don't want to charge the customer if something fails. But in the meantime, other customers are placing orders. Lots of orders, if you're fortunate. If the first customer's transaction later fails, what will happen to the orders placed in the meantime?

If the system isn't designed to isolate individual order failures, then the correct thing to do is to roll the system completely back to its original state. But considering this, that means we not only lose the first customer's order, but we also lose *every other* customer's order that was placed in the interim. Even if it's only two orders, that's not good. But if it's 10,000 orders...the loss of that amount of revenue can't be tolerated.

Of course, we'll retain those 10,000 orders and just deal with the first customer as an isolated event, but we're taking a chance in this case and intentionally breaking one of the four transactional properties to retain the revenue. It's a calculated risk, but often a risk we must accept in real-world situations.

The property that's being broken is actually atomicity, and for this reason people who write transactional processing systems strive to keep their transactions as short as possible. You do only what is required within your transactional bounds and no more, and you do so as efficiently as possible so that the transaction completes quickly.

Now let's throw in another complication—the Internet. Your customer is ordering online, and networks are notorious for slow speeds and even disconnections. So transactional processing over the Internet is questionable if only because sooner or later a transaction will run overlong and put our online ordering system in a transactional bind.

Compensation as a Solution

It is precisely this situation that created the need for a *compensated* transaction. If I give you five apples using an XA-style transaction and the transaction fails, time itself rewinds to the point I started to give you the apples. In a sense, history is rewritten such that the five apples were never given in the first place. But if I give you five apples in a compensated transaction and that transaction fails, to compensate (so that we maintain a determinate application state), you must return five apples to me. It might seem like a subtle difference, but there is a definite difference between the two styles of transactions.

When writing XA-style transactions, the responsibility for rolling back failed transactions falls to the resource, such as your database. Conversely, when a compensated transaction fails, you—as a transactional participant—are responsible for compensating by providing a compensation function for your part of the transaction. If you debited an online consumer's credit card and were later told to compensate, you would immediately credit the customer's account with the same amount of money you originally debited. In an XA-style transaction, the account would never have been debited in the first place. With the compensated transaction, you initiate two actions—one to debit the account and one to later credit it.

> **Note** Make no mistake, it would be a rare system that could successfully perform XA-style transactions over the Internet. (I would argue that no system can, but I would be doing just that—starting an argument—so I accept the fact that some systems will try and even succeed in some cases.) Compensation is generally called for. But craft your compensation functions very carefully. Pay attention to details. If you don't, you could be making a bad situation worse by injecting error upon error. It is often not easy to write accurate compensation functions.

Initiating Transactions in Your Workflows

In general, initiating transactions in WF is as simple as dropping a transaction-based activity into your workflow. If you're using transactional activities, however, there is a little more you should know.

Workflow Runtime and Transactional Services

When you use a transaction-based activity in your workflow, two workflow-pluggable services are required. First, because the two out-of-the-box transaction-based WF activities are both decorated with the *PersistOnClose* attribute (mentioned in Chapter 6, "Loading and Unloading Instances"), you must also start the *SqlWorkflowPersistenceService*. If you do not, WF won't crash, but neither will your transactions commit.

Perhaps more interesting for this chapter is the *DefaultWorkflowTransactionService* that WF starts on your behalf when the workflow runtime is started. This service is responsible for both starting and committing your transactional operations. Without such a service, transactions within the workflow runtime are not possible.

> **Note** Although it's beyond the scope of this chapter, you can create your own transactional services. All WF transactional services derive from *WorkflowTransactionService*, so creating your own service is a matter of overriding the base functionality you want to change. In fact, WF ships with a customized transactional service for shared Microsoft SQL Server connections, *SharedConnectionWorkflowTransactionService*. You can find more information at *msdn2.microsoft.com/en-us/library/ms734716.aspx*.

Fault Handling

Although it isn't required that you handle faults in your workflow due to transactional failures, it's good practice. But I don't mention it here simply because it could be considered a best practice. I mention it because it is possible for you to write your own transactional service that automatically examines the exception and retries the transaction before actually failing. Although demonstrating how to do this is outside the scope of this chapter, you should know this is possible.

Ambient Transactions

The transaction-based activities all work with something known as the *ambient transaction*. When your workflow enters a transactional scope, the workflow transactional service automatically creates a transaction for you. There is no need to try and create one yourself. The activities embedded in a transactional scope all belong to this one ambient transaction and are committed or rolled back (or compensated) if the transaction succeeds or fails.

Using the *TransactionScope* Activity

XA-style transactions in WF are implemented by the *TransactionScope* activity. This activity is closely aligned with the .NET *System.Transactions* namespace, and in fact it initiates a *Transaction* as the ambient transaction when the activity begins execution. The *Transaction-Scope* activity even shares data structures (*TransactionOptions*) with *System.Transactions*.

Using the composite activity-based *TransactionScope* is truly as easy as dropping it into your workflow. Any activity you place inside the *TransactionScope* activity automatically inherits the ambient transaction and operates as typical transactions do when using .NET's own *System.Transactions*.

Note   You cannot place a *TransactionScope* activity within another transactional activity. Nesting of transactions is not permitted. (This rule holds true for *CompensatableTransaction-Scope* as well.)

Transactional options dictate more precisely how the ambient transaction will operate. These options, supported by the *System.Transactions.TransactionOptions* structure, allow you to set the isolation level and timeout that the ambient transaction will support. The timeout value is self-explanatory, but the isolation level might not be.

Note   The timeout values have limits, which are configurable. There is a machine-wide setting, *System.Transactions.Configuration.MachineSettingsSection.MaxTimeout*, and a local one, *System.Transactions.Configuration.DefaultSettings.Timeout*, which set the ceilings on the maximum value to allow for a timeout. These values override anything you set using *TransactionOptions*.

A transaction's isolation level defines to a large extent what the transaction can do with data to be transacted. For example, maybe you want your transaction to be able to read uncommitted data (to preclude being locked out by a previous transactional database page lock). Or the data you are writing might be critical, and therefore you allow the transaction to read only committed data, and moreover, you disallow other transactions to work with the data while your transaction is executing. The isolation levels you can select are shown in Table 15-1. You set both the isolation level and timeout using the *TransactionOptions* property of the *TransactionScope* activity.

Table 15-1   Transactional Isolation Levels

Isolation Level	Meaning
Chaos	Uncommitted and pending changes from transactions using higher isolated level cannot be overwritten.
ReadCommitted	Uncommitted data cannot be read during the transaction, but it can be modified.
ReadUncommitted	Uncommitted data can be both read and modified during the transaction. However, keep in mind that the data may change—there is no guarantee that the data will be the same on subsequent reads.
RepeatableRead	Uncommitted data can be read but not modified during the transaction. However, new data can be inserted.
Serializable	Uncommitted data can be read but not modified, and no new data can be inserted during the transaction.
Snapshot	Uncommitted data can be read. But prior to the transaction actually modifying the data, the transaction verifies that another transaction has not changed the data after it was initially read. If the data has been changed, the transaction raises an error. The purpose of this is to allow a transaction to read the previously committed data value.
Unspecified	A different isolation level from the one specified is being used, but the level cannot be determined for some reason. If you try to set the transactional isolation level to this value, an exception is thrown. Only the transactional system can set this value.

When you drop an instance of the *TransactionScope* activity into your workflow, the isolation level is automatically set to *Serializable*. Feel free to change this as your architecture dictates. *Serializable* is the strictest isolation level, but it also limits scalability to some degree. It's not uncommon to select *ReadCommitted* as the isolation level for systems that require a bit more throughput, but this is a decision only your system can dictate based on your individual requirements.

Committing Transactions

If you're used to working with SQL Server transactions, or perhaps COM+ transactions, you know that once the data has been inserted, updated, or deleted you must commit the transaction. That is, you initiate the two-phase commit protocol and the database permanently records or removes the data.

However, this is not necessary with the *TransactionScope* activity. If the transaction is successful (no errors while inserting, updating, or deleting the data), the transaction is automatically committed for you when the workflow execution leaves the transactional scope.

Rolling Back Transactions

How about rolling back failed transactions? Well, just as transactions are committed for you, so too will the data be rolled back if the transaction fails. What is interesting about this is the rollback is silent, at least as far as WF is concerned. If you need to check the success or failure of your transaction, you need to incorporate logic for doing so yourself. *TransactionScope* doesn't automatically throw an exception if the transaction fails. It merely rolls back the data and moves on.

Using the *CompensatableTransactionScope* Activity

If an XA-style transaction won't do, you can instead drop the *CompensatableTransactionScope* activity into your workflow and provide for compensated transactional processing. The *CompensatableTransactionScope* activity, like *TransactionScope*, is a composite activity. However, *CompensatableTransactionScope* also implements the *ICompensatableActivity* interface, which gives it the ability to compensate for failed transactions by implementing the *Compensate* method.

Also like *TransactionScope*, the *CompensatableTransactionScope* activity creates an ambient transaction. Activities contained within *CompensatableTransactionScope* share this transaction. If their operations succeed, the data is committed. However, should any of them fail, you generally initiate the compensation by executing a *Throw* activity.

> **Tip** Compensated transactions can enlist traditional resources, such as databases, and when the transaction commits, the data is committed just as if it were an XA-style transaction. However, a nice feature of compensated transactions is that you do not have to enlist an XA-style resource to store data. Sending data to a remote site using a Web service is the classic example for a nonenlistable transactional resource. If you send data to the remote site but later must compensate, you need to somehow communicate with the remote site that the data is no longer valid. (How you accomplish this depends on the individual remote site.)

Throw causes the transaction to fail and calls into execution your compensation handler for your *CompensatableTransactionScope* activity. You access the compensation handler through the Smart Tag associated with the *CompensatableTransactionScope* activity in much the same way you would add a *FaultHandler*.

> **Note**   Although throwing an exception kicks off the transactional compensation, the *Throw* activity itself is not considered handled. You can also decide to place a *FaultHandler* activity in your workflow to preclude premature workflow termination.

Using the *Compensate* Activity

When you are compensating a failed transaction implemented by *CompensatableTransaction-Scope*, the compensation handler is invoked. If you have multiple compensatable transactions, the transactions are compensated in a default order, starting with the deepest nested transaction and working outward. (You'll see how this might be accomplished in the next section.) When your logic calls for compensation, you can place a *Compensate* activity in your compensation handler to initiate compensation of all completed activities supporting *ICompensatableActivity*.

It will always be the case that exceptions will cause compensation, so the use of the *Compensate* activity is not required. Why have it then? Because you might have nested more than a single compensatable transaction in a *CompensatableSequence* activity. If one transaction fails and is to be compensated, you can initiate the compensation of the other transaction even if that transaction previously completed successfully.

> **Note**   The *Compensate* activity is valid only in compensation handlers, cancellation handlers, and fault handlers.

You should use the *Compensate* activity only when you need to compensate activities in an order other than the default compensation order. Default compensation invokes compensation for all nested *ICompensatableActivity* activities in the reverse order of their completion. If this ordering doesn't fit your workflow model, or if you want to selectively invoke compensation of completed compensatable child activities, the *Compensate* activity is the tool of choice.

> **Note**   The *Compensate* activity uses its *TargetActivityName* property to identify which compensatable activity should be compensated. If more than one compensatable activity should be queued for compensation, you need to use more than one *Compensate* activity. If you decide not to compensate a given transaction, simply do nothing in the compensation handler for that transaction or in the enclosing parent activity.

The *Compensate* activity provides you control over the compensation process by allowing you to decide whether you want to compensate an immediate child activity that supports compensation or not. This ability enables your workflow to explicitly perform compensation on a nested compensatable activity according to your process's needs. By specifying which compensatable activity you want to be compensated in the *Compensate* activity, any compensation code in that compensatable activity will be executed as long as the compensatable activity previously successfully committed.

If you want to compensate more than one nested compensatable activity, you add a *Compensate* activity in your handler for each compensatable activity you want to compensate. If the *Compensate* activity is used in a handler of a compensatable activity that contains embedded compensatable activities, and if *TargetActivityName* for that *Compensate* activity is assigned to the parent activity, compensation in all child (compensatable) activities that committed successfully is invoked. Try saying that three times, fast.

Using the *CompensatableSequence* Activity

The preceding section might leave you wondering why the *Compensate* activity exists. After all, you can't nest compensated transactions. You can't nest any type of WF-based transaction.

But let's look at it in a different way. How would you tie two compensatable transactions together so that the failure of one triggers compensation in the other, especially if the other already completed successfully? The answer is you pair the compensated transactions in a single instance of the *CompensatableSequence* activity. Then, in the compensation or fault handler for the *CompensatableSequence* activity, you trigger compensation of both child transactional scope activities if either one of them fails. Even more interesting is the situation where you tie three compensatable transactions together in a single *CompensatableSequence* activity and allow one transaction to succeed even if the others fail and are compensated. The *Compensate* activity gives you this control.

This highlights the intent of the *CompensatableSequence* activity. The *CompensatableSequence* activity, at its core, is a *Sequence* activity, and you use the *CompensatableSequence* activity in the same way you would any sequential activity. The major difference is that you can embed multiple compensatable activities in a single *CompensatableSequence* activity, effectively tying related transactions together. Coupling the *CompensatableSequence* activity with both the *CompensatableTransactionScope* and *Compensate* activities provides you with powerful transactional control in your workflow.

Note   *CompensatableSequence* activities can be embedded within other *CompensatableSequence* activities, but they cannot be children of *CompensatableTransactionScope* activities.

Tip   When combining multiple compensatable transactions in a single compensatable sequence, you do not have to assign compensation functions to the individual transacted activities. Compensation flows to the parent activity if called for, so you can collect your compensation activities in the enclosing compensatable sequence activity if you want to.

Creating a Transacted Workflow

I've created an application that simulates an automated teller machine (ATM), one where you provide your personal identification number, or PIN as it's called, and make deposits to or withdrawals from your bank account. Deposits will be embedded in an XA-style transaction, while withdrawals will be compensated if the action fails. To really exercise the transactional nature of the application, I placed a "force transactional error" check box in the application. Simply select the check box and the next database-related operation will fail.

The workflow for this application is a state-based one, and it is more complex than the application you saw in the previous chapter (Chapter 14, "State-Based Workflows"). I've shown the state machine I based the workflow on in Figure 15-1. Most of the application has already been written for you. You'll add the transactional components in the exercises to follow.

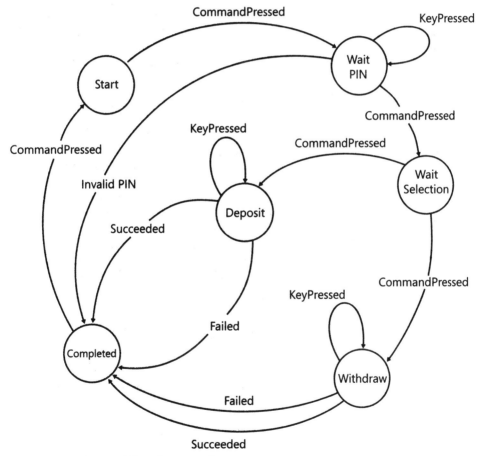

Figure 15-1   The WorkflowATM state diagram

The user interface for the application is shown in Figure 15-2. This is the initial application state, akin to the ATM's state prior to inserting your bank card. Clearly, the sample can't deal with a true bank card, so clicking the B key transitions the user interface (and application state) to the PIN verification state (shown in Figure 15-3).

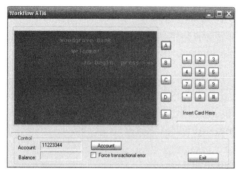

Figure 15-2   The WorkflowATM initial user interface

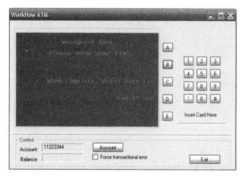

Figure 15-3   The WorkflowATM PIN verification user interface

You enter your PIN using the keypad to the right. Once the four-digit code is entered, you click the C key to kick off a database query to verify the PIN. If the PIN is verified (and note the account number in the lower-left corner; the PIN must be valid for that account number), the user interface transitions to the activity selection state, shown in Figure 15-4. Here you decide to either deposit funds to or withdraw funds from your account.

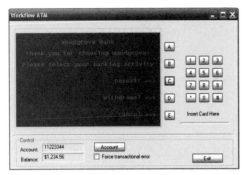

Figure 15-4   The WorkflowATM activity selection user interface

The application user interface for depositing and withdrawing funds is similar, so I've shown only the deposit user interface in Figure 15-5. You again use the keypad to enter a monetary value and then click a command key, the D key, to make the deposit or withdrawal or the E key to cancel the transaction.

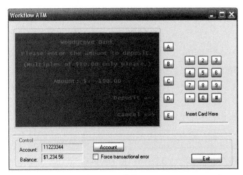

Figure 15-5   The WorkflowATM transaction deposit user interface

If the transaction was successful, you are rewarded with the screen you see in Figure 15-6. If not, you see the error screen shown in Figure 15-7. Either way, clicking the C key starts the workflow over again.

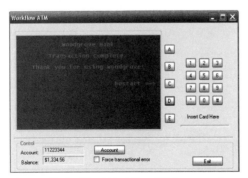

Figure 15-6   The WorkflowATM transaction successful user interface

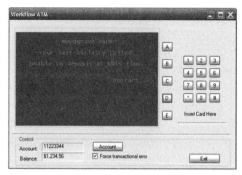

Figure 15-7   The WorkflowATM transaction failed user interface

The application requires a database to fully test WF's transactional capabilities. Therefore, I created a simple database used to store both user accounts with PINs and account balances. Several stored procedures are also available to help with the database interactions. All the stored procedures that involve a database update are required to execute within a transaction—I check @@trancount, and if it is zero, I return an error from each stored procedure. What this should prove is that the ambient transaction is being used if I fail to provide any ADO.NET code to initiate my own SQL Server transaction. What this also means is you need to create an instance of the database, but that's easily accomplished because you've learned how to execute queries in SQL Server Management Studio Express in previous chapters. In fact, let's start with that task because we'll soon need the database for application development and testing.

> **Note**   Before I forget to mention it, the database creation script creates a single account, 11223344, with the PIN 1234. The application allows you to change accounts and provide any PIN value you like, but unless you use this account (11223344) and this PIN (1234), or create your own account record, you will not be authorized to make deposits or withdrawals.

Creating the Woodgrove ATM databases

1. You should find the *Create Woodgrove Database.sql* database creation script in the \Workflow\Chapter15 directory. First find it and then start SQL Server Management Studio Express.

> **Note**   Keep in mind that the full version of SQL Server will work here as well.

2. When SQL Server Management Studio Express is up and running, drag the Create Woodgrove Database.sql file from Windows Explorer and drop it onto SQL Server Management Studio Express. This opens the script file for editing and execution.

Note   If SQL Server Management Studio Express requests a new connection to your database engine, make the connection and continue. The "Creating a SQL Server 2005 tracking database" procedure from Chapter 5, "Workflow Tracking," describes this process in detail if you need a refresher.

3. The script both creates the Woodgrove database and populates it with data. If you did not load SQL Server in the default directory, C:\Program Files\Microsoft SQL Server, you might need to edit the creation script to change the directory in which the database will be created. The fifth and seventh lines of the creation script indicate the database's directory and filename. Feel free to modify those as required to work within the bounds of your system. In most cases, you should not need to make changes. Click the Execute button to run the script and create the database. (You do not need to specify which database the query will run against since it creates an entirely new database.)

4. While you're using SQL Server Management Studio Express, if you didn't already work through the steps indicated in Chapter 6, "Loading and Unloading Instances," in the section "Setting Up SQL Server for Persistence," to install the workflow persistence database, do so now.

After completing these four steps, you'll have two databases ready to use: the Woodgrove database for banking information and the WorkflowStore database for workflow persistence. Now let's write some transacted workflow code.

Adding an XA-style transaction to your workflow

1. You should find the WorkflowATM application in the \Workflow\Chapter15\ WorkflowATM directory. As usual, I placed two different versions in the Chapter15 directory—an incomplete version and a completed version. If you're interested in following along but don't want to perform the steps outlined here, open the solution file for the completed version. (It will be in the WorkflowATM Completed directory.) If you're interested in working through the steps, open the WorkflowATM version instead. To open either solution, drag the .sln file onto an instance of Microsoft Visual Studio to open the solution for editing and compilation. For either version of the sample application, you might need to change the connection strings in the App.Config file to match your SQL Server installation.

2. So that the custom activities show up in the Visual Studio Toolbox, press F6 to compile the entire solution. You can, alternatively, choose Build and then Build Solution from Visual Studio's main menu. The application will compile without error.

3. Although the WorkflowATM application is moderately complex, it follows the pattern we've used throughout the book. The Windows Forms application itself communicates with the workflow via a local communication service, using custom activities I created with *wca.exe*. The service is housed in the BankingService project, while the workflow is maintained in the BankingFlow project. The only code we'll concentrate on is in the

workflow itself. Locate the Workflow1.cs file in the BankingFlow project, and double-click it to open it for editing in the visual workflow designer. The workflow should appear as you see here. Does it look somewhat like Figure 15-1?

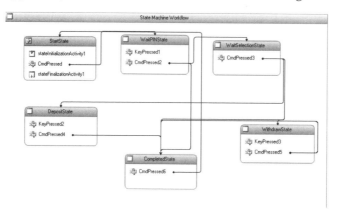

4. To insert the XA-style transaction, first double-click the *CmdPressed4 EventDriven* activity in the *DepositState* activity. This opens the *CmdPressed4* activity for editing.

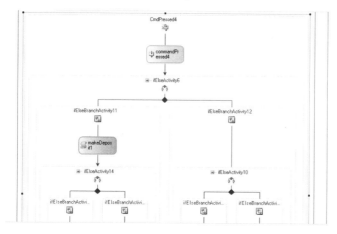

5. Looking to the left, you should see the *Code* activity named *makeDeposit1*. Between this *Code* activity and the *ifElseBranchActivity11* title above *makeDeposit1*, drag an instance of the *TransactionScope* activity from the Toolbox and drop it.

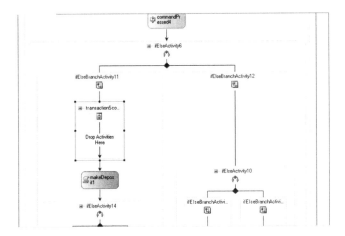

6. Drag *makeDeposit1* from below the transaction scope activity you just inserted, and drop it inside so that the *makeDeposit1 Code* activity will execute within the transactional scope.

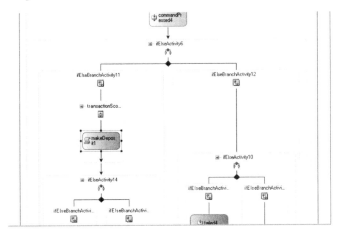

> **Note**   Feel free to examine the code contained in the *MakeDeposit* method, which is bound to the *makeDeposit1* activity. The code you find there is typical ADO.NET database access code. An interesting thing to see is that no SQL Server transaction is initiated in the code. Instead, the ambient transaction will be used when the code is executed.

7. Compile the entire solution by pressing F6 or by selecting Build Solution from the Visual Studio Build menu.

8. To test the application, press F5 or select Start Debugging from Visual Studio's Debug menu. The account should already be set. Click the B key to access the PIN verification screen, and then type **1234** (the PIN). Click the C key to verify the PIN and proceed to the activity selection screen.

> **Note** If the application fails to verify the PIN, assuming you typed the correct PIN into the application, it might be because the connection string for the Woodgrove database is not correct. (The error handling is such that the application should not crash.) Verify that the connection string is correct, and run the application again. Chapter 5 has some suggestions for building connection strings.

9. Because you added the transaction to the deposit logic, click the C key to make a deposit.

10. Type **10** to deposit $100 (10 multiples of $10.00) and then click the D key to initiate the transaction. The transaction should succeed, and the screen now indicates the transaction is complete. Because the Woodgrove database creation script loaded the fictitious bank account with $1234.56, the balance now indicates $1334.56. Note you can read the balance in the lower-left corner of the application. Click the C key to return to the starting screen.

11. Now let's force the transaction to fail. The Deposit stored procedure takes as a parameter a value that causes the stored procedure to return an error. Selecting the Force Transactional Error check box assigns a value that causes the Deposit error. So click the B key to access the PIN verification screen yet again, then type **1234**, and then click the C key to access the banking activity selection screen.

12. Again, click the C key to make a deposit and enter **10** to deposit another $100, but this time select the Force Transactional Error check box *before* clicking the D key.

13. After clicking the D key, the application indicates a transactional failure, but notice the balance. It indicates the current balance is still $1334.56, which was the balance prior to the transaction. Both the successful transaction (step 10) and the failed transaction (step 12) were handled by the *TransactionScope* activity you placed in the workflow in step 5.

This is a phenomenal result! By including a single WF activity, we gained automatic (XA-style) transactional control over database updates. Can implementing a compensated transaction be as easy? As it happens, more work is required, but it's still not difficult to add compensated transactions to your workflow.

Adding a compensated transaction to your workflow

1. With the WorkflowATM solution open for editing, again open the Workflow1.cs file in the visual workflow designer. Look for the *WithdrawState* activity in the lower row of state activities and double-click the *CmdPressed5* activity you see there. This opens the *CmdPressed5* activity for editing, and once it's opened, you should see the *makeWithdrawal1 Code* activity on the left side of the workflow.

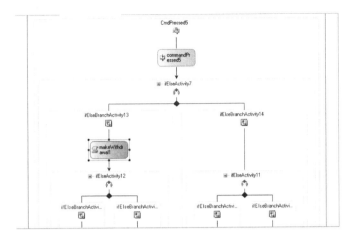

2. Similar to what you did with the preceding transaction, drag an instance of *CompensatableTransactionScope* from the Visual Studio Toolbox and drop it between the *makeWithdrawal1* activity and the *ifElseBranchActivity13* title above *makeWithdrawal1*.

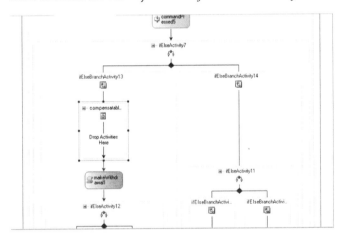

3. Drag the *makeWithdrawal1 Code* activity from below the *compensatableTransactionScope1* activity, and drop it into the transaction scope. The *MakeWithdrawal* method, which is bound to the *makeWithdrawal1* activity, now executes its ADO.NET code within an ambient transaction just as the deposit activity did.

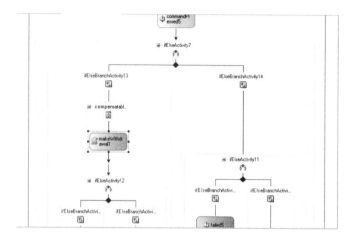

4. However, unlike the deposit functionality, you must provide the compensation logic. The transaction isn't rolled back in the traditional sense. Instead, you need to access the *compensatableTransactionScope1* compensation handler and add the compensating function yourself. To do that, move the mouse over the Smart Tag beneath the *compensatableTransactionScope1* title in the visual workflow designer and click it once to drop the view menu associated with this activity.

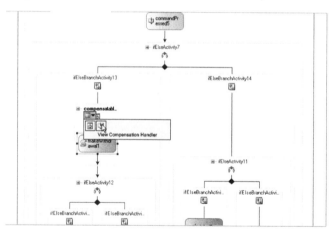

5. Click the right icon, View Compensation Handler, to activate the compensation handler view.

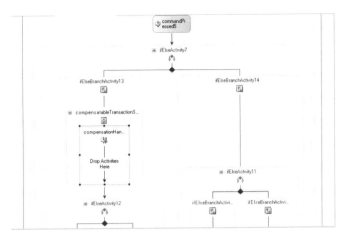

6. Drag an instance of the *Code* activity from the Visual Studio Toolbox, and drop it into the compensation handler activity.

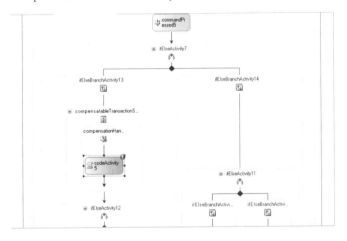

7. For the *Code* activity's *ExecuteCode* property, enter **CompensateWithdrawal**. Visual Studio inserts the method into your source code and switches you to the code editor.

8. Add the following code to the *CompensateWithdrawal* method you just inserted:

```
// Here, you "undo" whatever was done that did succeed. The
// code that withdrew the money from the account was actually
// successful (there is no catch block), so this compensation
// is forced. Therefore, we're safe in depositing the amount
// that was withdrawn. Note we can't use MakeDeposit since
// we require a SQL Server transaction and this method is
// called within the compensation handler (i.e., we can't drop
// a TransactionScope activity into the compensation to kick
// off the SQL Server transaction). We'll create the transaction
// ourselves here.
//
// Craft your compensation handlers carefully. Be sure you know
// what was successfully accomplished so that you can undo it
// correctly.
string connString =
    ConfigurationManager.ConnectionStrings["BankingDatabase"].
                                           ConnectionString;

if (!String.IsNullOrEmpty(connString))
{
    SqlConnection conn = null;
    SqlTransaction trans = null;
    try
    {
        // Create the connection
        conn = new SqlConnection(connString);

        // Create the command object
        SqlCommand cmd = new SqlCommand("dbo.Deposit", conn);
        cmd.CommandType = CommandType.StoredProcedure;

        // Create and add parameters
        SqlParameter parm = new SqlParameter("@AccountNo", SqlDbType.Int);
        parm.Direction = ParameterDirection.Input;
        parm.Value = _account;
        cmd.Parameters.Add(parm);
        parm = new SqlParameter("@ThrowError", SqlDbType.SmallInt);
        parm.Direction = ParameterDirection.Input;
        parm.Value = 0;
        cmd.Parameters.Add(parm);
        parm = new SqlParameter("@Amount", SqlDbType.Money);
        parm.Direction = ParameterDirection.Input;
        parm.Value = CurrentMoneyValue;
        cmd.Parameters.Add(parm);
        SqlParameter outParm =
                    new SqlParameter("@Balance", SqlDbType.Money);
        outParm.Direction = ParameterDirection.Output;
        outParm.Value = 0; // initialize to invalid
        cmd.Parameters.Add(outParm);

        // Open the connection
        conn.Open();
```

```
            // Initiate the SQL transaction
            trans = conn.BeginTransaction();
            cmd.Transaction = trans;

            // Execute the command
            cmd.ExecuteNonQuery();

            // Commit the SQL transaction
            trans.Commit();

            // Pull the output parameter and examine
            CurrentBalance = (decimal)outParm.Value;
        } // try
        catch
        {
            // Rollback... Note we could issue a workflow exception here
            // or continue trying to compensate (by writing a transactional
            // service). It would be wise to notify someone...
            if (trans != null) trans.Rollback();
        } // catch
        finally
        {
            // Close the connection
            if (conn != null) conn.Close();
        } // finally
    } // if
```

9. With the compensation code added to your workflow, return to the visual workflow designer and drop an instance of the custom *Failed* activity into the compensation handler, following the *Code* activity you just entered. Note Visual Studio might reformat and return you to the top-level state activity layout as you return to the visual workflow designer. If this happens, simply double-click the *CmdPressed5* activity in *WithdrawState* once again to access the *compensatableTransactionScope1* activity, and once again select the compensation handler view from its Smart Tag.

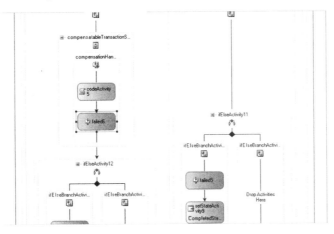

10. For the *Failed* activity's error property, type **Unable to withdraw funds**.

11. Following the *Failed* activity you just placed in your workflow, drag and drop an instance of *SetState*. For its *TargetStateName* property, select *CompletedState*.

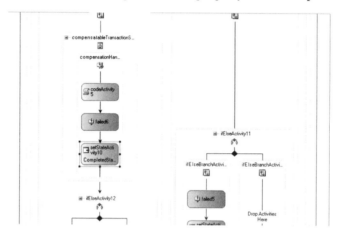

12. To again test the application, press F5 or select Start Debugging from Visual Studio's Debug menu. After the application begins execution, click the B key to access the PIN verification screen, and then type **1234** (the PIN). Click the C key to verify the PIN and proceed to the activity selection screen.

13. Click the D key to make a withdrawal.

14. Press **10** to withdraw $100 (10 multiples of $10.00) and then click the D key to initiate the transaction. With no other intervention on your part, the transaction should succeed and the screen should now tell you the transaction is complete with a balance of $1234.56.

15. Now let's again force the transaction to fail. Click the C key to restart the ATM and then click the B key to access the PIN verification screen once more. Type **1234**, and then click the C key to access the banking activity selection screen.

16. Once again, enter **10** to withdraw another $100, and select the Force Transactional error check box. Then click the D key to initiate the transaction.

17. After you click the D key, the application indicates a transactional failure and displays the current balance ($1234.56). Because there is no *catch* block in the *MakeWithdrawal* method, we know the withdrawal was made. (If it was not, the application would have terminated with a critical error.) This means the account was in fact debited the $100 and that the compensating function ran, which added $100 back into the account.

> **Note**   There are other ways to see the account debited and then credited as well. You could set a breakpoint in the compensating function, or you could even execute SQL Server Profiler, if you're familiar with that application and are using the full retail version of SQL Server.

If you want to continue to the next chapter, keep Visual Studio 2005 running and turn to Chapter 16, "Declarative Workflows." WF is capable of loading workflows declared in an XML format, and you'll see how that's accomplished in the next chapter.

If you want to stop, exit Visual Studio 2005 now, save your spot in the book, and close it. The next chapter introduces workflow in a slightly different way, and one you might find quite interesting, but there is certainly no hurry.

Chapter 15 Quick Reference

To	Do This
Introduce XA-style transactions into your workflow	Drop an instance of the *TransactionScope* activity into your workflow. You then should place all the transacted activities within the transactional scope. The ambient transaction will be applied to all, and should any one fail, all child activities will be rolled back. Otherwise, all will commit.
Introduce compensated transactions into your workflow	Drag and drop an instance of the *CompensatableTransactionScope* activity into your workflow. As with the *TransactionScope* activity, you then drop transacted child activities into the transactional scope. If all succeed, the transaction is considered successful and the child activities are committed. If not, the compensation handler is invoked and the code you place there to "undo" the transaction is executed.
Change the default order of compensation, or control which child transaction is compensated	Drop a *Compensate* activity into your compensation handler, cancellation handler, or fault handler. Assign the *TargetActivityName* property to the name of the activity to be compensated for.
Collect compensated transactions into a single work entity	Use the *CompensatableSequence* activity, and drop instances of the *CompensatableTransactionScope* activity into the compensated sequence. Keep in mind you can control which transactions are compensated using the *Compensate* activity. Individual compensated transactions do not require their own compensation function if the enclosing compensated sequence will provide for compensation.

Chapter 16

Declarative Workflows

After completing this chapter, you will be able to:

- Understand the primary differences between imperative and declarative workflow models

- Create declarative workflows

- Use the XAML XML vocabulary to build workflows

- Call XAML-based workflows into execution

Many developers probably don't realize that Microsoft Windows Workflow Foundation (WF) is able to execute workflows based on both imperative definitions (using the visual workflow designer) and declarative definitions (workflows defined using XML).

There are advantages to each style. When you create a workflow application using the techniques we've used throughout this book, the workflow model is actually compiled into an executable assembly. The advantage there is the execution is fast, as is the loading of the workflow itself.

But this style is also inflexible. Although there are dynamic capabilities built into WF (which are not covered in this book), in general your workflows remain as you compiled them. If your business process changes, unless you're using declarative rules for making workflow decisions (as discussed in Chapter 12, "Policy and Rules"), you will have to edit your workflow definition, recompile, and redeploy, as well as perform all the associated testing and validation that typically goes with that.

However, the workflow runtime is capable of accepting nearly any form of workflow definition. You just have to write some code to translate the definition you provide into a model the workflow runtime can execute. This is, in fact, precisely what WF does with XML-based workflow definitions.

As you might expect, recording your workflow in an XML format allows for very easy modification and redeployment. Instead of recompiling your workflow in Microsoft Visual Studio, you simply edit the XML-based workflow definition using any XML editor (even Notepad in Windows) and provide that to the workflow runtime as it creates the workflow model. You can even have the best of both worlds by compiling your XML workflow definition using the WF workflow compiler. We'll explore these topics in this chapter.

Declarative Workflow—XML Markup

To begin, there is a rich history of declarative application definition in .NET 3.0 (which includes Windows Presentation Foundation, or WPF). WPF from the start provided a declarative capability that could either be entirely declarative or partially so. You could encapsulate your application completely within the XML markup in a vocabulary known as *XML Application Markup Language*, or *XAML* (pronounced "zammel"). Or, by using special XAML-based constructs, you could compile some of your application into assemblies and call this into execution through XAML. You can even write C# code and embed it into your XAML definition for later execution, or place your C# code in a *code-beside* file.

> **Note**   You cannot find a better treatise on XAML and WPF than Charles Petzold's latest work, *Applications = Code + Markup* (Microsoft Press, 2006). You should especially review Chapter 19 in his book if you're interested in a very detailed XAML discussion.

In fact, just for fun try this. Create a new text file on your system, and name it **Button.xaml**. Type the code you see in Listing 16-1 into the file and save it. Then double-click the file. Because you must have installed the .NET 3.0 components to create workflow applications, you will have registered the .xaml file extension. Windows then knows to load the XAML file into your Web browser and display it. (Note you may be asked to download a browser-extension control from Microsoft to do so.) Although it's merely a button, this is a full-fledged WPF application, albeit a simple one. Figure 16-1 shows the button as it is rendered on Windows XP using Microsoft Internet Explorer 6.0.

Listing 16-1   Example XAML-based application displaying a single button

```xml
<?xml version="1.0"?>
<Button xmlns="http://schemas.microsoft.com/winfx/2006/xaml/presentation"
 Margin="36" Foreground="Blue" FontSize="36pt">
    Hello, World!
</Button>
```

Figure 16-1   A XAML-based button in action

The WF team took this concept and incorporated it into WF as well. While the WF XML follows the XAML namespace conventions, filenames containing WF-related XML are customarily named using a *.xoml* file extension. This approach allows for automated tools to interpret the file as a workflow file instead of as a presentation file. In fact, a tool we'll use in this chapter, the workflow compiler (*wfc.exe*), demands the .xoml file extension when creating workflows based on XAML.

Even though Listing 16-1 isn't a workflow declaration, take a closer look at the XML you see. Notice the XML element name is the same as the supporting .NET WPF class, which in this case is *Button*. Also worth noting are the attributes the button will have assigned once the XAML file is interpreted: *FontSize*, *Margin*, and *Foreground*. By changing these or adding others, we very easily change the nature of the button.

Workflow-based XAML files exhibit the same characteristics. The XML element name represents the activity type, such as *CodeActivity* or *IfElseActivity*. And as you might expect, each element can contain properties and their values. As for workflow structure, composite activities will have child XML elements, while basic activities will not.

Declaring Namespaces and Namespace Association

XML in general is very sensitive to namespaces, and XAML is no different. Several namespaces are critical, including workflow-related namespaces and namespaces associated with .NET itself.

The primary namespace your XAML file must include is *http://schemas.microsoft.com/winfx/ 2006/xaml*, which customarily uses the prefix *x*. In XML, the namespace declaration looks like this:

```
xmlns:x="http://schemas.microsoft.com/winfx/2006/xaml"
```

Workflow-based XAML files must also include the workflow namespace, *http://schemas. microsoft.com/winfx/2006/xaml/workflow*. If there is a namespace prefix, by convention it will be *wf*, but in workflow-based XAML files you typically make the workflow namespace the default namespace (by omitting the prefix):

```
xmlns="http://schemas.microsoft.com/winfx/2006/xaml/workflow"
```

It's a rare workflow that doesn't need to access the .NET runtime, but how is this done from an XML file? Well, actually the file doesn't invoke anything related to the .NET runtime—the workflow runtime does that for you. The XML file merely needs to identify the .NET common language runtime (CLR) components it requires, whether those objects are provided by .NET itself or are custom objects you include with the XML-based workflow. For this identification action, there is a special syntactical nomenclature used to create an XML namespace.

The CLR namespace that XAML will use is created using two keywords: *clr-namespace* and *assembly=*. For example, if you wanted to use *Console.WriteLine* from within your XAML-based workflow, you would need to create a namespace for the .NET namespace *System*:

```
xmlns:sys="clr-namespace:System;assembly=System"
```

The XML namespace is then a concatenation of the .NET namespace, followed by a semicolon, followed again by the assembly name that hosts the .NET namespace. Keep in mind this holds true for both .NET assemblies and assemblies you create.

But when you create custom assemblies you want to use in XAML-based workflows, it isn't enough to merely create the assembly, provide it with a namespace, and include it with the workflow. The workflow runtime will load the assembly you specify, but it requires the use of an additional attribute—the *XmlnsDefinition* attribute—to actually call objects into execution.

For example, consider this activity you want to use within your XAML-based workflow:

```
public class MyActivity : Activity
{
. . .
}
```

Assuming the class is contained within the *MyNamespace* namespace in the *MyAssembly* assembly, the code to introduce it to the XAML-based workflow is shown in Listing 16-2.

Listing 16-2 Example use of XmlnsDefinition attribute

```
using System;
using System.Collections.Generic;
using System.Text;
using System.Workflow.ComponentModel;
using System.Workflow.Activities;

[assembly:XmlnsDefinition("urn:MyXmlNamespace", "MyNamespace")]
namespace MyNamespace
{
    public class MyActivity : Activity
    {
        // Not a very active activity...!
    }
}
```

The XML to reference this class would then be as follows:

```
xmlns:ns0="urn:MyXmlNamespace"
```

Perhaps surprisingly, the string the namespace uses isn't important. What is important is that the string defining the namespace in *XmlnsDefinition* is the same as the namespace string used in the XML file when that namespace is declared, and the namespace must be unique within the XML file that uses the namespace. That is, they must match and not already identify an existing namespace in use in the XML file. We'll gain more experience with this in the following sections.

> **Note**   If you are new to XML namespaces, the following may be helpful: *http://msdn. microsoft.com/XML/Understanding/Fundamentals/default.aspx?pull=/library/en-us/dnxml/html/ xml_namespaces.asp*.

Creating and Executing XAML-Based Workflows

Workflow definitions defined in an XML file can be executed in one of two ways: through direct execution by the workflow runtime or as compiled assemblies in their own right. To execute a workflow contained in an XML file directly, simply call the workflow runtime's *CreateWorkflow* method using an *XmlTextReader* as a parameter, after first loading the XML into the *XmlTextReader*. Compiling XML files involves the use of the workflow compiler, *wfc.exe*. Let's look at both cases using the simple workflow you see in Figure 16-2.

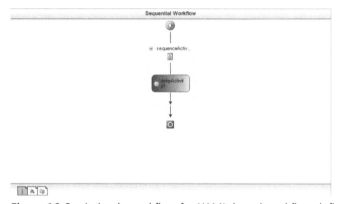

Figure 16-2   A simple workflow for XAML-based workflow definition experimentation

Creating a new workflow application with direct XML execution

1. I've provided two versions of the sample application: a completed version and an incomplete version, both found in \Workflow\Chapter16\. The DirectXmlWorkflow application is incomplete, but it requires only the workflow definition. The DirectXml-Workflow Completed version is ready to run. If you'd like to follow the steps I've outlined here, open the incomplete version. If you'd rather follow along but not type in code or drag activities, then open the completed version. To open either version, drag the .sln file onto Visual Studio and it will open it for you.

2. Before we modify the Program.cs file to execute our workflow, let's create the workflow itself. Right-click the DirectXmlWorkflow project name in Visual Studio's Solution Explorer, select Add, and then select New Item. When the Add New Item dialog box appears, select XML File from the list and name it **Workflow1.xml**. Click Add.

> **Note**   Visual Studio will create the file using the .xml file extension. Do not change that to .xoml just yet. Doing so will cause the XML file to be edited in the visual workflow designer, whereas you'll type the XML in directly for this sample. The .xoml file extension is a convention and not a requirement for WF runtime execution, so we're really just using Visual Studio as a convenient XML editor. (Any XML editor will do.) Just make sure the XML file is copied to the executable directory when the application runs so that the code will find the file.

3. Select the Workflow1.xml file in Solution Explorer to activate its file properties in the Properties pane.

4. Change the Workflow1.xml file's Copy To Output Directory option from Do Not Copy to Copy If Newer.

5. When Visual Studio created Workflow1.xml, it should have opened the XML file for editing. Add the following XML to the file and then save it:

```
<SequentialWorkflowActivity x:Name="Workflow1"
 xmlns:x="http://schemas.microsoft.com/winfx/2006/xaml"
 xmlns="http://schemas.microsoft.com/winfx/2006/xaml/workflow">
    <SequenceActivity x:Name="sequenceActivity1">
        <DelayActivity TimeoutDuration="00:00:05" x:Name="delayActivity1" />
    </SequenceActivity>
</SequentialWorkflowActivity>
```

6. Open the Program.cs file for editing. Add the following *using* statement to the end of the list of existing *using* statements:

```
using System.Xml;
```

7. Scan through the code and find this line of code:

```
Console.WriteLine("Waiting for workflow completion.");
```

8. So that you actually invoke the XAML-based workflow you just created, add the following lines of code after the line you found in the preceding step:

```
// Load the XAML-based workflow
XmlTextReader rdr = new XmlTextReader("Workflow1.xml");
```

9. To create a workflow instance, add this code following the line of code you just inserted:

```
// Create the workflow instance.
WorkflowInstance instance =
   workflowRuntime.CreateWorkflow(rdr);

// Start the workflow instance.
instance.Start();
```

10. Compile the solution by pressing F6, correcting any compilation errors.

11. Execute the application by pressing Ctrl+F5, or F5 if debugging is desired. If you don't run the application from within an open command window, you might have to set a breakpoint in *Main* to see the output.

You can create some rather complex workflows in this manner. However, it is limited in the following ways. First, although there is a mechanism for executing C# code from within the workflow when invoked in this way, it's far preferable to create custom assemblies that, if nothing else, house the code you want to execute. And second, you can't pass parameters into the workflow without first creating a custom root activity to accept them. At some point in the future that might change, but for now this is how WF operates. We'll create a custom assembly for this purpose later in the chapter.

However, an intermediate step is to compile your XAML-based workflow into an assembly you can reference for execution. To compile the XAML-based XML, we'll use the workflow compiler, *wfc.exe*.

> **Note** To learn a bit more about *wfc.exe*, see *msdn2.microsoft.com/en-us/library/ ms734733.aspx.*

Creating a new workflow application with compiled XML execution

1. Once again, I've provided two versions of the sample application: a completed version and an incomplete version, both found in \Workflow\Chapter16\. The CompiledXmlWorkflow application is incomplete, but it only requires the workflow definition. The CompiledXmlWorkflow Completed version is ready to run. If you'd like to follow the steps I've outlined here, open the incomplete version. If you'd rather follow along but not type code or drag activities, then open the completed version. To open either version, drag the .sln file onto Visual Studio and it will open it for you.

2. Add a new Workflow1.xml file as you did in step 2 of the preceding sample. Because you'll be compiling the workflow with the workflow compiler, you don't need to change the compiler settings for this file (steps 3 and 4 of the preceding section).

3. Add the following XML to the Workflow1.xml file and then save it:

    ```
    <SequentialWorkflowActivity x:Name="Workflow1" x:Class="Workflow1"
     xmlns:x="http://schemas.microsoft.com/winfx/2006/xaml"
     xmlns="http://schemas.microsoft.com/winfx/2006/xaml/workflow">
      <SequenceActivity x:Name="sequenceActivity1">
        <DelayActivity TimeoutDuration="00:00:05" x:Name="delayActivity1" />
      </SequenceActivity>
    </SequentialWorkflowActivity>
    ```

    Although this might look like the XML you added in the preceding sample, there is a minor difference: the inclusion of the *x:Class* attribute. This is required by the workflow compiler because the compiler will need to name the new class when the workflow is compiled.

4. Change the file extension from .xml to .xoml in Solution Explorer. If Visual Studio issues a warning about changing file types, ignore the warning and click Yes. The *wfc.exe* tool won't accept XML files with the .xml file extension. They must have the .xoml file extension. Save the file by choosing Save Workflow1.xoml from the File menu or by pressing Ctrl+S.

5. Open a command window. In Windows XP, you can click the Start button and then Run. After the Run dialog box appears, type **cmd** and click OK. If you're using Windows Vista, from the Start button access Accessories from All Programs and select Command Prompt.

6. Type **cd \Workflow\Chapter16\CompiledXmlWorkflow\CompiledXmlWorkflow** at the command prompt, and press Enter to change directories. The Workflow1.xoml file is now directly accessible in this directory.

7. Type **"C:\Program Files\Microsoft SDKs\Windows\v6.0\Bin\Wfc.exe"** **workflow1.xoml** at the command prompt, and press Enter. Of course, this assumes the Windows SDK was installed on your C drive in the Program Files directory. If you installed the Windows SDK elsewhere, use that directory instead.

8. The workflow compiler should execute without error. When its compilation processing is complete, it produces a dynamic-link library *workflow1.dll*, located in the same directory as Workflow1.xoml. You now need to reference that library, as it contains the workflow identified in the XML file you created in step 3. To do that, right-click the CompiledXmlWorkflow project name in Solution Explorer and select Add Reference. When the Add Reference dialog box pops up, select the Browse tab, select workflow1.dll from the list, and then click OK.

9. The workflow is now complete, so let's finish the main application. Open the Program.cs file for editing. Scan through the file, and find this line of code:

```
Console.WriteLine("Waiting for workflow completion.");
```

10. Add this code following the line of code you just found:

```
// Create the workflow instance.
WorkflowInstance instance =
    workflowRuntime.CreateWorkflow(typeof(Workflow1));

// Start the workflow instance.
instance.Start();
```

11. Compile the solution by pressing F6, correcting any compilation errors.

12. Execute the application by pressing Ctrl+F5 or F5. Again, you might have to set a breakpoint in *Main* to see the output if you don't run the application from within an open command window.

Although for this sample we didn't use one, you could also create a *code-beside* file and include code to be compiled into your workflow assembly. By convention, if the XML file uses the .xoml file extension, the code-beside file uses .xoml.cs. The *wfc.exe* tool accepts both a list of .xoml files and an associated list of .xoml.cs files, and it will compile everything together into a single workflow assembly, assuming there are no compilation errors.

Although it's seemingly a minor detail, this detail will prevent you from compiling your workflow. The only difference between the workflow in the first sample and the second sample is the addition of the *x:Class* attribute to the markup. XAML-based workflows lacking the *x:Class* attribute are candidates for direct execution only. Merely adding the *x:Class* attribute means you must compile the XAML-based workflow using *wfc.exe*. If you try to directly execute your XML-based workflow and generate a *WorkflowValidationFailedException* as a result, this is the most likely problem.

The instance in which compiling your XAML-based workflow makes the most sense occurs when you need to pass initialization parameters into your workflow. Directly executed XAML-based workflows can't accept initialization parameters. To demonstrate this, let's return all the way to Chapter 1, "Introducing Microsoft Windows Workflow Foundation," and re-create the postal code validation sample application. However, we'll host the workflow in XML rather than directly in C# code. We'll want to use a code-beside file because we'll have conditions to evaluate and code to execute.

> **Note**   You could place the code directly into the XML markup using the *x:Code* element. If this is interesting to you, see *msdn2.microsoft.com/en-gb/library/ms750494.aspx*.

Creating a new workflow application with compiled XML that accepts initialization parameters

1. Again, I've provided two versions of the sample application: a completed version and an incomplete version, both found in \Workflow\Chapter16\. The PCodeXaml application is incomplete, but it requires only the workflow definition. The PCodeXaml Completed version is ready to run. If you'd like to run through the steps here, open the incomplete version. If you'd rather follow along but not deal with coding the solution, then open the completed version. To open either version, drag the .sln file onto an executing copy of Visual Studio and it will open the solution for editing.

2. Add a new Workflow1.xml file as you did in each of the preceding samples. You don't need to change the file's compiler settings. In fact, once the XAML-based workflow is complete and compiled, we'll remove this file (as well as the code-beside file) from the project to prevent inadvertent compiler warnings.

3. Add the following XML to the Workflow1.xml file and then save it:

```xml
<SequentialWorkflowActivity x:Class="Workflow1" x:Name="Workflow1" xmlns:x="http://
schemas.microsoft.com/winfx/2006/xaml" xmlns="http://schemas.microsoft.com/winfx/2006/
xaml/workflow">
  <IfElseActivity x:Name="ifElseActivity1">
   <IfElseBranchActivity x:Name="ifElseBranchActivity1">
    <IfElseBranchActivity.Condition>
     <CodeCondition Condition="EvaluatePostalCode" />
    </IfElseBranchActivity.Condition>
    <CodeActivity x:Name="codeActivity1" ExecuteCode="PostalCodeValid" />
   </IfElseBranchActivity>
   <IfElseBranchActivity x:Name="ifElseBranchActivity2">
     <CodeActivity x:Name="codeActivity2" ExecuteCode="PostalCodeInvalid" />
   </IfElseBranchActivity>
  </IfElseActivity>
</SequentialWorkflowActivity>
```

4. Change the Workflow1.xml file extension from .xml to .xoml in Solution Explorer and save the file.

5. Next add the code-beside file. Right-click the PCodeXaml project name in Solution Explorer, select Add, and then select Class. Type **Workflow1.xoml.cs** in the Name field, and click Add.

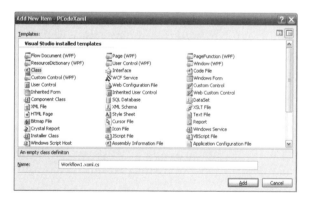

6. Add the following code to the file, completely replacing what Visual Studio added for you. Save the files you just created.

```csharp
using System;
using System.Workflow.Activities;
using System.Text.RegularExpressions;

public partial class Workflow1 : SequentialWorkflowActivity
{
    private string _code = "";
```

```
public string PostalCode
{
    get { return _code; }
    set { _code = value; }
}

private void EvaluatePostalCode(object sender, ConditionalEventArgs e)
{
    string USCode = @"^(\d{5}$)|(\d{5}$\-\d{4}$)";
    string CanadianCode = @"[ABCEGHJKLMNPRSTVXY]\d[A-Z] \d[A-Z]\d";

    e.Result = (Regex.IsMatch(_code, USCode) ||
                Regex.IsMatch(_code, CanadianCode));
}

private void PostalCodeValid(object sender, EventArgs e)
{
    Console.WriteLine("The postal code {0} is valid.", _code);
}

private void PostalCodeInvalid(object sender, EventArgs e)
{
    Console.WriteLine("The postal code {0} is *invalid*.", _code);
}
}
```

> **Note**   If this code looks familiar, it should. I literally cut and pasted it from the original PCodeFlow application and workflow found in Chapter 1.

7. Choose Save All from the File menu, or press Ctrl+Shift+S.

8. Open a command window, type **cd \Workflow\Chapter16\PCodeXaml\PCodeXaml** at the command prompt, and press Enter to change directories.

9. Type **"C:\Program Files\Microsoft SDKs\Windows\v6.0\Bin\Wfc.exe" workflow1.xoml workflow1.xoml.cs** at the command prompt, and press Enter.

10. The workflow compiler crunches both the XML and C# files. When it is complete, it again produces a dynamic-link library *workflow1.dll*, which you now should reference. Right-click the PCodeXaml project name in Solution Explorer, and select Add Reference. When the Add Reference dialog box pops up, select the Browse tab, select workflow1.dll from the list, and click OK.

11. Turning to the main application, select the Program.cs file for editing. Select it, and scan through the code to find this line:

```
Console.WriteLine("Waiting for workflow completion.");
```

12. Add this code following the line of code you just found:

```
// Create the execution parameters
Dictionary<string, object> parms = new Dictionary<string, object>();
parms.Add("PostalCode", args.Length > 0 ? args[0] : "");

// Create the workflow instance.
WorkflowInstance instance =
    workflowRuntime.CreateWorkflow(typeof(Workflow1), parms);

// Start the workflow instance.
instance.Start();
```

13. There is a slight problem with the project as it stands. You referenced the workflow1.dll assembly, but yet there is code to create the *Workflow1* class resident in the code-beside file. This sets up a conflict as there are two instances of a class named Workflow1. Because you want the class defined in the compiled assembly, right-click the Workflow1.xoml and Workflow.xoml.cs files in Solution Explorer and select Exclude From Project to remove them from the compilation process.

14. Compile the solution by pressing F6, correcting any compilation errors.

15. To test the application, we'll use the command prompt window that should still be open from the workflow compilation. Change directories to the Debug directory (or Release if you compiled the application in Release mode). To do so, from the command prompt type **cd bin\Debug** and press Enter (substitute *Release* for *Debug* if you compiled in Release mode).

16. At the command prompt, type **PCodeXaml 12345** and press Enter. You should see the following application output:

17. To try a negative application response, at the command prompt type **PCodeXaml 1234x** and press Enter. You should get the following output:

The final sample we'll create in this chapter involves a custom class so that we can exercise *XmlnsDefinition*.

Creating a new XAML-based workflow application with a custom activity

1. As I have for the previous sample applications, I've again provided two versions of this sample: a completed version and an incomplete version, both of which you'll find in \Workflow\Chapter16\. The XmlnsDefFlow application is incomplete, but it requires only the workflow definition. The XmlnsDefFlow Completed version is ready for you to execute. If you'd like to follow the steps here, open the incomplete version. If you'd rather just follow along, then open the completed version. To open either version, drag the .sln file onto Visual Studio and it will open the solution you selected for you.

2. Add a new Workflow1.xml file. You don't need to change the compiler settings for this file or rename it just yet.

3. Add the following XML to the Workflow1.xml file, and then save it:

```
<SequentialWorkflowActivity x:Class="Workflow1" x:Name="Workflow1"
 xmlns:x="http://schemas.microsoft.com/winfx/2006/xaml"
 xmlns="http://schemas.microsoft.com/winfx/2006/xaml/workflow"
 xmlns:custom="urn:PrintMessage">
  <custom:PrintMessageActivity x:Name="printMessageActivity1"
    custom:Message="Hello from the custom assembly!"/>
</SequentialWorkflowActivity>
```

4. Change the file extension from .xml to .xoml in Solution Explorer, again ignoring the warning. Save the file. The workflow is now complete, but notice the reference to *Print-MessageActivity* in the XML markup. This is a new, custom activity you need to create. To begin, right-click the solution name in Solution Explorer, select Add, and then select New Project. From the Workflow project types, select Workflow Activity Library, and in the Templates pane select Workflow Activity Library, type **XmlnsDefLib** into the Name field, and click OK.

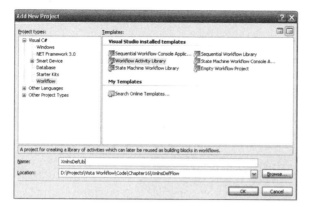

5. Visual Studio creates a workflow activity named *Activity1*. Rename the Activity1.cs file to be PrintMessageActivity.cs in Solution Explorer. Visual Studio will ask whether it's OK to also rename the class. Click Yes.

6. Open the activity source file for editing in the code editor. Select the PrintMessageActivity.cs file in Solution Explorer, and click the View Code toolbar button.

7. The activity currently derives from *SequenceActivity*. Change the base class to *Activity*. The class definition then appears as follows:

```
public partial class PrintMessageActivity: Activity
```

8. Following the constructor, add this code:

```
protected override ActivityExecutionStatus
        Execute(ActivityExecutionContext executionContext)
{
    // Print message to screen...
    Console.WriteLine(this.Message);
    return ActivityExecutionStatus.Closed;
}

public static DependencyProperty MessageProperty =
    DependencyProperty.Register("Message", typeof(System.String),
    typeof(XmlnsDefLib.PrintMessageActivity));

public string Message
{
    get
    {
        return ((System.String)(base.GetValue(
            XmlnsDefLib.PrintMessageActivity.MessageProperty)));
    }
    set
    {
        base.SetValue(
            XmlnsDefLib.PrintMessageActivity.MessageProperty, value);
    }
}
```

9. And now the secret ingredient—adding the *XmlnsDefinition* attribute. Just before the namespace declaration, insert this code:

```
[assembly: XmlnsDefinition("urn:PrintMessage", "XmlnsDefLib")]
```

> **Note**   If you're developing the activity for use in a large application or for distribution to customers or other external users, use a namespace URI that includes your company name, product group, and project or another typically unique value to disambiguate namespaces. This is considered a general best practice when working with XML.

10. Compile the XmlnsDefLib project so that you create a DLL that can be referenced by the workflow compiler. Note whether you compiled the assembly using Debug or Release settings because you'll need to reference the DLL later and the directory in which the DLL resides depends on the compilation setting.

11. Even though we'll be executing a XAML-based workflow, the workflow runtime still needs to access the *PrintMessage* activity we just created. Therefore, add a project reference for XmlnsDefLib to XmlnsDefFlow by right-clicking the XmlnsDefFlow project name in Solution Explorer and selecting the Add Reference option. When the Add Reference dialog box comes up, click the Project tab and select XmlnsDefLib from the list. Click OK.

12. Open a command window as with the previous sample applications.

13. Type **cd \Workflow\Chapter16\XmlnsDefFlow\XmlnsDefFlow** at the command prompt, and press Enter to change directories. The Workflow1.xoml file is now directly accessible in this directory.

14. Type **"C:\Program Files\Microsoft SDKs\Windows\v6.0\Bin\Wfc.exe" workflow1.xoml /r:..\XmlnsDefLib\bin\Debug\XmlnsDefLib.dll** at the command prompt, and press Enter. As before, if you installed the Windows SDK elsewhere, use that directory instead in the command to execute *wfc.exe*. Also substitute *Release* for *Debug* if you compiled the XmlnsDefLib project with Release settings.

15. The workflow compiler should execute without error. Assuming this is so, it produces a dynamic-link library *workflow1.dll* located in the same directory as Workflow1.xoml.

You now need to reference that library from your main application, as it will contain the workflow defined by the XML file you created in step 3. To do that, right-click the XmlnsDefFlow project name in Solution Explorer and select Add Reference. When the Add Reference dialog box pops up, select the Browse tab, select workflow1.dll from the list, and click OK.

16. With the workflow completely finished, let's turn to the main application. Select Program.cs in Solution Explorer, and open it for editing if it's not already open. Scan through the file, and find this line of code:

```
Console.WriteLine("Waiting for workflow completion.");
```

17. Add this code following the line of code you just found:

```
// Create the workflow instance.
WorkflowInstance instance =
    workflowRuntime.CreateWorkflow(typeof(Workflow1));

// Start the workflow instance.
instance.Start();
```

18. Compile the solution by pressing F6, correcting any compilation errors.

19. Execute the application by pressing Ctrl+F5 or F5. As is typically the case, you might have to set a breakpoint in *Main* to see the output if you don't run the application from within an open command window.

> **Note**   Even with the four sample applications we created here, I didn't come close to explaining everything there is to know about declarative workflow definitions. If you're interested in reading more, you can link to a great article in MSDN Magazine on the topic at *msdn.microsoft.com/msdnmag/issues/06/01/windowsworkflowfoundation/*.

If you want to continue to the next chapter, keep Visual Studio 2005 running and turn to Chapter 17, "Correlation and Local Host Communication." Correlation's the name, deconflicting workflow instances is the game. We'll dig into how you can keep data coming from multiple workflow instances straight.

If you want to stop, exit Visual Studio 2005 now, save your spot in the book, and close it. I'd go and try some more declarative workflows if I'd just read this chapter too. Chapter 17 will be here when you get back.

Chapter 16 Quick Reference

To	Do This
Create declarative workflow definitions	Use the XAML XML vocabulary to create fully featured workflow definitions.
Execute XAML-based workflow definitions directly	Load the XAML-based workflow into an instance of *XmlTextReader*, and assign that to the workflow runtime's *CreateWorkflow* method. Note that not all workflow definitions can be executed in this manner.
Compile XAML-based workflow definitions into .NET assemblies for execution	Use the *wfc.exe* workflow compiler tool to compile the XAML-based workflow definition. If you've created custom assemblies, you can reference and use those as well.
Assign an XML namespace to a custom assembly	Use the *XmlnsDefinition* attribute.
Pass initiation parameter values into your declarative workflow	Create a custom *SequentialWorkflow* or *StateMachineWorkflow* activity, and provide public properties to match the values you want to send into the workflow.

Part IV
External Data Communication

Chapter 17
Correlation and Local Host Communication

After completing this chapter, you will be able to:

- Understand workflow correlation and—where it's necessary—why it's important
- Use the workflow correlation parameters
- Build and use a correlated local communication service

The applications you've seen throughout this book have had a single architecture in common, aside from performing work in workflow instances supported by the Microsoft Windows Workflow Foundation (WF). There has always been a one-to-one correspondence between the application and its workflow instance. If you communicate with a workflow instance, you do so with the assurance that any data that passes between the application and workflow couldn't be confused in any way. One application, one workflow.

Another situation is possible, however, at least when applications and workflows execute in the same AppDomain. Your sole application could invoke multiple copies of the same workflow. What happens to data shipped back and forth then?

Clearly, somebody needs to keep track of which workflow is working with what piece of data. Often we can't mix and match. Once a workflow instance is created and queued for execution, if it is bound to a given data identifier, using that workflow to process information for a different data identifier could present problems with data integrity.

And, in fact, WF provides us with some internal bookkeeping to help prevent data-integrity issues. In WF terms, it's called *correlation*, and WF has very strong correlation support that is also easy to use.

Host and Workflow Local Communication

Before we get into correlation, let's briefly review the entire host and workflow communication process. Chapter 8, "Calling External Methods and Workflows," introduced the *CallExternalEvent* activity and used a local communication service to send data from the workflow to the host application. Chapter 10, "Event Activities," used the *HandleExternalEvent* activity for the reverse process–the host could send data to the workflow.

No matter which way data is passed, we first create an interface. Methods in the interface are destined to be *CallExternalEvent* activities, while events in the interface become

HandleExternalEvent activities. We used the *wca.exe* tool to create custom activities for us based on our interface. (We could have used the *CallExternalEvent* and *HandleExternalEvent* activities directly, providing each with the interface and method or event to process, but creating custom activities highlights their use in our workflows.)

With the interface in hand, we then created a local service that we plugged in to the workflow runtime to manage our local communications needs. The local service consisted of a data connector and a service class.

When the application needed to send data to the workflow, it requested the service from the workflow runtime and then raised the events supported by the interface. Your workflow instance would then handle those events, assuming you dropped the event handler into the workflow and invoked the event at an appropriate time (for example, when the workflow anticipated the event and was ready and waiting with the correct event handler).

The workflow, on the other hand, had no such need to query the workflow runtime for the local communication service. By dropping instances of *CallExternalMethod* in your workflow's processing path, the host would automatically be told of the data's arrival—again assuming the host application hooked an event handler into the local communication service for the received data event. The workflow runtime keeps track of workflow instances and their association with the local communication service and therefore the host application.

Correlation

Consider that last paragraph again. The workflow instance didn't need to rummage around to find the service that communicates with the host application. Yet the host application did need to query for the local communication service. Although this, in part, is due to the nature of host interaction with the workflow runtime, the process also underscores the one-to-many relationship between the host application and workflow instances.

The host application needs to identify which workflow instance it wants to communicate with because there might be many to choose from. However, a workflow instance has no such choice—there is only one host application.

I'm not saying the need for correlated data flow drove the WF team to architect the host application's access to the local communication service in this way. The host always queries the workflow runtime for services in this fashion, and the local communication service is just one service you might want to access. However, the reverse is certainly true. The workflow is bound to the local communication service with no regard for host application identification, and this is a direct result of an architecture designed around having many workflow instances in one host application. There can be no more than one host application, so there is no need to identify it. Therefore, the workflow runtime provides the workflow instance with the local communication service, and the workflow instance calls external methods at will.

So is it enough for the host to use the workflow instance identifier as the way to correlate data flow? That is, if you keep track of a workflow instance and try to send data back and forth to and from that workflow, wouldn't merely having the workflow's instance ID be enough to uniquely identify the workflow and the data?

Yes, if you had but a single data flow. But it's possible to have multiple data paths into and out of your workflow. For this reason, correlation was born.

When you use correlated workflow communication, in the end the workflow runtime creates a storage container for bits of information necessary to identify the workflow and data in question. This *correlation token* is consulted when the host and workflow pass data back and forth. If the correlation token indicates that both sides of the conversation are in sync, meaning the correct workflow instance and bound activity are communicating the correct piece of data, communication can proceed. However, if the correlation token indicates a problem, the workflow runtime does not allow the data communication to proceed and throws an exception. Problems might include using an incorrect workflow instance, communicating the wrong data, calling an activity bound to a different correlation token, or trying to send data without first creating the correlation token.

The correlation token is maintained by the *CorrelationToken* class. When you drop copies of the *CallExternalMethod* or *HandleExternalEvent* activity into your workflow, and if correlation is involved, you need to assign a correlation token. Correlation tokens are shared by name, so by assigning a correlation token with the same name to more than one correlated activity, you effectively bind those activities together from a data-conversation perspective. The token's name is nothing more than a string, the value of which is meaningless. It only matters that activities that share a correlation token share it by identifying the token using the same name.

A good question now is, Why didn't correlation tokens come into play earlier in the book? After all, we certainly have used both *CallExternalMethod* and *HandleExternalEvent* activities in previous work.

The answer is we chose not to invoke correlation. Correlation isn't required in all cases, and this was true for every workflow you created up until this chapter. When you have one-to-one mapping between the application and workflow instance, correlation is unnecessary overhead, and happily you can omit it and enjoy slightly increased performance.

Even when you have multiple workflow instances working with a single host application, you can work without correlation. However, when you use correlation, WF prevents you from inadvertently mixing up data, and in many cases, this is a very desirable feature.

To activate the correlation infrastructure, you use specific WF-based attributes when you create your host communication interface. The good news is the process to perform the host communication doesn't change by much. The effect the change has on your workflow can be dramatic, however.

The *CorrelationParameter* Attribute

If you think about situations where a single host application might orchestrate multiple workflow instances, you will probably find that methods and events that pass data also pass some sort of unique identifier. An order processing system might pass a customer ID, or a packaging system might pass a lot number. This type of unique identifier is a perfect candidate for identifying unique instances of data, and in fact, that's precisely what happens.

When you design the methods and events in your communication interface, you design into their signatures a data correlation ID. The data correlation ID doesn't have to be unique for all space and time, like a *Guid*. However, if it isn't a *Guid*, it must be used uniquely for the duration of the workflow instance's execution.

> **Note**   Perhaps surprisingly, it isn't an error if you create two correlated workflow instances that run simultaneously using the same correlation parameter value (akin to creating two workflows working with the same customer ID). Correlation merely associates a single workflow instance with a single correlation parameter value. Calling methods or events to exchange data with a workflow created with one correlation parameter value using a different correlation value is where the error lies, and this is where WF helps you keep things straight.

You tell WF what method parameter carries this data correlation ID value by including the *CorrelationParameter* attribute in your interface definition (placed there alongside the *ExternalDataExchange* attribute). WF can then examine the contents of the parameter as the data is moved about the system. If your logic attempts to mix customers or lot numbers, for example, WF will throw the *System.Workflow.Activity.EventDeliveryFailedException*.

This exception is your friend, because it indicates processing logic on your part that could conceivably cross-match data. One customer could be charged for another's purchase, for instance. Obviously, this result is not desirable. If you receive this exception, you need to check your application logic for incorrect logical operation.

The *CorrelationParameter* attribute accepts a string in its constructor. This string represents the name of the parameter used throughout your interface to contain the unique ID. If you elect to rename the parameter for a given method, you can rename it for a selected event or method using the *CorrelationAlias* parameter. You'll read more about this parameter later in the chapter.

The *CorrelationInitializer* Attribute

WF also needs to initialize the correlation token when data communications commence. To facilitate this, you place the *CorrelationIntializer* attribute on the method or event that kicks off the data communication, and there might be more than one. Any attempt to send correlated data back and forth before executing the method or event marked as the correlation initializer results in an exception.

The *CorrelationAlias* Attribute

When you build correlated services, the *CorrelationParameter* attribute identifies by name the method parameter that is used to convey the data correlation identifier. For your interface methods, this means you must have a method parameter named using the same name as the correlation parameter name.

But this can break down for events. If your delegate is created such that the correlation parameter is in the delegate definition, there is no problem. It's baked into the event handler's method signature just as if it were any other interface method.

The problem arises when you use a delegate that includes event arguments, and those event arguments convey the correlated parameter. For example, imagine your correlation parameter was named *customerID*. Then consider this delegate:

```
delegate void MyEventHandler(object sender, MyEventArgs e);
```

If the event that used this delegate were placed into your communication interface, the *customerID* parameter wouldn't appear in the event handler and WF would throw an exception stating correlation was misapplied when you executed your workflow. However, if *MyEventArgs* has a property that contains the customer ID, you can use the *CorrelationAlias* attribute to identify that. For this example, if the *MyEventArgs* customer ID property were named *CustomerID*, the correlation parameter's alias would be *e.CustomerID*.

An important thing to keep in mind is that once you initialize a correlated data path for a single workflow instance, you cannot change the data correlation ID for the lifetime of the workflow instance without generating an error. For example, once you communicate with a workflow data associated with one customer ID, you can't later communicate data regarding another customer ID to the same workflow instance. What this means is that if your process involves creating customer IDs, such as when inserting information into new database table rows, you need to pre-create the customer ID. You can't allow the database to generate those for you because your communications would be initialized using no customer ID, or a default "empty" one, only to later begin using the newly created ID. The IDs in question would differ, and your workflow would throw an exception.

Building Correlated Workflows

When it comes right down to it, in this chapter I've introduced the concept of correlation and mentioned only three attributes. Is this all there is to it?

In a word, yes. However, our local service grows a bit more complex because we must account for different data flows. Remember, the local communication service is a singleton service in the workflow runtime, so all data requests to the various workflow instances are made through this one local communication service. By necessity, that service has to keep track of the known workflow instances and correlation parameters so that when the host requests data from a given workflow, the service returns the correct data.

> **Note**   How you architect your local communication service is up to you. I'll show you how I build them later in the chapter, but in the end there is no rule that says you have to build your services as I do. The only requirement is that you return the correctly correlated data from your service.

So that you understand the bigger picture, I'll first introduce the application you'll modify and explain why it uses correlation.

The classic example of a correlated workflow is an order-processing system that uses unique customer IDs to keep track of customer orders. But I wanted a different example if only to be different. This chapter's sample application simulates an application a trucking company might use to track its vehicles.

Today, many long-haul trucks are equipped a with Global Positioning System (GPS) that is able to report the truck's position to the shipping company. Wherever the truck happens to be, you can track it and monitor its progress towards its destination.

This sample simulates that type of tracking application, the user interface for which is shown in Figure 17-1. Four trucks are shown, traveling to various destinations (as indicated by the Active Trucks list). The trucks themselves are animated, moving from origin to destination. As they arrive at their destination, they're removed from the list of active trucks.

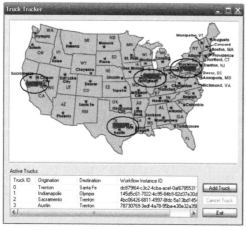

Figure 17-1   The TruckTracker application user interface

Each truck you see is supported by its own workflow instance. (Because it might be difficult to see the trucks in a two-color book, I circled them.) The heart of the workflow asynchronously updates the truck's geographic location. When updates are made, the workflow communicates the new coordinates to the host application, which then visually updates the truck's position in the user interface. Of course, we're simulating the GPS reception, and the simulation moves the trucks at a speed far greater than real vehicles could sustain. (It would be silly to run the sample for four days just to see whether a truck actually made it to New Jersey from California.) The true point of the application is to use correlated workflow instances when communicating data with the host application.

The trucks follow specific routes to their destinations, driving though other cities on the map. You select the truck's route when you click Add Truck, the supporting dialog box for which is shown in Figure 17-2. The routes themselves are stored in an XML file that is read as the application loads. The trip from Sacramento to Trenton, for example, has the truck pass through waypoints Phoenix, Santa Fe, Austin, and Tallahassee.

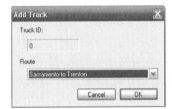

Figure 17-2   The Add Truck dialog box

The application's main program has been completed for you. What remains is completing the service and creating the workflow. We'll begin by creating the service interface.

Adding a correlated communications interface to your application

1. You should find the TruckTracker application in the \Workflow\Chapter17\ TruckTracker directory. As usual, I placed two different versions of the application in the Chapter17 directory—an incomplete version for you to work with, and a completed version that you can execute right now. If you want to follow along but don't want to actually perform the steps, open the solution file for the completed version. (It will be in the TruckTracker Completed directory.) If you do want to work through the steps, open the TruckTracker version. To open either solution, drag the .sln file onto an executing copy of Microsoft Visual Studio to open the solution for editing and compilation.

2. The solution contains two projects: TruckTracker (the main application) and TruckService. Looking at the TruckService project in Visual Studio's Solution Explorer window, open the ITruckService.cs file for editing by double-clicking the filename or selecting it and clicking the View Code button on the Solution Explorer toolbar. Note you might have to expand the TruckService project's tree control node to see the project files.

3. Between the braces delimiting the interface, add this code:

```
// Workflow-to-host communication
[CorrelationInitializer]
void ReadyTruck(Int32 truckID, Int32 startingX, Int32 startingY);
void UpdateTruck(Int32 truckID, Int32 X, Int32 Y);
void RemoveTruck(Int32 truckID);

// Host-to-workflow communication
[CorrelationAlias("truckID", "e.TruckID")]
event EventHandler<CancelTruckEventArgs> CancelTruck;

[CorrelationInitializer]
[CorrelationAlias("truckID", "e.TruckID")]
event EventHandler<AddTruckEventArgs> AddTruck;
```

4. Just prior to the *ExternalDataExchange* attribute (which you should find decorating the interface), insert the *CorrelationParameter* attribute:

```
[CorrelationParameter("truckID")]
```

5. Save the file.

Looking back at the code you inserted in step 3, which is repeated in Listing 17-1, you see each of the attributes discussed in this chapter. The *truckID* method parameter carries a unique truck identifier, and it's present in all methods in the interface. The *CorrelationParameter* attribute, then, tells WF that this method parameter is the one to use for correlation purposes.

Listing 17-1 ITruckService.cs completed

```
using System;
using System.Collections.Generic;
using System.Text;
using System.Workflow.ComponentModel;
using System.Workflow.Activities;

namespace TruckService
{
    [CorrelationParameter("truckID")]
    [ExternalDataExchange]
    public interface ITruckService
    {
        // Workflow-to-host communication
        [CorrelationInitializer]
        void ReadyTruck(Int32 truckID, Int32 startingX, Int32 startingY);
        void UpdateTruck(Int32 truckID, Int32 X, Int32 Y);
        void RemoveTruck(Int32 truckID);

        // Host-to-workflow communication
        [CorrelationAlias("truckID", "e.TruckID")]
        event EventHandler<CancelTruckEventArgs> CancelTruck;

        [CorrelationInitializer]
        [CorrelationAlias("truckID", "e.TruckID")]
        event EventHandler<AddTruckEventArgs> AddTruck;
    }
}
```

The two events, *AddTruck* and *CancelTruck*, use a *CorrelationAlias* attribute to reassign the correlation parameter from *truckID* to the name *e.TruckID* because the event arguments carry the correlation identifier for those events. *e.TruckID* is used for this sample, but any event argument that carries the correlation parameter could have been used. That is, you could alias *truckID* to any parameter that also carries the correlation value to the workflow.

And there are two ways to initialize the correlation mechanism in this interface: the workflow can call *ReadyTruck*, or the host application can invoke the *AddTruck* event. Either one kicks off correlated communications because both are decorated with the *CorrelationInitializer* attribute. Invoking any other method or event prior to the initialization results in a workflow runtime exception.

The service project typically carries with it the local communication service, and this sample application is no different. Because the connector class *TruckServiceDataConnector* is derived from *ITruckService*, it makes sense to complete that class at this time.

Completing the correlated data connector

1. Turning again to the TruckService project, look for the TruckServiceDataConnector.cs file and open it for editing.

2. The *TruckServiceDataConnector* class is empty, but it clearly derives from *ITruckService*. So, at the very least, you add the methods and events from the interface to this class. Before you do, however, let's add some supporting code. First, add the following fields just after the opening class brace:

```
protected const string KeyFormat = "{0}.Truck_{1}";
protected static Dictionary<string, string> _dataValues =
                                new Dictionary<string, string>();
protected static Dictionary<string, WorkflowTruckTrackingDataService>
    _dataServices =
        new Dictionary<string, WorkflowTruckTrackingDataService>();
private static object _syncLock = new object();
```

3. Because the data connector keeps track of data items and is a singleton in the workflow runtime, we'll add a pair of static methods to both register and retrieve registered data services. Add these methods following the fields you just inserted:

```
public static WorkflowTruckTrackingDataService
    GetRegisteredWorkflowDataService(Guid instanceID,
                                     Int32 truckID)
{
    string key = String.Format(KeyFormat, instanceID, truckID);

    WorkflowTruckTrackingDataService serviceInstance = null;
    if (_dataServices.ContainsKey(key))
    {
        // Return the appropriate data service.
        serviceInstance = _dataServices[key];
    } // if
```

```
        return serviceInstance;
    }

    public static void
       RegisterDataService(WorkflowTruckTrackingDataService dataService)
    {
        string key = String.Format(KeyFormat,
                                    dataService.InstanceID.ToString(),
                                    dataService.TruckID);
        lock (_syncLock)
        {
            _dataServices.Add(key, dataService);
        } // lock
    }
```

4. Once a data service is registered, which occurs in the main application when a new work-flow instance is started (one data service per workflow instance), it stores correlated data in the data connector. We need to have a way to retrieve the data. Previously, we used a property, but that won't work for us now because we have to pass in both a workflow instance ID and the correlation value (a truck identifier in this case). To retrieve data, then, add this method following the static registration methods:

```
public string RetrieveTruckInfo(Guid instanceID, Int32 truckID)
{
    string payload = String.Empty;

    string key = String.Format(KeyFormat, instanceID, truckID);
    if (_dataValues.ContainsKey(key))
    {
        payload = _dataValues[key];
    } // if

    return payload;
}
```

5. With that last method, the housekeeping code is complete. Now let's add the methods from the *ITruckService* interface. These follow the data-retrieval method from the preceding step:

```
// Workflow-to-host communication methods
public void ReadyTruck(Int32 truckID, Int32 startingX, Int32 startingY)
{
    // Pull correlated service.
    WorkflowTruckTrackingDataService service =
                        GetRegisteredWorkflowDataService(
                        WorkflowEnvironment.WorkflowInstanceId,
                        truckID);

    // Place data in correlated store.
    UpdateTruckData(service.InstanceID, truckID, startingX, startingY);
```

```
        // Raise the event to trigger host activity.
        if (service != null)
        {
            service.RaiseTruckLeavingEvent(truckID, startingX, startingY);
        } // if
    }

    public void UpdateTruck(Int32 truckID, Int32 X, Int32 Y)
    {
        // Pull correlated service.
        WorkflowTruckTrackingDataService service =
                                GetRegisteredWorkflowDataService(
                                WorkflowEnvironment.WorkflowInstanceId,
                                truckID);

        // Update data in correlated store.
        UpdateTruckData(service.InstanceID, truckID, X, Y);

        // Raise the event to trigger host activity.
        if (service != null)
        {
            service.RaiseRouteUpdatedEvent(truckID, X, Y);
        } // if
    }

    public void RemoveTruck(Int32 truckID)
    {
        // Pull correlated service.
        WorkflowTruckTrackingDataService service =
                                GetRegisteredWorkflowDataService(
                                WorkflowEnvironment.WorkflowInstanceId,
                                truckID);

        // Remove truck from correlated store.
        string key = String.Format(KeyFormat, service.InstanceID, truckID);
        if (_dataValues.ContainsKey(key))
        {
            // Remove it.
            _dataValues.Remove(key);
        } // if

        // Raise the event to trigger host activity.
        if (service != null)
        {
            service.RaiseTruckArrivedEvent(truckID);
        } // if
    }
```

6. Following the methods in *ITruckService* are the events, so add those as well, following the methods from step 5:

```
// Host-to-workflow events
public event EventHandler<CancelTruckEventArgs> CancelTruck;

public void RaiseCancelTruck(Guid instanceID, Int32 truckID)
{
    if (CancelTruck != null)
    {
        // Fire event.
        CancelTruck(null, new CancelTruckEventArgs(instanceID, truckID));
    } // if
}


public event EventHandler<AddTruckEventArgs> AddTruck;

public void RaiseAddTruck(Guid instanceID, Int32 truckID, Int32 routeID)
{
    if (AddTruck != null)
    {
        // Fire event.
        AddTruck(null, new AddTruckEventArgs(instanceID, truckID, routeID));
    } // if
}
```

7. Looking back at the methods entered in step 5, you see a helper method used to insert the correlated data into the appropriate dictionary slot. The data itself must be converted to XML, so rather than proliferate this code in the three external methods, it's wrapped up in the *UpdateTruckData* helper method. Add that method now, following the events you just added:

```
protected Truck UpdateTruckData(Guid instanceID, Int32 truckID, Int32 X, Int32 Y)
{
    string key = String.Format(KeyFormat, instanceID, truckID);
    Truck truck = null;
    if (!_dataValues.ContainsKey(key))
    {
        // Create new truck.
        truck = new Truck();
        truck.ID = truckID;
    } // if
    else
    {
        // Pull existing truck.
        string serializedTruck = _dataValues[key];
        StringReader rdr = new StringReader(serializedTruck);
        XmlSerializer serializer = new XmlSerializer(typeof(Truck));
        truck = (Truck)serializer.Deserialize(rdr);
    } // else

    // Update values.
    truck.X = X;
    truck.Y = Y;
```

```
    // Serialize values.
    StringBuilder sb = new StringBuilder();
    using (StringWriter wtr = new StringWriter(sb))
    {
        XmlSerializer serializer = new XmlSerializer(typeof(Truck));
        serializer.Serialize(wtr, truck);
    } // using

    // Ship the data back...
    _dataValues[key] = sb.ToString();

    return truck;
}
```

8. Save the file.

The entire *TruckServiceDataConnector* class is shown in Listing 17-2. Again, keep in mind that the purpose of this class is to store correlated data coming from the various workflow instances. The data is stored in a *Dictionary* object, the key for which is an amalgam of the workflow instance identifier and the truck identifier. Therefore, the data is keyed in a correlated fashion. The data connector class is a singleton service in the workflow runtime, so we have registration methods the individual workflow instance data services will use to identify themselves and establish their presence as far as data communication is concerned.

> **Note**   You might wonder why the data being transferred is in XML rather than the data objects themselves. WF doesn't serialize objects when passed between workflow and host, or the reverse. As a result, copies of the objects are not created (undoubtedly to boost performance). Exchanged objects are passed by reference, so both workflow and host continue to work on the *same* object. If you don't want this behavior, as I did not for this sample application, you can serialize the objects as I have or implement *ICloneable* and pass copies. If this behavior doesn't affect your design, you don't need to do anything but pass your objects back and forth by reference. Keep in mind, though, that your objects will be shared by code executing on two different threads.

Listing 17-2   TruckServiceDataConnector.cs completed

```
using System;
using System.Collections.Generic;
using System.Text;
using System.Threading;
using System.Workflow.Activities;
using System.Workflow.Runtime;
using System.Xml;
using System.Xml.Serialization;
using System.IO;

namespace TruckService
{
    public class TruckServiceDataConnector : ITruckService
    {
```

```
protected const string KeyFormat = "{0}.Truck_{1}";
protected static Dictionary<string, string> _dataValues =
                            new Dictionary<string, string>();
protected static Dictionary<string, WorkflowTruckTrackingDataService>
                    _dataServices = new Dictionary<string,
                        WorkflowTruckTrackingDataService>();
private static object _syncLock = new object();

public static WorkflowTruckTrackingDataService
                GetRegisteredWorkflowDataService(Guid instanceID,
                                                    Int32 truckID)
{
   string key = String.Format(KeyFormat, instanceID, truckID);

   WorkflowTruckTrackingDataService serviceInstance = null;
   if (_dataServices.ContainsKey(key))
   {
      // Return the appropriate data service.
      serviceInstance = _dataServices[key];
   } // if

   return serviceInstance;
}

public static void
   RegisterDataService(WorkflowTruckTrackingDataService dataService)
{
   string key = String.Format(KeyFormat,
                        dataService.InstanceID.ToString(),
                        dataService.TruckID);
   lock (_syncLock)
   {
      _dataServices.Add(key, dataService);
   } // lock
}

public string RetrieveTruckInfo(Guid instanceID, Int32 truckID)
{
   string payload = String.Empty;

   string key = String.Format(KeyFormat, instanceID, truckID);
   if (_dataValues.ContainsKey(key))
   {
      payload = _dataValues[key];
   } // if

   return payload;
}

// Workflow-to-host communication methods
public void ReadyTruck(Int32 truckID,
                    Int32 startingX,
                    Int32 startingY)
{
```

```
    // Pull correlated service
    WorkflowTruckTrackingDataService service =
                        GetRegisteredWorkflowDataService(
                            WorkflowEnvironment.WorkflowInstanceId,
                            truckID);

    // Place data in correlated store.
    UpdateTruckData(service.InstanceID,
                    truckID,
                    startingX,
                    startingY);

    // Raise the event to trigger host activity.
    if (service != null)
    {
        service.RaiseTruckLeavingEvent(truckID, startingX, startingY);
    } // if
}

public void UpdateTruck(Int32 truckID, Int32 X, Int32 Y)
{
    // Pull correlated service.
    WorkflowTruckTrackingDataService service =
                        GetRegisteredWorkflowDataService(
                            WorkflowEnvironment.WorkflowInstanceId,
                            truckID);

    // Update data in correlated store.
    UpdateTruckData(service.InstanceID, truckID, X, Y);

    // Raise the event to trigger host activity.
    if (service != null)
    {
        service.RaiseRouteUpdatedEvent(truckID, X, Y);
    } // if
}

public void RemoveTruck(Int32 truckID)
{
    // Pull correlated service.
    WorkflowTruckTrackingDataService service =
                        GetRegisteredWorkflowDataService(
                            WorkflowEnvironment.WorkflowInstanceId,
                            truckID);

    // Remove truck from correlated store.
    string key = String.Format(KeyFormat,
                            service.InstanceID,
                            truckID);
    if (_dataValues.ContainsKey(key))
    {
        // Remove it.
        _dataValues.Remove(key);
    } // if
```

```
        // Raise the event to trigger host activity.
        if (service != null)
        {
            service.RaiseTruckArrivedEvent(truckID);
        } // if
    }


    // Host-to-workflow events
    public event EventHandler<CancelTruckEventArgs> CancelTruck;

    public void RaiseCancelTruck(Guid instanceID, Int32 truckID)
    {
        if (CancelTruck != null)
        {
            // Fire event.
            CancelTruck(null,
                        new CancelTruckEventArgs(instanceID, truckID));
        } // if
    }


    public event EventHandler<AddTruckEventArgs> AddTruck;

    public void RaiseAddTruck(Guid instanceID,
                              Int32 truckID,
                              Int32 routeID)
    {
        if (AddTruck != null)
        {
            // Fire event.
            AddTruck(null,
                     new AddTruckEventArgs(instanceID, truckID, routeID));
        } // if
    }

    protected Truck UpdateTruckData(Guid instanceID,
                                    Int32 truckID,
                                    Int32 X,
                                    Int32 Y)
    {
        string key = String.Format(KeyFormat, instanceID, truckID);
        Truck truck = null;
        if (!_dataValues.ContainsKey(key))
        {
            // Create new truck.
            truck = new Truck();
            truck.ID = truckID;
        } // if
        else
        {
            // Pull existing truck.
            string serializedTruck = _dataValues[key];
            StringReader rdr = new StringReader(serializedTruck);
            XmlSerializer serializer = new XmlSerializer(typeof(Truck));
            truck = (Truck)serializer.Deserialize(rdr);
        } // else
```

```
        // Update values.
        truck.X = X;
        truck.Y = Y;

        // Serialize values.
        StringBuilder sb = new StringBuilder();
        using (StringWriter wtr = new StringWriter(sb))
        {
            XmlSerializer serializer = new XmlSerializer(typeof(Truck));
            serializer.Serialize(wtr, truck);
        } // using

        // Ship the data back...
        _dataValues[key] = sb.ToString();

        return truck;
    }
  }
}
```

From Chapter 8, you might recall that the local communication service also has a service component used by the workflow to interface with the data connector. In fact, this service, *WorkflowTruckTrackingDataService*, is what is registered with the connector class we just created. The service primarily implements helper methods to fire events for host consumption, such as when data is available, and when using correlation, it helps to keep correlated values straight.

Completing the correlated data service

1. Looking at the TruckService project, you should find a source file named WorkflowTruckTrackingDataService.cs. Once you've located it, open it for editing.

2. The first things to add are the private fields the service requires to perform its tasks. Place this code following the opening brack of the *WorkflowTruckTrackingDataService* class:

```
private static WorkflowRuntime _workflowRuntime = null;
private static ExternalDataExchangeService _dataExchangeService = null;
private static TruckServiceDataConnector _dataConnector = null;
private static object _syncRoot = new object();
```

3. Follow the private fields with the events the service will fire. These events are fired as a result of the workflow instance invoking a *CallExternalMethod* activity (which you see in the *TruckServiceDataConnector* class):

```
public event EventHandler<TruckActivityEventArgs> TruckLeaving;
public event EventHandler<TruckActivityEventArgs> RouteUpdated;
public event EventHandler<TruckActivityEventArgs> TruckArrived;
```

4. Next add two fields and property pairs you'll need to identify correlated service instances:

```
private Guid _instanceID = Guid.Empty;

public Guid InstanceID
{
    get { return _instanceID; }
    set { _instanceID = value; }
}

private Int32 _truckID = -1;

public Int32 TruckID
{
    get { return _truckID; }
    set { _truckID = value; }
}
```

5. Now we'll add two static methods: one to register the service and configure it within the workflow runtime, and another to retrieve a registered service instance:

```
public static WorkflowTruckTrackingDataService
    CreateDataService(Guid instanceID,
                      WorkflowRuntime workflowRuntime,
                      Int32 truckID)
{
    lock (_syncRoot)
    {
        // If we're just starting, save a copy of the workflow.
        // runtime reference.
        if (_workflowRuntime == null)
        {
            _workflowRuntime = workflowRuntime;
        } // if

        // If we're just starting, plug in ExternalDataExchange service.
        if (_dataExchangeService == null)
        {
            _dataExchangeService = new ExternalDataExchangeService();
            _workflowRuntime.AddService(_dataExchangeService);
        } // if

        // Check to see if we have already added this data.
        // exchange service.
        TruckServiceDataConnector dataConnector =
            (TruckServiceDataConnector)workflowRuntime.GetService(
                                        typeof(TruckServiceDataConnector));
        if (dataConnector == null)
        {
            _dataConnector = new TruckServiceDataConnector();
            _dataExchangeService.AddService(_dataConnector);
        } // if
        else
        {
```

```
                  _dataConnector = dataConnector;
            } // else

            // Pull the service instance we registered with the connection
            // object.
            return WorkflowTruckTrackingDataService.
                        GetRegisteredWorkflowDataService(instanceID, truckID);
        } // lock
    }

    public static WorkflowTruckTrackingDataService
        GetRegisteredWorkflowDataService(Guid instanceID,
                                         Int32 truckID)
    {
        lock (_syncRoot)
        {
            WorkflowTruckTrackingDataService workflowDataService =
                TruckServiceDataConnector.GetRegisteredWorkflowDataService(
                                            instanceID, truckID);
            if (workflowDataService == null)
            {
                workflowDataService =
                    new WorkflowTruckTrackingDataService(instanceID, truckID);
                TruckServiceDataConnector.RegisterDataService(
                                            workflowDataService);
            } // if

            return workflowDataService;
        } // lock
    }
```

6. Now add a constructor and destructor:

```
private WorkflowTruckTrackingDataService(Guid instanceID, Int32 truckID)
{
    this._instanceID = instanceID;
    this._truckID = truckID;
}

~WorkflowTruckTrackingDataService()
{
    // Clean up.
    _workflowRuntime = null;
    _dataExchangeService = null;
    _dataConnector = null;
}
```

> **Note** As you might recall from Chapter 8, the destructor is required to break circular links between the service and connector classes. Implementing *IDisposable* won't work for this because the *Dispose* method isn't called when the service is removed from the workflow runtime.

7. Following the class destructor, add the correlated data read method:

```
public string Read()
{
    return _dataConnector.RetrieveTruckInfo(InstanceID, TruckID);
}
```

8. Finally add the event implementations:

```
public void RaiseTruckLeavingEvent(Int32 truckID,
                                   Int32 startingX,
                                   Int32 startingY)
{
    if (_workflowRuntime == null)
        _workflowRuntime = new WorkflowRuntime();

    // Loads persisted workflow instances.
    _workflowRuntime.GetWorkflow(_instanceID);
    if (TruckLeaving != null)
    {
        TruckLeaving(this, new TruckActivityEventArgs(_instanceID,
                                                      truckID,
                                                      startingX,
                                                      startingY));
    } // if
}

public void RaiseRouteUpdatedEvent(Int32 truckID,
                                   Int32 X,
                                   Int32 Y)
{
    if (_workflowRuntime == null)
        _workflowRuntime = new WorkflowRuntime();

    // Loads persisted workflow instances.
    _workflowRuntime.GetWorkflow(_instanceID);
    if (RouteUpdated != null)
    {
        RouteUpdated(this, new TruckActivityEventArgs(_instanceID,
                                                      truckID,
                                                      X, Y));
    } // if
}

public void RaiseTruckArrivedEvent(Int32 truckID)
{
    if (_workflowRuntime == null)
        _workflowRuntime = new WorkflowRuntime();

    // Loads persisted workflow instances.
    _workflowRuntime.GetWorkflow(_instanceID);
    if (TruckArrived != null)
    {
        TruckArrived(this, new TruckActivityEventArgs(_instanceID,
                                                      truckID));
    } // if
}
```

9. Save the file, and compile the TruckService project by pressing Shift+F6 or by selecting Build TruckService from Visual Studio's Build menu. Correct any compilation errors you receive.

With the completion of the service class, the full listing for which is shown in Listing 17-3, the TruckService local communication service is done and ready to use. What we don't have is a workflow that uses the service. We'll also need to use the trusty *wca.exe* tool to create custom *CallExternalMethod* and *HandleExternalEvent* activities for us.

Listing 17-3   WorkflowTruckTrackingDataService.cs completed

```
using System;
using System.Collections.Generic;
using System.Text;
using System.Workflow.Activities;
using System.Workflow.Runtime;

namespace TruckService
{
    public class WorkflowTruckTrackingDataService
    {
        private static WorkflowRuntime _workflowRuntime = null;
        private static ExternalDataExchangeService _dataExchangeService =
            null;
        private static TruckServiceDataConnector _dataConnector = null;
        private static object _syncRoot = new object();

        public event EventHandler<TruckActivityEventArgs> TruckLeaving;
        public event EventHandler<TruckActivityEventArgs> RouteUpdated;
        public event EventHandler<TruckActivityEventArgs> TruckArrived;

        private Guid _instanceID = Guid.Empty;

        public Guid InstanceID
        {
            get { return _instanceID; }
            set { _instanceID = value; }
        }

        private Int32 _truckID = -1;

        public Int32 TruckID
        {
            get { return _truckID; }
            set { _truckID = value; }
        }

        public static WorkflowTruckTrackingDataService
            CreateDataService(Guid instanceID,
                            WorkflowRuntime workflowRuntime,
                            Int32 truckID)
        {
            lock (_syncRoot)
            {
```

```
                // If we're just starting, save a copy of the workflow
                // runtime reference.
                if (_workflowRuntime == null)
                {
                    _workflowRuntime = workflowRuntime;
                } // if

                // If we're just starting, plug in ExternalDataExchange
                // service.
                if (_dataExchangeService == null)
                {
                    _dataExchangeService =
                        new ExternalDataExchangeService();
                    _workflowRuntime.AddService(_dataExchangeService);
                } // if

                // Check to see if we have already added this data
                // exchange service.
                TruckServiceDataConnector dataConnector =
                    (TruckServiceDataConnector)workflowRuntime.
                        GetService(typeof(TruckServiceDataConnector));
                if (dataConnector == null)
                {
                    _dataConnector = new TruckServiceDataConnector();
                    _dataExchangeService.AddService(_dataConnector);
                } // if
                else
                {
                    _dataConnector = dataConnector;
                } // else

                // Pull the service instance we registered with the
                // connection object.
                return WorkflowTruckTrackingDataService.
                    GetRegisteredWorkflowDataService(instanceID,
                                                     truckID);
            } // lock
        }

        public static WorkflowTruckTrackingDataService
            GetRegisteredWorkflowDataService(Guid instanceID,
                                             Int32 truckID)
        {
            lock (_syncRoot)
            {
                WorkflowTruckTrackingDataService workflowDataService =
                    TruckServiceDataConnector.
                        GetRegisteredWorkflowDataService(instanceID, truckID);
                if (workflowDataService == null)
                {
                    workflowDataService =
                        new WorkflowTruckTrackingDataService(
```

```
                                          instanceID, truckID);
            TruckServiceDataConnector.RegisterDataService(
                                          workflowDataService);
        } // if


        return workflowDataService;
    } // lock
}


private WorkflowTruckTrackingDataService(Guid instanceID,
                                         Int32 truckID)
{
    this._instanceID = instanceID;
    this._truckID = truckID;
}


~WorkflowTruckTrackingDataService()
{
    // Clean up.
    _workflowRuntime = null;
    _dataExchangeService = null;
    _dataConnector = null;
}


public string Read()
{
    return _dataConnector.RetrieveTruckInfo(InstanceID, TruckID);
}


public void RaiseTruckLeavingEvent(Int32 truckID,
                                   Int32 startingX,
                                   Int32 startingY)
{
    if (_workflowRuntime == null)
        _workflowRuntime = new WorkflowRuntime();

    // Loads persisted workflow instances.
    _workflowRuntime.GetWorkflow(_instanceID);
    if (TruckLeaving != null)
    {
        TruckLeaving(this, new TruckActivityEventArgs(_instanceID,
                                                      truckID,
                                                      startingX,
                                                      startingY));
    } // if
}


public void RaiseRouteUpdatedEvent(Int32 truckID, Int32 X, Int32 Y)
{
    if (_workflowRuntime == null)
        _workflowRuntime = new WorkflowRuntime();
```

```
            // Loads persisted workflow instances.
            _workflowRuntime.GetWorkflow(_instanceID);
            if (RouteUpdated != null)
            {
                RouteUpdated(this, new TruckActivityEventArgs(_instanceID,
                                                               truckID,
                                                               X, Y));

            } // if
        }

        public void RaiseTruckArrivedEvent(Int32 truckID)
        {
            if (_workflowRuntime == null)
                _workflowRuntime = new WorkflowRuntime();

            // Loads persisted workflow instances.
            _workflowRuntime.GetWorkflow(_instanceID);
            if (TruckArrived != null)
            {
                TruckArrived(this, new TruckActivityEventArgs(_instanceID,
                                                               truckID));

            } // if
        }
    }
}
```

Creating the correlated data exchange workflow

● Creating the workflow in this case is no different from how you created workflow projects in the past. Simply right-click the TruckTracker solution name in Visual Studio's Solution Explorer, select Add, and then select New Project. When the Add New Project dialog box appears, expand the Visual C# tree control node if it isn't already expanded and select Workflow. From the Templates list, select Sequential Workflow Library. Type **TruckFlow** into the Name field, and click OK.

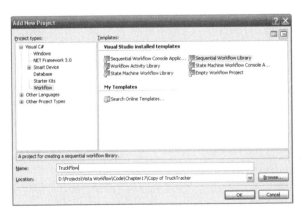

With the workflow project created, we can now use the *wca.exe* tool to generate the custom activities we'll need to communicate between workflow and host application, and vice versa. We're going to follow the same recipe we used in the Chapter 8 "Creating the communication activities" procedure.

Creating the custom data exchange activities

1. Before you begin, make sure you didn't skip step 9 of the earlier "Completing the correlated data service" procedure. The *wca.exe* tool will need a compiled assembly when it executes.

2. Click the Start button and then the Run menu item to activate the Run dialog box.

3. Type **cmd** in the Open combo box control, and click OK to activate the Windows Command Shell.

4. Change directories so that you can directly access the *TruckService* assembly you previously created. Typically, the command to type is as follows:

   ```
   cd "\Workflow\Chapter17\TruckTracker\TruckService\bin\Debug"
   ```

   However, your specific directory might vary.

5. Next execute the *wca.exe* tool by typing the following text at the command-line prompt (including the double quotes):

   ```
   "C:\Program Files\Microsoft SDKs\Windows\v6.0\Bin\Wca.exe" TruckService.dll /
   n:TruckFlow
   ```

   Press the Enter key. The tool's output should be similar to the following:

6. The *wca.exe* tool created two files for you, each of which you'll rename and move to the workflow directory. (Renaming isn't required but makes for easier source code tracking, I think.) Type **ren ITruckService.Invokes.cs ExternalEventActivities.cs** at the command prompt, and press Enter to rename the file. This file contains the generated *CallExternalEvent* activities.

7. Because the file we just renamed is a workflow activity, we need to move it from the current directory into the TruckFlow directory for compilation and use. At the command prompt, type **move ExternalEventActivities.cs ..\..\..\TruckFlow** and press Enter.

8. Now we'll do the same for the external event activities. Type **ren ITruckService.Sinks.cs ExternalEventHandlers.cs** at the command prompt, and press Enter to rename the file. This file contains the generated *CallExternalEvent* activities.

9. To move the file, at the command prompt, type **move ExternalEventHandlers.cs ..\..\..\TruckFlow** and press Enter.

10. The external data exchange activities are now created. As a final step, let's add them to the workflow project. Right-click the TruckFlow project in Solution Explorer, select Add, and then select Existing Item. When the Add Existing Item dialog box appears, select both external event activity source files from the list and click Add.

To briefly review, you created an interface that identified methods and events your workflow and application will use to communicate information. The interface is decorated with correlation attributes, so each method and event must in some way convey the correlation parameter. Then you built the local communication service you'll use to communicate the information between the host and workflow. Finally, you ran *wca.exe* to build custom activities you can use in your workflow to perform the data communications. Now it's time to build the workflow itself.

Completing the correlated workflow

1. With the external data communications activities now a part of your workflow project, the first thing to do is add a reference to the communication service project. Right-click the TruckFlow project name in Solution Explorer, and select Add Reference. On the Projects tab, select TruckService from the list and click OK.

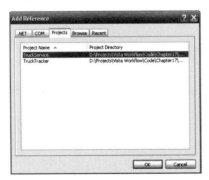

2.   Compile the workflow project (not the entire solution) so that the custom activities will be loaded into Visual Studio's Toolbox for use in the visual workflow designer. Press Shift+F6, or select Build TruckFlow from Visual Studio's main Build menu.

3.   If the visual workflow designer isn't active (for editing Workflow1.cs), select Workflow1.cs from the TruckFlow project and click the View Designer toolbar button.

4.   The first activity to place in your workflow is an instance of the *ReadyTruck* activity. Drag a copy from Visual Studio's Toolbox, and drop it into your workflow.

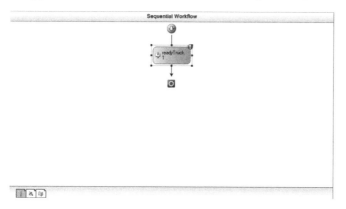

5.   You need to set several properties for this activity, the first of which is the information associated with the correlation token. In the Properties pane, type **TruckIDCorrelation** into the *CorrelationToken* property and press Enter.

6.   In the Properties window click the plus sign (+) next to the *CorrelationToken* property to expand the *OwnerActivityName*. Using the arrow, drop the selection list and select *Workflow1* (the only option present for this sample application).

7. You need to bind the data properties, starting with the *startingX* property. Select the *startingX* property in the Properties pane, and click the browse (...) button to activate the Bind 'startingX' To An Activity's Property dialog box. Select the Bind To A New Member tab, and type **CurrentX** into the New Member Name field. Click OK.

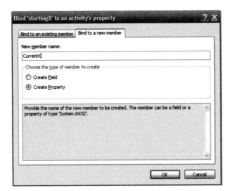

8. Do the same for the *startingY* property. Click the *startingY* property and then the browse (...) button to activate the Bind 'startingY' To An Activity's Property dialog box. Select the Bind To A New Member tab, and type **CurrentY** into the New Member Name field. Click OK.

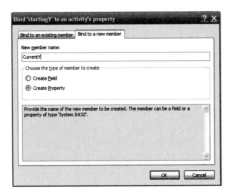

9. Finally, bind the *truckID* property by again selecting the *truckID* property in the Properties pane. Click the browse (...) button to activate the Bind 'truckID' To An Activity's Property dialog box. Select the Bind To A New Member tab, type **TruckID** into the New Member Name field, and then click OK.

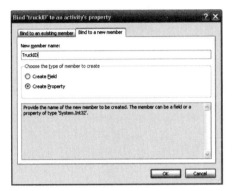

10. Returning to the visual workflow designer, drag a copy of the *While* activity onto the designer's surface and drop it below the *readyTruck1* activity you just placed there.

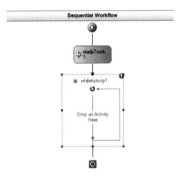

11. You need to add a conditional expression, so select the *Condition* property and choose Code Condition from the list. Expand the plus sign (+) next to the *Condition* property and type **TestAtDestination** into the secondary *Condition* property's edit control and press Enter. Visual Studio inserts the *TestAtDestination* method and places you in the code editor. Return to the visual workflow designer view.

12. Drag an instance of the *Listen* activity onto the visual workflow designer's surface, and drop it inside *whileActivity1*.

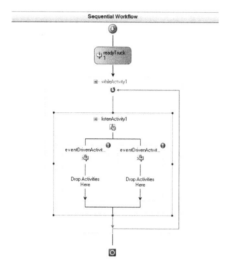

13. The *Listen* activity you just inserted performs two functions, the first of which you'll begin working with here. Drag an instance of *CancelTruck* from the Toolbox, and drop it into the left *EventDriven* activity, *eventDrivenActivity1*.

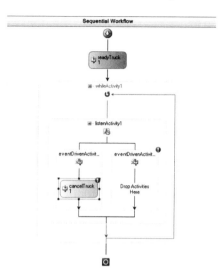

14. You need to establish the correlation token for *cancelTruck1*. To do so, simply drop the arrow associated with *cancelTruck1*'s *CorrelationToken* property and select the **TruckIDCorrelation** option. If the arrow isn't visible, select the *CorrelationToken* property to activate it.

15. *cancelTruck1* needs to have the truck identifier established, so click the browse (...) button in the *truckID* property. If the browse (...) button isn't present, click the property once to activate it as you might have just done for the correlation token property. Once the Bind 'truckID' To An Activity's Property dialog box is showing, select *TruckID* from the list of existing properties and click OK.

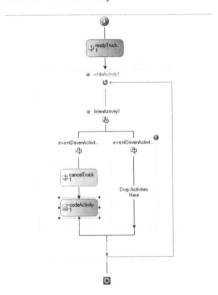

16. To perform some processing after the *CancelTruck* event is handled, drag and drop a copy of the *Code* activity onto the designer's surface, placing it just below the *cancelTruck1* activity.

17. Assign *codeActivity1*'s *ExecuteCode* property to be **CancelTruck** (press Enter). Return to the visual workflow designer after Visual Studio inserts the *CancelTruck* method for you.

18. With the visual workflow designer once again showing, drop a *Delay* activity into the right *EventDriven* activity, *eventDrivenActivity2*. This is the second function the *Listen* activity performs—executing the simulated GPS truck location scan.

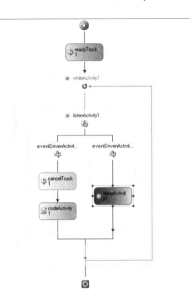

19. Set *delayActivity1*'s *TimeoutDuration* to be 1 second. This represents the refresh rate your workflow will use to update the user interface.

20. Drag a *Code* activity onto the designer's surface, and drop it below the delay activity you just placed. Change its name to **updatePosition**, and assign its *ExecuteCode* property to be **UpdateTruckPosition** (press Enter).

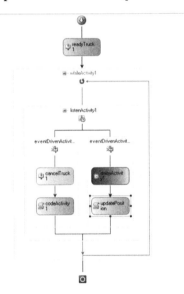

21. Return to the visual workflow designer. The *updatePosition Code* activity performs the truck location determination simulation, the result of which needs to be issued to the host application for visual processing. To issue the result to the host application, drag a copy of *UpdateTruck* activity onto the designer's surface and drop it below the *updatePosition* activity.

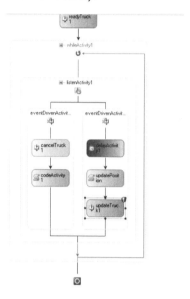

22. Assign *updateTruck1*'s *CorrelationToken* property to be **TruckIDCorrelation** by selecting it from the selection list, after clicking the down arrow. You might have to select the *CorrelationToken* property with a single mouse click to activate the down arrow.

23. Click the *truckID* property once to activate the browse (...) button so that you can assign the correlated truck identifier to the *updateTruck1* activity. Click the button, select *TruckID* from the list of existing properties in the Bind 'truckID' To An Activity's Property dialog box, and click OK.

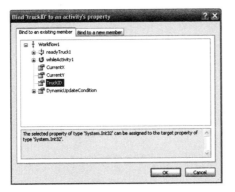

24. For *updateTruck1*'s *X* property, again click the browse (...) button and assign *X* to the existing *CurrentX* property. Do the same for the *Y* property, binding it to the *CurrentY* property.

25. The simulation runs until either you cancel a truck or the truck reaches its destination. Either condition causes *whileActivity1* to break its loop. At that point, the user interface needs to remove the truck from consideration. Therefore, drop an instance of the *RemoveTruck* activity onto the visual workflow designer and drop it below *whileActivity1*.

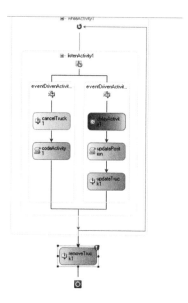

26. Select *removeTruck1*'s *CorrelationToken* property to activate the down arrow. Click the down arrow to display the token selection list, and set the token to **TruckIDCorrelation**.

27. Also select *removeTruck1*'s *truckID* property to activate the familiar browse (...) button. Click the browse button, select *TruckID* from the list of available existing properties, and click OK.

28. With that last property, you're finished with the visual workflow designer. Now it's time to add some code. Select Workflow1.cs in Solution Explorer, and click the View Code toolbar button to activate the code editor.

29. With the Workflow1.cs file open for editing, add the following using statements to the end of the list of existing using statements at the top of the file:

```
using System.IO;
using System.Xml;
using System.Xml.Serialization;
```

30. Scroll down through the source for *Workflow1* and locate the constructor. Following the constructor, add these fields:

```
private bool _cancelTruck = false;
private TruckService.RouteInfo _routes = null;
private TruckService.Truck _myTruck = null;
private TruckService.Route _myRoute = null;
private TruckService.Destination _currentOrigin = null;
private TruckService.Destination _currentDestination = null;
```

31. Following the fields you just added, you need to add two properties used for workflow initialization:

```
public string Routes
{
    set
    {
        // Deserialize route information.
        using (StringReader rdr = new StringReader(value))
        {
            XmlSerializer serializer =
                new XmlSerializer(typeof(TruckService.RouteInfo));
            _routes = (TruckService.RouteInfo)serializer.Deserialize(rdr);
        } // using
    }
}

public string TrackedTruck
{
    set
    {
        // Deserialize truck information.
        using (StringReader rdr = new StringReader(value))
        {
            XmlSerializer serializer =
                new XmlSerializer(typeof(TruckService.Truck));
            _myTruck = (TruckService.Truck)serializer.Deserialize(rdr);
        } // using

        // Assign the truck ID.
        TruckID = _myTruck.ID;

        // Pull the route so we can retrieve the starting coordinates.
        foreach (TruckService.Route route in _routes.Routes)
        {
            // Check this route to see if it's ours.
            if (route.ID == _myTruck.RouteID)
            {
                // Ours, so save...
                _myRoute = route;
                break;
            } // if
        } // foreach

        // Pull origin.
        _currentOrigin = FindDestination(_myRoute.Start);
```

```
        // Pull destination or first waypoint.
        if (_myRoute.Waypoints.Length > 0)
        {
            // Pull first waypoint.
            _currentDestination =
                        FindDestination(_myRoute.Waypoints[0].ID);
        } // if
        else
        {
            // No waypoints.
            _currentDestination = FindDestination(_myRoute.Stop);
        } // else

        // Assign the X and Y coordinates.
        CurrentX = _currentOrigin.X;
        CurrentY = _currentOrigin.Y;
    }
}
```

32. The setter for the *TrackedTruck* property used a helper method, *FindDestination*. Add that following *TrackedTruck*:

```
private TruckService.Destination FindDestination(Int32 id)
{
    // Loop through the route destinations, looking for the
    // one we want...
    TruckService.Destination retVal = null;
    foreach (TruckService.Destination destination in _routes.Destinations)
    {
        // Check this destination.
        if (destination.ID == id)
        {
            // Got it.
            retVal = destination;
            break;
        } // if
    } // foreach

    return retVal;
}
```

33. Scroll down through the dependency properties Visual Studio added, and locate the *TestAtDestination* method. To *TestAtDestination*, add the following:

```
// Check for cancel...
if (_cancelTruck)
{
    // Cancel immediately.
    e.Result = false;
}
else
{
    // If the truck is within 3 pixels for both X and Y, we're at the
    // destination...
    e.Result = true;
    if (Math.Abs((double)_currentDestination.X - (double)CurrentX) < 3.0 &&
```

```
        Math.Abs((double)_currentDestination.Y - (double)CurrentY) < 3.0)
    {
        // Check for waypoints...
        if (_currentDestination.ID != _myRoute.Stop)
        {
            // Copy former destination to origin, and then
            // look up next waypoint destination.
            _currentOrigin = _currentDestination;
            TruckService.Waypoint waypoint = null;
            for (Int32 i = 0; i < _myRoute.Waypoints.Length; i++)
            {
                // Check to see if this is the current waypoint
                waypoint = _myRoute.Waypoints[i];
                if (waypoint.ID == _currentOrigin.ID)
                {
                    // Found the current waypoint, so assign the next.
                    // waypoint to be the new destination.
                    if ((i + 1) == _myRoute.Waypoints.Length)
                    {
                        // Last waypoint, head to true destination.
                        _currentDestination =
                            FindDestination(_myRoute.Stop);
                    } // if
                    else
                    {
                        // Next waypoint
                        _currentDestination =
                            FindDestination(_myRoute.Waypoints[i + 1].ID);
                    } // else
                    break;
                } // if
            } // for
        } // if
        else
        {
            // We've arrived...
            e.Result = false;
        } // else
    } // if
} // else
```

34. To the *CancelTruck* method, add this code:

```
// Set the cancel flag.
_cancelTruck = true;
```

35. Finally, add the simulation code itself to *UpdateTruckPosition*:

```
// Calculate slope for linear interpolation.
//      Y1 - Y2
// m =  -------
//      X1 - X2
//
// Solve for b: y = mx + b, so b = y - mx
double m = ((double)_currentDestination.Y - (double)_currentOrigin.Y) /
           ((double)_currentDestination.X - (double)_currentOrigin.X);
```

```
double b = (double)_currentDestination.Y -
              (m * (double)_currentDestination.X);

// With slope and intercept, we increment x to find the new y.
Int32 multiplier = (_currentDestination.X - _currentOrigin.X) < 0 ? -1 : 1;
CurrentX += (multiplier * 2);
CurrentY = (Int32)((m * (double)CurrentX) + b);
```

36. Save all open files.

37. The workflow is now complete, but one last task remains for you to execute the application. The main application, TruckTracker, requires a reference to the workflow. So right-click the TruckTracker project, and select Add Reference. From the Projects tab, select TruckFlow and click OK.

38. Now you can compile the entire solution by pressing F6 or by selecting Build Solution from Visual Studio's Build menu option. Correct any compilation errors you encounter.

39. To execute the application, press Shift+F5, or just press F5 to run the application in debug mode. Add a truck by clicking Add Truck, selecting a route, and clicking OK. Add as many trucks as you like. To remove a truck, select it in the listview control and click Cancel Truck.

The application's code isn't very different from what you saw in Chapters 8 and 10. The one difference is when accessing the data for a given truck, you need to pass in the truck identifier for that vehicle. In some cases, that's even provided for you in the event arguments.

If you want to continue to the next chapter, keep Visual Studio 2005 running and turn to Chapter 18, "Invoking Web Services from Within Your Workflows." We've been working with single-computer data long enough...it's time to branch out and hit the Web.

If you want to stop, exit Visual Studio 2005 now, save your spot in the book, and close it. I'm sure you're as excited about using Web services from your workflow as I am, but man doesn't live by work alone. Time for a break!

Chapter 17 Quick Reference

To	Do This
Add correlation to your external workflow data processing	Add the workflow correlation parameters to your communication interface. WF then automatically inspects workflows and data exchanges and throws exceptions if there is a data-correlation problem.
Build a correlated local communication service	However you choose to architect your local communication service, you must first make sure the method or event that is declared as the initializer is called before other correlated data paths are used (or you'll receive an exception). Also, you must return data in a correlated fashion, so saving data for use by using the workflow instance ID and the correlation parameter makes sense.

Chapter 18
Invoking Web Services from Within Your Workflows

After completing this chapter, you will be able to:

- Invoke a Web service from your workflow
- Add and configure Web service proxies
- Manage sessions in your workflow

Speaking personally, something about sending and receiving data over networks struck a chord with me, and I've enjoyed writing communications-based code for years because of it. When I saw that Microsoft Windows Workflow Foundation (WF) had built-in capabilities to both connect to and act as a Web service, well, that was something I just had to dig into a bit deeper.

WF ships with several XML Web service–based activities, the client side of which we'll examine in this chapter. (We'll work with the server-side activities in the final chapter, "Workflow as Web Services.") Before actually working with the *InvokeWebService* activity, I thought I'd describe how Web services work, as we'll need to understand the terminology as we progress through this and the final chapter.

Web Services Architecture

One could argue that any Internet-based server that performs work at your request is a Web service. However, I'll use the term in both this and the next chapter as measured against a more strict interpretation. Here, I'll be referring to an *XML Web service*, which is a service based on the *SOAP protocol*.

> **Note** Originally, "SOAP" was an acronym that stood for the *Simple Object Access Protocol*, which is an XML-based communications framework. However, with the release of the current version of SOAP, the protocol is simply known as the SOAP protocol. You can find the latest SOAP specification here: *http://www.w3.org/TR/soap/*.

The basic idea that drove the creation of the SOAP protocol was the notion that intrinsic data types and even complex data structures could be converted from their native binary format into XML, and that the XML could then be sent over the Internet in much the same way Web pages are sent using the Hypertext Markup Language (HTML). The original SOAP specification clearly outlined the "serialization format" for everything from integers and strings to enumerations to arrays and complex structures. Later specifications relaxed the serialization format with the advent of serialization description languages. Currently, the serialization description language of choice is the Web Service Description Language, or WSDL.

WSDL allows you to format the contents of your SOAP message as you see fit. You simply describe the contents in WSDL format and provide users your WSDL, from which they can interpret the structures and methods your Web service exports and, therefore, use your services. While the original SOAP specification intended SOAP to be used for remote method invocation, the latest specification, coupled with WSDL, allows for a more message-based architecture, with the contents of the message being anything you can serialize into XML (which in one form or another is just about anything).

Therefore, when you reference a remote Web service, you'll download and interpret the WSDL the service provides you. When using .NET, tools that ship with the .NET Framework do this interpretation for you and create for you a C# class you can use to invoke the remote service's methods. This C# class is known as a *proxy* because it acts in place of the actual service. Ultimately, except for communication latency, your software should not even be aware of the fact it's talking to a service over the Internet. The proxy makes it appear as if the service is housed within your local computer.

To review, you make a reference to a Web service, at which time it sends you its WSDL. .NET creates for you a proxy you can use to communicate with the remote server according to the remote server's specification (per its WSDL). When you communicate, the data you transmit is converted into XML and sent over the wire using the SOAP protocol. The remote server interprets your request and responds. When you receive the server's response, the response XML is converted back into binary form for your code to use.

> **Note**   It would be all too easy for me to go on and on discussing Web services and how they're implemented, but we truly need to move on and dive into workflow. However, should you like to learn more, many books and online references are available. A great place to start is *http://msdn.microsoft.com/webservices/*.

Using the *InvokeWebService* Activity

WF's built-in client-facing XML Web service support comes in the form of the *InvokeWebService* activity. In many respects, the *InvokeWebService* activity merely fronts a proxy for you, but it does have added capability to control multiple invocations using a single session cookie.

The crucial properties you need to work with when using the *InvokeWebService* activity are shown in Table 18-1.

Table 18-1   Critical *InvokeWebService* Activity Properties

Property	Purpose
MethodName	Gets or sets the method to be invoked when the activity is executed. This property represents the method name of the remote method you want to call.
ProxyClass	Gets or sets the type name for the proxy class. Either you can provide this yourself or WF will help you by creating a proxy class for you when you drop the activity into your workflow.
SessionId	Gets or sets the session to be used. You use this mechanism to tie different XML Web service invocations together. I discuss this property further in the "Working with Sessions" section.
URL	Gets or sets the URL to be used for communicating with the XML Web service. The URL itself is stored in your workflow project's Settings property bag, although you can easily change it using the Properties pane for your *InvokeWebService* activity instance.

In addition to these properties, you might also from time to time need to provide event handlers for the *Invoking* and *Invoked* events. You'll see why you might need these when you configure your proxy in this chapter's "Configuring the Proxy" section.

Using the *InvokeWebService* activity is simply a matter of dropping it into your workflow. When you do, Microsoft Visual Studio helps you configure the activity by requesting the server information so that it can retrieve the WSDL and create the proxy. If you want to create the proxy yourself, simply cancel the dialog box Visual Studio pops up. If you want Visual Studio to create the proxy, you'll recognize the dialog box as the same dialog box Visual Studio uses for selecting a Web reference for a typical Visual Studio project, as you see in Figure 18-1.

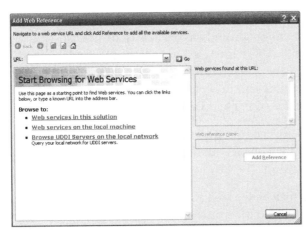

Figure 18-1   Visual Studio's Add Web Reference dialog box user interface

Once you add the Web reference, you need to assign the *MethodName* from the list of available methods and bind any parameters that might be required. Once you do, you're ready to go.

Adding the Web Reference

As Figure 18-1 indicates, there are four ways to assign an XML Web service binding to your *InvokeWebService* activity. The three links are clear: Select a Web service from your current solution, select a Web service from your local machine, or use something known as UDDI to locate a Web service hosted on a server in your local network. The fourth way, of course, is to type the URL directly in and press the Go button.

> **Note** UDDI is the Universal Description, Discovery, and Integration protocol, which is used to publish the existence and capabilities of XML Web services. At one time, it was intended for Internet-wide use, but that idea has since fallen short of expectations. However, you can use UDDI on your local network if you're using Windows Server 2003. The following online information source tells you how: *http://www.microsoft.com/windowsserver2003/technologies/idm/uddi/default.mspx.*

If you select the local solution link (the first link in the list of options), Visual Studio inspects your current solution for XML Web service projects. If any are found, they're presented to you and you can choose one to bind to (by clicking the Add Reference button, which will be enabled once you select a service).

Choosing a service from your local server tells Visual Studio to scan the local Internet Information Services (IIS) metabase for XML Web services configured to execute under local IIS control. If any are found, they're presented in a list for you to select the service you desire. Again, once you select a service, the Add Reference button is enabled. Click it and Visual Studio creates your proxy for you. Note if you want to reference a WSDL file located on your local hard drive, you need to type that into the URL field by hand using the file protocol (*file://{filename}*).

As for using UDDI, if you select this option and there is at least one UDDI server available in your local network, you can use the UDDI services it provides to seek and select an XML Web service of interest. Having found one, UDDI provides Visual Studio with the relevant service URL, and Visual Studio again creates your proxy for you.

Something to keep in mind when you add Web service references is that you have the option of assigning names to the proxies when you select the service. This option can be useful, especially when you reference more than one service. The name you provide becomes part of the proxy's namespace.

If your Web service is truly out there in the land of the Internet, you need to provide the URL yourself by typing it into the URL field that you see at the top of the dialog box shown in Figure 18-1 and clicking the Go button. Visual Studio queries the URL for its WSDL and builds the proxy just as if the XML Web service were local to your system.

Configuring the Proxy

Once you add the *InvokeWebService* activity, which in many respects is similar to adding a Web reference to a typical Visual Studio project, you need to configure the proxy. There are two ways this can be accomplished: static and dynamic configuration.

Static Proxy Configuration

Static proxy configuration is performed by setting the properties of the *InvokeWebService* activity using Visual Studio's Properties pane. When you add a new *InvokeWebService* activity and bind to a Web service (using the Add Web Reference dialog box we've been discussing), nearly everything is complete and ready to use. The URL is known and saved in the workflow project's Settings property bag, and the proxy type is assigned. (The *ProxyClass* property will have a value.) The exception is the *MethodName* property.

Visual Studio "knows" what methods are available to you when it interprets the WSDL and creates the proxy. Specifying a method to invoke is then as simple as dropping a list of available methods and selecting one. Unless that method has bindable parameters, your configuration is complete. If there are parameters, either into or from the method, you need to bind a local field or dependency property to those parameter values. With the *MethodName* established and the method properties bound, you truly are ready to access the XML Web service using *InvokeWebService*.

Dynamic Proxy Configuration

However, as soon as anything is statically set, it always seems like we need to dynamically reconfigure it. Perhaps you want to algorithmically assign a URL rather than use one baked into Settings. Or maybe you need to assign credentials to the invocation to gain access to a secured Web service. None of these things is available through statically configured parameters in Visual Studio.

The solution lies in handling the *Invoking* event. If you provide an event handler for the *InvokeWebService* activity's *Invoking* event, you are given access to the proxy class itself via the event's *InvokeWebServiceEventArgs*. *InvokeWebServiceEventArgs* has a property named *WebServiceProxy* that is the instance of the proxy the *InvokeWebService* activity is using to invoke the XML Web service. By simply casting this object to the proxy type you're using, you can change any dynamic value you require, including the URL and credentials.

> **Note**   For information regarding how you gain access to the Internet when it is protected by a proxy server, see *http://msdn2.microsoft.com/en-us/library/system.net.configuration. proxyelement(VS.80).aspx*. For information describing accessing secured XML Web services, see *http://msdn.microsoft.com/library/default.asp?url=/library/en-us/dnnetsec/html/SecNetch10.asp* (especially the "Passing Credentials for Authentication to Web services" section).

Working with Sessions

Sessions, in Web parlance, are sets of connected request-response pairs. That is, if you make a request of a Web resource in one invocation, you expect the next invocation to keep track of the previous invocation. This is definitely not how the HyperText Transfer Protocol (HTTP) works under the covers. HTTP was developed to support a single request-response pair. Any knowledge of prior dealings with the server are completely forgotten.

However, as Web users, we demand that Web request-response pairs be remembered. The most obvious example is the Web-based shopping cart. When you place orders for goods over the Internet and those goods are collected into a virtual shopping cart, you expect the things you selected will be available for checkout at a later time. How do we reconcile the disparity between what HTTP expects to support and what we, as users, demand?

The answer is Web applications maintain *session state*. When you begin using a Web application, you initiate a session. That session is tracked until you cease using the Web application, either by logging out of the application (if it's secured) or by simply closing your browser.

A common way to track session state is through the use of a *cookie*. Cookies are auxiliary data containers that ride along with your HTTP request-response in the HTTP packet, along with the actual payload (SOAP-based XML, HTML, or whatever). On the server, they're typically extracted into memory and are accessible by your Web application for whatever reason you're tracking session information. On the client, they're commonly stored as files. When you access the given Web resource, any cookies destined for that resource are retrieved from the cookie folder and shipped back to the server. Although this process is not the only way to maintain session information, it is a common scenario.

XML Web services are a little different, however. For one thing, they're not invoked using a browser, at least not when using WF. (Other technologies most certainly do invoke XML Web services from a browser.) Because of this, the cookies associated with an XML Web service are not file-based but merely exist in memory or on the wire when transferred back and forth to the server. They're not stored in files on the client.

Another way they differ is that they might not always be present, so you can't depend on their existence. If the XML Web service isn't configured to send session-based cookies, session continuance isn't possible.

> **Tip** If you're writing your XML Web service using the .NET Framework and you want sessions to be in effect, be sure to enable session management using the *EnableSession* key in the *WebMethod* attribute identifying your Web-based methods. By default, the session management subsystem is deactivated in .NET XML Web service operations.

There is at least one good reason to enable session management within your workflow—workflows can take time to complete, and in some cases, significant amounts of time. If the XML Web service is long-running, you need to tie related queries together to retrieve the results of the long-running service.

Long-Running XML Web Services

Workflows that involve people are, by nature, long-running. Quite often you'll persist your workflow while waiting for somebody to respond or take some action.

If an XML Web service for some reason requests human intervention, or if by design it takes a long time to complete (such as waiting for an order to be fulfilled), your client workflow becomes a long-running workflow too. Rather than keep everything tied up, it's often easiest to cease processing, wait awhile, and then query the XML Web service again to see if it's complete. (There are specifications out there for Web-based notification, such as *WS-Eventing*, but .NET doesn't implement those as yet.)

Imagine you make a request of an XML Web service, stop processing for a while, and then start back up and query the service again. If you don't use the same session, generally the server will most likely throw an exception unless some other mechanism to relate server queries is used.

It's up to you, then, to retrieve the session cookie created by the first XML Web service invocation, copy its information, and save that for later use. Assuming that session cookies are enabled, to make a copy, you provide an event handler for the first *InvokeWebService* activity's *Invoked* event that is patterned after the following:

```
private void FirstWebMethodInvokedHandler(object sender,
                                 InvokeWebServiceEventArgs e)
{
    MyWebServiceProxy ws = e.WebServiceProxy as MyWebServiceProxy;
    foreach (System.Net.Cookie cookie in
                    ws.CookieContainer.GetCookies(new Uri(ws.Url)))
    {
        // The following values must be saved in order to re-create
        // the cookie. There should be only one cookie, but just in
        // case, you can examine them all if there is more than one.
        string a = cookie.Name; // (persist values for later recall)
        string b = cookie.Path;
        string c = cookie.Value;
        string d = cookie.Domain;
    }
}
```

You save the string values in the *a*, *b*, *c*, and *d* variables for later use. Subsequent invocations destined to use the same session cookie then use the information formerly stored in *a*, *b*, *c*, and *d* to re-create the cookie for the next invocation, perhaps to request status or results. In the following example, the subsequent *InvokeWebService*'s *Invoking* event is handled:

```
private void NextWebMethodInvokingHandler(object sender,
                                          InvokeWebServiceEventArgs e)
{
    // Create the cookie from persisted values.
    System.Net.Cookie cookie = new System.Net.Cookie();
    cookie.Name = a; // (values from previous Invoking handler)
    cookie.Path = b;
    cookie.Value = c;
    cookie.Domain = d;

    // Add the cookie to the cookie collection going to the
    // remote server.
    MyWebServiceProxy ws = e.WebServiceProxy as MyWebServiceProxy;
    ws.CookieContainer.Add(cookie);
}
```

Note that this effort is required only if the workflow instance was persisted or otherwise removed from memory. If two session-related *InvokeWebService* activities are used within the same workflow instance execution, the cookie is carried forward to each XML Web service method invocation for you as long as they share the same *SessionId* value.

Building a Workflow That Uses an XML Web Service

With all that background information, isn't it about time to give the *InvokeWebService* activity a spin? I created an application that contains several projects: a console application to drive the workflow, a Web service that returns stock quote information, and a basic sequential workflow library. I called the solution QuoteRetriever, and it uses the same three stock symbols you used in Chapter 10's sample application. Let's work with this sample and call an XML Web service from the workflow.

Adding an *InvokeWebService* activity interface to your workflow

1. The QuoteRetriever application is in the \Workflow\Chapter18\QuoteRetriever directory, and as usual, I placed two different versions of the application there. The incomplete version for you to work with is in the QuoteRetriever directory, while the completed version is in the QuoteRetriever Completed directory. If you want to work through the steps, open the QuoteRetriever version. If not, open the completed version and follow along. To open either solution, drag the .sln file onto an executing copy of Visual Studio to open the solution for editing and compilation.

2. Find the Workflow1.cs file in the QuoteFlow project, and click the View Designer button on the Solution Explorer toolbar. This opens the visual workflow designer.

3. The workflow is empty at this time, so let's add its first activity. Drag an instance of *InvokeWebService* activity onto the designer's surface and drop it.

4. Although you might expect to see the behavior you've seen throughout this book—a rounded rectangle appearing on the designer's surface—what you are presented with instead is the Visual Studio Add Web Reference dialog box. Because you've not identified a previous Web reference suitable for use in this project, let's complete the addition of the Web reference and the initial *InvokeWebService* activity property settings. Click the Web Services In This Solution link to proceed.

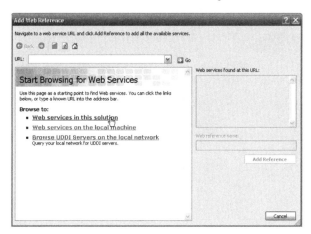

5. The only XML Web service present in the solution is for the QuoteService. Click the QuoteService link to proceed.

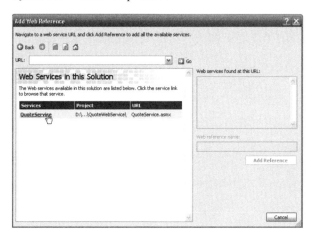

Note   QuoteService prepopulates a *Dictionary* object with the three stock symbols used in Chapter 10 along with their initial values. Then it places the *Dictionary* object in the ASP.NET cache for use when the XML Web service is invoked. (See Global.asax for the code that initializes the cache.)

6. Visual Studio works for a moment—it's loading the WSDL for the service and parsing it for methods the service exports. Once it has loaded the WSDL and presented you with the methods the service exposes, the Add Reference button is enabled. Click it to add the Web reference to your project.

Visual Studio also adds the familiar rounded-corner rectangle to the visual workflow designer, this being the instance of *InvokeWebService* you just dropped into your workflow.

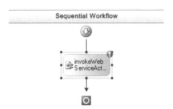

7. Most of the settings for *invokeWebService1* have been established for you by Visual Studio. However, you must tell Visual Studio what method you want to call with this instance of the *InvokeWebService* activity. In the Properties pane, select the *MethodName* property to activate the down arrow, and then click the down arrow. Select *GetQuote* from the list.

8. Selecting the method name causes Visual Studio to examine the method and add the parameters the method supports to the Properties pane. Select the (Return Value) property to activate the familiar browse (...) button. Click the browse button to activate the Bind '(Return Value)' To An Activity's Property dialog box. Click the Bind To A New Member tab, and type **StockValue** in the New Member Name field, making sure the Create Property option is selected. Click OK to add the *StockValue* dependency property to your workflow.

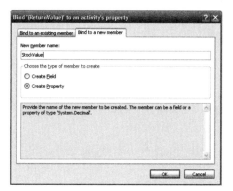

9. Do the same for the *symbol* property, naming its dependency property **Symbol**.

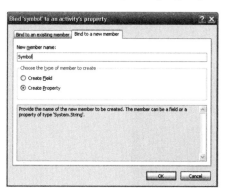

10. The *InvokeWebService* activity is now fully configured for this workflow, so drag a copy of the *Code* activity onto the visual workflow designer's surface and drop it below *invokeWebService1*. Assign its *ExecuteCode* property to be **DisplayQuoteValue**.

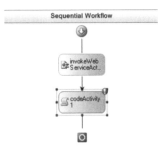

11. Visual Studio adds the *DisplayQuoteValue* method and switches you to the code editor. Add this code to the *DisplayQuoteValue* method Visual Studio just added:

```
if (StockValue >= 0)
{
    // Found the stock value.
    Console.WriteLine("The value for '{0}' is: {1}",
                        Symbol, StockValue.ToString("C"));
} // if
else
{
    // Unknown stock.
    Console.WriteLine("Stock symbol '{0}' is unknown...please try" +
                        " again using a valid stock symbol.", Symbol);
} // else
```

12. Compile the entire solution by pressing F6, or by selecting Build Solution from Visual Studio's Build menu. Correct any compilation errors that might appear.

13. The main application expects a stock ticker symbol as the only command-line argument. The XML Web service has information for only three ticker symbols: CONT, LITW, and TSPT. Therefore, these are the only three values you can pass into the application. If you execute the application and pass in the CONT stock symbol, the program's output appears something like the following:

The output value for the stock will vary because random numbers are used in the simulation the XML Web service implements, but the application should still execute and retrieve the stock value from the XML Web service. If there is a problem, the returned exception is shown for debugging purposes. Generally, restarting the Web server is all you'll need to do.

If you want to continue to the next chapter, keep Visual Studio 2005 running and turn to Chapter 19, "Workflows as Web Services." In this final chapter, we'll look at the converse of this chapter, which is how workflows can host an XML Web service.

If you want to stop, exit Visual Studio 2005 now, save your spot in the book, and close it. I couldn't blame you...*InvokeWebService* is a great activity and very useful. No doubt you want to experiment. We'll see you in the last chapter.

Chapter 18 Quick Reference

To	Do This
Call an XML Web service from your workflow	Use the *InvokeWebService* activity. Although you can use a *Code* activity with a Web reference and proxy, using *InvokeWebService* brings the invocation into the workflow designer instead of hiding it within a *Code* activity. You also can bind properties to the activity, which is handy.
Dynamically reconfigure your proxy prior to making the XML Web service invocation	Provide an event handler for the *Invoking* event, and access the *InvokeWebServiceEventArgs WebServiceProxy* property (cast to your proxy type) to gain access to any of the typical proxy properties.
Tie separate *InvokeWebService* calls to a single session	Provide the same *SessionId* value to each instance of *InvokeWebService*. The session cookie can then be used to connect the method calls together within a single session.

Chapter 19
Workflows as Web Services

After completing this chapter, you will be able to:

- Understand how the various workflow activities designed to expose your workflow as an XML Web service are used

- Understand what is required to host workflow in ASP.NET

- See how faults are handled in XML Web service–based workflow

- Configure your XML Web service–based workflow for various conditions

In the previous chapter, "Invoking Web Services from Within Your Workflows," you saw how to call XML Web services from your client-side workflow using the *InvokeWebService* activity that Windows Workflow Foundation (WF) provides for this purpose. The XML Web service in that chapter's sample application, however, was a typical ASP.NET XML Web service—nothing special.

In this final chapter, you'll learn how to take workflow processes and automatically expose the workflow as an XML Web service for clients to consume. It's not as simple as creating a workflow assembly library and referencing that from a Web service project, but then again, it's not difficult to do once you understand some essential concepts and see it accomplished in a sample application.

> **Note** This chapter focuses on integrating WF into ASP.NET for use as an XML Web service. But there are many critical issues you should be aware of when exposing XML Web services, not the least of which is security. A full discussion of security is well beyond what I can present here, but this link should get you started: *http://msdn.microsoft.com/library/default.asp?url=/library/en-us/dnnetsec/html/THCMCh12.asp*. If you're going to expose your workflow as an XML Web service, I strongly encourage you to review ASP.NET security best practices, especially practices that are centered around XML Web services.

Exposing a Workflow as an XML Web Service

Part of the reason you can't directly execute the workflows you've seen throughout the book in an ASP.NET environment is that the workflow runtime, by default, executes workflow instances asynchronously. In fact, that's a particularly valuable feature when working with workflow in non-Web applications.

But in a Web-based scenario, this presents a problem. If an ASP.NET request comes in, whether it's for an XML Web service or even an ASP.NET Web page, the workflow instance begins execution and the runtime returns control to ASP.NET. Your XML Web service or ASP.NET page immediately continues preparing output and likely finishes before the workflow instance completes. Because the workflow instance is asynchronous, executing in parallel with your ASP.NET application, your ASP.NET code could easily finish and return a response to the caller without ever completing the workflow processing.

> **Tip** Properly executing workflow instances within ASP.NET Web pages really calls for ASP.NET asynchronous Web pages, the discussion of which is beyond the scope of this book. However, this link gives you some details: *http://msdn.microsoft.com/msdnmag/issues/05/10/WickedCode/*.

This behavior presents at least two challenges for us. First, we need to disable, or at least work around, the asynchronous execution of our workflows. We need for them to execute synchronously such that they use the same thread our page or XML Web service is using so that the Web application doesn't return a response to the caller until we're finished. Of course, this leaves open the question of long-running workflows, which is the second challenge we'll need to address.

The challenge long-running workflows present is centered around the nature of Web-based applications themselves. From the last chapter, you know that Web applications are by nature stateless. Requests made milliseconds apart are completely unaware of each other unless we build a framework to provide that awareness. Web applications also execute on Web servers, which are normally very expensive systems designed to serve a great many clients. If a workflow takes a long time to complete, it ties up the Web server and reduces the application's scalability (the ability to serve a greater number of client requests).

The solution to both state management and long-running workflows is persistence. If your workflow process completes over the span of more than one Web-based invocation (ASP.NET page request or XML Web service), you must persist the workflow instance and reload it during the next execution cycle. This is also the reason why I mentioned regenerating the session-state cookie in the previous chapter's "Long-Running XML Web Services" section, because the client must also be aware of this possibility and make allowances for more than a single request-response.

Internet Information Services (IIS) in particular, however, is quite adept at conserving system resources. In a typical client application, and in fact in every application you've seen in the book so far, the workflow runtime is started when the application begins execution and runs throughout the lifetime of the application. IIS, though, recycles applications to reclaim server resources. This means two things to us as ASP.NET programmers.

First, we have to somehow decide where and how to start the workflow runtime. Different requests for the same ASP.NET application are processed on different threads, but they execute in the same AppDomain. As you might recall, you can have only a single instance of the WF workflow runtime executing per AppDomain. So it isn't as simple as creating an instance of the workflow runtime whenever your ASP.NET application receives a request. Doing so could result in a workflow runtime exception.

And second, we need to find a way to execute our workflow in a synchronous manner. Or, if our workflow is long-running, we need to synchronously begin workflow instance execution, stop execution, persist the workflow instance, and report back to the client the current workflow status. To do that, we need to replace the default workflow runtime thread scheduling service. To replace the thread scheduling service, we need to reconfigure the workflow runtime.

Creating the Workflow Runtime

If you look at the previous chapter's XML Web service, you see that I added a special file to the sample ASP.NET application—Global.asax. This file contains event handlers for important events in the ASP.NET application's lifetime. One of the events handled in Global.asax is the application starting event fired by ASP.NET when it creates an instance of *HttpApplication*. You could, if you wanted, start the workflow runtime in the *Application_Start* event handler. (I did something similar in the previous chapter with the static *Dictionary* object for stock lookups.)

> **Note**   If you'd like to learn more about the application life cycle in ASP.NET, check out *msdn2.microsoft.com/en-us/library/aa485331.aspx* for some details.

The problem you'll face is you then need to provide some mechanism for individual Web resource requests to access the workflow runtime. The obvious solution to this is to reference the workflow runtime from a container class you create and then stuff that into the ASP.NET cache. In fact, this is very nearly what happens.

The WF team knew people would want to use the workflow runtime from ASP.NET applications, and they knew that starting the workflow runtime could be problematic, so they created for us the *WorkflowWebRequestContext* class.

WorkflowWebRequestContext neatly solves a couple of problems for us. For one, it maintains a singleton instance of the workflow runtime. When you use its *Current.WorkflowRuntime* accessor, it creates the workflow runtime for you if the singleton instance of the workflow runtime is *null*. If the workflow runtime has already been created, the cached workflow runtime is returned. This is exactly the pattern we've been using throughout the book with the *WorkflowFactory* class introduced in Chapter 2, "The Workflow Runtime." The other problem it solves is all Web resources have access to *WorkflowWebRequestContext* and can therefore gain access to the workflow runtime.

Configuring Services

With a mechanism in place for retrieving the single workflow runtime destined to be used by our ASP.NET application (good for pages or XML Web services), we now need to turn to adding the services we require. We require at least one service, but more could be necessary. The service we need to add to the runtime is the manual thread scheduling service, but the persistence and transactional services are also commonly added.

You might at first believe that services are added in the same way we've added them throughout the book. That is, you might think the following approach would work:

```
WorkflowRuntime workflowRuntime =
    WorkflowWebRequestContext.Current.WorkflowRuntime;

. . .

string connString = ConfigurationManager.
    ConnectionStrings["MyPersistenceDB"].ConnectionString;
workflowRuntime.AddService(new SqlWorkflowPersistenceService(connString));
```

However, in an ASP.NET environment this fails. By the time we have access to the workflow runtime, it has already been started by *WorkflowWebRequestContext*. Once the workflow runtime is started, you can't add some specific services, persistence being one. Moreover, in an ASP.NET environment, other workflow instances might already be using the workflow runtime, so you can't just elect to stop it, add the desired services, and then restart it. Therefore, there must be some other way to perform workflow runtime configuration.

And in fact there is, and the term "configuration" is more apropos than you might have guessed. The services to be added are read from the ASP.NET application configuration file, Web.config. A special section is devoted to workflow configuration, delimited by the *<WorkflowRuntime />* XML element defined by WF. Because the workflow runtime uses a custom configuration section, you would expect there to also be a section identifier in the *<configSections />* element as well. Services themselves are configured using the *<Services />* element found in *<WorkflowRuntime />*.

I'll show you a typical Web.config file in a moment, but before I do, there is one more thing to consider. What creates the *WorkflowWebRequestContext* object? This object isn't a part of the out-of-the-box ASP.NET implementation, so something, somewhere, must be responsible for its lifetime. It's also the case that XML Web service invocations for specific workflow instances (remember *SessionId*?) must be mapped to those instances, and if the instances happen to be persisted, they must be rehydrated for execution.

The object responsible for all this is an ASP.NET *HttpModule* called the *WorkflowWebHostingModule*. ASP.NET *HttpModules*, as you might know, are extensibility objects you can place in the request-response path of your Web-based application. They're used for just this type of thing—adding extensible functionality to your ASP.NET applications. As it happens, you configure additional ASP.NET *HttpModules* via your application's Web.config file as well.

> **Note**   To learn more about *HttpModules* and how they enhance the ASP.NET HTTP request-response pipeline, see *http://msdn2.microsoft.com/en-us/library/ms178468.aspx*.

Listing 19-1 provides you with a basic Web.config file, common to many WF-based applications hosted in ASP.NET environments. Note it contains information specific to hosting WF in your ASP.NET application—you still need to add any ASP.NET configuration that's appropriate for your application (such as to the *<system.web />* section).

> **Note**   Listing 19-1 is valid for the release of WF current at the time of this writing. However, if new releases become public, the version numbers and potentially the public key token values in your configuration files will require updating. You might also need to update the connection string to match your SQL Server installation.

Listing 19-1   Web.config with workflow extensions

```xml
<?xml version="1.0"?>
<configuration xmlns="http://schemas.microsoft.com/.NetConfiguration/v2.0">
  <configSections>
    <section name="WorkflowRuntime" type=
      "System.Workflow.Runtime.Configuration.WorkflowRuntimeSection,
      System.Workflow.Runtime, Version=3.0.00000.0, Culture=neutral,
      PublicKeyToken=31bf3856ad364e35"/>
  </configSections>
  <WorkflowRuntime Name="WorkflowServiceContainer">
    <Services>
      <add type=
        "System.Workflow.Runtime.Hosting.ManualWorkflowSchedulerService,
        System.Workflow.Runtime, Version=3.0.00000.0, Culture=neutral,
        PublicKeyToken=31bf3856ad364e35"/>
      <add type=
        "System.Workflow.Runtime.Hosting.SqlWorkflowPersistenceService,
        System.Workflow.Runtime, Version=3.0.00000.0, Culture=neutral,
        PublicKeyToken=31bf3856ad364e35"/>
      <add type=
        "System.Workflow.Runtime.Hosting.DefaultWorkflowTransactionService,
        System.Workflow.Runtime, Version=3.0.00000.0, Culture=neutral,
        PublicKeyToken=31bf3856ad364e35"/>
    </Services>
  </WorkflowRuntime>
  <appSettings/>
  <connectionStrings>
    <add name="MyPersistenceDB"
      connectionString=
"server=(local)\SQLEXPRESS;database=WorkflowStore;Integrated Security=true"
      />
  </connectionStrings>
  <system.web>
    . . .
    <httpModules>
```

```
        <add type="System.Workflow.Runtime.Hosting.WorkflowWebHostingModule,
          System.Workflow.Runtime, Version=3.0.00000.0, Culture=neutral,
          PublicKeyToken=31bf3856ad364e35" name="WorkflowHost"/>
      </httpModules>
    </system.web>
  </configuration>
```

Workflow Housekeeping

Everything discussed so far in this chapter has revolved around ASP.NET's architecture and its requirements for hosting WF-based applications. Before we get to the WF XML Web service–based activities themselves, let's spend a little time discussing how workflow-based XML Web service applications are architected.

When you use *ExternalDataExchange* and a local communication service, at least as I've described the process in this book, the first thing you do is create an interface. This interface identifies methods and data to be used for transferring information between your application and workflow, and it serves as the foundation for the entire communication process.

XML Web service workflows follow a similar model. You create an interface, the methods of which become Web-based service methods (*Web methods*, as we call them when using .NET). Both the interface and the workflow are typically housed in a separate assembly you reference from an ASP.NET host application. (ASP.NET has the ability to dynamically compile code for use over the Web. We'll circumvent that by using a precompiled assembly.) Later, when I mention associating the WF XML Web service–based activities with an interface and method, it's this interface we will have generated to which I am referring.

Something else to remember is that typical .NET XML Web services are exposed through an .asmx file. This file, or its code-behind file, will contain a class definition generally deriving from the *System.Web.Services.WebService* base class. Individual methods destined to be Web methods are decorated with the *System.Web.Services.WebMethod* attribute. The .asmx file itself contains, at a minimum, the *<%@WebService %>* directive, which informs ASP.NET that this is an XML Web service, rather than a Web page, and it provides some specific information regarding where the Web methods are found using its *Class* and possibly its *CodeBehind* attributes.

WF-based XML Web services require .asmx files like any other XML Web service, including the Web service directive, because this is how ASP.NET and IIS identify XML Web services. The good news is we won't need to build the actual ASP.NET XML Web service project ourselves. WF adds a menu item to Microsoft Visual Studio that publishes the workflow as an ASP.NET project and places it in our solution for us. This is a wonderful feature, and we'll give it a try later in the chapter.

Using the *WebServiceInput* Activity

OK, let's dig in. WF-based XML Web services require at least one *WebServiceInput* activity and one or more *WebServiceOutput* activities. The input and output activities are related—each output activity must be associated with an input activity. (This is true of the *WebServiceFault* activity as well.) You can't drop in an instance of *WebServiceInput* and have no outputs or faults, and you can't have outputs or faults without at least one *WebServiceInput*. Either case presents you with a validation and compilation error.

When you place an instance of *WebServiceInput* into your workflow, you need to set several properties and perhaps handle at least one event. The properties of interest are shown in Table 19-1. The event, *InputReceived*, allows you to establish initial conditions for the workflow. The properties serve to configure the *WebServiceInput* activity.

Table 19-1 Critical *WebServiceInput* Activity Properties

Property	Purpose
InterfaceType	Gets or sets the interface data type used to identify the methods potentially available as Web methods.
IsActivating	Gets or sets the activation status for the activity. If multiple *WebServiceInput* activities exist in your workflow, you identify the one that activates the workflow itself by setting this property to *True*. One *WebServiceInput* activity in your workflow must have this property set to true. If more than one *WebServiceInput* activity has this set to *True*, then more than one Web service call can start the workflow. If the two *WebServiceInput* activities are tied by session cookies, the second call blocks (waits) until the first completes.
MethodName	Gets or sets the method to be exported as a Web method. This method must also be a method defined by the interface assigned to *InterfaceType*.

The three properties in Table 19-1 must have assigned values, although *IsActivating* defaults to *False*. Omitting any property assignments results in validation and compilation errors.

IsActivating allows you to control secondary Web service calls into your workflow. The primary call, the Web Service method call that kicks off the workflow, should have *IsActivating* set to *True*. If your workflow then allows secondary calls from the client, such as when accepting inputs that act as events in a state-based workflow, the secondary *WebServiceInput* activities should have *IsActivating* set to *False* or else the workflow starts anew. If you allow a second instance of your workflow to start, the second instance will block if it shares session state with the first workflow instance and potentially cause a deadlock. Therefore, use multiple activating *WebServiceInput* activities with great care.

When you assign the *MethodName*, keep in mind that the method parameters associated with that method also need to be bound or otherwise assigned. In Visual Studio, when you select a method to act as the *MethodName*, the method's parameters automatically appear in the activity's Properties pane for you to bind using the property binding dialog box you've used throughout the book. You'll see this when working with the sample application for this chapter.

Using the *WebServiceOutput* Activity

The *WebServiceOutput* activity completes the XML Web service's processing by returning the value identified by the *MethodName* in the *WebServiceInput* activity. For this reason, you must assign the *WebServiceOuput*'s *InputActivityName* property to be one of the *WebServiceInput* activities present in your workflow. Failing to assign the input activity name results in both validation and compilation errors.

WebServiceOutput has a single method parameter to bind—that being the return result if any is indicated by the method in the interface bound to the *WebServiceInput* activity this output activity is tied to. If the method returns *void*, no return value binding is possible. The *WebServiceOutput* activity then is reduced to signaling the end of the workflow processing for this Web method invocation.

Interestingly, you can have multiple outputs for a single input, as might happen if the output activities are placed within separate *Parallel* activity execution paths, or in different branches of an *IfElse* activity. Different paths through your workflow might result in different outputs. What you cannot do is have multiple output activities in the same execution path. (The same holds true for the *WebServiceFault* activity as well.) If WF determines that more than one *WebServiceOutput*, or *WebServiceFault* combined with a *WebServiceOutput*, is in the same execution path, WF invalidates the activities and you need to correct the execution logic by moving or removing the offending activity or activities.

Using the *WebServiceFault* Activity

The *WebServiceFault* activity is closely related to the *WebServiceOutput* activity. Both indicate the termination of workflow processing for the particular invocation they happen to be supporting. And, as it turns out, *WebServiceFault* is used just as *WebServiceOutput* is used.

WebServiceFault is also tied to a single *WebServiceInput* activity. Like its cousin the *WebServiceOutput* activity, *WebServiceFault* has a single output property you must bind, in this case *Fault*. *Fault* is bound to a field or property based on *System.Exception* that represents the exception to report back to the client. Ultimately, *Fault* is translated into a *SoapException* and sent over the wire to the client. But any exception you care to bind is acceptable. ASP.NET translates the exception you provide into *SoapException* automatically.

Creating a Host Web Service Project

The final sample application for the book is one we'll create entirely from scratch. We'll begin by creating a simple console application, which does not need to reference the WF assemblies. This is because the workflow will be housed in an ASP.NET XML Web service, the workflow assembly for which we'll create next. With the workflow assembly ready, we'll publish the workflow as an ASP.NET Web service project, make some tweaks, and then add the code to invoke the workflow from the original console application. I mention the application creation process here before we start simply because it's circular and might appear odd at times because of its circular nature. Armed with the bigger picture, let's get started.

Creating the basic workflow application

1. Start an instance of Visual Studio. Click its File, then New, and finally Project menu items.

2. When the resulting New Project dialog box appears, select Windows in the Project Types pane. (First expand the Visual C# tree control node if it isn't already expanded.) Select Console Application from the Templates list.

3. Type **QuoteGenerator** into the Name field and **\Workflow\Chapter19** into the Location field. Click OK.

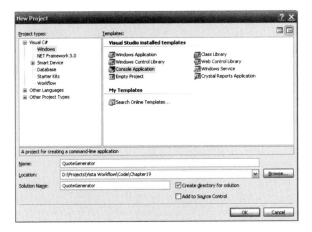

This creates both the console application you'll use to test the XML Web service and a solution file to which you can add more projects. The next step is to create a new sequential workflow library project and the stock quote workflow.

Adding the sequential workflow library

1. With Visual Studio still running, right-click the QuoteGenerator solution name in Solution Explorer to activate the context menu. From the context menu, select Add and then New Project.

2. This activates the Add New Project dialog box. Expand the Visual C# tree control node if it's not already expanded, select Workflow from the Project Types pane, and then select Sequential Workflow Library from the Templates list. Type **GeneratorFlow** in the Name field, and click OK.

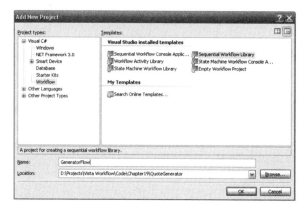

3. Visual Studio adds the new sequential workflow project to the QuoteGenerator solution and opens the visual workflow designer for your use. However, before creating the workflow, let's create the interface you'll need. Right-click the GeneratorFlow project, and select Add from the resulting menu. From there, select Class. When the Add New Item dialog box appears, type **IGenerateQuote.cs** in the Name field and click Add.

4. Change the class definition Visual Studio created for you to the following:

    ```
    public interface IGenerateQuote
    ```

5. Add the following method to *IGenerateQuote* and then save the file:

    ```
    decimal GetQuote(string symbol);
    ```

6. Now that you have an interface to build from, return to the visual workflow designer by selecting Workflow1.cs in the GenerateFlow project and then clicking the View Designer button from the Solution Explorer toolbar.

7. Drag an instance of *WebServiceInput* from the Visual Studio Toolbox, and drop it into your workflow definition.

8. Now let's set *webServiceInputActivity1*'s properties. To begin, click the *InterfaceType* property to activate the browse (...) button. Click the browse button, which activates the Browse And Select A .NET Type dialog box. *GeneratorFlow.IGenerateQuote* should already be inserted into the Type Name field because it belongs to the current project and is the only interface available. Click OK.

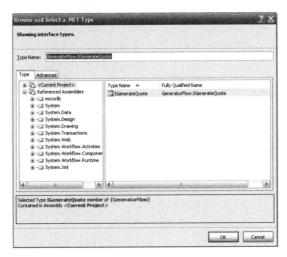

9. Click the *IsActivating* property to activate the down arrow. Click the down arrow, and select *True* from the list of available options.

10. Select the *MethodName* property to activate its down arrow. Click the down arrow, and select the only option, *GetQuote*. Once you make this selection, notice that the *symbol* property is added to the properties for this activity.

11. Select the *symbol* property that was just added to activate the familiar browse (...) button. Click the browse button to bring up the Bind 'symbol' To An Activity's Property dialog box. Click the Bind To A New Member tab, and type **Symbol** in the New Member Name field. After making sure the Create Property option is selected, click OK. The *webServiceInputActivity1* activity continues to indicate there is a validation error (that is, the exclamation mark in the red circle remains active). This is because you've not paired the input with an output, which is something you'll remedy shortly.

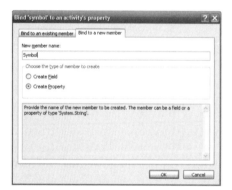

12. We'll need to do some initialization when the XML Web service executes for the first time, so type **CreateStocks** in *webServiceInputActivity1*'s *InputReceived* property and press Enter. Visual Studio inserts the *CreateStocks* event handler for you and switches you to the code editor. Return to the visual workflow designer to finish the workflow.

13. Drag a *Code* activity from the Toolbox, and drop it below *webServiceInputActivity1*.
    Enter **UpdateMarketValues** as its *ExecuteCode* property. Return to the visual workflow
    designer once Visual Studio inserts the *UpdateMarketValues* event handler for you.

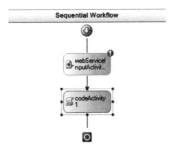

14. The next workflow activity to insert is an instance of the *IfElse* activity. Drag this onto the
    designer's surface, and drop it below the *Code* activity you just placed.

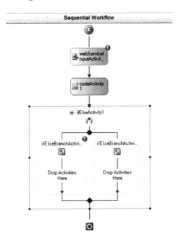

15. Select the left branch in *ifElseActivity1*, and click its *Condition* property to activate the
    down arrow. Select *Code Condition* from the options and then expand the plus sign (+)
    next to the *Condition* property. Type **TestKnownStock** into the secondary *Condition*

property and press Enter. Once Visual Studio again adds the event handler for you, return to the visual workflow designer.

16. Drag a copy of the *Code* activity onto the designer's surface, and drop it into the left *ifElseActivity1* branch. Enter **RecordStockValue** as its *ExecuteCode* property, and return to the visual workflow designer once Visual Studio adds the event handler.

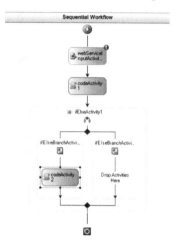

17. Now drag an instance of the *WebServiceOutput* activity, and drop it below the *Code* activity you just inserted.

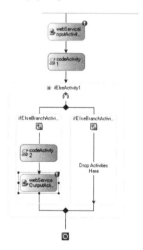

18. Assign *webServiceOutputActivity1*'s *InputActivityName* to be *webServiceInputActivity1* by clicking the *InputActivityName* property once to activate the down arrow, and then by clicking the down arrow to select the *webServiceInputActivity1* activity. Note (*ReturnValue*) is added to the list of *webServiceOutputActivity1* properties.

19. Because we do want to return a stock value, we need to bind a workflow property to the *(ReturnValue)* property of *webServiceOutputActivity1*. Select the *(ReturnValue)* property once to activate the browse (...) button, and then click the browse button. When the Bind '(ReturnValue)' To An Activity's Property dialog box appears, select the Bind To A New Member tab and type **StockValue** into the New Member Name field. Make sure the Create Property option is selected, and then click OK.

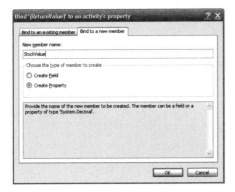

20. The last activity you should add is an instance of *WebServiceFault*. Drag a copy of the *WebServiceFault* activity onto the visual workflow designer's surface, and drop it into the right branch of *ifElseActivity1*.

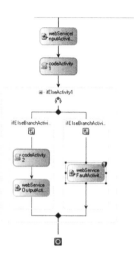

21. As you did with *webServiceOutputActivity1*, you need to assign *webServiceFaultActivity1*'s *InputActivityName* property. Select its *InputActivityName* property to activate the down arrow, and then choose *webServiceInputActivity1* from the list. (It will be the only option available.)

22. You then need to provide *webServiceFaultActivity1* with an appropriate fault, so select its *Fault* property to activate the browse (...) button. Click the browse button to again bring up the Bind 'Fault' To An Activity's Property dialog box. Click the Bind To A New Member tab, and type **StockFault** into the New Member Name field. Make sure the Create Property option button is selected, and click OK.

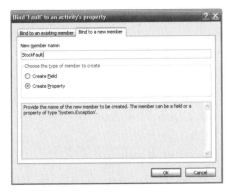

23. The workflow is now complete from a visual design perspective, so open the Workflow1.cs file for code editing. Select Workflow1.cs in Solution Explorer, and click the View Code toolbar button.

24. The first bit of code to add will be a pair of *using* statements that allow us to access some ASP.NET structures. Add these to the end of the existing list of *using* statements:

```
using System.Web;
using System.Web.Caching;
```

25. Next let's complete the *CreateStocks* event handler. Scroll down until you find *CreateStocks*, and add the following lines of code to that method:

```
System.Collections.Generic.Dictionary<string, decimal> stockVals =
    HttpContext.Current.Cache["StockVals"] as
    System.Collections.Generic.Dictionary<string, decimal>;
if (stockVals == null)
{
    // Create and cache the known stock values.
    stockVals =
        new System.Collections.Generic.Dictionary<string, decimal>();
    stockVals.Add("CONT", 28.0m);
    stockVals.Add("LITW", 22.0m);
    stockVals.Add("TSPT", 24.0m);

    // Add to the cache.
    HttpContext.Current.Cache.Add("StockVals", stockVals, null,
                          Cache.NoAbsoluteExpiration,
                          Cache.NoSlidingExpiration,
                          CacheItemPriority.Normal, null);
} // if
```

26. Scroll down further and locate the *UpdateMarketValues* event handler. To the *UpdateMarketValues* handler, add the market update simulation code:

```
// Iterate over each item in the dictionary and decide
// what its current value should be. Normally we'd call
// some external service with each of our watch values,
// but for demo purposes we'll just use random values.
//
```

```csharp
// Note this is essentially the same simulation code as
// found in Chapter 10...
Random rand = new Random(DateTime.Now.Millisecond);
System.Collections.Generic.Dictionary<string, decimal> currentStockVals =
    HttpContext.Current.Cache["StockVals"] as
    System.Collections.Generic.Dictionary<string, decimal>;
System.Collections.Generic.Dictionary<string, decimal> newStockVals =
    new System.Collections.Generic.Dictionary<string, decimal>();
foreach (string key in currentStockVals.Keys)
{
    // Pull the item's value.
    decimal currentPrice = (decimal)currentStockVals[key];

    // Set up the simulation.
    decimal newPrice = currentPrice;
    decimal onePercent = currentPrice * 0.1m;
    Int32 multiplier = 0; // no change

    // We'll now roll some dice. First roll: does the
    // market value change? 0-79, no. 80-99, yes.
    if (rand.Next(0, 99) >= 80)
    {
        // Yes, update the price. Next roll: will the
        // value increase or decrease? 0-49, increase.
        // 50-99, decrease.
        multiplier = 1;
        if (rand.Next(0, 99) >= 50)
        {
            // Decrease the price.
            multiplier = -1;
        } // if

        // Next roll, by how much? We'll calculate it
        // as a percentage of the current share value.
        // 0-74, .1% change. 75-89, .2% change. 90-97,
        // .3% change. And 98-99, .4% change.
        Int32 roll = rand.Next(0, 99);
        if (roll < 75)
        {
            // 1% change
            newPrice = currentPrice + (onePercent * multiplier * 0.1m);
        } // if
        else if (roll < 90)
        {
            // 2% change
            newPrice = currentPrice + (onePercent * multiplier * 0.2m);
        } // else if
        else if (roll < 98)
        {
            // 3% change
            newPrice = currentPrice + (onePercent * multiplier * 0.3m);
        } // else if
        else
        {
            // 4% change
```

```
                newPrice = currentPrice + (onePercent * multiplier * 0.4m);
            } // else if
        } // if
        else
        {
            // No change in price
            newPrice = currentPrice;
        } // else

        // Update the data store.
        newStockVals.Add(key, newPrice);
    } // foreach

    // Add to the cache.
    HttpContext.Current.Cache["StockVals"] = newStockVals;
```

27. We need to add logic to test the stock's symbol, as it might not be a symbol we recognize. Search the Workflow1.cs code for the *TestKnownStock* event handler, and add this code to the body of that method:

```
// Retrieve the cached stock values.
System.Collections.Generic.Dictionary<string, decimal> stockVals =
    HttpContext.Current.Cache["StockVals"] as
    System.Collections.Generic.Dictionary<string, decimal>;

// Check to see if the ticker symbol is in the
// known stock list. Fault if not...
e.Result = true;
if (String.IsNullOrEmpty(Symbol) || !stockVals.ContainsKey(Symbol))
{
    // We don't have the desired stock in our list,
    // so return a fault.
    e.Result = false;
    StockFault = new System.Exception("The desired stock ticker symbol" +
                                      " is unknown.");
} // if
```

28. The last few lines of code to add are the code to assign the stock value to the return value property. The *RecordStockValue* method handles that, so locate the *RecordStockValue* method and add the following lines:

```
// Place updated stock value in the dependency property
// for return to the caller.
System.Collections.Generic.Dictionary<string, decimal> stockVals =
    HttpContext.Current.Cache["StockVals"] as
    System.Collections.Generic.Dictionary<string, decimal>;
StockValue = (decimal)stockVals[Symbol];
```

29.   The workflow itself is now complete. Save all open files, and compile the workflow by pressing Shift+F6 or by selecting Build GeneratorFlow from the Visual Studio Build menu. Correct any compilation errors you encounter before moving on.

The workflow is now ready to be placed into an ASP.NET setting so that external clients can connect to the service and request stock values. Although you could create a new ASP.NET application and perform all the configuration magic yourself, the WF team kindly provided you with a superb feature that builds the ASP.NET project for you, error free. It could hardly be easier to use, too.

Creating the ASP.NET Web application

1.   This is so easy they should give the WF developer who came up with the idea a pay raise. Simply right-click the GeneratorFlow project name in Solution Explorer, and select Publish As Web Service. Visual Studio will grind for the briefest of moments and then display a confirmation dialog box. Click OK to dismiss this confirmation dialog box.

2.   Because that was entirely too easy, let's rename the .asmx file. (The name Visual Studio selects is a bit overwhelming.) Right-click the newly created Generator-Flow.Workflow1_WebService.asmx file's name in Solution Explorer, and select Rename. Change its name to **QuoteService.asmx**.

3.   Just to be sure, you can press Shift+F6 or select Build Web Site from the main Build menu. This step isn't required, but it will precompile the Web application so that when you reference it to retrieve its WSDL you'll save a bit of time at that point. If there were any errors, you could correct them, but you should find none. If you receive schema warnings for the values Visual Studio placed for you into the Web.config file, ignore those.

The final task is to return to the original program file, add a Web Reference to its project, and test the XML Web service. That's next.

Creating the XML Web Service client application

1.   Right-click the QuoteGenerator project name in Solution Explorer, and select Add Web Reference.

2. When the Add Web Reference dialog box appears, click the Web Services In This Solution link.

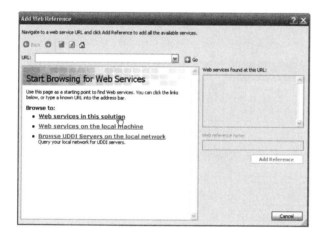

3. As there is only one XML Web service in the QuoteGenerator solution, the QuoteService XML Web service is the only service that appears. Click the QuoteService link to continue.

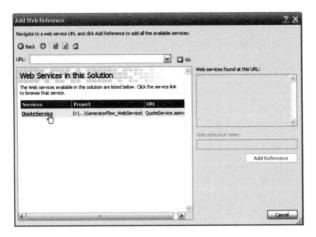

4. Visual Studio invokes the WSDL generation capabilities of the QuoteService XML Web service and displays the methods it finds. In this case, there is only one method. You could, if you like, click the method name and test the method. For now, click Add Reference to add the Web Reference to the QuoteGenerator project.

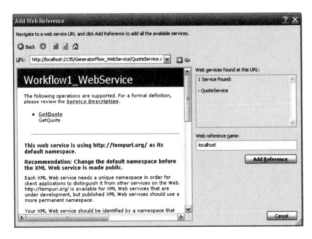

Note The Web Reference Name field contains the value *localhost*. If you had multiple Web References, you could change this to a more meaningful value to ease maintenance and Web service tracking.

5. With the Web Reference in place, open the Program.cs file for editing. Select the Program.cs file in Solution Explorer, and click the View Code toolbar button.

6. Look for the *Main* method. To the *Main* method, add this code:

```
// Create the proxy.
QuoteGenerator.localhost.Workflow1_WebService ws =
    new QuoteGenerator.localhost.Workflow1_WebService();

try
{
    // Call the service a few times to
    // test its logic.
    decimal val = ws.GetQuote("CONT");
    Console.WriteLine("The latest value for CONT is: {0}",
                                        val.ToString("C"));

    val = ws.GetQuote("LITW");
    Console.WriteLine("The latest value for LITW is: {0}",
                                        val.ToString("C"));

    val = ws.GetQuote("TSPT");
    Console.WriteLine("The latest value for TSPT is: {0}",
                                        val.ToString("C"));

    // Error test
    val = ws.GetQuote("ABC");
    Console.WriteLine("The latest value for ABC is: {0}",
                                        val.ToString("C"));
} // try
catch (Exception ex)
{
    Console.WriteLine("Error checking stock value: {0}", ex.Message);
} // catch
```

7. Compile the solution by pressing F6 or by selecting Build Solution from the Visual Studio Build menu. Correct any compilation errors.

8. Execute the application by pressing Shift+F5, or simply F5 for debugging mode. The output should appear as you see here. If the output scrolls by too quickly and the console window disappears before you have a chance to see the output, set a breakpoint in the *Main* method and step through until you see all the output.

With this application, your quick tour of WF is complete.

Chapter 19 Quick Reference

To	Do This
Lay out methods your workflow-based XML Web Service will implement	Create a new interface with the methods you desire.
Begin workflow processing in your workflow-based XML Web service	Drag and drop an instance of the *WebServiceInput* activity into your workflow. Assign it your interface and desired method name. Set its *IsActivating* property to *true*.
Return values from your workflow-based XML Web service	Drag and drop an instance of the *WebServiceOutput* activity onto the workflow designer's surface, and assign it the corresponding *WebServiceInput* activity it is to be paired with. Bind the return value to a workflow field or property, and assign that field or property a value prior to executing *WebServiceOutput*.
Return an exception (fault) from your workflow-based XML Web service	Drag and drop a copy of *WebServiceFault* activity into your workflow, and assign it the corresponding *WebServiceInput* activity and bound *Fault* property. Be sure to create an exception and assign it to the bound *Fault* property prior to executing *WebServiceFault*.
Create an ASP.NET Web-based project in Visual Studio that uses workflow definitions that include the WF XML Web service activities	With the workflow created and successfully compiled, right-click the workflow assembly's project name in Solution Explorer and select Publish As Web Service.
Bind client applications to your workflow-based XML Web service	Add a Web Reference in the traditional Visual Studio way. Workflow-based XML Web services are no different from any other XML Web service as far as the client is concerned.

Index

Kenn Scribner

Kenn is a software developer who happens to write books as an excuse to learn new technologies. There is nothing quite like a deadline to get those creative neurons firing. He's been working with computers since he built a breadboarded Z-80 in college a few too many years ago. (Happily the Z-80 survived the encounter.) While he fondly remembers writing 6502 assembly language on his Apple][, he's quite happy writing complex C# applications today, both for the Web and for the desktop. This is his fifth computer book—his second solo effort—and he truly hopes you'll enjoy reading it and learning Windows Workflow Foundation. His personal Web site is *www.endurasoft.com*.

What do you think of this book?

We want to hear from you!

Do you have a few minutes to participate in a brief online survey?

Microsoft is interested in hearing your feedback so we can continually improve our books and learning resources for you.

To participate in our survey, please visit:

www.microsoft.com/learning/booksurvey/

...and enter this book's ISBN-10 number (appears above barcode on back cover*).
As a thank-you to survey participants in the United States and Canada, each month we'll randomly select five respondents to win one of five $100 gift certificates from a leading online merchant. At the conclusion of the survey, you can enter the drawing by providing your e-mail address, which will be used for prize notification only.

Thanks in advance for your input. Your opinion counts!

*Where to find the ISBN-10 on back cover

ISBN-13: 000-0-0000-0000-0
ISBN-10: 0-0000-00000

0 000000 000000

Example only. Each book has unique ISBN.

Microsoft
Press

www.microsoft.com/learning/booksurvey/